TEN YEARS
—IN THE—
SADDLE

TEN YEARS
—IN THE—
SADDLE

The Memoir of
WILLIAM WOODS AVERELL

Edited by
Edward K. Eckert
and
Nicholas J. Amato

Presidio Press
SAN RAFAEL • LONDON

Copyright © 1978 by Presidio Press

Published by Presidio Press of San Rafael, California,
and London, England, with editorial offices at
1114 Irwin Street, San Rafael, California 94901

Library of Congress Cataloging in Publication Data

Averell, William Woods, 1832–1900.
  Ten years in the saddle.

  Bibliography: p.
  Includes index.
    1. Averell, William Woods, 1832–1900.   2. United
States—History—Civil War, 1861–1865—Personal
narratives.   3. Soldiers—United States—Biography.
4. Frontier and pioneer life—New Mexico.   5. Indians
of North America—New Mexico—Wars.   I. Amato,
Nich J., 1922-   II. Eckert, Edward K.,
1943–   III. Title.
E601.A85   357′.1′0924 [B]   77-73551
ISBN 0-89141-024-4

Maps on pages 82 and 109 reprinted from The Atlas
of American History *by James Truslow Adams with
the permission of Charles Scribner's Sons. Copyright
1943 Charles Scribner's Sons.*

Book design by Joe Roter

Dust jacket design by Tom Blakeley

Printed in the United States of America

3-1-79

CONTENTS

ILLUSTRATIONS

MAPS

FOREWORD

Ten Years in the Saddle is the previously unpublished memoir of William Woods Averell, a Union cavalry general from Bath, New York. Averell, a West Point graduate, served in the wild New Mexico territory and early in the Civil War was placed in command of a cavalry regiment. Although successful in battle, he lacked the drive to make his victories complete. Averell's innate caution meant that he would never achieve a place of renown in the annals of war. Yet his memoir is one of the most fascinating reminiscences to emerge from that conflict. It is full of details about life in the cavalry, battlefield action and a thrilling mission through Confederate territory to warn a Union garrison of impending attack.

Averell began collecting material in the early 1880s for at least several articles and probably a full-scale autobiography. In 1881 he wrote that he planned to write a paper on the cavalry in the Civil War in order to correct erroneous statements that had been published.[1] In March, 1883, a close friend, Marcus A. Reno, learned of Averell's decision to write a book about his military experiences.[2] By this time Averell had received numerous requests for long reports concerning his cavalry service which others were incorporating into their own stories. Occasionally he gave speeches, and he also wrote short articles for the "Battles and

---

[1]W. W. Averell to General [illegible] (September 16, 1881), New York State Library, Manuscript and Special Collections, "William W. Averell Collection," (HU 12349), box 4, folder 4). (Hereinafter this collection is cited as NYSL.)

[2]M. A. Reno to W. W. Averell (March 15, 1883), NYSL, box 5, folder 4.

Leaders" series published by *The Century Magazine*. Averell contributed a chapter to *The History of the Third Pennsylvania Cavalry*, entitled "With the Cavalry on the Peninsula." (This chapter is included in the memoir.)

Averell began work on his memoir manuscript in 1891, by which time he already had named it "Ten Years in the Saddle," and word of its preparation appeared in the newspapers.[3] He was a busy man with his businesses, patents and legal problems, so the memoir was a labor of love. By the time of his death on February 3, 1900, the manuscript had not been completed.

The majority of the chapters had been typed, except for "West Point" and the preface, both of which Averell apparently added as an afterthought. The chapter entitled "The Third Pennsylvania Cavalry" was completed but the last pages have been lost. "A Long and Perilous Ride" was a story which he told to delighted nephews and nieces, and to which he often referred in speeches. A version of this tale appeared in a newspaper; Averell kept the clipping but had failed to identify either the name of the paper or the date.[4] The last chapter, "Conduct of the War" is unlike the rest of the memoir. It does not deal with cavalry exploits, but is instead an explanation of Averell's opinions and prejudices.

The copy of the manuscript used by the editors was typewritten and clear except for occasional marginal additions by Averell. Very few changes have been made as the editors wished to retain the flavor and charm of the original. For the sake of readability, spelling has been corrected, capitalization has been made consistent, and paragraphing has been imposed. But the book is Averell's. The editors have interrupted the author's style as infrequently as possible.

Averell's style of writing (as well as his penmanship) changed little throughout his long life. An early letter to his brother is typical of his flowing, conversational style: "I cannot hardly realize that I have left my old home for good but I fear I never can be home only upon visits which may be long or short they are not living at home. I can't believe my boyish days are all gone. I wish I could live some of them over. Oh happy days quickly gone."[5]

The editors have identified individuals more completely and have checked Averell's sources for authenticity. Unless noted, Averell's figures

---

[3][Illegible] to W. W. Averell (April 4, 1891), NYSL, box 6, folder 1.
[4]Unidentified clipping in NYSL, box 9, folder 3.
[5]W. W. Averell to O. J. Averell (July 26, 1851), NYSL, box 1, folder 2.

and dates are correct. No doubt he was aided by the very complete diaries that he kept throughout his adult life.

Averell and his family were great savers. Thousands of letters, bills, menus, orders, calling cards and miscellaneous papers are in the collections. Little doubt exists as to the accuracy and authenticity of the memoir since Averell kept most of his official orders along with corroborating evidence such as letters from friends and diary entries. He must have spent a great deal of his time writing, yet still found time to conduct military campaigns and conclude business deals.

In 1928 William M. Stuart, the postmaster of Canisteo, New York, proposed writing a biography of the general, and he requested the family's aid. William S. Crandall, spokesman for the family, advised Stuart that "I shall insist on editing that portion of it . . . to show up the conspiracy of that old bird [Amazi L. Barber] in a way that will show his criminal duplicity for all time."[6] Stuart could not find a publisher and Averell's story remained hidden for another generation. Neither Stuart nor Crandall proposed editing the memoir for publication.

Lucy Henica, the Averells' niece and adopted daughter, inherited the memoir along with about half of the general's papers. She kept the latter in a carpetbag in an unused coal bin of her home in Westchester County, New York. Another collection of Averell's papers made its uncharted way to the New York State Library in 1950. Miss Henica's holdings passed to her grandnephew, William E. Dascomb, of Allegany, New York, who generously permitted the editors to research the papers and publish the memoir. Interestingly, both the Dascomb and the New York State Library collections have similar material. Each has extensive holdings in all phases of Averell's life except his three years as the American consul general to Canada. These papers, except for the official diplomatic records which are in the National Archives, have disappeared. The editors are convinced that many personal items from this period also have disappeared. Perhaps they now lie in someone's attic or basement, waiting to tell their tale.

St. Bonaventure, New York   Edward K. Eckert
February, 1977   & Nicholas J. Amato

---

[6]William E. Dascomb collection of the papers of William W. Averell; these letters are filed in a folder labeled "Biography."

ACKNOWLEDGMENTS

Indispensable as the raw sources are to editors and writers of history, no work can be adequately completed without the advice, direction and assistance of librarians, colleagues, family and friends. Therefore, the editors would like to acknowledge a number of substantial debts—to the librarians and archivists of the New York State Library, the National Archives, the St. Bonaventure University Library and to Mr. William E. Dascomb, who not only made the Averell manuscript available, but, more than any other individual, understood its significance and usefulness for an understanding of the history of the period.

A sabbatical leave granted in 1971 by St. Bonaventure University provided one of the editors with the opportunity to assess the material and begin the research and editing of the Averell manuscript. To former president Reverend Reginald A. Redlon, O.F.M., who initiated the sabbatical leave policy at St. Bonaventure University, a considerable debt is owed. A grant from the Academic Research Committee of St. Bonaventure University provided a stipend used to complete the research and editorial work on the manuscript.

Much of the account of Averell's Civil War years is based on an article entitled "William W. Averell: Sheridan's Scapegoat General?", published in *By Valor & Arms*. The editors gratefully acknowledge permission to incorporate this information in their Introduction and Epilogue.

The editors are deeply grateful to Linda Corroum Eckert who read and commented upon the entire manuscript. To our colleagues, Professors

Helen F. Jones and Peter G. Marron, we owe an equal debt for they readily gave of their time and knowledge in assisting the editors in the preparation of the manuscript for publication.

Finally, the quiet help and encouragement forthcoming from the respective families of the editors cannot be measured in any possible way.

To all we are grateful, for without their help, this manuscript could not have been completed.

[EDITORS' INTRODUCTION]

William Woods Averell was born in the town of Cameron in Steuben County, New York, on November 5, 1832. Like many people in this area, his family was descended from seventeenth-century New Englanders who moved to upstate New York following the American Revolution. William's father, Hiram Averell, was born at Harpersfield, New York, on November 21, 1795, on his father's farm.[1]

In 1825 Hiram purchased a small farm of his own in the town of Cameron. He held a number of minor political and appointive offices, including justice of the peace, postmaster and constable. His first wife, Elizabeth Young, bore him two daughters, one of whom died in infancy. Elizabeth died in 1826, and four years later Hiram married Huldah Hemenway. Huldah bore five children, two boys and three girls. William was their second child and first son.

William was educated in local public schools. He believed much of his later success stemmed from the example of his father, to whom he seemed much closer than his mother. While at West Point, William wrote his father, "I owe all my education and improvement (little enough)

---

[1]Clara A. Avery, *The Averell-Averill-Avery Family—A Record of the Descendents of William and Abigail Averell of Ipswich, Mass.* vol. 1, pp. 490-92 and vol. 2, pp. 700-03.

1

to the ambition you inspired in me by well chosen stories of persons who made themselves by their own exertions &c."[2]

A few years before his entry at West Point, William had moved from the family farm to the nearby village of Bath, where he worked as a clerk in a drugstore. But William Averell's ambition could not be fulfilled as a drugstore clerk. He sought appointment to the United States Military Academy where he could receive the college education that his own family could not afford. In December of 1850 Congressman David Rumsey of Bath gained an appointment for Averell for the following summer.

At West Point, Averell began to keep a diary of daily events. These recordings would be invaluable years later when he began his memoir. Averell enjoyed cadet life at West Point where he tasted the pleasure of youth despite the disciplined environment. He was never a model cadet, but his lighthearted ways made him many friends. A close companion at the academy was Fitzhugh Lee, whose later correspondence with Averell indicates an ease of manner and personal knowledge typical of youthful comrades.

Like all schoolboys, Averell frequently wrote home asking for food or clothes. On the other hand, since he was being paid by the government while at West Point, Averell's family would occasionally ask him for money to supplement their meagre earnings. Although he was usually happy during his cadet years, he frequently experienced pangs of loneliness. At the beginning of his third year at the academy, Averell wrote to his younger brother Oscar about his depression. "Sometimes when classmates are around me and fun is on the [illegible] I am quite contented in my forgetfulness—but the feeling returns to [sic] often—a kind of desolation sort of blues that I guess you never have enjoyed."[3]

Averell was an average student, near the middle of his class in all subjects except horsemanship, where he stood first. His riding ability would save his life more than once during his military career. His personal ambition at West Point was not to be a career soldier but rather a successful civilian. Before leaving for the academy he wrote Oscar that he planned to follow his four years at West Point with "3 years as a topographical engineer."[4] His view of pre-war military life was realistic but negative. During his second year he reflected on a soldier's life:

[2]NYSL, box 1, folder 2 (October 2, 1852).
[3]W. W. Averell to O. J. Averell (September 11, 1853), NYSL, box 1, folder 3.
[4]W. W. Averell to O. J. Averell (December 30, 1850), NYSL, box 1, folder 1.

If after graduating I could get a R.R. to build or a canal or a dock or in fact any civil post that would bring me a salary of $1000 or more, I would "scoot" from the army most d—d quick—when the prospect is being sent out near sunset to spend five years with the aborigines, where all the glory of war is boiled down to being shot with an arrow in a running "fight from a funeral," being buried in a ditch, and having my name printed wrong in the newspaper that deigns to notice the affair by laying all the blame on my shoulders and having as an expression of the world's regret, "served him right."[5]

Averell graduated in 1855, twenty-sixth in a class of thirty-four, and was commissioned a brevet second-lieutenant of mounted rifles. Initially he was assigned to the Cavalry School at Jefferson Barracks, Missouri, but was shortly transferred to Carlisle Barracks, Pennsylvania. There he served as the adjutant to the post commandant, Col. Charles A. May.

Antebellum life for a bachelor officer at Carlisle was pleasant. Averell received many invitations from young ladies in the community who enjoyed his company. "Swell," as he was generally known to his friends, was a popular guest in many of the homes in Carlisle. The nickname was an early recognition of his ambitious personality. It was taken from Shakespeare—"I have seen the ambitious ocean swell"—and Averell was known to his classmates by this name for the rest of his life.[6] Garrison duty was onerous for Averell, especially the supervision of enlisted men who had more time on their hands than they could properly use. He was not unhappy to be transferred with a detachment of recruits to the New Mexico territory.

In 1857 New Mexico still remained Spanish in tone and temper. Averell found the customs of the people strange, particularly the behavior of the women, who not only smoked cigarettes but danced with anyone at a ball even before proper introductions had been made. Such a free-and-easy attitude made garrison life a pleasure for young Averell. He had a large number of women friends, some of whom were his lovers.[7] Life was exciting on the frontier and the young lieutenant felt he was at last a part of the real army.

In 1859 a serious leg wound made it necessary for him to be sent

---

[5]W. W. Averell to O. J. Averell (November 26, 1852), NYSL, box 1, folder 2.

[6]Dozens of letters in the Averell collections begin "Dear Swell." The quote was mentioned by C. Van Camp to W. W. Averell (July 29, 1855), NYSL, box 1, folder 4. It is from *Julius Caesar*, Act 1, Scene 3, 11. 6-7.

[7]G. Granger to W. W. Averell (January 19, 1859), William E. Dascomb Collection of the papers of William W. Averell (hereinafter cited as the Dascomb Collection).

home on convalescent leave. For the next two years Averell remained with his family in Bath. As his leg grew stronger he visited friends in New York City, Philadelphia and the northern watering spots. He was still on leave when the batteries in Charleston fired on Fort Sumter. Bored with inactivity and anxious to be of service, Averell presented himself to the War Department on April 16, 1861, for assignment. Having made the acquaintance of Lt. Gen. and Mrs. Winfield Scott while he was a cadet, the ambitious lieutenant volunteered his services to the general.

Averell's first assignment in the Civil War was as exciting as it was unique. The government was worried about the isolated garrisons in the West and feared another disaster like that in Texas where the senile Col. David E. Twiggs had surrendered United States troops to state authorities without a fight. Averell was sent to Fort Arbuckle, 300 miles beyond the western border of Arkansas, to order commander William H. Emory to destroy all property which could not be transferred to Fort Leavenworth and then to leave the post with his troops. Averell's ride to Fort Arbuckle provided one of the most exciting, although unknown, chapters in the war.

After his return to Washington, Averell had little to do until June 7, 1861, when he was ordered to Elmira, New York, to muster volunteers. He found the recruits, and especially their officers, a distasteful lot of country boys with little knowledge of soldiers and less inclination to be one. The lack of professional military men to lead the motley mass appalled the West Pointer. He had little sympathy with the idea of appointing prominent politicians as officers, and he blamed the Union's early military disasters on the lack of trained personnel. In less than a month Averell was ordered to report to Brig. Gen. Irvin McDowell, who was preparing the First Manassas campaign.

Averell relished his appointment as assistant adjutant general to the brigade of regulars under Col. Andrew Porter, where he found professional military men like himself. During the battle Averell acted as a courier, relaying messages between McDowell and Porter and ordering units to different positions on the field. But confusion and lack of training bore sad results, and the Union army turned tail and dashed back to Washington. The disorganized retreat made Averell feel ashamed, and he was disgusted with the Republican administration for encouraging a premature action. The young officer anticipated better results when George B. McClellan was ordered to leave the scene of his success in western Virginia and assume command of the demoralized Army of the Potomac.

Averell was in many ways a mirror of McClellan. Like McClellan, he saw the war as an elaborate chess game which demanded careful planning and preparation before any move could be undertaken. The pieces— regiments, brigades and divisions—needed careful training in order to be ready to perform their duties. It was all too obvious to both men what would happen when an untrained army took the field. Consequently, McClellan and Averell would take time to reorganize, reequip and retrain their forces even if it meant stopping the momentum of battle. Lack of a visceral desire to aim for the jugular of the defeated enemy eventually would cost both men their commands. They would hold back reserves needed on the field—McClellan at Antietam and Averell at Kelly's Ford—and afterward each would return to camp rather than pursue the enemy. A final similarity was in political views. Both Averell and McClellan regarded the Republican administration as, at best, a necessary evil, whose advice should not be taken very seriously. In their opinion the war had been caused by bungling politicians who were continuing to mismanage, and professional military men should be allowed to save the nation. Fighting for political reasons was contrary to their grain and seemed to violate everything they had been taught at West Point.

For two months after Manassas, Averell served on the staff of the provost marshal in Washington. Although he found his duties intriguing, he longed for a chance to demonstrate his abilities as a commander. The opportunity arose on October 7, 1861, while he was waiting to make a report to the assistant secretary of war. Into the office came a group of civilians from the Virginia side of the Potomac to complain of the depredations of the unruly Kentucky Cavalry Regiment under Col. William H. Young. Someone remarked that he wished a colonel could be found to handle the regiment, and Averell volunteered. An order was immediately issued to allow him to assume the command of this cavalry unit, lately redesignated the Third Pennsylvania Cavalry.

The unit, with a majority of members from Pennsylvania, was commanded by Young, a Kentuckian, who gave it its nickname and thus provided confusion for all future historians. The regiment had been mustered into service in August and was scattered about northern Virginia from a point opposite Georgetown to Alexandria. The dispersion of the unit prevented proper discipline and instruction and made the job of the untrained officers practically impossible. Averell was then only twenty-nine, but his career as an instructor at the cavalry school and as an officer in the mounted rifles had sufficiently prepared him to head a cavalry regiment. He reorganized the unit and trained the men. The spectacle of a regimental camp complete with flags, bugles and discipline quickly provided the Third Pennsylvania with a unity it had failed to experience before.

Averell's success with the Third Pennsylvania was recognized almost immediately and he was assigned to train the Eighth Pennsylvania Cavalry as well. The two units formed the First Brigade of Volunteer Cavalry, which Averell commanded while at the same time keeping his position as colonel of the Third. Due to his knowledge of the cavalry, he was also appointed to a board to review the qualifications of cavalry officers. By June, 1862, Averell had a well organized and trained cavalry unit.

The cavalry was the most prestigious unit of the Civil War armies, but its duties were often onerous and boring. The men served primarily as scouts, couriers and the rear guard. Unlike the dragoons, a sort of mobile infantry which usually got into the thick of battle, the cavalry generally waited on the periphery to attack at the crucial moment (which often never occurred) to drive the enemy off the field. The cavalry was not expected or trained to fight like infantry. Colorful and inspiring to behold was the galloping charge of a cavalry regiment with sabres drawn. Yet when the noise and the excitement had cleared, casualties were insignificant compared with those of a typical infantry engagement. This provoked Union General Joseph Hooker to remark, "Who ever saw a dead cavalryman?" One of the best uses of the cavalry was raiding and harassing the enemy, often behind his own lines. Although such attacks were sometimes felt to be uncivilized or ungentlemanly, they caused unwarranted fear in the enemy, as when the Confederate Cavalry leader, Lt. Gen. Jubal A. Early, rode to the very gates of Washington in 1864.

In March of 1862 the Third Pennsylvania was transferred to the Virginia peninsula via ship. The geography of this land was not suited to cavalry operations. The lack of broad fields meant that the cavalry could not actively engage enemy units. The almost constant spring rains produced swollen creeks and rivers and made it impossible for the horses to move rapidly in the ankle-deep mud. The Third Pennsylvania was placed on the army's left flank. Near Williamsburg they captured some Confederate skirmishers and artillery. By the 25th of May the army was about seven miles from Richmond, with the Third Pennsylvania Cavalry still on the left flank. In this position the regiment maintained communication with the federal gunboats in the James River at City Point.

While waiting for some action to develop, Maj. Gen. James E. B. Stuart's Confederate cavalry made a bold and dramatic ride around the entire Union army. Although embarrassed by the success of this raid, the Union cavalry did little to hinder the Confederates. On June 29th the First North Carolina and the Third Virginia Cavalry probed the Union left flank but were successfully blunted by Averell and the Third Pennsylvania. This attack was part of the great Confederate push under Gen. Robert E. Lee which has come to be known as the Seven Days' Battles. During the fight for Malvern Hill on July 1, the Third Pennsylvania was drawn up in the rear of the Union forces with orders to allow no Union soldier to pass back unless he could show blood.

On the day after the battle, Averell's cavalry was assigned to protect the rear of the Army of the Potomac as it made its way toward safety at Harrison's Landing. The enemy had suffered terribly in the assaults on Malvern Hill and would not attack the retreating Union army. With the arrival of the Union forces at Harrison's Landing, Averell was appointed an acting brigadier general.

Averell's manuscript ends at this point in his career, August, 1862, with the conclusion of the Peninsular campaign. He had planned to take his memoir through the end of the Civil War. Hence the title, "Ten Years in the Saddle," was intended to reflect his service career from 1855 to 1865.[8] But the unpleasant circumstances surrounding his removal from command by Gen. Sheridan—a totally unjust and illegal action in Averell's opinion—made it too painful for him to recall objectively these last years of his military service.

---

[8] Although Averell set out to recount the ten years of his military career that loom as the most significant in his life, he nonetheless gave some indication of preparing a fuller autobiographical account. The hand and typewritten pages of Averell's original manuscript include his West Point years, and additional handwritten pages suggest an even broader span of years. Furthermore, his diaries of 1890, 1891 through 1897 (1897 being the last in the Dascomb Collection) include notations referring to his "book," his "reminiscences," and his "memoirs."

INTRODUCTION

No feeling of egotism inclines one to write the experiences of "Ten Years in the Saddle" in the military service of the Republic. On the contrary the apprehension of the possible ascription of such a motive has been one of the obstacles which has deterred me from the undertaking. To a great extent it must be an autobiography. A single life, however eventful, seems nothing in a multitude of two million soldiers whose days and deeds are already covered with a thickening oblivion which obscures the vision of the rapidly succeeding and busy generations. Yet the experiences of an individual however inconspicuous may have a more important interest than could be derived from any personal considerations by shedding light upon situations and conditions whose existence and relations have been forgotten or misunderstood, by revealing influences which have been hidden or unappreciated, by satisfying the curiosity which suggests research into the details and characteristics of a country and its people in former days, and by contributing to the public record the names of men who merited remembrance.

The solicitations of many unselfish friends have moved me toward what seems a duty to the gallant soldiers and men whom I had the honor to organize, lead, or command. Many delays have been occasioned by data which was difficult or impossible to find. The irreparable loss or destruction of important reports or correspondence should be taken into account whenever there seems a want of completeness.

The ten years to which the title refers was from 1855 to 1865. In the first year the writer was graduated from the West Point Military Academy; in the last, his service in the United States Army was terminated. No decade since the beginning of the history of civilization was pregnant with more stupendous events.

The first eighteen years of my life were spent in Steuben County, New York, where I was born on November 5, 1832. My father, Hiram Averell, was a pioneer farmer in that region when it was a wilderness. He was born in Delaware County, New York, from whence my grandfather, Ebenezer Averell, removed in 1806 and established himself as a farmer and merchant at Black Rock near Buffalo. He was a native of Connecticut and an officer in the revolutionary army. General Scott's army encamped upon his farm previous to the Battle of Lundy's Lane and in the *Archives of Congress* may be found an Act passed about 1820 making an appropriation to reimburse him for supplies furnished to the army at that time. My grandmother on my father's side in this country came from the Turner and Bartlett families of Massachusetts and New Hampshire whilst from my mother's ancestry the Scotch-Irish blood of the Heminway, Gilbert and Thomas families was drawn. I saw four generations at my father's table: my great-grandmother, grandmother, mother, sister and nephew. Our homestead in Cameron, Steuben County, is about three hundred miles west of New York City and one hundred southeast of Buffalo. Such education as the Cameron Schools furnished I readily acquired and when thirteen years old was sent for a term to the Elmira Academy in an adjoining county. My reading embraced the ancient histories, books of travel and exploration, the philosophical works of Dr. Dick,[1] a few romances, and the current magazine literature of that day. My parents being devout Christians, my attendance at church and Sunday School was regular and habitual. At the age of ten I had committed the four gospels to memory and took great pleasure in the commentaries of Dr. Adam Clarkson.[2]

During the winters of 1847-8 and 1848-9, when fifteen and sixteen years of age, I taught a school of about fifty scholars over half of whom

---

[1] John Dick, D.D. (1764-1833), Scottish minister, teacher and theological writer. He received the D.D. degree from Princeton College, New Jersey, in 1815. His writings placed emphasis on the literal acceptance of Scriptures and use of the *Bible* as the sole source of inspiration. His writings include "Essay on the Inspiration of the Scriptures" (1800), "The Conduct and Doom of False Teachers" (1788) and a posthumous collection in four volumes of his theological lectures (1833).

[2] While a number of Clarksons are listed in *Catalog of the British Museum*, the editors have been unable to locate a Dr. Adam Clarkson.

were older than myself and broke, if I did not enliven, the tedium of the long winter by giving the scholars and their parents lectures upon astronomy, geography and other subjects.

Having learned surveying I found pleasant and profitable occupation during the summers in surveying land. The government system of surveying lands in ranges or sections from an established lease-line had been first applied in Steuben and adjacent counties of New York. The first settlers had taken up larger areas than they could possibly cultivate and it became necessary when children had grown of age, or parents had deceased, or, for other reasons, to divide the lands. In the progress of improvements during twenty-five years many landmarks had disappeared along with the forests, and the magnetic needle had varied so that surveyors from a distance were sometimes baffled in their search for an old line and confidence in their work was weakened or lost. By careful observations of the North Star the existing variations were ascertained and by applying it to a few well-known lines the changes which had taken place since the survey was made was found so that I experienced no difficulty in finding old lines. These were pleasant days and one of the happiest of them was when, after making a partition of a large estate among five heirs so that each should have the same quantity of woodland, hill-land, cultivated fields, and frontage, my work was questioned and experienced surveyors were brought to go over it and it was approved without changing a stake. After that my work was arduous and never questioned.

The most pleasant memory I have of this work is of the reestablishment of the old county road through my native town of Cameron a distance of about eight miles. The road had been diverted from its original line in many places and, as the land along it had become valuable, disputes had arisen between farmers living on opposite sides. To adjust these, commissioners were appointed, and they employed me to resurvey it which was done with the greatest care and the work proved in the presence of the commission and the parties interested. That which is remembered better than all else was when I in my roundabout jacket and accompanied by the commissioners and rodmen and chainbearers ran the line by our home and my mother had some cool milk brought out for us to drink.

I was appointed to West Point by C. M. Conrad, Secretary of War.[3]

---

[3]Charles M. Conrad of Winchester, Virginia, served as secretary of war from 15 August 1850 to 7 March 1853 under President Millard Fillmore.

West Point

Again in deepning beauty, ye float near,
Forms dimly imaged in the days gone by,
Ye throng before my view, divinely clear
Like Sunbeams conquering a cloudy sky!

During the last days of May and the first half of June 1851 I lingered about my home in Cameron trembling with the dread of the leave-taking which drew near with unrelenting rapidity. The recollection now of our filial love and veneration and of the home sentiment that had bound the children's lives so closely together from their beginning until then, is to me the sweetest of all reminiscences. My father and mother and brother and sisters were as glad and proud as myself that I was going to West Point but the exhilaration arising from any consideration of my future welfare did not render the grief of parting less poignant. It was the easier for me, for diversion and novelty awaited me, but to the dear ones I must leave there was nothing new but the never-ending strain of my absence upon their hearts and minds.

At last, after the final feverish struggle of parting was over, I found myself one morning in a railway coach for the first time in my life, speeding away on the Erie Railroad which had then not long been completed. I am quite sure now that no more unsophisticated youth had ever set out for the United States Military Academy. I had never been beyond forty miles from home and knew nothing by experience of the world. Of West Point and the education to be acquired there I knew next to nothing. My day's journey of three hundred miles ended shortly after dark at Newburgh on the Hudson, twenty miles above West Point, where I spent the night at a hotel built against the hillside where the acclivity was so great that from my bed chamber in the second story back, one could step out of the window onto the ground. With the perfect health of youth and the fatigue of the unusual experience of the day, I quickly found sound and refreshing sleep.

The following day was glorious with bright sunshine and soft balmy airs. It was destined to be crowded with novel and trying experiences for me. The first great and new sensation was the view of the broad and deep river breaking through the high mountain barriers a few miles below. For about eighteen years, indeed, all my life thus far, had been passed in a beautiful landscape of hills, some of them bold, and of valleys, some of them deep, but agriculture was gradually spreading its checkering fields over a large proportion of it, and a boy could throw a stone across our rivers which were not navigable except for rafts of lumber on the spring freshets after the ice gorges had been broken and carried away. But here were mountains up to the sky whose chief use in nature was to exhibit their inspiring and eternal grandeur, and a river upon whose bosom ships and boats with tall spars and great white sails were gracefully gliding like soaring birds. To my senses, always attuned to rural prospects, this was an absorbing enchantment which enraptured me during the morning hours. It seemed to me an intrusion when the magnificent harmony of the picture was disturbed by a swift steamboat which passed through it, tossing aside the lovely reflections in the water with the directness, power and indifference of an agent of the business world and with a noise like the rush of a gale in the forest. Taking a train on the Hudson River Railroad about midday, I was soon dropped off and left alone with my trunk at the Cold Springs Station opposite West Point. There was then no ferryboat to cross the river, but an oarsman, whose trained sagacity enabled him to divine my necessities, came to me and offered to row me over to the Point in his skiff.

The water was as smooth as a mirror and for awhile the silence was only broken by the regular dip of the oars and their clutter in the rowlocks. But as soon as the boat had passed by the head of Constitution Island, the rugged outlines and rocky slopes of West Point opened out through the clustering cedars, and wafts of music from a great band reached my ears. The flag was seen billowing lazily and proudly against the blue sky from a staff that rose above the trees, and now and then figures in uniform could be descried moving upon the heights. When condemned criminals approach the supreme moment of their execution, their senses become abnormally acute and no object or incident however trivial escapes their observation. I was rapidly entering that mental condition. When the boat was quitted an omnibus was in waiting, the driver of which, after putting my trunk on board without any remark, opened the door for me to enter. Questioning him about the hotels, he said there was but one on the Point, from which the omnibus was sent when a boat with passengers was seen coming over the river. Up the wide zigzag road the vehicle slowly mounted giving one opportunity to note the freshness and fragrance of the well-kept slopes and shrubbery, and the sodded fieldworks with yawning embrasures, the enormous mortars and huge columbiads with pyramids of balls and shells, such as I had seen in pictures.[1] The moral effect of these symbols of war was a mixture of curiosity and dreadful appreciation.

My self-confidence was shaken. As the verge of the plain was reached my attention was attracted to the stately array of buildings away across the broadest and smoothest lawn I had ever seen. Half hidden by lofty elms, there were the immense gray stone barracks with towers and sallyport, the academic building, the chapel, the library with a dome from which the flag was floating. The quick and varied sensations aroused by my first glimpses of this great institution received a new and keen animation as the omnibus neared Roe's Hotel and I saw its broad piazzas enlivened with groups and couples of ladies and gentlemen, sitting or walking, and talking. A glance showed me that the ladies in fresh, flowing summer costumes seemed mostly young and lovely and that the gentlemen were in blue uniform frock coats with bright buttons with straps on the shoulders and with immaculate white trousers and that they had fine upright figures with an easy military deportment. Right in front of this gay throng the omnibus stopped, and so for a moment did the activities and conversation on the porch, and I alighted. The driver kindly indicated the direction of the office, and in mounting the steps and crossing the piazza I imagined I overheard some murmured remarks upon the advent of a new cadet. It was my purpose, momentarily formed, to remain at the hotel a day or two to enable me to look about the place before surrendering myself to the con-

---

[1]Columbiads are large, smoothbore cannons usually found in forts.

trol of the authorities. This dream was quickly disputed the moment my name was written on the hotel register. The sagacious clerk promptly asked if I was a new cadet. Rather flattered by the interest my appearance had awakened in him, I kindly informed him that such was the case and asked for a room. He thereupon informed me to my great astonishment and disappointment that the regulations of the Academy did not permit any cadets, new or old, to have rooms at the hotel and that his orders were to direct me to the Superintendent's office down across the plain in the library building.

Not a step of my walk of a quarter of a mile along the wide, hard road across the plain under the glare of the midday sun is forgotten after forty years. My mind at first was full of painful and racking confusions. My natural freedom was flitting away. I felt myself already enmeshed by an invisible but controlling authority. Being alone and without the guiding advice or counsel of anyone who had ever been here, I was troubled with an agitation difficult to repress. But the grand scene around me claimed my attention and did much to calm and divert me. The towering mountains on my right, uplifting summer's splendors of leaf and vine to the skies, the wide and profound gorge of the Hudson down below on my left, and this grand plain of West Point, matchless in the grace and precision of its embellishments, and the associations thronging about the place hallowed with the names of Washington and his heroic compatriots, the stain of the traitor Arnold and the awful tragedy of Major Andre, all these and more which crowded my memory, were enough on first experience to make a boy, even an egotistical, if unsophisticated plebe, to forget his own anxieties for the moment.

Halfway down to the library, a cadet, I was quite sure from his uniform which I had heard was gray, was coming up the road and excited my greatest curiosity. He was tall and slim and came on with an elastic regular step such as I had never before seen; with elegant, sweet figure, square shoulders, a jaunty blue cap with glistening visor, three rows of bright buttons on a gray coat which fitted him like the bark of a birch tree, white trousers creased in front and rear, shining shoes and white thread gloves—a dainty, well-trained youth with an air of complete self-possession.[2] I ventured to address this being by asking, "Will you please

---

[2]For further information on cadet uniforms, see Frederick P. Todd, *Cadet Gray: A Pictorial History of Life at West Point as Seen through Its Uniforms*, pp. 38-55.

tell me, sir, where the Superintendent's office is?" Pausing, with a bright
and kindly expression on his face, not destitute of a certain cognition such
as one might cast on a stray dog hunting his master, he half turned and
pointed towards the library and without a word resumed his stride toward
the hotel. Thus, slightly paralyzed, and feeling as though I weighed two
or three hundred, I proceeded. In front of the entrance in the shadow of a
tree, a young man in a bright scarlet coat, tall hat with pompon and
bright brass ornaments was walking to and fro. He wore white crossbelts,
waist belt and small sword. At first sight of his gorgeous apparel it
appeared to me that this might be the Superintendent himself. So I respectfully inquired of him for the entrance to the Superintendent's office,
whereat he went with polite alacrity and opened the door, ushering me
into the presence of a gentleman with short-cropped red hair, a friendly
face and quick business manner and speech. He wore a blue frock coat
with a single row of gilt metal buttons and with straps on the shoulders.
Seeing my look of inquiry he politely asked if I was a new cadet and
informed me that he was the Adjutant, Lieut. Seth Williams, and after
registering my name and asking me a few questions for the purpose of
identification, he called, "Orderly!" and the scarlet-coated personage
before mentioned appeared and received orders to show me to the nearest
cadet barracks.

It was all over in five minutes and I was escorted to a room in the
western, or L wing, of the barracks where I found myself in the presence
of Cadet Lieutenant [George W.] Rose. After registering here again I was
shown to a room and the door closed behind me. Thus closed the simple
ceremonies. All preliminary anxieties were at an end; I had arrived. I had
expected a chamber something like the one I had occupied at Newburgh
the night previous. Here was a room fourteen by twenty-two feet with one
large window looking out on the face of the mountain, over some flowers
and vegetable gardens beyond a wide alley. Within the room was a fireplace with an iron mantel, two alcoves at the inner end separated by a
partition with hooks on each side of it for hanging clothing, and not an
article of furniture of any description, and nothing but the window sill on
which one might sit. I soon after learned that the iron bedstead had been
removed for renovation and would have been of no use without mattresses
which were not issued until after summer encampment. The room was
perfectly clean. A solitude of two hours in this vacant and barren room
was a pretty severe test and ordeal to pass through upon the threshold of a
new life. How well misery loves company I realized when the door was

opened and a little fellow, who seemed his mother's own boy, was ushered in and the door closed. It was James Wheeler Jr. from Central New York. We became well acquainted and formed a friendship which lasted throughout his life. The next to come in was a great awkward, laughing youth from Pennsylvania named [Henry W.] Freedley, a jolly fellow who seemed amused at everything, and lastly came a red-haired, austere young man with a pale face and thin lips, named [William R.] Likens from Mississippi.[3] Whilst we were making each other's acquaintance there came a sharp knock at the door, which was opened at once without our bidding and in stepped a cadet corporal. I sprang from the window, and we all began salutations of welcome which were suddenly interrupted by the corporal exclaiming, "ATTENTION!," which of course was Greek to us. The corporal had the sharpest voice and the most exacting. His attitude and expression were awfully military. In two minutes we were subdued to silence and taught the position of a soldier at "attention." In addition to the confusing humiliation of being told how to behave in a dozen different ways, I was informed that a grave infraction of the regulations had been committed by me in sitting on the window sill.

We were "turned out" and marched by the corporal down to "Old Tim O'Makers," the military storekeeper, for our "kit." We were placed in single file in the order in which we had reported, which brought me in front, "Pony" Wheeler next, followed by Freedley with Likens in rear. The care that Freedley had to exercise to prevent his long legs striding over little Wheeler and which frequently made it necessary for him to reach over Wheeler to my shoulders to prevent himself from falling upon him led to trouble which caused the corporal paroxysms of admonitory energy. We walked, or rather stumbled over each other, in a vain effort to take the lockstep, the corporal shouting at us as though he were commanding a battalion, all the way down to the store, about half a mile. Freedley's irrepressible tendency to burst out laughing at every stumble would bring forth stentorian injunctions from the corporal to "Stop laughing in ranks, sir," with a variety of instructions such as "Little fingers on the seam of your pants," "Heads up," "Draw in your chin," "Breast out," "eyes fifteen paces to the front on the ground," and our

---

[3]James Wheeler, Jr., was cashiered from the United States Army in May, 1862, by which time he was a captain. Henry W. Freedley had a more distinguished career. He was appointed brevet major in May, 1863, for gallant and meritorious service in the Battle of Chancellorsville and lieutenant colonel in July, 1863, for gallant and meritorious service in the Battle of Gettysburg. Freedley retired with the rank of colonel in September, 1868. William R. Likens did not graduate from West Point.

earnest but ineffectual attempts to comply seemed to attract the attention of ladies and gentlemen who were strolling along the neighboring walks, and the spectacle evidently being made of us aggravated an embarrassment and increased our mortification.

A "kit" for a cadet as I recollect, consisted of a pair of heavy gray blankets, a bucket and broom, washbasin, pillow, cocoanut dipper, candlestick, a pound of candles, a box of matches, a cake of soap and a small looking-glass. Loaded with the articles above mentioned and presenting an appearance something like a band of immigrants leaving Castle Garden, convoyed by a runner for a boarding house, we were marched back to the barracks by the Corporal whose passionate entreaties to remember that we were disgracing the Academy and ourselves by our unsoldierlike conduct were discouraging. On reaching the barracks we were disenchanted enough to think about home to which our thoughts reverted all the more readily on finding that our trunks had arrived at our room during our absence. After this came the terrible ordeal of being formed in ranks again with about sixty of our fellows and marched or worried to supper in the old mess-hall by several Corporals. The few first classmen or seniors who had general charge of us were entirely too dignified and exalted to embarrass us with any notice. We had an hour of freedom after supper in which we got a little acquaintance with each other. Then at the bugle call "to quarters" we repaired to our room and interchanged experiences since we left our homes. At the call for "tattoo" we turned out and fell in ranks again and answered to our names as the roll was called. During the fifteen minutes that intervened between tattoo and "taps" we spread our blankets, adjusted ourselves to the floor and extinguished the lights. And thus ended the first day at West Point.

Although the floor was hard we slept soundly until aroused by reveille. Hastily dressing we hurried forth to find that wild, weird musical disturbance was made by a dozen drums and fifes in the hands of boys in uniform gathered in a group at the centre of the great area in the rear of the barracks. After playing a few minutes in that position they began a march at quick step across the quadrangle, back and forth, and at the end of ten minutes resumed their first position and brought their performance to a conclusion by three prolonged rhythmic swirls. The Orderly Sergeants and other cadet officers of the four companies of old cadets appeared about the middle of the reveille and took their positions opposite the rear entrances to the barracks, and cadets came out leisurely and took their places in the lines already marked by the Sergeants until just before the concluding swirls of the drums, when the tardy ones came hurrying out, and the ranks were formed in the twinkling of an eye and at the last emphatic tap of the drums they were as motionless as a gray wall. Our despots, the Corporals, were on hand and supervised our formation and attitudes as we came out of our quarters. At the last tap, the command "attention" rang along the lines and then the voices of the Sergeants calling the rolls of the corps and of the new cadets were echoed from the walls. The Sergeants saluted the cadet captains and reported and the companies broke ranks and returned to quarters.

The peculiar effect of that inexorable, mournful reveille upon me has never died away. Whenever I have chanced to hear it in my life it has awakened an impulse to "fall in" for roll call. The military calls at West Point have a penetrating, irresistible force which contributes largely to the unyielding rigor which, rain or shine, characterizes the discipline of the corps of cadets.

The majority of my class had arrived some days before me and had been studying and attending recitations, with old cadets as instructors, in the branches upon which our preliminary examination would be made. Eighty-one candidates had been appointed in 1851 of which number seven had failed to report before the 20th of June. From the time of their arrival the new cadets had been undergoing the setting-up process inculcated and rigorously enforced by daily squad drills, but the more or less unavoidable mortifications, harassments and humiliations incident thereto caused but momentary annoyance to the majority and were overshadowed by anxiety concerning the ordeal of the approaching primary examination. The Academic Board, sitting in grand array, resplendent with full dress uniforms and epaulettes, was not an assemblage to be faced by an unsophisticated youth alone, with perfect tranquillity. Every condition of the examination was very trying to the nerves of the candidate. Its impressiveness amounted to a shock. Imagine a dozen young men sitting on a bench alongside the entrance to the audience chamber. The name of one is called and repeated by an orderly. The youth rises, passes around the flank and in front of a line of large blackboards on great easels, takes his position in front of the centre and becomes painfully conscious that he is the cynosure of twenty-five pairs of keen, investigating eyes. A clear head and a quiet heart are the only things on earth he now needs for a fair showing. The kind voices and paternal manner of a venerable professor go far to reassure him. He is requested to take a book and read, then to write from dictation. Another professor leads him gently through elementary mathematics and so on here and there testing his common-school acquirements. Nearly all of our class had received a good common-school education, a dozen or more had been prepared for college, and two or three were collegiates. The Surgeon's examination immediately followed. This was very carefully and thoroughly conducted. Every vital organ and every sense and every muscle was tested. At evening parade, where we stood in a herd by ourselves, the names of those who had passed the examinations were read by the Adjutant; and there were three who had been rejected for want of some qualifications. We were now "conditional cadets" of the Fourth Class, or "plebes," in the cadet vernacular. Before this examination we had been only "things."

Five of our classmates did not join until September 1: [Jesse K.] Allen, [William B.] Hazen, [Marcus A.] Reno, [George D.] Ruggles and [Alfred T. A.] Torbert. Seven members were added from the class above; so that the roll was as follows:

LIST OF CADETS ADMITTED TO THE U.S. MILITARY ACADEMY IN 1851.

1.	Abbot, Ephraim P. - Ohio.	24.	Gardiner, George F. - At Large.
2.	ALLEN, JESSE K. - Ill.	25.	Gillespie, Zadock R. - Tenn.
3.	AVERELL, WILLIAM W. - N.Y.	26.	GREGG, DAVID McM. - Pa.
4.	BENNETT, CLARENCE E. - N.Y.	27.	HARTZ, EDWARD L. - Pa.
5.*	BIGGS, HERMAN - N.Y.	28.	HAZEN, WILLIAM B. - Ohio.
6.	BRECK, SAMUEL, Jr. - Mass.	29.	HILL, ROBERT C. - N.C.
7.	BRYAN, TIMOTHY M. Jr. - Pa.	30.	HILL, JAMES H. - At Large.
8.	Bursley, Allen A. - Mass.	31.	Holbrook, James B. - Conn.
9.	CHILDS, FREDERICK I. - At Large.	32.	Huston, George W. - Va.
10.	Church, John R. - Ga.	33.*	JACKSON, GEORGE - Va.
11.	COLBURN, ALBERT V. - Vt.	34.	Larned, Charles T. - Mass.
12.	Collins, Thomas E. - N.Y.	35.	Leigh, Arthur K. - Md.
13.	COMSTOCK, CYRUS B. - Mass.	36.	Likens, William R. - Miss.
14.	CUNNINGHAM, ARTHUR S. - At Large.	37.	Littlefield, Chas. S. - Me.
15.	Drum, William F. - At Large.	38.	McHenry, John H. Jr. - Ky.
16.	DU BOIS, JOHN VAN DEUSEN - N.Y.	39.	McNutt, John W. - Tenn.
17.	ELLIOT, GEO. H. - Mass.	40.	MERRILL, LEWIS - Pa.
18.	Emery, Chas. D. - Pa.	41.	Montague, Mickelboro' L. - Ala.
19.	Faison, Jas. A. - N.C.	42.	Newton, John W. - Ark.
20.	Folsom, Andrew J. - N.Y.	43.	NICHOLLS, FRANCIS R. T. - La.
21.*	FORSYTH, JAMES W. - Ohio.	44.	Nowland, Wm. B. - At Large.
22.	Fort, James E. - N.Y.	45.	Palmer, Benj. H. - Ky.
23.	FREEDLEY, HENRY W. - Pa.	46.	PEASE, WM. R. - N.Y.
		47.	Peck, Henry W. - Ohio.
		48.	Powell, Conrad H. - Va.

49. Powers, Longworth - At Large.
50. Price, Leonidas L. - Tenn.
51. Randall, John C. - La.
52.‡ RENO, MARCUS A. - Ill.
53. RUGGLES, GEORGE D. - N.Y.
54. Russell, Leonidas - Ind.
55.° Salisbury, Charles L. - N.Y.
56. SHOUP, FRANCIS A. - Ind.
57. SMALL, MICHAEL P. - Pa.
58. Stanton, Henry T. - Ky.
59. Ten Eyck, Samuel - N.Y.
60. THOMAS, CHARLES W. - At Large.
61. TORBERT, ALFRED T. A. - Del.
62. TURNER, JOHN W. - Ill.
63. VAN CAMP, CORNELIUS - Pa.
64.* VINTON, FRANCIS L. - At Large.
65. Watson, Chas. B. - At Large.
66. WEBB, ALEXANDER S. - N.Y.
67. WEITZEL, GODFREY - Ohio.
68. WHEELER, JAMES, Jr. - N.Y.
69. WHEELER, JUNIUS B. - N.C.
70. Whistler, James A. - At Large.
71. Williams, Edward - D.C.

LISTS OF CADETS ADMITTED TO THE ACADEMY IN 1850, WHO WERE TURNED-BACK TO JOIN THE CLASS OF 1855.

1. Black, J. Logan - S.C.
2. DICK, GEORGE McG. - Pa.
3. GAY, EBENEZER - N.H.
4. Green, Jackson W. - Cal.
5. LAZELL, HENRY M. - Mass.
6. Scott, William P. - Md.
7. Wood, Robert C., Jr. - At Large.

REJECTED BY THE ACADEMIC BOARD - 1851

1. Jeffries, Benjamin F. - Mo.
2. Lyman, Hamilton - N.Y.
3. Woods, Cornelius C. - Tenn.

FAILED TO REPORT - 1851

1. Caldwell, H. Clay - Iowa.
2. Eaker, F. - Ky.
3. Pentecost, W. P. - Ind.
4. Powers, L. - At Large.
5. Screvens, Richard D. - At Large.
6. Tew, William H. - Ohio.
7. Vickery, Francis - Ky.

1. Fort, James E. - died at West Point, June 15, 1853.

Names of graduates are in Capitals.
*Graduated with class of 1856.
‡Graduated with class of 1857.
°Resigned July '51.

By the time our trunks were stored and we were settled in camp the members of our class had become generally acquainted with each other and the spirit of comradeship began to take hold of us. These young men were fairly representative of the communities from which they came. The characteristics of the quiet puritan and the self-confident cavalier abounded. As between the city and the country the latter was represented by a large majority. The accents and idioms of all the older states were distinguishable and those of Virginia, Kentucky, Pennsylvania and the states of New England were easily recognized. New York has no peculiar accent nor idiom—it mixes and blends all.

Just at the beginning of our lives at West Point it was noticeable that southern men seemed to *junta* more together than with northern men and that northerners as a rule broke up into small parties or couples according to their inclinations during hours of recreation. The prominence of the family in the social structure of the South was easily perceived in the conversation of southern men as well as a certain acquaintance with political questions in which the South had a positive interest. I presume this slight but significant tendency to segregation has not been observed since the war. As it was, even then, when it was a natural, if an unconscious outgrowth of conditions which are now dead and forgotten, it quickly faded out of sight and our common purposes, needs and studies soon welded our personal friendships into a union which was never broken.

We experienced the usual "hazing" which was then in vogue, but it rarely received serious consideration from old or new cadets and was soon forgotten. There are two ways of viewing the matter. One involving the survival of the fittest; that a youth so sensitive and tender that he cannot endure the surprises and shocks of an innocent hazing without injury has mistaken his career in the endeavor to become a soldier. I have heard the inventors, promoters or excusers of hazing go so far as to draw an illustration from the life and example of our Lord by claiming that He was not always "meek and lowly" but most intensely positive in His character, and, instance His scourging the money changers out of the temple. Those opposed to hazing in any and all degrees believe that anything which tends to wound the self respect of a youth undergoing the formative process of character and habits, inflicts an unnecessary and cruel wound, the scar of which will remain in the victim, and, what is equally deplorable, will foster and encourage in him who inflicts it an indifference to the feelings of others which should never have place in the character of a gentleman. Undoubtedly some degree of callousness is inevitable in the sensibilities of those who indulge in hazing and to the school in which it is tolerated. I have seen illustrations of this latter effect carried on into the army and revealed even in prominent commanders.

There were, as all graduates remember, occasional personal difficulties, but no one can recollect any quarreling. There was a quiet, unavoidable way of settling such difficulties which corrected all tendencies to careless or reckless expressions. Such settlements were conducted with dignity and deliberation and with the aid of one or two seconds for each principal and sometimes an umpire at Koscinsczko's Garden or other secluded spot, and the results were usually satisfactory. Friendship was generally restored and there was hardly ever any open talk about such affairs. The net result of this adjudication of differences was to lead men to fully understand the responsibility of language.

Our tactical officers during the first encampment were of the best in the army and well remembered. The commandant of the corps was Captain B.[Bradford] R. Alden who was a courteous and considerate gentleman of the old school,[4] and his assistants were Lieutenants J.[John] M. Jones, Henry B. Clitz, D.[David] R. Jones and Charles T. Baker who had all distinguished themselves in the Mexican War. Judged even by the experiences of after years, they were model soldiers and gentlemen. Our drills at infantry and in the school of the piece in artillery were almost continuous. We were out in the morning before the dew was off the grass. Drill, drill, drill until our muscles were brought to a rhythmic and uniform motion.

It was a great day for us when our uniforms were ready; and besides the general effect which we welcomed in our appearances, there was a particular result which was curious in the difficulty we at first experienced in recognizing each other. Before we had donned the gray, the differences in our various garbs, in cut and color, had afforded ready means for distinguishing any one of us; and now these means were restricted to size, shape, walk or carriage at distances beyond which the faces could not be recognized. It was wonderful how keen our sight soon became in these particulars. A cadet who has been at the Academy a year could name any cadet in his own class, and a majority of those in the classes above and below it, almost as far as he could well see him. A stranger could not distinguish one cadet from another at a hundred yards.

There are some beneficent results produced by uniform clothing in a school that are worthy the careful consideration of our colleges and great

---

[4]Bradford R. Alden served as commandant of cadets at West Point from 1845 to 1852. The following year he was wounded in the Oregon Indian war, which prevented him from serving in the Civil War.

schools. Every youth in uniform soon perceives that the object of the school is to cultivate that which is inside his clothing and under his hat. External display is impossible—clothing all the same in quality and quantity; no pockets, no use for them; no money; and no needs unprovided for by the "Order Book" under the approval of the Superintendent. Young men would then stand together, at the threshold of life's opportunities, as they should start in a democratic republic. The military training in other schools would not need be so complete and thorough as it is at West Point, but enough of it for organization and discipline would be found advantageous for inculcating self-government and developing all manly attributes.

It is a fact, not always recognized even by those acquainted with the Military Academy, that the corps of cadets governs itself. If every officer of the army, every professor or instructor were temporarily absent from the post, the discipline of the corps would be maintained. The principles of honor and truth were held so high and sacred that the words "lie" and "liar" were never heard, even in playful conversation. A cadet's word was always accepted without question.

Life in our first encampment is well remembered—the arduous hours of drill through which we moved with the untiring regularity of the hands of a clock; the marches to and from the mess hall to the music of the drum and fife; the morning parade and guard mount; the "evening for colors"; the evening parade and trooping spectators; the sunset gun and the falling flag; the strolling hour after supper; the swim in the river and the furtive smoke; the soft illumination of the tent-lighted camp from which breathed forth the music of the violin and guitar, banjo and flute; and the murmur of voices in story and song until all were hushed after "tattoo" and "taps" into the silence of night when the quiet tread of sentinels tolled as to our dreams.

By the end of August when we broke camp and marched into barracks, we were physically in pretty good shape. The class, as yet, had not been graded at all; and when together, our names had been called in alphabetical order. Now, we were classified into sections of about a dozen each which remained unchanged during the month; then and afterward at the end of every month, transfers were made up and down according to our marks in studies; and before January the class had become settled into an order which was not much changed until June, the end of our first year. The studies of the first year's course excepting French were not new to me, and I soon fell into the habit of resorting to the great library where

I found a world of opportunities which I embraced with avidity and un-bounded pleasure. This unrestrained habit of reading, to which every new book lent a fresh zest and a larger capacity for enjoyment, doubtless affected my class standing by a diminution of that attention which my regular studies should have received; yet so long as my final graduation was not thereby imperilled, I could not resist it. And I have never since regretted any loss of rank I may have suffered on that account. First going through a strictly historical course of reading wherein I came across the fitting places for the fragments which I had gathered in earlier years, I then set out to read in proper chronological order the poetry and general literature of the world from the *Iliad* down to Tennyson and Longfellow and embracing some from the Scandinavian, Teutonic and Romantic languages that had been translated into English.

There were several good readers with trained and discriminating tastes in my class whose interesting talk and appreciative views, even if immature, served as a guide and spur to my progress. The prescribed studies of the four years' course provided the strong and essential warp of our mental development, but at the end, only thirty-four men of our class held unbroken threads. The rich and varied treasures of the library fur-nished the woof which patterned and gradually formed and variegated our intellectual fabric, and which left to us the most pleasing and enduring memories of our little *noctes ambrosianae*, where, as nowhere else in the cadet life, we saw revealed the true, real individual personal character of each—the father of the man. There the bright faces, the genial smiles, merry conceits, brilliant fancies, unaffected tones of voice—all the infinite diversities of action and expression which distinguished and endeared our classmates—made faithful and unfading portraits on my memory. Al-though I have met the majority of them since our graduation, and before they joined the "Great Majority," yet the strongest and most welcome remembrances of them leaps over the intervening recollections of forty years to the days when we were cadets together.

> "WHAT IS, in the far distance seems to be,
> THE PAST, the PAST alone is true to me."

The examinations were the principal and most trying events of our cadet life, and I remember best the first one, in January 1852. The scene as I recall it was a large, carpeted hall over the library, one side of which was occupied by tall glass cases containing the philosophical instruments and apparatus, in front of which were arranged on easels, four long black-boards. On the opposite side was a slightly elevated platform upon which in front of the centre stood an elaborate table behind which sat a tall man in full uniform, with snow-white hair, a benevolent kindly face and eyes —Captain Henry Brewerton of the Corps of Engineers, the Superinten-dent of the Military Academy. On a line with him to the right and left were seated the Academic Board of Professors, Assistant Professors and Instructors to the number of twenty or more. Among those I remember best there were on his right the spare figure, scholarly, wrinkled face, ample hair of iron gray and inclined to curl of D.[Dennis] H.[Hart] Mahan, Professor of Engineering. Next to him, a short corpulent man with large head, round face, small mouth turned up at the corners, and eyebrows ever lifting high as he threw his glasses back onto his bald head when asking questions, was the presentment of the formidable Professor of Mathematics, Albert E. Church.

Then followed on the right Assistant Professor [John J.] Peck and Instructors [John A.] Mebane, [Delavan D.] Perkins and [Chauncey] McKeever, all officers of the army. The latter was a well-made man of medium size, with ruddy complexion and restless nervous manner and a tendency, when asking questions, to go off at half cock and repeat them with modifications before they could be answered, the questions and repetitions lapping onto each other like skirmishers running up into line. On the left of the Superintendent sat Assistant Professor E. Kirby Smith, the prominent features of whose long earnest face were deep set and serious eyes below a high, doric brow. Our eye was arrested in its sweep by the grand symmetrical figure which next appeared, with massive head and noble face with well-trimmed beard and a general expression of strong life and high intelligence, whose voice cadets were used to hearing in the wild rush of a flying artillery drill like the roar of a lion, and in whom the corps always recognized the original of "War" in the great picture of "Peace and War" above the chancel in the Chapel. This was Major George H. Thomas, Instructor of Ordnance and Artillery. The familiar figure of the Commandant of the Corps, Captain B. R. Alden, came next—a gen-tleman of dark complexion, perfect soldierly bearing and high-bred man-ner. Then a line of distinguished looking officers sat behind the first row.

The examination began with Lieutenant McKeever firing off the names: "Mr. Averell," "Mr. Fort," "Mr. Hartz" and "Mr. Powell" who took their places in front of the blackboards, facing the battery of aca-demic eyes. We received our several problems and turned to our work whilst another of the section was called up and questioned. I had "General Theory" and Powell next to me had "Logarithms." After a little while Powell whispered to me, "Averell I can't do it. Shall have to 'fess.' " I told him to keep his head, that he could do it. A minute or two later there was a low moan and a tumble. Powell was down in a dead faint. The Superintendent touched a bell, an orderly appeared and supported him out of the hall and the examination proceeded. When the results had been announced on parade, a day or two later, nine men of our class took off their uniforms, put on their "cits" and started for their homes. As one, [Charles L.] Salisbury, had resigned in July, we had after the first January examination but sixty-one survivors who on February 7 received their warrants on taking the oath of allegiance.

To perform this ceremony the class was marched to the library in side arms and dress caps and seated. The Academic Board was called to order by the Superintendent, and the nature and obligations of the oath were explained to us in a letter from the Secretary of War which was read by Lieut. D. R. Jones, Acting Adjutant, and then six of the first on the roll of the class were called up and seated around a table on which lay the full form of their oaths which they signed and then proceeded to another table upon which lay a large, open Bible behind which stood the Magistrate. Laying their hands on the sacred volume they listened to the reading of the oath and kissed the book, whereupon their warrants were handed them by the Commandant Captain Alden. The scene was one of great dignity and solemnity.

In March '52 there was a change among our tactical instructors which resulted in Lieutenant D. R. Jones having Company A, Lieutenant H. B. Clitz Company B, Bvt. Captain E.[Edmund] K. Smith Company C, and Lieutenant J. M. Jones Company D.

Our studies continued the same, Mathematics, English Studies and French, gradually increasing in volume and in exacting rigor of recitations until the end of our first year.

On the 26th of May I remember a swift whisper ran along the ranks at evening parade, "There's Jenny Lind." The queen of song, just married, had arrived at the Point that day and her carriage halted in front of the Superintendent's house to look at parade. The band serenaded her at the hotel that evening, but we never saw her more nor heard her voice.

At the June examination in '52 our class was further reduced to fifty-two members. A few were turned back into the next class, but the greater number were discharged.

Our third class encampment was, to me, the least notable of all. We were only emancipated plebes, and had plenty of hard work with no control of the gayeties. We were taught dancing to be sure and enjoyed the hops in a subordinate manner.

The chief servants of our Alma Mater, the Academic Staff—their personal appearance and characteristics—furnished abiding memories to her children. Those officers could not know, except by remembering their own experience, how thoroughly and well cadets "sized them up," how accurately all traits of character, manner and habit were noted. No photograph could be more faithful than the composite mental picture which resulted from cadet observations. Nothing could excite a more intense interest among cadets than a change in the academic staff. These were not frequent but were always notable. The change which produced the most profound sensation while we were at the Academy was made in the autumn of 1852 when the Superintendent was relieved by Colonel Robert E. Lee and the Commandant of Cadets, Captain Alden, by Major R.[Robert] S. Garnett, and Captain J. M. Jones, the Senior Tactical Instructor, by Lieutenant C.[Cadmus] M. Wilcox and Capt. E. K. Smith by Lieut. Milton Cogswell. The Academic Staff then became as follows:

ACADEMIC STAFF

Superintendent and Commandant: Bvt. Col. Robert E. Lee, Captain Engineers

Professor of Military and Civil Engineering: Dennis H. Mahan, L.L.D.

Assistant Professor of Engineering: Bvt. Capt. Gustavus W. Smith, 1st Lieut. Engineers.

Acting Assistant Professors of Engineering: 2d Lieut. Charles S. Stewart, Engineers; Bvt. 2d Lieut. Newton F. Alexander, Engineers.

Professor of Natural & Experimental Philosophy: William H. C. Bartlett, L.L.D.

Assistant Professor of Philosophy: 1st Lieut. Joseph J. Reynolds, 3d Artillery.

Acting Assistant Professors of Philosophy: 1st Lieut. Edward D. Stockton, 1st Infantry; 2d Lieut. Joseph H. Wheelock, 4th Artillery.

Professor of Mathematics: Albert E. Church, L.L.D.

Assistant Professor of Mathematics: 1st Lieut. William G. Peck, Top. Engineers.

Acting Assistant Professors of Mathematics: 2d Lieut. Delavan D. Perkins, 4th Artillery; 2d Lieut. Chauncey McKeever, 3d Artillery; 2d Lieut. John A. Mebane, 2d Artillery; 2d Lieut. Alexander J. Perry, 2d Artillery.

Professor of Chemistry, Mineralogy, and Geology: Jacob W. Bailey, A.M.

Assistant Professor of Chemistry, Mineralogy, and Geology: Bvt. Capt. Edward C. Boynton, 1st Lieut. 1st Artillery.

Acting Assistant Professors of Chemistry, Mineralogy, and Geology: 2d Lieut. Caleb Huse, 1st Artillery; Bvt. 2d Lieut. George T. Balch, Ordn.

Chaplain, and Professor of Ethics, and English Studies: Rev. William T. Sprole.

Assistant Professor of Ethics, and English Studies: Bvt. Capt. Henry Coppée, A.M., 1st Lieut. 1st Artillery.

Acting Assistant Professors of Ethics, and English Studies: 1st Lieut. Charles C. Gilbert, 1st Infantry; 2d Lieut. Beekman DuBarry, 3d Artillery.

Professor of Drawing: Robert W. Weir, N.A.

Assistant Professor of Drawing: 1st Lieut. Richard S. Smith, 4th Artillery.

Acting Assistant Professor of Drawing: Bvt. Capt. Truman Seymour, 1st Lieut. 1st Artillery.

Instructor of Practical Military Engineering: Capt. George W. Cullum, Engineers.

Assistant Instructors of Practical Engineering: 2d Lieut. Andrew J. Donelson, Engineers; 2d Lieut. James C. Duane, Engineers;.

Professor of the French Language: Hyacinth R. Agnel.

Assistant Professor of the French Language: 1st Lieut. Theophilus D'Orémieulx, 1st Infantry.

Acting Assistant Professor of the French Language: 1st Lieut. John H. Grelaud, 4th Artillery.

Commandant of Cadets, and Instructor of Infantry Tactics: Bvt. Maj. Robert S. Garnett, Capt. 7th Infantry.

Assistant Instructors of Infantry Tactics: 1st Lieut. David R. Jones, 2d Infantry; 1st Lieut. Henry B. Clitz, 3d Infantry; 1st Lieut. Cadmus M. Wilcox, 7th Infantry; 2d Lieut. Milton Cogswell, 8th Infantry.

Instructor of Artillery, and Cavalry: Bvt. Major George H. Thomas, 1st Lieut. 3d Artillery.

Assistant Instructor of Artillery: Bvt. Major Fitz John Porter, 1st Lieut. 4th Artillery.

Assistant Instructors of Cavalry: 1st Lieut. Delos B. Sacket, 1st Dragoons: 2d Lieut. Roger Jones, Md. Riflemen.

Instructor of the Sword Exercise: Patrice de Janon.

MILITARY STAFF

Adjutant: **Bvt. Capt. Seth Williams**, 1st Lieut.
1st Artillery.
Surgeon: **John M. Cuyler**, M.D.
Assistant Surgeon: **James Simons**, M.D.
*Assistt. Commy. of Subsistence, Quarter Master, and
Treasurer:* **1st Lieut. Richard S. Smith**, 4th
Artillery.

Colonel Lee was then about forty-four years old, six feet in height and his figure in form and proportions was a realization of perfect manly symmetry. His natural unaffected dignity and grace of manner and motion presented a personal equilibrium which nothing could invade or disturb. I remember, cadets living in the front rooms of barracks were apt to go to the windows to see him walk by on the opposite side of the street on his way to and from his office. It was not that our eyes were idle, but because there is nothing more attractive than a superb man in motion. There were several strong resemblances of person and character between Colonel Lee and Major George H. Thomas. And I heard in after years that they held each other in high esteem which was once illustrated by a little incident that occurred on the march of the Second Cavalry to Texas in 1855. One night, Major Thomas was visiting Colonel Lee at his campfire, and when he had said good night and gone, Colonel Lee was heard to exclaim, musingly, "Corinthian Thomas! Corinthian Thomas!" In an effort to account for the divergence of these two great soldiers, both from Virginia, at the outbreak of the Civil War, I have sometimes conjectured that the ownership of slaves by one of their families and not by the other might have given unconsciously to each a differing bent to their determinations.

Major Garnett, our new Commandant, at once impressed himself with restless and resistless energy upon the corps as the most forceful drill-master and strictest disciplinarian the Academy had ever known. He cut our hair very short and introduced a new style of dress cap and a new manual of arms with Hardee's tactics. His voice moved our ranks like an electric shock, but our hands, arms and feet were never quite quick enough to suit him. He was merciless in giving us demerit marks. Alas! a few years later and that ringing voice, to the sound of which our battalion had responded with lightning evolutions on the plain at West Point, was hushed forever beside a stream at the foot of Cheat Mountain, West Virginia, when General Garnett fell at the rear of his column retreating before the Union forces of McClellan.[5]

After our furlough in '53 there were frequent evening meetings of members of our class before "call to quarters" in one or other of our rooms where satisfactory entertainment was found in stories, recitations and songs. A few possessed some musical accomplishments and could play upon the violin, flute, guitar and banjo. Hartz could pick a banjo with a skill and taste equal to that of any minstrel. New songs were often contributed by Vinton, Van Camp and Gay, who were our leading poets, and some of the more atrocious rhymes were charged to me. A song of Van Camp's, inspired by the Garnett revolution, before we had learned to appreciate and esteem the Major's methods, began:

> Oh my dear Commandant 'tis no wonder you frown,
>> Och home, Major Bob G.
> Popularity for you is fast going down,
>> Och home, Major Bob G.
> How altered our air with these dress caps we wear,
> And you've cut off our hair which should be flowing full,
> Thure's no longer a churl who can boast of a curl,
>> Och home, Major Bob G.

At the examination in January '53 I can remember that the problem given me was to draw a tangent plane to a hyperboloid of revolution at a given point of the surface. I had previously had an amusing tussle with my instructor in the section room concerning the same problem, when I knew little about it, which ended in a draw, but a much better mark than I deserved which was .5. I then took the trouble to learn it thoroughly so that I was fortunately quite prepared at the examination. After that examination we began to count the days to furlough and there was a calendar in all the rooms—in some rooms two—from which a day was erased every evening. No Cossack returning from war ever hailed the first glimpse of the Steppes with more delight than did we, on March 26, '53, the order to be measured for our furlough uniforms. When the last day had been scratched off the calendar, forty-odd half-crazy youths dragged their

---

[5]Garnett's death on 13 July 1861 gave him the dubious distinction of being the first general officer on either side to die from battle in the Civil War.

forgotten trunks out of the storerooms and had them packed and themselves arrayed in their new uniforms hours before the time to leave, and the irksome wait was filled by embracing each other and everyone in reach. All, excepting the few going up the river, sailed away for New York City on board the steamboat *Alida* and the echoes of the highlands were aroused with our songs and cheers. I remember we all put up at the Metropolitan Hotel kept by Simeon Leland and after dinner went to Franconi's Hippodrome, in an amphitheater erected on a vacant lot where now stands the Fifth Avenue Hotel, and enjoyed the chariot races. In coming out through a crowded passageway, Merrill had his pocket picked, which awakened our astonishment. A clean slit had been made in the breast of his new uniform coat and his pocket book extracted therefrom. Van Camp and I went also to the World's Fair away up out of town near the reservoir above 40th Street and had as much enjoyment as I have ever experienced since in visiting such exhibitions. We enjoyed a veritable enchantment at Niblo's Garden in the evening.

The raptures of nearly three months furlough after a close seclusion of two years may be imagined but cannot be easily described. The recollection of my own homecoming is vivid. Although expected, the time of my arrival was not exactly known, so there was no one to meet me at the station one glorious morning in June and I had a delightful walk of three miles to the summit of Cameron Hill and entered my home without being seen until I was among my people. The younger ones after a burst of joyous exclamations seemed rather afraid to touch my lovely uniform, but my mother in her supreme happiness regarded it not at all.

The class reassembled at the Metropolitan in New York on Aug. 26. The next morning after breakfast, Ruggles and I went to the World's Fair and spent half the day. I remember we were greatly impressed with the statuary, especially *Power's Greek Slave*, *Sue* and *The Fisher Boy*. The large equestrian statue of Washington we thought very grand. We joined Van Camp and others of the class at luncheon in Taylor's gilded saloon on Broadway, and in the evening went to see the famous Ravels at Niblo's Garden. We were off at 7 A.M. on the 28th by train for West Point and reported at 3 P.M. and slept in camp that night.

The examination in June '53, before our furlough, had left but forty-three members in our class.

The studies of the Second Class year, which included Astronomy, Chemistry and Philosophy, were the most interesting and satisfying of the entire course. A man knows but little of earth and less of heaven until he has learned something of Chemistry and Astronomy, and our minds had been prepared by the thorough training of the first two years to grasp and enjoy the unfolding wonders of the two infinities—the great and the small.

At the end of our Second Class course, and of our third year in June '54, our class was the first one for a number of years to pass the examination in Philosophy without the loss of a man. The class above us the previous year had lost seven members on their examinations. The Board of Visitors, the Professors and the Instructors all expressed high opinions of our class in its studies, military qualifications and deportment, and we were further gratified by an especial commendation of Major Fitz-John Porter that we had excelled all other classes which had passed through the Academy within his experience in artillery studies and practice. This encomium drawn from that accomplished instructor and ideal soldier was remembered with pride. But our best display was of our drawings with pencil and watercolors, which when mounted and exhibited in the gallery were pronounced the best that had been shown in twenty years. I was rather proud of having nine watercolor and ten pencil drawings admitted of my own. My highest standing in drawing was 3, obtained in topographical sketches. The bump of "locality," as the phrenologists call it, was largely developed in my head and served me well in later life. James Whistler was easily at the head of our class in graphic art and Vinton, Gay, Webb, Larned, Du Bois, Thomas, Merrill and half-a-dozen others showed promise of becoming good artists. Whistler excelled in ink etching in a wonderful style of his own. He was remarkably nearsighted, which caused astonishingly novel effects in his colors—harmonious and beautiful, but unnatural to the normal eye. His abnormal vision may have influenced his work in after years and given rise to his "Nocturnes" and "Symphonies" in different tones of a single color, which occasioned his controversy with Mr. Ruskin in London.[6] We had only nine months in drawing: from September 1, 1853 to June 1, 1854. That coordination of the eye and the hand which enables one to transfer accurately the picture or image on the retina or in the mind to canvass is an uncommon gift. Whistler could look at an object and at once draw it correctly; he could even create characters and situations from memory or from his ideals of

---

[6]Whistler had settled in England in the 1860s where he became a leading figure in the art world, although his colors and shapes were too advanced for English taste. John Ruskin, an English critic who disliked non-didactic, amoral art, accused Whistler of "flinging a pot of paint in the public's face." Whistler sued Ruskin.

them. One of Whistler's pictures which was done at that time yet hangs, I believe, in the gallery of the Academy. It represents the great door of an English church, opening upon a churchyard. Grand old trees cast their leafy shadows athwart the doorway and across the grass and tombstones. English country people, men, women, and children, are enjoying the intermission between morning and afternoon services. Some are in groups, enjoying their luncheon. The faithfulness and tenderness of the entire scene, in its large effects and minute details, strikes one as remarkable when it is considered that it was all done with a reed pen and India ink. We often saw the old master, Robert Weir, standing behind "Jimmy" Whistler and watching his rapid work. Poor fellow, he was "found" in Chemistry and, when asked about the difficulty, replied laughingly, with an implied reproach upon nature, "Oh it was because silicon was not a gas."

During the autumn of '53 Mrs. Winfield Scott visited West Point and on the evening of September 24 gave a party at Roe's Hotel to which twenty cadets of the First and Second classes were invited. General Winfield Scott, Commander in chief, was very gracious and sociable and called us his young friends. The madame was arrayed in a costume of oriental splendor and her head was surmounted with a wonderful creation of silver filigree. She graciously called us her children and was most happy when surrounded by a half dozen of us listening to her really spirited and clever talk. On October 1 the entertainment was repeated and we felt sincerely grateful to the General and Mrs. Scott for a diversion so rare and agreeable. The General with his immense proportions and impressive manner inspired us with a feeling of genuine veneration almost amounting to awe. I believe there was an unconscious and unexpressed belief that General Scott had always been so. That he had ever been born, or had ever been young, did not occur to any of us. Neither did the thought exist that he would not always be the Commander in chief. He was especially kind to me and spoke of the Battle of Lundy's Lane just before which he encamped upon my grandfather's place at Black Rock near Buffalo, N.Y.

Another lady whom I remember meeting on these occasions was Mrs. Walworth, who was the widow of the eminent Chancellor, and had been born an Averell.[7]

My roommate from September '53 until our June examination in '54

---

[7]Maria Ketchum Averill had died before this date. She was married to Reuben Hyde Walworth (1788-1867) who was the last chancellor of New York. Averell could have met Walworth's second wife (Ellen Smith Hardin) but it would be more than a decade before she would be widowed.

was David McM. Gregg who became the intrepid cavalry commander in the Army of the Potomac who brought the Battle of Gettysburg to a fitting and glorious close by attacking and defeating the main body of the Confederate cavalry on our right. On the evening of the 8th of June, the class held a jollification in our room to celebrate our success in passing the examinations.

The hard work of the previous year, together with the memories of the social enjoyments of former seasons in which we had participated to some extent, made our first-class encampment eagerly welcomed by us. The hotels, both Roe's on the Point and Cozzens down below, were crowded with visitors. Because we controlled and directed its diversions, perhaps it was the gayest camp life we had ever seen. Notwithstanding our hard work during the day at practical military engineering and swift artillery drills, we were always ready every evening when there was pleasant weather to entertain the throngs of visitors to our campground. Eben Gay had always ready a new topical song which would never fail to provoke roars of laughter.[8] We had minstrelsy, dancing, and fantastic entertainments to our hearts' content and the apparent delight of our visitors. As many as four hundred guests sometimes attended our balls; and being one of the managers, I had many agreeable opportunities to make delightful acquaintances. Mrs. Winfield Scott arrived in August with her daughter Mrs. H. L. Scott and sent for me to act as her intendant at a *soirée dansante*, as she was pleased to call it, which she was about to give at the house of Professor Bailey. The madame entrusted to me some delicate negotiations with a distinguished lady whose attendance she desired and who for certain reasons she feared would not come. When I reported the result to Mrs. Scott and the causes of the hesitation of the lady, the madame interrupted me with the exclamation, "Oh! we may count upon her coming for as my old friend Jean Jacques Rousseau says, 'A woman who hesitates is lost!' " which was the first time I had ever heard the saying quoted, and the sequel proved its truth. Mrs. H. L. Scott was young and one of the loveliest women I ever saw. Among the many distinguished visitors to West Point during these gay summer days were Hon. James Watson Webb and family, ex-governor Bradish and Governor

[8]Ebenezer Gay of New Hampshire served in the Union Army in the Civil War. He was made a brevet major in October, 1862 for gallant and meritorious service in the Battle of Perryville, and a lieutenant colonel in September, 1864, for similar service during the Atlanta campaign.

Seymour with their families, Recorder Tillon of New York, Mr. Charles Bonapart and family of Baltimore, the Adams family of Augusta, Ga., Robb of New Orleans, Amory of Boston, Oakley and Rhinelander of New York, Bishop Kip of California, Mr. Geo. W. Curtis of N.Y., and the Colemans of Penna. On the evening of the 28th of August we had the largest ball that had ever been given in the academic building. There were not less than four hundred ladies present and all the halls were thronged. Dancing was kept up until midnight. In the capacity of floor manager that evening I had the honor of receiving General Scott and family and the families of ex-governor Bradish and Governor Seymour. About 10 o'clock, I remember, Mrs. Scott sent for me and presented me to several ladies from Washington.[9]

The last I remember of that camp is that I was officer of the day when the tents were struck and was the last man to leave the old camp-ground when the battalion marched away to barracks.

The studies of the last year were of the highest interest and included Military Engineering, Field and Permanent Fortifications, Army Organization, Strategy, Advanced Guards and Outposts, Civil Engineering, Bridge Building, Railroads and Canals, Stone Cutting, Machines, Motive Powers, Architecture, Geology and Mineralogy, Gunpowder, Projectiles and Pyrotechny, Artillery, Cavalry and Fencing, Practical Instruction in Construction and Fabrication, Moral Science, Logic and Kent's Commentaries. The course also included working drawings in colors of Fortifications and Public Works. Our capacities for study had been so trained and enlarged that we entered upon this formidable course with easy alacrity and found more leisure for general reading, perhaps, than in the previous years.

I was now First Lieutenant of Company D and Eben Gay was my roommate. Our room was in the same division with the one I had first occupied on my arrival at the Academy three years before. Gay was a strong, handsome, spirited fellow with an active brain and a little inclined

---

[9]Identifiable persons mentioned are: George W. Curtis (1824-1892) author, editor for *Harper's New Monthly Magazine*, and reformer; James Watson Webb (1802-1863) journalist and U.S. minister to Brazil from 1861-1869; Luther Bradish (1783-1863) New York politician, lieutenant governor from 1839 to 1843, and unsuccessful candidate for governor in 1842; Horatio Seymour (1810-1886) New York politician, governor from 1853 to 1863, and Democratic presidential candidate in 1868; William I. Kip (1811-1893) first bishop of the Episcopal diocese of California in 1853; James Robb (1814-1881) New Orleans banker and merchant; and Charles Bonaparte (1803-1857) scientist and author of many books on birds.

to recklessness in taking risks of demerit and "running" to Benny Havens'.[10]

"Running the limits" was a risky enterprise and sometimes men were found absent by unexpected inspections. About Christmas '54, Weitzel, Gregg, J. H. Hill, Elliott, Colburn and Freedley were all "hived" absent for an hour by inspections, and the first four, who were cadet officers, were reduced to the ranks and the others had some "extras" to walk on Saturday afternoons.

Any retrospect of West Point which did not include any reminiscences of Benny Havens would be incomplete. Benny Havens, who kept a picturesque little sylvan resort on the bank of the river below Buttermilk Falls about two miles below West Point, was a singular character. He was of uncertain age, over fifty and under eighty, with a ruddy clean-shaven face which displayed soft little wrinkles about his eyes and mouth, and was full of wise saws and quaint stories about prominent army officers who had been cadets during the previous twenty-five years, which he would relate with a merry twinkle of his eyes and a genial quaver of voice that made them fascinating to youngsters. He had three grown daughters, loyal children, who waited upon us at sequestered and sometimes nocturnal banquets of chicken, cakes and small beer. These daughters of Benny were invested by cadets with all the charms of Dulcineas del Toboso. In cadets who visited Benny's place two dominant traits were exhibited—chivalry and hunger. The first is recorded in the West Point classic:

"Oh Ryders is a perfect 'fess' and Cozzens all the go,
And officers as thick as hops infest the Falls below,
But we pass them all so slyly by as once a week we go
To toast the lovely flowers that bloom at Benny Havens O."

To be known well enough to be called by name, or inquired about by Benny or his daughters, was an honor to which no cadet was indifferent.

---

[10]Benny Havens was the closest tavern to West Point, located below Buttermilk Falls which today is known as Highland Falls. It was a favorite albeit illegal meeting place for cadets in the last half of the nineteenth century. The cadets were so fond of the inn that they composed a drinking song in its honor:

To our comrades who have fallen, one cup before we go,
They poured their life blood freely out *pro bono publico*;
No marble points the stranger to where they rest below
They lie neglected far away from Benny Havens, Oh!
Oh Benny Havens, Oh! Oh! Benny Havens, Oh!
So we all sing reminiscences of Benny Havens, Oh!

(Quoted in Hudson Strode, *Jefferson Davis: American Patriot*, p. 41.)

Hunger! We were always hungry although bountifully fed at the mess hall. At no period of our lives, before or after, could we consume so much food as when we were cadets. Besides the demands of rapid growth, the incessant exercise of every physical and mental function created a waste which required an almost constant supply. We were trained down to the physical limits with rapid infantry and artillery drills, active fencing, riding and engineering labor—sometimes overtrained until boils would afflict us. Nineteen of these "Job's Comforters" scattered over my back and limbs at one time impressed these considerations on my memory.

Riding, while the most enjoyable of all our exercises, was also the most violent and exhaustive. When we returned to quarters from cavalry drills our clothing was commonly "wringing wet" with perspiration; and we would have to strip, dry ourselves with quick towel rubbing and get into a dry suit throughout and be ready in ten minutes, often in less time, for the "dinner call." A large proportion of the horses were good for ordinary cavalry work and some of them were fine, but many of them were restive and a few vicious, chiefly from the constant changing of the riders in the second and third classes. In our first-class year, each cadet, according to his standing in riding, selected his horse. My choice was "Duroc," the swiftest horse in the squadron. From childhood I had been accustomed to the use of horses and was fond of them. There were several men in the class with similar experience: Gregg, Colburn, Bennett, Van Camp, Vinton, Weitzel, Merrill, Gay, Reno, Hartz, Webb, Shoup and Allen were all strong riders and half of them were finished, graceful horsemen. There were quite a number who indulged the ambition to come out at the head in horsemanship and I was among them.

There was a horse misnamed "Quaker" in the squadron, a bright, handsome bay with an eye all black, that was generally as vicious as he knew how to be; and he was a very intelligent animal. He had thrown almost everyone who had tried to ride him. The previous year he had thrown Darant of South Carolina, the strongest rider in the class before us, three times and the last time had torn the clothing off his back and lacerated it by pitching him down the slopes of "Execution Hollow." Half-a-dozen others had been hurt by the horse. So that for a long time he was withdrawn from the squadron. It was an unwritten law that no man who had been fairly thrown from a horse should ever be graduated "first." My "marks" justified my hope of coming out first until one day in October '54 when we went out to drill on the plain, to our astonishment there was Quaker in the rear of the squadron, restive and champing his bit. To my momentary dismay, Captain Sackett, our instructor, said, "Mr. Averell, you may ride Quaker." There were but two difficulties about riding the horse: the first was to mount him and the second to remain mounted. An attempt to vault was futile for he was quicker than a cat and never took his eye off a man trying it and in case of failure he would generally get away and run to the stables. After examining the girths and adjusting the stirrup straps, Webb and Weitzel, who were mounted, kindly endeavored to attract or divert his attention by patting his head and face. Fixing the hold of my left hand in his mane without the slightest pull and carrying the reins lightly to the cantle with my right, I attempted to take the stirrup and saddle in one motion, but Quaker's spring was quicker than mine. Like a flash he whirled to the right nearly taking Weitzel off his horse, brushed me violently against the rear of the squadron, and shot across the plain toward the river with terrific speed. Clinging to his side, the wind whistling about my ears, I felt my left hand slipping its hold in the mane, when he suddenly doubled to the left, like a fox, in the direction of the stables on the north side of the Point, which enabled me to throw my right leg over and get my seat. I never was made so happy in one second of time. Crossing my stirrups in front for rough riding, I adjusted my cap and gathered up the reins. Quaker was already half a mile on the way to the stables when I had recovered my breath and began to take him up. Then began the struggle with buck-jumps, whirling, staggering, rearing and plunging. He hit me once a stunning blow on my cheek with his head which raised a lump. I let him have the spur without mercy until he was completely conquered, and then made him take all the paces—walk, trot and gallop and the hurdles over towards Dade's Monument, without dodging, and even made him stop champing his bit. He was reduced to abject fear. Then I took the risk of dismounting, out on the plain alone with the horse, and remounted again without trouble to my great gratification. When I was quite sure of Quaker's behavior I rode down to the squadron, and Captain Sackett sang out, "Very well done, Mr. Averell, very well done sir," which was a deal for him to say and very agreeable for me to hear.

My memory teems with reminiscences of the Riding School and its exciting incidents. The wildest riding of the circus was tame in comparison. There was no play in it. The cutting of heads and taking of rings, in half-a-dozen different positions in our circuit of the hall at the swiftest pace, and the bareback riding aroused the eager emulation of the class to the highest pitch. The warning voice of the master in stern injunction was sometimes required to restrain the exhilaration of the manège, and accidents and casualties were hardly noted until after the dismount. When Gay's horse fell headlong with him one day and two or three dragoons ran in and carried him out, we did not know that his leg was badly broken until we heard from the hospital an hour later. When a horse named "Minor" compelled Van Camp to do the Mazeppa act one day across the plain,[11] we lost sight of him and forgot him until we learned from the hospital that his jaw had been split at the chin on the "Western Gate." Only four years later a similar experience carried this beloved and accomplished classmate of ours far in advance of his troop into the midst of a hostile Indian camp in Texas, and an arrow through his heart ended his most promising life. There was a horse in the squadron very appropriately named "Cycloid" which no curb could check when he felt like running away. He would let his chin fall back against his neck and in that position the hardest pulling had no effect on his mouth. With Colburn in the saddle Cycloid would occasionally set out on an excursion and describe cycloidal curves all over the plain. Sandy's red hair, as he leaned back in a dead pull, lended a meteoric effect to the movement. There were not half-a-dozen poor riders in the class but they all had to ride, or try to, and they occasionally furnished amusing incidents. I remember Whistler's remark in our Second-Class year, when after having been picked up the third time from a fall off his horse he said, "I don't see how people can ever ride for pleasure."

When at the end of the year the battalion listened with eager ears to the reading of the standing of the men in the four classes, and Horsemanship in the First Class was announced, and the voice of Van Camp, the Adjutant, rang out, "First, Averell," I felt a thrill of satisfaction. It was not strictly an intellectual triumph, nor did it count for much in general standing, but I was glad to be graduated head in something.

In our time there were no societies in the corps of cadets, such as exist in most colleges, only a literary society called "The Dialectic" composed of members of the First Class. It was the custom to organize this society every year by that class upon the return of the battalion from

---

[11]The Mazeppa act was developed by Cossack horsemen in the 17th century. At a full run the rider would somersault over the head of the horse who would be trained to stop.

camp to barracks by the election of officers, and the president would deliver the opening address at the first meeting. David McM. Gregg was elected president in the Autumn of '54, but he could not be persuaded to deliver the usual address. Thereupon the class honored me with that misery. The opening night arrived. Colonel Lee and the Academic Staff with their families occupied the front rows of seats on the right and cadets filled the others. The venerable G. W. P. Custis, the step-son of Washington and father of Mrs. Robert E. Lee, was present with some of General Zachary Taylor's family and several other distinguished people. The utter terror, the shivering fright that I experienced when seated on the platform while the audience assembled will never be recalled by me without a shudder. The preliminary exercises were completed all too soon and I tremblingly rose to my feet with a consciousness of helpless inanity. My heart stood still. Just then my eye rested on the face of Van Camp, who leaning forward and looking straight at me, delivered a quick meaning smile, combined with a willful wink of the eye, which conveyed volumes, as much as to say, "This is the happy moment I've been looking forward to, etc." Instantly my blood rushed again, my tongue found my theme, which, merciful shades of Cicero, Demosthenes, Patrick Henry and Daniel Webster, was "Eloquence"! I had not then read Emerson's essay on that subject or I might not have tackled it. Van Camp had read and approved my "Screak," as he irreverently termed it, and came to my room after it was over and endeavored with Gay and others to soothe me with assurances of acceptability. Thanks to a quick oblivion it was not laid up against me.

In November '54 Mr. Jefferson Davis, the Secretary of War, visited the Academy and with Colonel Lee inspected everything in the institution. I remember their visit to the drawing academy while our class was at work and their pausing to inspect my drawings, shaded in color, of a Vauban front.[12] By their remarks to each other they seemed pleased to recognize the various parts of the work. Mr. Davis was a slender gentleman, about forty-seven years of age, and had the formal air of a public man conscious of being under constant observation. There was little variety of expression in his clear-cut, sharp, refined face and his carriage and occasional slight smile seemed studied. I observed him closely as he

---

[12]Sebastien le Prestre Marqui de Vauban (1633-1707) was a French military writer and engineer who wrote the classic work on siege warfare, *Memoire pour servir d'instruction dans la conduit des sieges*.

was already a notable man. I do not remember seeing him again until 1867, when I was U.S. Consul General in British North America at Montreal. I received a message from him through ex-governor Westcott of Florida asking if it would be agreeable to me that he should attend the consecration ceremonies of the English Cathedral in which I was to take part. My reply was, of course, in the affirmative and that I had no reason or right to object, and he was seated near me during the consecration.

Our last year at the Academy, whilst the happiest of our cadet life, was the hardest in discipline. To enforce rigid discipline and compel the closest attention to studies, there was the most relentless reporting of cadets for every offense however slight and every apparent neglect however trivial, and our demerit marks accumulated rapidly. No man was without them and about forty men had over the one hundred in the six months ending January 1, '55. Although I was a Cadet Lieutenant, and after New Years one of the four Cadet Captains, yet it seemed impossible for me to avoid having 108 demerits at the end of the six months. Colonel Lee sent for me and asked me if I was aware of the number of my demerits and of the consequences. To this there could be but one answer. The Colonel then suggested that I examine the records and ascertain if I had excuses for any of the reports which would justify the officers making them in recommending their removal. It was found by the search that seven marks had been given me on reports of Major Fitz-John Porter and Captain Sackett. I called on these officers and told them the reports were just and that I had no excuse, that I had not intentionally committed the faults, that they were the result of carelessness and inattention, and asked them to recommend their removal. After a few kind words of admonition they promised to make the recommendation. The next day I called on Colonel Lee again at his office, and he informed me that the number of my demerits over the limit had been reduced to one. I then reminded the Colonel of the rule that when only one demerit was incurred by a cadet in a month that it was removed without excuse, and that this one was the only one standing against me in the month of December, and that as I had no reasonable excuse, except carelessness, it must rest entirely on the clemency of the Superintendent. The Colonel with the suspicion of a smile on his grim face remarked, "Well, Mr. Averell, if I were in your place I would not run such risks—I will remove this one." On the 27th of March '55, an order of the Secretary of War, Mr. Jefferson Davis, was published suspending seven cadets until the first of the following July for having over 100 demerits on January 1, and among them were Vinton and Reno who had

120 and 158 respectively. The effect of this was to postpone their graduation one year.

Every class at West Point acquires a character of its own and no two classes were ever alike. Notwithstanding the same rules of conduct, process of discipline, courses of study—all the educational and formative forces of the Academy are applied in the same precise and uniform manner to all the classes—yet there will be marked differences between any two classes during any given period of their cadet lives in their social tone, intellectual development and personal deportment. As the general and dominating expression of a composite photograph made up from thirty or forty faces exposed in the same focus is determined by the images derived from half-a-dozen of the strongest faces which were nearest alike in features, so the general character of a class of cadets is determined by half-a-dozen of its leading members. In our day, classes were known and commonly referred to by the names of their head men: thus Andrews' class was graduated in '51, the year we entered; Casey's class in '52; McPherson's in '53; Custis Lee's in '54; and after ours, Comstock's in '55; followed Syder's, Palfrey's and Paine's; so that we had acquaintance with six classes besides our own.

Casey's class of '52 is best remembered because it was the First Class when we were plebes. Casey and Bonaparte were roommates in their first-class year and occupied the tower room, fourth floor in "A" Company, and my room that year was opposite theirs in the same Hall with Bennett, my roommate. It is not easy to realize that Casey, now a General, has a son graduated from the academy who occupied the same room that his father had before him. Thos. L. Casey was the first Captain of the Corps and Bonaparte was Adjutant and both were ideal cadets.[13]

I well remember the curious sensation I experienced on witnessing for the first time the arrest of a cadet. It occurred at breakfast in the old mess hall in May '52. Browne and Howard from Maine, and both of the

---

[13]Thomas L. Casey remained a career soldier in the Corps of Engineers until he retired in 1895, at which time he held the rank of brigadier general as chief of engineers. In this position he worked on new headquarters for the State, War and Navy Departments and completed the construction of the Washington Monument.

Jerome Napoleon Bonaparte, Jr., was the grandson of Jerome Bonaparte, the youngest brother of Napoleon. After graduating from West Point in 1852, he served in the French Army from 1854 to 1870. He participated in the Battle of Inkerman, 5 November 1854, a bloody battle during the Crimean War, when the combined French and British forces defeated a Russian attack.

Third Class, had some dispute across the table which culminated in angry words, and in a fit of uncontrollable rage Browne threw a glass tumbler which struck Howard on the forehead, cutting it and causing the blood to flow freely. The slight noise which attended the incident attracted attention, but not a man moved excepting the first Captain Casey, who came sailing down the Hall and said, "Mr. Browne, go to your quarters in arrest, sir." And Browne went without a word. Howard, who had fainted, went to the hospital on recovering consciousness. I wondered why a man in arrest was not accompanied by an officer and soon learned that the force of the principle of honor was stronger and more watchful than all the officers in the world. A man in arrest was bound by his honor to confine himself to his quarters. A breach of arrest was an impossibility. Suicide would have been easier.

Bonaparte was the finest Adjutant the corps had in our time—tall, well made and graceful with a handsome, well-poised head and a sonorous, agreeable voice which could be heard in reading orders or giving commands at parade to the farthest limits of the plain. The Adjutants who immediately succeeded him were Boggs, Custis Lee and Van Camp, all selected for their qualifications and fitness, but none equalled the perfection of Bonaparte.

I remember the thrill of pride and pleasure we experienced in December '54 on hearing of Bonaparte's conduct at the Battle of Inkerman where he served on the staff of Marshall Canrobert and was constantly passing between him and Lord Raglan, for which service he was preeminently well fitted, having the ability to speak English and French with equal fluency together with a military education. He was wounded in the arm during the battle. We had already learned the result of his examination by a board of officers in Paris and that their report sent to the Emperor had stated that his military education was unsurpassed in France. It is comforting to American spirit to reflect that during the Franco-Prussian War of '73, our Bonaparte was the only French officer to raise a regiment of volunteer cavalry, which he did at Rouen.

Ten members of the class became general officers during the Civil War: [Henry W.] Slocum, [David S.] Stanley, [Milo S.] Hascall, [George I.] Hartsuff, C. [Charles] R. Woods, Alex. [Alexander McD.] McCook, [August V.] Kautz, [George] Crook, [John P.] Hawkins and [Robert H.] Anderson, the latter joining the Confederacy. Most of these were great fighters and all achieved high reputations.

In the next class of '53, there were ten generals: [James B.] McPherson, [Joshua W.] Sill, [William R.] Terrill, W. [William] S. Smith, [John McA.] Schofield, Robert O. Tyler, [Philip H.] Sheridan, [Alexander] Chambers, [John B.] Hood and Thos. W. Jones. The first three were killed in battle and all the others, excepting Sheridan, were wounded. Only Jones and Hood joined the Southern Army. McPherson and Schofield won imperishable fame devoid of any factitious consideration. But for a disabling wound which shortened his life, Robert O. Tyler would have achieved great distinction.

McPherson proved an exception to the general lot of head men. Whilst he was an eminent engineer, he was also the greatest soldier of his class of good soldiers. He possessed intense and buoyant social characteristics, and was full of good humor and exuberant spirits. He had the love of every good man and the confidence and admiration of every good woman who knew him. McPherson would never have gained a baton from Napoleon had the length and prominence of his nose controlled the honor. Nature had been niggardly in furnishing that feature to him. The general expression of the face on busts of Pulaski remind me of McPherson's. The nose made its expression pleasantly piquant, and the frank earnestness of his bright blue eyes gave it vigor and enthusiasm. I recall him as the Orderly Sergeant of "D" Company, standing in front of it and rapidly calling the roll, turning his face to the right and left as we answered to our names. His own name and the names of a majority of the men he called are now chiseled on tombstones. He fell at the head of an army before Atlanta while resisting a sortie of the beleaguered enemy, after having "engineered" all the western battles in which he was engaged.

Custis Lee's class of '54 yielded ten general officers: [Thomas H.] Ruger, [Oliver Otis] Howard, [Stephen H.] Weed, [George Washington] Custis Lee, [John] Pegram, J. [James] E. B. Stuart, S. [Stephen] D. Lee, [William Dorsey] Pender, [Horace] Randal and [John T.] Mercer.[14] Only the first three remained in the Union Army. Howard lost an arm and Weed was killed in battle. Pegram, Stuart, Pender, Randal and Mercer were killed in battle or died of wounds. Custis Lee was a singularly modest man, a close student, methodical, precise and quiet. In his physical and mental presentment he strongly resembled his father, Col-

---

[14]John T. Mercer never became a general officer. He rose to the rank of colonel as commander of the Twenty-first Georgia Infantry and was killed in an attack against Plymouth, North Carolina, on 19 April 1864.

onel Robert E. Lee. Stuart was the opposite of Custis Lee in almost every characteristic. Vivacious, exuberant, romantic and overflowing with good spirits, but quick to provocation. There were several other men of this class who became distinguished in service, among them I best remember [Charles G.] Sawtelle [Jr.], the accomplished quartermaster, B.[Benjamin] F. Davis, the dashing cavalryman who was killed in a charge at Beverly Ford, Va., O.[Oliver] D. Green[e], the able Adjutant General, John R. Smead, the splendid artilleryman who was killed in battle, and the debonair and dimpled [John T.] Greble, who was sacrificed at Big Bethel.

In our class of '55, twelve men earned their stars and only three of these, Nicholls, J. H. Hill and Shoup, were in the Southern army arrayed against their classmates Weitzel, Gregg, Webb, Vinton, Turner, Torbert, Hazen, Forsyth and Averell. Several of these received more or less disabling wounds.

Frank Nicholls, sincere, gentle and a touchstone of honor and virtue, was the orator of our class on the Fourth of July '54. He was always ready, firm and undaunted where a sense of duty controlled him. He resigned within the first year after his graduation and began the study of law in New Orleans. The fortune of battle bereft him of a leg and an arm, but left enough of him to make the best governor Louisiana has had since the war.[15] We were tent mates during our last cadet encampment.

Godfrey Weitzel came to West Point a stout, modest German boy but little over five feet high in '51, but grew about three inches a year and was graduated a "six footer." His aptitude for original observation kept itself in proportion with his physical growth. He distinguished himself during a critical period of the war by subordinating himself with all his military and engineering abilities to one of those generals evolved from political life. After the war he originated and developed new and useful methods in hydraulic engineering and was employed on the improvement of the Mississippi River when he died.

Frank Vinton was one of the best endowed men of our class. He had genius. After his graduation he entered the Imperial School at Paris

---

[15]Francis R. T. Nicholls (1834-1912) resigned his commission in 1856 but volunteered his services to the Confederacy as lieutenant colonel of the Eighth Louisiana Infantry. He was made a brigadier general in October 1862, and lost a foot during the battle of Chancellorsville on 1 May 1863. He served two terms as governor of Louisiana (1879-1881 and 1891-1893, and served on the Supreme Court of Louisiana from 1892 to 1904.

whence he was graduated just before the breaking out of our Civil War. Reentering the army in August '61, he quickly earned his star. A bullet through his body at Fredericksburg gave him a hurt from which he never quite recovered. He was master of the best English and choicest French and was familiar with German literature in the original. As an artist he had a decided and effective style of his own. In his spacious and attractive atelier near Grace Church in New York City, whilst he was Professor in the School of Mines, Columbia College, one could meet of a Saturday afternoon some of the brightest men and women in the world. He was a poet and illustrated with his own etchings a volume of which he had a limited edition published for a few of his intimate friends. He played the violoncello in the Philharmonic in Brooklyn. Art appealed to him, and his life responded in work along all her various ways. And beyond all expressions of art and suggestions of Nature, he penetrated and sounded the profoundest depths of all the philosophies and reduced them to their simplest terms. He was the most companionable of men but destitute of the faintest interest in popular applause. To dine with Vinton at Delmonico's or in bivouac was all the same to the memory; the menu was always forgotten. He drew his last breath from the thin air of Colorado, eleven thousand feet above the sea, and the rough but reverent hands of miners closed his eyes when the daring light of his life had faded.

Torbert I remember as an amiable, industrious man who had always the appearance of being "dressed up." I can recollect several men that I have known who suffered the same lack of harmony with their habiliments. No effort of their own or of intimate friends could enable them to avoid having their attire the first thing observed whenever they came in view. General U. S. Grant illustrated this condition. Torbert cheerfully attempted many things that others could easily do, but was never depressed by failure, indeed, seemed to hardly realize any want of success. Besides those men in the classes I have mentioned who were distinguished as Generals, there were many who achieved equal or greater distinction in all the branches of the military services, especially the staff.

The relations between by class and the next one following it were of the most friendly character, and I remember many of its members with pleasure. Among the brilliant men who sprang from its graduates were eight general officers: [Orlando M.] Poe, [George D.] Bayard, [Samuel S.] Carroll, [William P.] Sanders, Fitzhugh Lee, W.[William] H. ["Reds"] Jackson, [Lunsford L.] Lomax and [James P.] Major. The latter half went South in the war.

The successful defense of Knoxville, Tenn., against Longstreet in '63 was chiefly due to Poe and Sanders, the former the engineer and the latter the undaunted fighter who was there mortally wounded.

Sprigg Carroll was a mixture of fire and affection. He had the luck of finding the bullet that had been moulded for him in several battles, but they never subdued his fearless and fiery spirit.

Fitzhugh Lee was a sturdy, muscular and lively little giant as a cadet. With a frank, affectionate disposition he had a prevailing habit of irrepressible good humor which made any occasion of seriousness in him seem like affectation. He was a good Indian fighter before the war, and when in '61 he was compelled to choose between his state and the Nation and we came to the parting of the ways, the tears which suffered his eyes and the lamentations that escaped his lips betrayed a depth of feeling which revealed a sincere character beneath his habitual cheerfulness.

Bayard was all his name implied—*sans peur et sans reproche*—a handsome, well-bred young man with a certain modest reserve, but cordial and strong in his social life. A painful wound in his face from a poisoned Indian arrow in '60 disfigured a cheek and would have invalided a man of less fortitude. He was an intrepid and dashing cavalryman of the greatest promise. He met a soldier's death at Fredericksburg and among those to whom he sent messages during his last minutes he kindly remembered me.

Lomax, who had been a roommate of Bayard at the Academy, became a Southern cavalry man after having been an Indian fighter and like Bayard always maintained the high character of the cavalry service.

W. H. Jackson became a cavalry commander in the southwest where the service was arduous but remote from popular observation.

The class which was graduated in '59 turned out a famous Southern cavalryman, Joseph Wheeler of Alabama.

My most unfading memories of West Point are of my classmates. We were harmonized by identical work and concurred habits of mind and body during four long years. We grew as alike and as different as leaves upon the same tree. Together we obeyed the same commands and signals and were exalted by the same triumphs and strained by the same trials. We brought to the Academy all sorts and conditions of early manhood. We presented diversities of blood and breeding as various as our names.

In the formative process of our Alma Mater there was found scant mercy. A faultless but friendless courtesy characterized the academic staff in our contact with them whether in drills or studies. Naturally, we turned to each other and loved and helped each other. We entered with seventy-one. We saw forty original members fall out of our ranks at different stages of the course with much the same emotion that we experienced a few years later when we saw stricken comrades carried from the line of battle. Five fell back into the next class and thirty-four went homeward. One, James E. Fort, died at West Point, June 15, '53, and Ruggles, Du Bois and myself were appointed a committee to attend to the erection of a monument to his memory at his home in Oswego, N.Y.

I do not remember my last day at West Point as well as the first day. It was too crowded with sensations: the realization of hope, the sweet triumph of graduation, the sad rending of a pleasing network of friendships, the dispersion of comrades forever. There was the last parade, the heart-stirring strains of "Home Sweet Home" and "Auld Lang Syne," the last salute as cadets, the visit in a body to the houses of the Superintendent and Academic Staff, the crowded chapel in the evening where, notwithstanding the brilliant lights, I saw my classmates through a dimming mist as each arose as his name was called and walked forward to the Superintendent and received his diploma, until my own was called, when with a curious dizzy feeling I gathered my diploma and walked out into the air and to the tree in front of the library where I had seen the orderly walking on my arrival four years before and sat down awhile to quell myself.

Thirty-four were graduated in our class of '55, but three of them had joined from former classes. We knew each other as no other men than cadets can know each other. Of course, every man holds a citadel within himself, an arcanum which none may penetrate or capture, and which he himself is powerless to surrender; but outside its mysterious confines we had full and welcome cognition of each other. Nearly forty years have passed since we left West Point. Its setting of the majestic river and towering highlands was our only horizon. As the seasons recurringly swept over it, our young eyes became fond and familiar with all its moods of sun and shadow, of softening verdure, of black isolation or of grandeur.

Forty years are but moments in the life of a race, a phrase in the history of a nation, a pulsation in human development, yet on the dial of civilization these last forty years have swept over more pregnant facts than had the forty centuries that looked down from the summits of the pyramids upon the legions of Napoleon. One tenth of this time—four years—was ample for the seven classes of cadets of my day to challenge fortune, to strive for the honor and a name which may not be found ordinarily in a long lifetime. Ample for some to grasp leadership and power, long enough for one half of them to meet death, gloriously, as they had been trained to do. The dozen that remain of my class can now look back from the serenity of three-score years and note the fading events without passion. One emotion will abide until the last of the friendly throng has departed: our love for our Alma Mater. Vinton's song at our graduation was prophetic:

> The purple shadows of the past are closing o'er the gray cadet
> And recollection bows at last in somberful regret,
> The voices of unselfish friends plead mournful echoes to the ear
> Far, far away the river bends that never was so dear.

[2]

The Cavalry School

T here was nothing notable in the three-months leave granted us after graduation except that it seemed to me very short. But the enjoyment of it was greater than had been that of our furlough two years before. Our status was now different. Doubts and anxieties had been dispelled by our success. We were now officers of the United States Army with all the responsibilities and considerations pertaining to that condition. Everywhere in this country an officer's commission in the army was an unquestioned credential and letter of credit, and it was never dishonored. No cadet left the Military Academy without realizing the *noblesse oblige* character that his commission in the army conferred.

This character came to be well realized during the war. Whenever it was desirable to be absolutely sure of any trust depending upon the integrity and honor of an official, then an officer of the regular army was found most available, but in matters that involved irregular contracts, the promotion of opportunities for speculation, the packing of courts-martial to convict or acquit, they were generally to be regarded as inconvenient. The inconvenience of this army character was shown by the sneers flung at it by the doughty General B. F. Butler in his notable book, wherein he relates his share in the contest for the preservation of the Union and alleges that some of his best efforts had been thwarted occasionally by the indirection, malicious interference and obstructive jealousy of officers of the regular army. The paradoxical disingenuousness of the General was later on revealed when after predicting a war in each generation he expressed purpose to prepare his son for the next one by sending him to

West Point to be educated in order that he might avoid the obstacles which had beset his father in the Civil War.[1]

The recollections of that graduation furlough are not altogether pleasant. Death has claimed most of the friends who helped me to enjoy it and the increasing infirmities and growing isolation of old age have overtaken the scattered survivors.

The seclusion of the Military Academy had been so complete that we soon found that there was a vast deal for us to learn immediately. Growth of any kind brings new experiences. Even our physical growth began anew from the date of our graduation. A part of my own physical description at that interesting period was height 5 feet 8¾ inches, weight 135 pounds, breast measure 36 inches, waist 26 inches. Three years later it was height 5 feet 10 inches, weight 165 pounds, breast measure 42 inches, waist 32 inches. Our mental cabinet contained more or less definite notions of all the instruments, tools, implements and apparatus required for scientific investigation or the development of any art. But our experience had been only elementary. We had now also to learn how to live. We had been delivered, so to speak, a second time helpless into our mother's arms. To get the proper outfit for a mounted officer that would last him forever and not weigh over 100 pounds at the start and to pack it in a medium-size sole-leather trunk, I remember was one of the problems that confronted me. With all the elements of science and rudiments of art with which we had been loaded during the four years, we were, most of us, now to be used simply and solely to supervise the living and disciplining of soldiers and to train them in the art of killing Indians and other enemies.

My classmate, John V. Du Bois, with myself had been assigned to the Regiment of Mounted Riflemen, now the 3d Cavalry, as Brevet Sec-

---

[1]Benjamin F. Butler, antebellum Democratic senator from Massachusetts, politically appointed major general and postwar radical Republican, wrote his autobiography and reminiscences under the title *Butler's Book*. Butler, not used to making temperate remarks, was highly critical of regular officers (p. 863):

> During my whole service in the army it was always thrown in my face by the regular officers that I had no technical military education. That meant that I had not been to West Point. Now a West Pointer if he graduated very high never was employed in the army in managing troops until our war. But during the Rebellion all was changed. It was assumed that West Point officers knew the whole art of war and were ready-made generals. . . . It is wonderful how soon this claim of theirs burst out after the war commenced, and even then how little ambition for fighting these men had.

ond Lieutenants.[2] The companies of the regiment were dispersed among the widely separated Military Posts of New Mexico and Texas. We were not to join at once but were ordered to report in person on the 30th day of September to Colonel Charles A. May, 2d Dragoons, U.S. Army, Superintendent of the Cavalry School at the Recruiting Depot, Jefferson Barracks, Mo., for a tour of duty, generally two years in length, previous to joining our regiment. This post-graduate assignment of young officers attached to mounted regiments served several important purposes. One was to permit them to acquire practical experience in the instruction and management of soldiers and in all the details of camp and garrison life before undertaking their exacting and responsible duties with their regiments which would subject them at once to the most critical observation in the world—that of the keen-eyed veterans of the frontier, who awaited the coming of every new officer with anxious curiosity. Another object was that these officers might take charge of the instructed recruits that were sent to the different regiments from time to time, and also that when joining their regiments they might avail themselves of these detachments as escorts without which the frontier could not then be penetrated very far.

On the 24th of September 1855 I set out from my home in Cameron, New York, to obey my orders. My brother accompanied me as far as Niagara Falls where Du Bois joined me pursuant to appointment. We stopped at the Cataract House and in the full moonlight wandered around Goat Island and visited the old stone tower above the horseshoe fall, ventured out on every brink and reclined on all the inviting banks, unwilling that any sight or sound should escape our senses. We were so fortunate as to see a lunar rainbow bending above the abyss which recalled the classic of Chateaubriand. The memory of the mournful story of Atala aroused imagination.[3] Transitions are awakening. My own life, having just quitted the rigorous seclusion of four-years hard study and training

---

[2]Averell, Du Bois and most of his class were brevet second lieutenants, that is, acting second lieutenants, because the army had no way at that time of adding new officers to the ranks each year. Since there was no effective retirement system and since almost all promotions were based on seniority, an officer literally had to wait until someone died or left the service before he could be promoted. The Regiment of Mounted Riflemen were dragoons, infantrymen mounted on horses for transportation. They were expected to fight as infantry rather than as cavalry. Because of Averell's partiality to the cavalry, he does not always make the distinction clear.

[3]François René de Chateaubriand (1768-1848) was one of the founders of French romanticism. He visited the United States in 1791 and saw Niagara Falls. *Atala* (1801) was a novel concerned with the noble savage in conflict with white civilization.

and now entering upon a new and adventurous career, made me an easy victim to the supreme allurements of the hour. The spectacle as revealed and softened by the flooding moonlight was indescribably grand and beautiful. Every cataract has its own note, but none of Niagara could be found for ears so near its deafening roars. I fancied that an infinite variety of notes could be heard—that all the tones of the numberless cascades falling from the myriad lakes of that vast region extending from the borders of the frozen zone to the upper chain of inland seas were here assembled and repeated in a chorus titanic. Its quavering diapason of thunders cannot be heard elsewhere and once heard cannot be forgotten. The following morning we examined the suspension bridge which we had studied and drawn on blackboards at the Academy. We knew, of course, every detail of its construction, but we found it novel and satisfactory to realize dimensions and weight. These things cannot be imagined of anything without realizing them through the senses, at least of one example.

On the 28th Du Bois and I parted from my brother at the suspension bridge and took passage on the Great Western Railway for Detroit where we arrived about sunset. It seemed to us that everybody in the country was traveling and we wondered at it. We reached Chicago the next morning and found that our classmate, Colburn, who was going to the same Post with us, had come from Vermont through Michigan on the same train. Chicago was a small but active town. I think I could have run around it in two hours. Now, forty years later, I am told it has streets twenty-two miles long. We went in the evening to hear a family of singers called "The Hutchinsons."[4] We started on the evening of the 28th and arrived at Alton about noon the next day and at St. Louis at 3 P.M. We found at the Planters House, Van Camp, Gregg and Merrill, our classmates, all on their way to Jefferson Barracks. Four of us, Van Camp, Gregg, Colburn and myself, secured a carriage to drive us to the Post, eleven miles distant. The driver lost the way for a time and we did not reach our destination until nearly midnight. Captain Travis of the 2d Cavalry kindly took care of us for the night.

---

[4]The Hutchinson Family of Singers was a well-known musical group in the nineteenth century. They regularly toured the lyceum circuit presenting a variety of temperance, sacred and abolitionist songs mixed with comic skits. The group sang to Union soldiers during the war; but in 1862 the Hutchinsons ran afoul of Maj. Gen. George B. McClellan who did not like abolitionist songs the group had sung to the Army of the Potomac. According to the Hutchinsons, however, President Lincoln had told them, "It is just the character of song that I desire the soldiers to hear." See Carl Sandburg, *Abraham Lincoln: The War Years*, vol. 1, p. 561.

On the morning of September 30, after witnessing with great interest the parade of the new regiment of the 2d Cavalry, we put on our new uniforms and sabers and reported to Colonel Charles A. May of the 2d Dragoons commanding the Cavalry School and the garrison. We had all heard of Colonel May as the dashing dragoon who had led the charge at Resaca in the Mexican war, capturing General La Vega and a battery of artillery. We found him a tall, graceful man, about six feet four, with a long flowing beard of a dark brown color and neatly trimmed, ample hair, a striking well-bred face capable of varied expressions and keen grey eyes which with his quick eyebrows made one suspect at first view that he was an emotional man and quick to anger—perhaps with a temper a trifle dangerous. He received us kindly and quickly gave directions and advice regarding our quarters. We also called on the field officers of the 2d Cavalry. After we were settled, which was a matter of very few minutes, we received calls from all the officers at the Post before night. In the evening we called at Colonel May's quarters to pay our respects to Mrs. May. Our reception was so agreeable and our entertainment so charming that we felt altogether satisfied and contented with our first day of army life. Mrs. May was a daughter of Hon. George Law of New York and was an ideal wife for a commanding officer.[5] Hospitable, always in perfect health with a sunny, sympathetic nature and lovely manners, she could make her home an oasis in any desert of a garrison.

We began regular duties on the day after our arrival and found them arduous. "Reveille" at 5 A.M., followed by "stable call" which we attended until 7 o'clock. We walked up and down the line while the men were grooming the horses and also inspected the stables. Each of us had charge of about thirty horses. While we were all up in the theory of these duties, it was for a few days fortunate for us and the service that we found the practice of instructing recruits in stable duties in the hands of old Sergeants. Guard mounting was called at 8 A.M., and at 9 mounted drill began and lasted until 11:30. At 1:30 P.M. there was a dismounted drill which lasted until 4:30 followed by stable call again at 5 o'clock. After that we had the evening to ourselves, those of us who were not on duty as

[5]George Law (1806-1881) was a wealthy contractor and transportation member of the Know-Nothing party and in 1855 received the support of the Pennsylvania legislature for that party's presidential nomination. When Millard Fillmore received the national Know-Nothing party's endorsement in 1856, Law attacked Fillmore and supported the Republican party's candidate, John C. Fremont.

Officer of the Day or Officer of the Guard. Sometimes, with leave, we used to gallop into the city, eleven miles, to social entertainments or to the theatre. The Planters House was a famous hostelry in those days and at no other have I ever felt quite so much at home. St. Louis was then distinguished among all cities west of Detroit for its social attractions. Its relations with the army had long been intimate and strong. There was a degree of "go" or personal force and adventurous spirit in the men and a frank courtesy, felicitous common sense with high breeding and an absence of affectation in the women, that made society particularly refreshing and enjoyable. We were made to feel glad that we had met wherever a meeting might have taken place, whether in their own homes, at the theatre or at social entertainments. Speaking of the play, I remember that pretty much all of us at that time were enamored of Agnes Robertson, a young, beautiful and captivating actress who, it may be remembered by some people yet living, retained the admiration and esteem of all who knew her throughout her career.[6]

As young cavalrymen we enjoyed an uncommon advantage in witnessing the "setting up" and mounting of the 2d Cavalry. There was probably never a better officered regiment placed in the field. The subsequent history of most of its officers became sufficiently remarkable to justify me in recalling some of their names. Its Colonel was Albert Sidney Johnston; its Lieutenant Colonel, Robert E. Lee; its Majors, William J. Hardee and George H. Thomas. Among its Captains were E. [Kirby] Smith, James Oakes, Innis N. Palmer, George Stoneman, Theodore O'Hara, [Albert G.] Brackett, [Charles E.] Travis, [Charles J.] Whiting and Earl Van Dorn. Kenner Garrard was 1st Lieutenant and Adjutant. Other 1st Lieutenants were Richard W. Johnson, C. [Miles] W. Field, [William P.] Chambliss, [William B.] Royal and [Walter H.] Jenifer. John B. Hood and W.[illiam] W. Low were among the 2d Lieutenants. Junius B. Wheeler and [Cornelius] Van Camp of my class were at the foot of the Seconds.

It will be remembered Colonel Lee, Major George H. Thomas, Captain E. K. Smith and Lieutenant Garrard had been on duty at West

---

[6]Agnes Robertson (1833-1916) was a British actress, the adopted daughter of the actor Charles Kean. She made her debut in 1851 at the Princess Theatre in London as Nerissa in *The Merchant of Venice*. Two years later she married the Irish playwright, Dion Boucicault, and came to the United States to star in his dramas.

Point, and their kindly remembrance of us as cadets made our meeting again here seem like the renewal of old acquaintance. As a cadet-manager of our balls when a first classman, I had met Stoneman when he was on a visit to the Academy and was glad to see him again. Lieuts. John B. Hood and W. W. Lowe we had known as cadets during the two years '51 and '53.

Regiments, in respect to the tone and bearing of their officers, are like clubs; there were never two alike. The 2d Cavalry through all the mutations of service and changes of officers it experienced, even through a change of name to the 5th, never lost the high tone which vibrated in all the impulses of its officers during its organization. Devotion to duty—the most rigorous, zealous, and enthusiastic—was the mainspring of their conduct. The records of half the officers were already among the brightest in the army. Some were authors of tactics or had devised or improved arms and equipments. I remember with pleasure the individual characteristics of several of them. O'Hara was a poet and could sing a good song. Jenifer had the best seat and was the most graceful rider I ever saw. He had invented a new saddle-tree and was devoted to the Cavalry Service. "Shanks" Evans was a bold dragoon who scorned sleep and would keep a "mess" laughing at his stories until reveille.

The great plain outside the Post presented the most attractive and animated spectacle during drill hours. Nearly a thousand mounted men were instructed there daily in all the schools—from that of a trooper mounted, to that of the squadron, and finally of the regiment. There was a demonstration of the results of a steady application of talent and instructive energy such as it was impossible to find elsewhere in any army. Within sixty days over eight hundred men and horses had been broken in and formed into coherent troops and squadrons. Every manoeuvre known to tactics could be executed with rapidity and precision. The men could use their arms and fight mounted or dismounted. And beyond all, for without it everything else would have soon disappeared, they had learned how to care for their horses, arms and equipments, how to pitch camp or establish bivouac and to guard it, how to handle their rations and the best way to prepare their food. It was a wonderful performance. It tested the qualifications of every officer to the utmost. The figures of Lee, Hardee and Thomas on horseback were always to be seen moving quietly through and about all the operations and movements upon the field, pausing here and there to approve some excellence or to suggest some modification.

There were many incidents to this active life, some amusing and some tragic, few of which I can recall. We had from one hundred to three hundred recruits in the depot going through the schools of instruction and above a hundred horses for their use. Among the latter was one named "Turk" that was a terror to recruits. He had his own views regarding the proper duration of riding exercises, and when that time had expired he could not be persuaded to remain any longer on the field but would break for the stables like a "quarter horse" generally leaving his rider on the ground more or less demoralized. One day he came out in Merrill's platoon. When Turk considered his time was up he made an effort to quit the Irishman who was on his back, but the rider under the emphatic exhorations of Merrill clung to him with desperation. At the end of a few seconds, however, the recruit was seated in the dust near the center of the disturbance while Turk was galloping off to the stables. Merrill asked the dizzy man on the ground, "Why didn't you keep the spurs out of his sides as I told you?" The poor fellow looking up replied, "Holy St. Patrick! Leftenant, if it hadn't been for the holders he'd tossed me the first lift."

Turk was brought back to the field by a stable guard and Merrill mounted him, remarking to the platoon, "I will now show you how this horse should be handled." And Turk *nolens volens* was made to take all his gaits and turns in the school. There were a few severe struggles, but the horse had found his master and apparently submitted. This seeming acquiesence was, however, a ruse, probably for deliberation. Having reached the conclusion that as he could not, in this instance, leave his rider behind, he would take him with him, he suddenly took the bit with his teeth and left the track on a tangent at the top of his speed for the stables. A part of the way there ran along the crest of a slope which curved around the head of an arroyo. As Turk was racing along this he suddenly doubled like a fox at right angles and Merrill, taken off his guard, went down the slope in a series of slices and tumbles. It was an unwritten law of the mounted service that any officer who was fairly thrown should forfeit a case of wine. Merrill called at the Sutlers on his way to his quarters and ordered a case, wherewith the wind of friendly "chaff" was tempered with his ruined uniform.

The regulations and customs of the service at that time had not been relieved of the brutal punishment of whipping for desertion, and I remember the abhorrence with which I witnessed two or three inflictions of that barbarous and cruel sentence. The command was formed in a hollow square about the whipping post with the officers near the center. The prisoners were brought in and the orders were read aloud by the Adjutant. The prisoners were stripped to the waist, one by one in turn, and tied to the post by the Sergeant of the Guard. The Surgeon then examined each and, if found able in his opinion to endure the infliction of the sentence, a bugler taking position at one side of the prisoner raised a small rawhide whip about a yard long high in the air, the Officer of the Day counted "one," the whip hummed through the air and creased the back of the man with a purple streak which brought a drop of blood sometimes at the end of it. The Adjutant tallied "one," the Officer of the Day counted "two," and so on to the end, generally 30 odd blows. Some would endure the infliction with very little writhing and few groans, others would yell and squirm from the first blow. The Surgeon forbade the whipping of one young prisoner with bright gleaming eyes but a deadly pallid face, and he was returned to the guard house on two occasions. Those who had been whipped were turned out of service to the tune of "The Rogues' March." These savage spectacles may have served to prevent desertion, but they were sickening to witness. The officers came away from these scenes silent and depressed, some muttering curses on the regulation which compelled them to officiate at them.

The 2d Cavalry left Jefferson Barracks on the march to Texas about the middle of November 1855. The day of their departure was clear and full of sunshine. Their wagons were packed and started, and as the long, white, covered train drew out across the plain and was lost to sight in the forest beyond, we began to feel the first of those breakings of army associations to which we afterward became accustomed. Our morning drills were suspended that day and we all rode out to see for the last time the parade of that fine regiment. The alignment was perfect, the colors and guidons were gently furling and unfolding in the morning air. Overcoats and blankets were rolled and strapped on the saddles and every buckle shone. The band played "Auld Lang Syne," and after the officers came up to the Colonel, we had an opportunity to bid them good-bye. Not satisfied with this, some of us rode to the edge of the plain where their way entered the forest. They soon began to pass by in a column of twos with perfect intervals and steady gait. I was waiting to see Van Camp once more. Debonair and smiling he rode out of the column saying, "I wish you were going with us," and put his arms around me and kissed me and galloped to his place. I never saw him again except in my dreams, and in them he appears always young.

Just four years later at Lancaster, Pennsylvania, I laid some flowers on his grave. He was killed in a fight with Comanche Indians near Wichita village, Texas, on October 1, 1858. He had gotten far ahead of his men in the attack. Captain Earl Van Dorn was wounded four times, twice with arrows, in the same combat. Seven years later I was a General of Cavalry and this same 2d Cavalry Regiment, renamed the 5th, was in my Cavalry division, but its officers were changed. Some of those belonging to the regiment in '55 were commanding armies in support of the Southern Confederacy while others of them were leading armies to its destruction.

Jefferson Barracks seemed desolate after the departure of the 2d Cavalry, but we met the situation with our little social rallies in the intervals of garrison duties and with hunting excursions in the vicinity of the Post. Our small society was frequently enlivened by the visits of officers coming from or going to their stations on the frontier.

I had been fond of hunting partridges and rabbits in my boyhood but had never learned to shoot birds on the wing. The first day that an opportunity and invitation offered, I went out with Captain Tyler of the 2d Dragoons who was a fine shot and had a couple of beautiful setter dogs. Discovering after an hour's trial that an untrained shot might be an embarrassing companion to a thorough sportsman, I struck off by myself and industriously beat up several coveys, but without getting a bird. Then I tried in vain to shoot a rabbit. My kind fellows of our mess had warned me before my coming out that a certain forfeit of wine and cigars was always imposed on a novice who could show no game on his return from his first day's hunting. I had resigned myself in despair to the inevitable and was making my way homeward quite tired and disgusted and with my gun at a slope under my arm, when almost from under my feet a covey of quail got up with a noise that startled me. In a hurried endeavor to use my gun, it was accidentally discharged and brought down one of the birds which I put in my bag with a sense of great relief. As I approached the western gate some of the future heroes of the Civil War, among whom were George Crook and [John W.] "Jowler" Davidson, were standing expectantly about the entrance stating their preferences in wine and cigars. It was plain to be seen that I was not loaded with game and as I declined to answer questions a forced search was instituted by them which brought forth my providential bird not yet cold, and the old proverb was fully sustained about the value of a "bird in hand."

The climate about St. Louis that autumn was glorious and every element and sensation of it quite different from the only climate I had ever experienced. The resultant of the complex conditions called *climate* can be measured only by a living human being with all his senses keenly efficient. The readings of all the known meters combined furnish an idea of it which is vague and deficient. It is a matter beyond any nameable sensation. It is recognizable but elusive to description. Colors, perfumes, flowers and music give us endless varieties of impressions which it is impossible to name. There are electrical conditions as changeable as the summer clouds or the mists revealed and lifted by the morning sun. To my feeling there are four distinct climates and endless differentiations of them to be found in crossing this continent. That of the Atlantic slope of the Alleghenies, of the Mississippi Valley, of the Valley of the Rio Grande and of the Pacific slope. Color helps to describe or indicate them. For the Atlantic slope, I would use different shades and tones of blue; for the Mississippi Valley, yellow; for the Rio Grande, violet; and the Pacific slope, orange. A climate map of the continent correctly expressed in colors would require no legend.

About the end of November, orders were received from the War Department to transfer the Cavalry School of practice to Carlisle, Pennsylvania. The garrison consisted of Colonel May, Surgeon Joseph J. B. Wright, Captain C. H. Tyler, 2d Dragoons, and Lieutenant Averell, Mounted Rifleman—Lieuts. Du Bois and Merrill having been sent with the recruits to Fort Riley. The ladies of the garrison were Mrs. May and Dr. Wright's three daughters. We had a "Permanent Party" of forty picked men, Sergeants, Corporals and Privates, a few recruits who had not been sent to regiments and a band of about twenty pieces. The new steamboat *Sir William Wallace*, which had before made but one trip, was chartered to convey us to Pittsburgh. We sailed on the 6th of December and were eleven days making the voyage. The golden Indian Summer prevailed all that time and made the passage the most pleasant journey of my life. Being in no hurry the boat was permitted to stop at various points along the Ohio to take on or discharge light freight. This afforded us an opportunity to go ashore and visit the towns and inspect their various and interesting activities. The lovely and ever-changing panoramas that were gliding by on either hand in the daylight and by moonlight with the autumn-tinted shores of the Ohio repeated in her placid waters, enlivened by the musical strains and echoes sometimes awakened by our band, left reminiscences of ideal travel which I cannot forget.

A short distance above Evansville, the Surgeon reported to Colonel May that one of the recruits, the one whom he had exempted from the flogging for desertion on two occasions, was sinking rapidly and would probably soon die. It appeared that the boat was about to pass his home which could be plainly seen upon the high bank to our left a mile ahead. The young man was lying on the lower deck in a position to see and recognize the familiar scenes about his home. Dr. Wright reported it as his opinion that the man would die when the boat should pass that point. The man had been regularly enlisted and could not be discharged except in accordance with his sentence by court martial and the orders thereon from the headquarters of the army. When the situation had been made known to the Colonel, who was a man not easily disturbed or diverted where orders and regulations pointed out his duty, he stood up and looked at the place ahead a minute and then sat down and called, "Orderly, ask the Captain to come here." To the Captain when he reported, he said, "Please land this boat as near that house," pointing it out, "as you can." The whistle was sounded for a landing and the boat headed for the shore below the house. Two women ran out from the dwelling and stood on the high bank in astonishment and evident perplexity. As the landing was made, one of the women ran down the zigzag pathway toward the shore. The landing stage was thrown out and the sick recruit was carefully carried on shore. He called out faintly, the girl heard and ran to him and then turning her face up the bank cried out wildly, "Mother, it's Jim," and the mother flew down and the three were united in a moment in a paroxysm of happiness. Their cries and exclamations were comingled.

The Colonel was a study. He had been tender and careful in getting the nearly dead man ashore, but when he saw the boy revive and heard the greetings of his mother and sister he became savage and ordered the planks on board and berated the men and stormed about their slowness. As the young man on shore saw the boat leaving, he fully realized that he was free, and striving to rise to his knees he feebly lifted up his hands, but we could not hear what he said. The Colonel had nothing at this moment that he could pretend to swear at and so called the sergeant leader of the band and told him passionately, "Play something and play it now"; and I remember the thrill that swept the boat as "Home Sweet Home" pealed forth from the band. When the Colonel had settled down, he asked the Surgeon if the boy would live. The doctor said that he believed now he would, that it was the worst case of nostalgia he had ever seen, but the boy had now the only sure cure—home and mother.

From Pittsburgh a train carried us to Carlisle via Harrisburg where we arrived about the 20th of December to find a steady, old-fashioned winter firmly established.

The historic town of Carlisle was then the most agreeable place in the country of its size for army people. Several of its leading families, including those of Judges [John B.] Gibson and [Frederick] Watts, Mr. William and Mr. Edward Biddle, Mr. [John] Brown Parker, Mr. Johnston Moore, Dr. [Alexander] Mahan, Mr. [Alexander K.] McClure, Judge [Robert M.] Henderson, Mr. [George] Blaney and Mr. [Peter F.] Fge were connected with the army more or less directly by marriage or otherwise. It had of itself almost an army society. So we felt quite at home. The markets were excellent and the garrison was only one mile from the center of town. The fields surrounding the Post were well adapted to cavalry exercises. The quarters were comfortable for both officers and the men. In the summer season two or three watering places within a few miles contributed to the social attractions of the neighborhood.

On our arrival I was appointed Adjutant of the Post, and the office duties and correspondence with recruiting stations at Albany, New York, Philadelphia, Richmond, Baltimore, Pittsburgh and other points, in addition to my equal share of garrison duties with the other officers, kept me well occupied. Captain D.[Dabney] H. Maury of the Regiment of Mounted Rifles, Captain [Newton C.] Givens, 2d Dragoons, 1st Lieutenant C.[Charles] W. Field 2d Cavalry, and Captain [James McQ.] McIntosh and Lieuts. Robert Ransom and [Alfred] Iverson 1st Cavalry were added to the garrison. Recruits came in squads every ten days and our morning reports sometimes afterward aggregated 600 men. It was a great school under Colonel May's administration. Going over and over again every line and precept of tactics and regulations as an instructor and the use of my voice daily at parades and guard mountings was of the greatest service to me in after years when it became my duty to prepare regiments, brigades and divisions for the field—to feed, clothe, mount and drill, to arm, equip and command them on the march and in battle.

Our commanding officer, Colonel May, while one of the most exacting men wherever the performance of duty was concerned, looked with favor on all spirited diversions of his officers when off duty and did not disapprove a streak of wildness and dash in our recreations. The cultivation of a luxuriant crop of wild oats in his youth terminated by an early appointment in the army by President Andrew Jackson had interfered with the Colonel's education and his literary enjoyments were now mostly limited to *Porter's Spirit of the Times* and *Charlie O'Malley, or the Irish Dragoon*. He kept a file of the former, it was said, and read the latter once a year. He was an undisputed authority on horses and all that pertained to racing as well as an accepted referee of all wagers. Social life to him was nothing if not that of a high-living club. He had been bred to army life in the old 2d Dragoons under Colonel [David E.] Twiggs along with such men as Fowler Hamilton, [Lawrence] Pike Graham, [John] Sanders and [George A. H.] Blake when they were young and restless. They were a remarkable set of men and the only man who could manage them without trouble was Twiggs. I was told by old officers that Colonel May had many of Twiggs' ways. One characteristic occasionally revealed was his readiness to lay a wager on anything. Once an old Dragoon officer who had just arrived at the garrison was observed measuring the circumference of some of the large shade trees in a surreptitious manner and when questioned about it replied, "May probably knows their measures from betting on them, and I want even chances with him."

The Colonel was a vivid raconteur and could upon occasion sing a good song. One that was written by Sanders of the 2d Dragoons was a favorite with him, and as I have never seen it in print I may be permitted to write it here from memory:

THE BOLD DRAGOONS

Oh the bold dragoon he scorns all care
As he roams around with his uncropped hair
He casts not a thought on the evil star
That sends him away to the Florida War.
His form in the saddle he lightly throws
And on the weekly scout he goes
Blithely humming some old time song
As o'er the trail he bounds along.

All night he camps in the dark pine wood
Lights his fire and cooks his food
His riding blankets around him close
And on the ground he seeks repose.
At the merry blast of the bugle horn
He's up and away at the break of morn
While the mists hang o'er each lake and dell
And the hoots of the owl through the wild woods swell.
Oh gay is the life that a soldier leads
And a lawless freedom marks his deeds
As he rides at will o'er the dark green sod
Where the foot of the white man never trod
If an anxious thought should sad his mind

'Tis of her he loves and has left behind
But well he knows that a soldier's fame
Will endear her more to her lover's name.

Oh sweet is the hour! oh passing sweet!
When the girl he loves again he'll meet
Of whom he hath dreamed both night and day
When "o'er the hills and far away."
Then courage, boys, the time will come
When we shall see our friends and home
When swarthy bronzed by a Southern sun
We'll spin long yarns of the deeds we have done.

Another important thing upon which the Colonel was high authority was the code duello which should control a gentleman's conduct in "difficulties." He kindly instructed us in the interesting and inexorable rules of procedure which were or had been the vogue among gentlemen of the South: the giving a deadly insult in a proper manner, the reception or recognition of it, the activity or passivity of the parties on either side, the rights as challengers or respondents to a challenge, and finally, and of higher importance than any preliminaries, how to select a field, place the men, give the word and—lastly and vastly most interesting—how to hit the other fellow. It should be understood that these instructions were neither proposed nor sought but came up naturally at our pistol practice. The Colonel was a remarkably good shot. I have seen him break the stem of a sherry glass at twelve paces at the word. The Colonel preferred the practice of holding the pistol vertical, muzzle up, and dropping it at the word, as the quadrant through which it would fall would not be so great as the one that would be described in raising it from a vertical position muzzle down to a level. There would be a saving of nearly half a second in favor of the drop. The Colonel had a younger brother named Julian May who was in my regiment, the Rifles, and who died in '57 with the memory of an affair of honor which had been settled with rifles wherein the other man had fallen dead at the first fire. I think it entered the minds of all who knew Julian whenever they saw him that he found that memory a burden.

One of the Colonel's precepts to which he attached high importance was that a principal in position on the field of honor should never take his eyes off his adversary. From this habit was derived the advantage of keeping the distance and line of fire constantly in the eye thus necessitating no change of focus at the word. It was related of General Jackson that he never took his eyes off the man whom he killed in a duel after they came on the field although his adversary's shot had first struck him. As everything must be a thought before it becomes a thing, I have no doubt that the study of the code by all gentlemen of the South through the generations before the war led to its familiar contemplation by its students and opened the tempting way to many a duel.

Lieut. D. H. Maury was a complete contrast to Colonel May. His height was about five feet nothing. Precise as a Virginia statesman in his manners, duties and habits, a great reader of the best literature, he was a conversationalist most bright, interesting and profitable. He was afterward the General commanding the Confederate forces at Mobile when that place was taken by Farragut and General Granger during the war.

Never did I serve at any garrison where such diversities of excellent character were found in the officers. Captain Givens, 2d Dragoons, was a tall, deliberate, impassable gentleman, cool in speech and action, the ideal "Count Considine."[7] His laugh was rare but his disposition genial. Captain C. H. Tyler was a handsome, courtly Virginian, a Chesterfield in manners, with dignity which was rendered very agreeable by a large and ready sense of humor. Lieut. C. W. Field, 2d Cavalry, was a living ideal of a Virginia Cavalier, a handsome horseman and a charming good-natured comrade.

Captain James McIntosh, 1st Cavalry, was a son of General James S. McIntosh, who was killed at the storming of Molino del Rey in the Mexican War, and a brother of General John B. McIntosh, a distinguished cavalry leader of the Union Army in the Civil War. The Captain was a thorough soldier and an entertaining messmate but he had a temper as hot and quick as Colonel May's. For some oversight in the performance of his duties which McIntosh regarded as too trivial to make the offering of an excuse necessary, the Colonel directed me to place him in arrest and confine him to his quarters. This was done with all proper formality. After two or three days the commanding officer found himself in an unpleasant position. The offence was hardly sufficient to justify him in asking for a general court-martial and McIntosh swore he would have a court-martial. It took me two or three days more to get these two high-tempered men into a proper frame of mind to yield toward each other in a slight degree, and I think in the end that an inclination to relieve me of

[7]Count Billy Considine is a character in the rollicking novel *Charles O'Malley*, written in 1840 by Charles James Lever (1806-1872), an Irish novelist.

the distress I experienced from the situation induced the commanding officer to consent to an interview with McIntosh and the latter to ask it. That was all that was necessary and I left them alone together. McIntosh told me afterward that when they were left alone the Colonel arose, extended his hand and said, "Captain, you needn't trouble yourself to say anything; my office hours are over this morning; let's go over to my house." That settled it.

It was one of the many illustrations of the horrors of the Civil War that the McIntosh brothers were divided by it. Captain James McIntosh, to whom I have alluded, was killed as a Confederate General at Pea Ridge, Arkansas, March 7, 1862, and John B. McIntosh as a Brigadier General in the Union Army lost a leg in leading a cavalry charge at Winchester, Va., on the 19 September 1864, and this shortened his life.

The Adjutant of a Post may do much to promote harmony and avoid friction in garrison life. He must have the absolute confidence of his chief and also of his messmates. He stands in no small degree as an unofficial exchange between the commander and his subordinates and it must be but little of the grain that he may drop of either side and none of the "chaff." He may restrain or delay action on one side or avert or prevent conduct on the other that would be prejudicial to military discipline and to social harmony. It is one of the most satisfactory memories of my army life that I was Adjutant nearly two years for the most difficult-tempered and exacting commanding officer whose subordinates included fifteen or twenty young officers who were accounted as lively and as high spirited as any in the army, some of them touching the borders of recklessness, without a single quarrel or arrest—excepting the McIntosh incident—and never at any Post were duties more faithfully performed.

There were one or two general courts-martial assembled at Carlisle Barracks during my tour of duty there for the trial of deserters, and Colonel Robert E. Lee was the President of one of them. As a matter of army etiquette we all called on the visiting officers soon after their arrival whether they stopped in the town or in the garrison and of course our calls were returned by the officers before their departure. I remember that when Colonel Lee returned my call he found me alone. It was a clear and cold winter day and a bright fire was burning in the grate. The Colonel wore a blue dress coat with metal buttons and stood on the rug with his back to the fire parting his coat-tails. He was bright, genial and easy, while I remember I was a little embarrassed. He stayed, perhaps half an hour, and we talked a little of West Point and of the Cavalry Service. I told him that after seeing him as Superintendent at West Point it seemed somehow incongruous to find him in the Cavalry Service. He asked me if I liked it and why, and after my reply said, "Well, I was always fond of horses and liked the service for the outdoor life the same as you. When in Mexico we young fellows of the engineers had to ride a great deal and were glad to get a mule sometimes." We all kept some excuse for a side-board and I ventured to ask him to have a biscuit and a glass of sherry or a cigar. He apologized for declining by saying, "I never acquired the habit of smoking at all nor of taking wine except with my dinner." And then he interjected a little precept in the most delicate manner by continuing, "If I were young again and had my life to live over I would take the same course."

The recruiting officers at the several stations made us short visits at least once a month when they brought in their recruits to the depot and contributed to our little social enjoyments for a day or two. Among these I remember 1st Lieutenant B.[Beverly] H. Robertson, 2d Dragoons, Captain R.[Richard] C. W. Radford, 1st Dragoons, and Lieutenant W.[William] B. Royall, 2d Cavalry. The last named had a novel experience in Philadelphia, where he had charge of the recruiting station, in which he came near terminating all imperial aspirations concerning Mexico. At the hotel where Royall was living, the old La Pierre House, there was also stopping Prince Iturbide of Mexico with whom Royall was not acquainted. One day on entering the cafe, Iturbide, who was entertaining a party of lively young men, accosted Royall and asked him to drink. He politely begged to be excused. The Prince insisted in an offensive and imperious manner and approached Royall as if to urge him with force, whereupon the latter let go a hard right fist actuated by some redundant and tough Missouri muscle and backed up with about 170 pounds of well-trained cavalryman, and the imperial hope of Mexico was prostrated for a minute or two. The horror-stricken friends of his Imperial Highness hastened to inform Royall of his rank. Royall remarked quietly that his rank furnished no excuse for not behaving like a gentleman. The Prince the next day ascertained who the stranger was, who had made such an impression upon him at first sight, and at once set himself right with an ample apology.[8]

---

[8]Augustin de Iturbide (1783-1824) was the self-proclaimed emperor of Mexico. His arbitrary and extravagant reign soon brought his empire to collapse exactly ten months after it began (19 May 1822-19 March 1823). Although he escaped into exile in Europe, he returned to Mexico in 1824 where he was captured and executed. The Prince Iturbide to whom Averell refers was Augustin's eldest son who hoped to establish a second empire.

The political campaign of 1856 created a lively interest among us although we took no part in it. I think without exception every officer of my acquaintance desired the success of Mr. Buchanan as against Colonel Fremont, for the reasons that they believed the former to be a conservative statesman whose election would promise tranquillity while no one believed that Fremont would be aught else than a tool in the hands of radical politicians whose election would bring on dangerous agitations. As an entertainment I went one day with Mr. Thomas Biddle to hear him address a political meeting in the country and had my faith in the capacity of the people for self-government, at that time, rudely shaken. The prejudices and passions of the people were appealed to and the "crisis" was painted in startling colors, but no other or better rule of action was recommended than that which was dictated by expediency.

There were of course conversations at our mess and in quarters upon the questions of the day, and the possibilities and results of a conflict between the North and South were prognosticated and discussed, and we occasionally went over the questions of the justice, rights, advantages and divine authority of Negro slavery. The views of all were crude and undeveloped. Whatever conflict might come would be within the Union. There was not then any expression, and I believe there was no thought, of any possible disunion of the States.

We were much diverted by a local contest for the legislature in Carlisle about this time. Among the solid men of the town were two brothers named John and Armstrong Noble. The first dealt largely in horses and beef cattle and the other, "Army" as we called him, was wealthy, kept an open house and was a man of leisure. Neither had received more than the rudiments of any education but were shrewd in business affairs. Colonel "Army" Noble was a favorite guest at garrison dinners and we always had a speech from him. I forget his politics, if he had any, but some of the "boys" in the town conceived the idea of running him for the legislature. The speeches, the posters, the charges and countercharges of that campaign surpassed belief. Candidates were nominated against him and withdrawn one after another, and the struggle was varied by frequent modifications of the Colonel's platform. At last he was elected, as the boys assured him, on a woman's-rights ticket. After he had occupied his seat in the legislature for a fortnight at Harrisburg, a committee waited upon him at his home and complained that he had as yet made no speech, and reminded him of the importance of the question which had induced his fellow citizens to send him to the legislature, and intimated that there were some dissatisfied people who went so far as to say he could not make a speech. "Army" arose in his wrath and told them that he would show them that he could make a speech, that he had the lungs to do it, at the same time striking his breast with his hand. Poor "Army," I suspect there have been in times past, statesman, even in the national legislature, no better equipped than were you. Well, it was settled that Mr. Tom Biddle should prepare a speech on woman's rights and that the member should commit it to memory and deliver it on an appointed day when a committee from Carlisle would be present to hear it.

The day arrived, the committee was on hand, and Noble was ready. There was a heavy discussion going on in the House on State canals. Some old members were invited to assist at the debut of the new member and "Army" was instructed that upon a given signal he should rise and make his speech and pay no attention whatever to the fellow in the chair with the hammer as he was not a friend of woman's rights anyhow and would try and stop the speech. The speaker did not realize the character of the interruption made by Noble's stentorian voice for at least ten seconds, when cries of "order" from various parts of the House were heard and the gavel beat a tattoo. It mattered not to the Colonel, who was warming to his theme. His voice filled the chamber. The storm of objections and cries of order expended itself in vain against his thunder and at last died away and the entire House, Speaker and members, became quiet. It began to dawn upon them that "something was up" and curiosity prompted them to hear what Noble was saying. The speech was in one of Tom Biddle's best veins of humor to which the serious manner of Noble lent additional and ineffable charms. It ended in an ovation to Colonel Noble who was carried off in triumph. The committee from his constituents made a favorable report, and a rousing welcome awaited the Colonel's return to his home.

Early in June '56 Captain Radford took 250 recruits to Kansas and was accompanied by Lieuts. Merrill and Du Bois. A few days before their departure Merrill was married at Columbia, Pa., and Captain Tyler and myself assisted him in the capacity of groomsmen.

At the end of September 1856 the new Second Lieutenants, who had been graduated from the Academy in June and attached to Cavalry regiments, reported at Carlisle for duty. They were 2d Lieuts. Fitzhugh Lee, Va., 2d Cavalry; William H. Jackson, Tenn., Regiment Mounted Rifles; James P. Major, Mo., 2d Cavalry; William Gaston, S.C., 1st Dragoons; L.[Lunsford] L. Lomax, Va., 1st Cavalry; Joseph H. Taylor, D.C., 1st Cavalry; John K. Mizner, Mich., 2d Dragoons; and Herbert M. Enos,

N.Y., Regiment Mounted Rifles—all most acceptable acquisitions to the mounted service. This infusion of young officers was far more welcome than would have been the arrival of the same number of old officers. The life of a garrison depends on incidents for its diversions—anything however trivial that will cause a ripple on dull monotony is gladly entertained. A veteran is mostly destitute of incident. He takes up his duties and performs them without comment. His form is not novel. To see half-a-dozen young fellows exhibiting their various styles of doing the same thing is an entertainment.

Our lives off duty were also brightened. We all had good horses, a few running ones, and some had fine sporting dogs. The few hours off duty were pleasantly filled with driving, riding and shooting parties. Having four married ladies, Mrs. May, Mrs. Maury, Mrs. Ransom and Mrs. Iverson, permanently at the Post together with the daughters of Surgeon Wright, and all these generally entertaining a few charming young ladies as guests, rendered us self-sustaining regarding the enjoyments of dinners and dancing, and the interchange of these social elements with those of the town, which was constantly going on, made the winter of '56-7 worth remembering.

A little episode about Christmastide '56 created a delightful memory for me. Colonel May desired to pass holiday week in Baltimore with his brother, Hon. Henry May, and other relatives and friends and asked McIntosh and myself to accompany him as his guests. We put up at the Gilmore House and had a large suite of rooms which were generally thronged with the Colonel's friends when we were at home. But we commonly used them only for dressing and a little sleeping. The old Maryland club suspended some of its rules during the week. It was the first opportunity I had ever enjoyed of city life. It has always seemed to me since that the warm glow and sparkling brilliancy of Baltimore dining rooms and the loveliness and grace of Baltimore women could never be surpassed. Moreover, to me there was for a long time no real terrapin or canvasback duck to be found elsewhere.

I remember Mr. Henry May as one of the most courtly and entertaining hosts I have ever known. During a trout fishing excursion with me the following spring I had an opportunity to perfect my acquaintance with him which increased my admiration for the noble traits of his character.

About the first of March '57 Lieut. W. H. Jackson and myself were granted a ten-days leave of absence to permit us to attend the inauguration of President Buchanan. Neither of us had ever visited Washington

City. We escorted two young ladies of our garrison, Miss Annie Wright and her guest Miss Mary Cosby of Kentucky, to Washington where they became the guests of Mr. Joseph Bradley, a prominent lawyer living on 4½ street, not far from the City Hall. Jackson and myself secured a room at Mrs. Harrison's on Pennsylvania Avenue nearly opposite Brown's Hotel and took our meals at Willards.

It would be tiresome, if it were possible, to relate all the sensations and happenings of this our first visit to the Capital. The war afterward educated at least two generations of Americans at once in the geography of our country and the topography of its Capital. They also became familiar with crowds of people. A man who has belonged to an army of a hundred thousand men can never be astonished nor even very much impressed afterward by any crowd. We could not then compare what we saw with any previous experience. To us the throngs were countless and we stuck together with fear of losing each other. Everybody was going everywhere, talking and wondering.

The impressive grandeur of the long and lofty colonnades of the great white marble buildings was felt by the multitudes which surged about them. They recognized the majesty of the unseen but supreme general government of the States and People. One could not see it, nor touch it, this government. Yet it was here. Its great officers were somewhere hidden from public sight. The feeling of awe which oppressed us as the resistless current of humanity bore us toward the President at his first reception, and we at last saw a weary, pallid, white-chokered old man with a large head inclined to one side, touched his hand and passed on and out into the cool, empty universe outdoors, can never be experienced but once.

During my tour of duty at Carlisle Barracks our small army society was interested in and modified by five weddings, in all but one of which I acted as best man to the groom. Tyler, Stanley, Field, Elliott and Merrill. The first two touched us most nearly as by them we lost two of the estimable daughters of Surgeon Wright who accompanied their husbands to Kansas to which territory we sent three hundred and twenty recruits on April 23d '57. At the same time J. H. Taylor and Mizner left us. The detachment was also accompanied by Griffin, Starr and Wheaton who had been in the States on duty or leave of absence.

The always interesting incidents which enliven the approach to a wedding were rendered almost exciting one day in the case of Captain Elliott of the Rifles, who was to marry a lady prominent in the society of

Carlisle. The Captain, actuated with a laudable purpose to delight his fianceé with a drive, asked the loan of my ponies and light wagon. The ponies were handsome thoroughbreds, bred by Governor Porter of Pennsylvania, and could easily do six miles in thirty minutes to my light wagon. They had run away twice with poor drivers but in an innocent and perfectly excusable manner. Elliott was the pink of perfection as to dress and personal equipment, and if there was anything he knew better than another it was driving. So my kindly warnings went for naught and he set forth with the ponies. A stable man from the "Mansion House" brought them back with the wreck of the outfit in about an hour. The Cumberland Valley railway runs directly through the main street of Carlisle. A train was coming behind Elliott as he swung into this street, and the ponies quite on the verge of a break, with the added scare of the locomotive, got away from him. In his embarrassment he simply remembered where he wished to stop on the same street and pulling to that idea ran the ponies into the front door which, like all Dutch built towns, opened directly on the walk. Fortunately no serious damage was done but I could never lend my ponies afterward.

Another remarkable runaway occurred in the same locality about the same time. Lieut. Fitzhugh Lee had a high bay horse which he called "Whalebone." His plan and elevation were attractive but his cross section showed a great lack of breadth, or thickness—he was too thin. Looking at him sideways he seemed the mezzo-relief of a horse. But he had high action and a tremendous stride. It was impossible to say what he was made for. Fitz imagined for a buggy and so equipped him. He pranced and curvetted like a gigantic English greyhound for a while about the drives in the garrison while the friends of Lee trembled, and then he started for the town. The subsequent cataclysm as described by the ostler of the Mansion House was as follows:

Leftenant Lee's horse was a comin' down the street with a buggy and the Leftenant was in it and the locomotive a comin' a little way after. The horse was a jumpin' awfully, like a cat and a goin' faster and faster, when the Leftenant just rolls over the seat backward onto the ground and lets him go. Then the Leftenant picks himself up and walks into the barroom and asks for a cigar and has the dirt brushed off his coat. In two minutes that horse comes a tearin' down the street agin with two pieces of the shafts and runs right into the barroom not hurt a bit, and one of the tires off a wheel of the buggy comes a rollin' in after him.

The horse had run around two blocks distributing the buggy along the way and finished his career at the Mansion House.

Once in the summer of '57 there came along a troupe of singers called "The Continentals" who gave public entertainments in the old Continental uniform. Some of them were collegiates on a vacation tour and having a purpose to earn some money for their college expenses. One of them was the son of an Episcopal Bishop, and all of them were well-bred young men. They were led by a professional instructor of vocal music named Franklin from Boston and sang patriotic songs, glees, solos and choruses in the most enchanting manner. Fitz Lee, Jackson and myself, who were in the habit of attempting something of this sort in a modest way as a trio, were captivated by the singers and had them out to the garrison, learned some of their songs and listened with unspeakable delight to some of their best selections as they rendered them in the quiet summer moonlight before Colonel May's house and other married officers' quarters. Colonel May would have undertaken to defend Bunker Hill single-handed and alone had there been any occasion of that kind on hand after listening to their song of its "sword." As it was, he surrendered, lighted up his house and had us all in at midnight for a glass of champagne. And when they chanted "The Raven" in front of Maury's, I remember Fitz Lee lying on the grass and quietly clutching it and pulling it up by the roots in the ecstasy of his enjoyment.

About midsummer '57, Lieuts. Oliver H. P. Taylor and William Gaston were sent to Fort Walla Walla, Oregon, where in the following spring they joined the ill-fated Spokane expedition under Colonel Steptoe and were both killed in that desperate and hopeless combat May 17, '58, aged thirty-three and twenty-four years respectively. They were both gallant cavalry men.[9] When Gaston received his orders at Carlisle he had to dispose at short notice of his horse which was an exceptionally valuable animal. He was known to have remarkable speed and across country no ordinary fence could stop him. He was a beautiful glossy black with a silky skin, a white star on his forehead, and one white foot. To help Gaston out, some gentlemen from town joined the officers in a rafffle for

---

[9]Troubles were common between the miners in eastern Washington and the Coeur d' Alene and Spokane Indian tribes. In 1858 Col. Edward J. Steptoe, commander of Fort Walla Walla, left the fort with only 158 men on a practice march. The Indians, having heard of a new road through their lands, were angry. More than 1,000 braves surrounded the small force about twenty miles south of the present city at Spokane and cruelly took their time picking off a few soldiers at a time. Leaving their supplies behind, the remaining soldiers sneaked away. The attraction of the loot caused the Indians to abandon the troops, thus permitting their escape.

the horse, twenty chances at $20 each. Nineteen were taken, that number being all there were present. Jackson and myself took the remaining chance. That chance won the horse. There was an immediate clamor to have us put him up again at the same price to which we yielded and in this Mr. Tom Biddle and myself took the odd chance. Strangely enough that chance won the horse a second time. As there was a little account in my favor between Mr. Biddle and myself, he proposed we should call it square and I take the horse which was acceded to, and I declined to put him up again.

Being a Saturday afternoon and no drills, several of us rode out with the party from town, Mr. John Noble being one of them. He had a dozen running horses in his stables and had formerly owned the black which he had sold to Gaston. A long, straight grassy lane which we passed prompted Mr. Noble to suggest a little trial of speed. He was riding the best horse he owned and I was riding my new acquisition, the black horse. His invitation was accepted and I loaned him my whip. In the brush his horse beat mine by half a length in five hundred yards. He used the whip and I rode carefully with my horse well in hand. My opinion was instantly formed that mine was the better horse, that he had probably been often raced with the other when Noble owned him and had formed the habit of being beaten by that particular horse, and that if properly ridden and waked up at the right moment he could come out ahead. I told Mr. Noble that my horse could beat his if properly ridden. He said if my opinion was correct a nice lot of money could be won on it. A race was at once made for 440 yards to be run on what was known as the Paxton Course about six miles from Carlisle, a fortnight later, and a forfeit was put up.

Colonel May tried to dissuade me from the race, saying, "Noble is an old and experienced horseman and knows exactly what both horses can do, and his son who will ride his horse is the best race rider in the State—has taken prizes for roughriding and good horsemanship, and weighs but 135 pounds; weight, however, goes for little in a quarter race." Everybody sympathized with me but not a single friend bet on my horse excepting Lieut. Lee. When Colonel May found that the race would come off, barring accidents, he gave me all the points in training he knew, and he knew them all. Lieut. Robert Ransom had a beautiful Arabian mare, a descendant from the Arabians presented to President Van Buren by the Imaum of Muscat, that was as swift as a bird. A boy weighing 93 pounds, who answered to the name of "Ike" and could ride anything, was found and kept with the horse in daily training and practice, I riding Ransom's mare against him. During the intervening fortnight a wide and increasing interest was developed in the coming race and money was offered on Noble's horse at 100 to 60 as a rule, but considerable was invested at longer odds. As the excitement and the stakes increased, it became necessary to carefully guard my horse and rider. No one outside of the garrison was permitted to see him or the boy. I had reason to think about this precaution afterward.

The day arrived and was bright and sunny and not too warm. History tells us that "a spectacle at the colosseum would empty ancient Rome." This was told, I suppose, to enable us to form a correct idea of the mighty dimensions of the colosseum and not to belittle Rome nor to enhance our ideas of the attractions of the spectacle. It is not presumed that a quarter race of the nineteenth century is as attractive as was a chariot race of the first, but it certainly may be claimed that it sustains a better and pleasanter ratio and relation to the population and civilization of Carlisle than did the rending of a group of Christian martyrs by wild beasts to the strength and moral development of old Rome. This particular race well-nigh depopulated Carlisle. Before 3 o'clock in the afternoon the town was at the course or as many of its citizens as vehicles could be found to transport thither.

At sunrise I had driven out leisurely with my rider and had the horse led behind with the grooms. The horse was stabled in a country barn at a little distance from the track and the doors kept closed and guarded until the time of the race. My judge at the start was Judge Henderson of Carlisle, a quick, decided man; and at the outcome, Lieut. Gus Nicholson of the U.S. Marine Corps. The crowd, of course, was at the finish line. While the distance was being measured, the Nobles' money was shaken in several hands at the throng and lengthening odds offered. I had everything up already. At this moment a well-dressed stranger appeared and began taking all the bets offered, and when he had silenced the clamorous offer of odds he soon brought the betting even and then marked foot lines across the track short of the end and offered feet as odds until the betting money seemed to be all up. Had I known this incident it would have encouraged me, but the saddling and the preparations for the start kept me at the other end.

Everything was ready and Noble seemed as confident as a dead-sure thing can make one appear. He with myself took position inside the fence halfway down to see the horses pass. From our position we could see that young Noble was jockeying to fret my horse when they were scoring for the word, as a running start had been insisted on by the father. Finally they got it and came away like two rockets. It was easy to see that Noble had the best of the start. My horse had his head on the flank of Noble's, his habitual position, as I had feared and conjectured. Noble was using the whip and rushing. The race was over unless I could make that forgetful boy hear me. It was like a flash, but stepping up a bar or two on the fence I cried out as they passed, "Hit him Ike." The little rascal shouted back, "I will," and gave the black one smart blow of the whip. In three strides he was ahead and at the outcome there were thirty-four open feet between head and tail. The breath that he drew when struck had caused the tongue of the buckle to his surcingle to rip the leather at the end an inch and a half. Three watches agreed that the black had covered the quarter of a mile in eighteen and three quarter seconds. When the cheers that went up announced the result, Mr. Noble and myself were starting down the track. He took off his hat and wiping his perspiring forehead with a red bandanna said, "You have the fastest quarter horse in this country and I didn't know it."

It was in the nature of a surprise to the people that Noble had been beaten. Everyone congratulated me, even those who had lost money. It was afterward ascertained that the stranger who had picked up a lot of money was a professional gambler from Philadelphia. How he came to know how to do it no one could ever find out. Not the least satisfactory of my winnings was a supper for twenty-five at Mount Holly Springs that evening.

The horse received an ovation as he was led home through the town, I was told, and ladies came from their houses to see him and pat his silken coat. Colonel May was gratifyingly relieved of great anxiety on my account and moreover shared the regret of many, which is quite common after a race, that he had not known which would win. This little event is still remembered in Carlisle.

These reminiscences of the cavalry school of practice at which I served one year and eleven months are only a few of those which throng my memory as I write. Many warm and cherished friendships were made which were never marred nor broken. But few are left of those who were then young and fair and strong. Life and nature smiled on us, our joys were many and our sorrows were few and soon forgotten.

Orders for Lieut. W. H. Jackson and myself to join our regiment in New Mexico came about the middle of August 1857. After a brief visit to my home in Western New York, which was saddened by the expectation of being absent four years and by the natural apprehensions that I would never see all of my father's family together again, my mind was occupied and diverted from the grief of parting by the preparations for the journey. Public conveyances westward then ended in Missouri. For a thousand miles beyond Leavenworth our way lay across prairies, which were then regarded as deserts, and forbidding mountain trails—a region infested with wandering tribes of unsubdued savages. Jackson and myself, guided by the advice of old frontiersmen, had us each make two strong oak chests with ironed angles, one for a complete mess kit and furniture, and the storage of food supplies, and the other for wearing apparel, blankets and books. I had secured small editions of my favorite authors, a traveller's set of chess men, some drawing materials and some emergency medicines. Our mess chests were marvels of protean possibilities: dining tables, writing desks, dressing tables, bedstead, and lounges were a few of the useful forms which might be produced from them.

Major [James H.] Carleton, 1st Dragoons, was to command a detachment of two hundred and fifty well-drilled recruits to be sent from Carlisle to Fort Union, New Mexico, and another larger detachment of recruits for the infantry from Fort Columbus was to join it at Leavenworth. Captain [Thomas] Duncan of the Rifles with Mrs. Duncan was to accompany our detachment. Other officers were to join at St. Louis and Fort Leavenworth. By the 27th of August, the day set for our departure, we were ready to say good-bye.

[3]

The Plains

We cross the prairie as of old
The pilgrim crossed the sea,
To make the West, as they the East,
The Homestead of the free.

A detachment of 250 recruits under the command of Major Carleton, 1st Dragoons, and accompanied by Captain and Mrs. Duncan, Lieut. W. H. Jackson and myself of the Rifles and Asst.-Surgeon J.[James] C. McKee,[1] left Carlisle by railway on the 27th of August 1857 en route to New Mexico via Fort Leavenworth. The special train was under the personal direction of Mr. T. Scott Stewart of the Pennsylvania R.R., a handsome, entertaining and prepossessing young gentleman, of whom I was destined to see a great deal a few years later. My brother accompanied us as far as St. Louis. The journey was made in two days without incident worthy of mention.

At St. Louis after the train had left the station, Captain Duncan, our immediate commander, who had observed the leave taking of my friends, said to me, "You might have remained in St. Louis three or four days with your friends as we have plenty of officers and shall be at Leavenworth a

---

[1]According to Francis B. Heitman, *Historical Register and Dictionary of the United States Army*, Vol. 1, p. 671, McKee only entered service as an assistant surgeon on 2 October 1858.

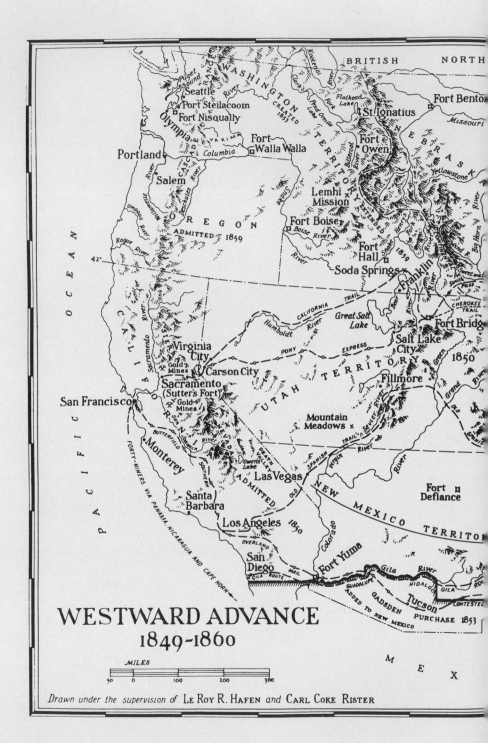

WESTWARD ADVANCE
1849-1860

MILES

50   0   100   200   300

Drawn under the supervision of LE ROY R. HAFEN *and* CARL COKE RISTER

82

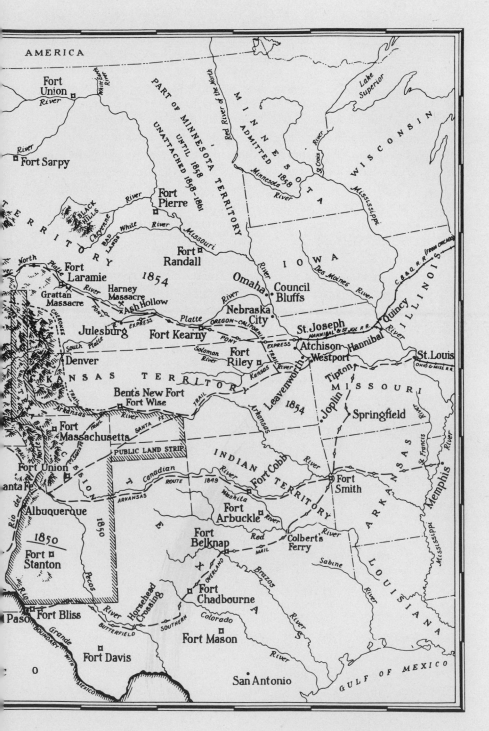

AMERICA

Fort Union
River
Fort Sarpy

TERRITORY

BLACK HILLS
Cheyenne River
BAD LANDS
WHITE River
Fort Pierre

Missouri

PART OF MINNESOTA TERRITORY
UNTIL 1858
UNATTACHED 1858-1861

Red River of the North
WHITE EARTH River

MINNESOTA
ADMITTED 1858

Lake Superior

St. Croix River

WISCONSIN

Mississippi

Minnesota River

Fort Randall
1854
Fort Laramie
Grattan Massacre
Harney Massacre
Ash Hollow
PONY EXPRESS
Julesburg
Fort Kearny
South Platte

North Platte
River
Platte

IOWA

Omaha
Council Bluffs
Nebraska City
OREGON-CALIFORNIA TRAIL
Platte

St. Joseph
Atchison
Westport
Hannibal

Quincy

ILLINOIS

C.B.& Q R.R. (FROM CHICAGO)

Des Moines River

River

HANNIBAL & ST JOE R.R.

St. Louis

OHIO & MISS R.R.

Denver

CHEROKEE TRAIL

KANSAS TERRITORY

Fort Riley
Solomon River
Kansas River

Leavenworth
1854

Tipton
Joplin
Springfield

MISSOURI

PONY EXPRESS

Bent's New Fort
Fort Wise
SANTA FE TRAIL

Arkansas River

Arkansas

ARKANSAS

St. Francis River

Memphis

Mississippi

Fort Massachusetts

EXCURSION

PUBLIC LAND STRIP

1850

Canadian River
ROUTE 1849
ARKANSAS

INDIAN TERRITORY
Fort Cobb
River

Fort Smith

Fort Union
Santa Fe
Albuquerque

Rio del Norte

Washita
Fort Arbuckle
River

LOUISIANA

1850
Fort Stanton

Pecos

Red River
Fort Belknap
MAIL
Colbert's Ferry
Sabine River

TEXAS

Rio Grande

Horsehead Crossing
BUTTERFIELD
OVERLAND
SOUTHERN

Fort Bliss
El Paso

River

Fort Chadbourne
Colorado
Brazos

Fort Mason

River

GULF OF MEXICO

Fort Davis

MEXICO
BOUNDARY 1854

San Antonio

83

week or more." I replied, "With your leave I will get off at the next station and return."

"All right," said he, and so off I got at Kirkwood, thirteen miles out. This was only a wood and water station. The country thereabouts was rough and rolling. Near by upon a knoll a hundred feet from the railroad stood a white cottage with a wing and a porch on which was sitting Lieut. William Craig, of the 8th Infantry, and his wife—old friends of mine. Craig was to be the commissary of our expedition across the plains and had established himself at this point for the collection and shipment of supplies for which he had advertised. I remained here not quite an hour before a train going to St. Louis took me on board for the city, but in that brief interval an incident happened which though deemed of little importance at the time, yet in the light of subsequent events and the possible bearing it may have had upon my military career is worth reminiscence.

While we were chatting on the porch, there came up the country road which skirted the railway a single horseman wearing a blue overcoat such as was worn by private soldiers and a black felt hat rather broken and worn. He carried a small "black-snake" whip which he applied to the little pot-bellied mare he was riding. The mane and tail of the animal, I noticed, were disfigured with burrs. The brownish-red face of the man was covered with a stubby, sandy beard. When he arrived near the gate in front of the cottage, he halted, dismounted and fastened his beast to the picket fence. Opening the gate he inquired for Lieut. Craig who arose and went down to meet him and walked out with him to the horse. After an earnest conversation of perhaps ten minutes Craig shook hands with the man who unfastened his animal, slowly mounted and rode away.

When Craig returned to the porch he remarked, "Averell, would you believe that man had ever belonged to the army?"

I replied, "Oh yes, might have been an old soldier."

"No," said Craig, "I mean as an officer and a graduate of the Military Academy."

I said, "He don't look it now, who is he?"

With an air of deep regret Craig answered, "That's Ulysses Grant who used to belong to the 4th Infantry. He wanted me to employ him as Commissary Clerk (to take charge of the supplies, superintend the herd of beef cattle and issue rations) in crossing the plains." And Craig went on to say that the regulations required him to use details of enlisted men for such duties. He said he was very sorry, as Grant wanted to get to New Mexico or Texas where he hoped to get appointed Sutler to some frontier post, and he needed something of the kind very much as he had a family out on a farm near St. Louis and they were in needy circumstances.[2]

I left St. Louis on the 31st with 1st Lieut. Orren Chapman, 1st Dragoons, and Lieut. J.[Joseph] G. Tilford, "Rifles," for Leavenworth. Colonel Crossman [Lieutenant Colonel George H. Crossman], the chief quartermaster at St. Louis, kindly assisted me in quickly obtaining exactly the kind and quantities of supplies we required and I reciprocated by taking charge of a lot of papers he desired delivered to Colonel [Charles] Thomas, the quartermaster at Leavenworth. He informed me that the command would be ready to start across the plains sooner than we had expected and it cut short my stay.

The railway westward then terminated at Jefferson City, Missouri, where we arrived at 9 P.M. and went immediately on board the *F. X. Aubry*. The river steamboat was yet almost the only means of travel and transportation in all the great west. If at that time one could have been lifted in imagination to an altitude from which a birds-eye view could have been obtained of that vast region known as the Mississippi Valley, he would have seen the "Father of Waters" with his fifty-nine navigable tributaries, some of them over a thousand miles above their mouths and all draining a territory as large as all Europe, leaving out Norway and Sweden; and lingering over their vexed waters, he would have noted the smoke of countless puffing, throbbing steamboats of all sizes from the stately St. Louis and New Orleans packet to the little toiling shell working its way like a huge tumblebug over the bars of the upper Missouri and Yellowstone. They were all of the same type, nearly flat bottomed for very light draft, "made to run on heavy dew," and sitting like a swan on the water. They had what was called a boiler deck cabin and hurricane decks upon which latter was an officers' cabin called the "Texas." They were propelled with a stern wheel much like the undershot mill wheel. These boats had well known, *sui generis* characters and reputations which were quite independent of their Captains' or owners'. They were commonly spoken of as living, sentient beings by the people of the river towns. The voices of the *Prairie Belle* or the *Annie Laurie*, when their hoarse steam whistles sounded a landing, were listened for and recognized from afar.

---

[2]This story of the Grant incident can be most recently found in Lloyd Lewis, *Captain Sam Grant*, p. 346. Grant was frequently around Jefferson Barracks in St. Louis seeking odd jobs to help support his family which lived near there on a small farm which Grant called "Hardscrabble."

The people spoke of what the boat could or would do, would not do, without any reference to her Captain. By our running waters the people were commingled and their interests interwoven. Did the waters of Canada reach the ocean through the United States, she would doubtless have been a part of the Union and would have no foreign interests not in common with our own. The force of running water before the Railroad Era was very potent in its influences upon the social and political conditions of the people who lived along its courses. Now, the Western steamboat is as much a thing of the past as the Indian and the buffalo. The railroad has killed all of them together. They have vanished and become silent. The mighty tread of the iron horse covers the land in which they flourished, and even the names of many rivers are now forgotten and their courses unknown.

The first four days in September were occupied in pushing the *F. X. Aubry* up the Missouri to Fort Leavenworth. This season of the year in this yellow climate was most enjoyable on a steamboat. With pleasant companions not long known to each other and with widely different experiences in army life, our intercourse was fresh and agreeable. Orren Chapman had an army reputation as a wit and a good storyteller, second only to Derby or "John Phoenix,"[3] and there was a store of quaint unconscious humor in Tilford. Such companions are best appreciated during the dreary hours a steamboat is hanging on a sand bar. The *Aubry* was a fine, commodious boat, one of the best on the river, and its officers capable and untiring. There was not an abundance of water and it was necessary to spar the *Aubry* over several bars. Sometimes this was a matter of minutes and one lift, but often it required a tedious and continuous effort of hours.

For the benefit of those who never have seen and never will see a western steamboat, a brief description of the method of "sparring" may not be out of place. The spars used were straight, strong, round sticks of timber from twenty to forty feet in length, and from six to ten inches in diameter at the larger end. The pilot when approaching a bar would steer for the best water and shortest crossing, and when the boat struck the sandy bottom and stuck fast, a spar was put over on one or both sides of the boiler deck forward and elevated nearly to a verticle position by lines

---

[3]George Horatio Derby (1823-1861) was graduated from West Point in 1846. He served in the Mexican War, after which he was assigned to the U.S. Topographical Service in California. While there, Derby wrote a series of sketches for the San Francisco magazine *Pioneer*. In 1855, these essays were collected and published under the title *Phoenixiana*, hence the sobriquet "John Phoenix."

and pulleys. The top, which was inclined slightly forward, had rigged to it a double or treble block through which ran lines to another block hooked to a strong ring in the lower deck near the guards, the free end of the line in the blocks being carried to the capstan and wound around it. The capstan was turned, on small boats, by men with hand-spikes, and on the larger boats with a donkey engine. It was astonishing how quickly all the spars and rigging would be placed in position when needed. The effect was, as soon as the spars had sunk to a firm footing, to lift the boat forward and permit the wheel to propel her. As she slowly proceeded, foot by foot, other pairs of spars were set in advance and sometimes in rear to push so that the boat would, with half a dozen spars, have the appearance of a gigantic "daddy long-legs." The profuse and picturesque profanity of the mates who directed and encouraged the crew was considered an indispensable and inevitable factor in the work.

The officers and crews were the most tireless and indefatigable boatmen I ever saw. No obstacle could daunt them and no peril could make them hesitate. Since the English occupied Egypt I have believed that the Missouri steamboat with its crew would be the correct outfit for the Nile, to carry and supply expeditionary forces. The guards of the boats could be easily arranged to protect the crew and cargo from a shore fire. We used cotton bales for that purpose during the war.

I recollect when the boat made Westport Landing, which I believe is now swallowed up and forgotten in Kansas City, that we went upon the highest bluffs to get a glimpse of the country beyond. At that time a month's pay account would have secured a considerable tract of land in that vicinity if we could have found an owner of whom to make the purchase and had thought of it at all. But army officers in those days on the frontier, although having the "first show," never looked about them with the faintest idea of seeing anything valuable or of making money. They did not dream that enough settlers would reach the Rocky Mountains within a single generation, or in many generations, to form a State. And making money per se was never thought of nor talked about. If an officer ever did make an investment or was even noticeably economical, nothing but advancing years or a large family would ensure him from some comment.

Our river voyage ended on the evening of the 4th of September. We found Fort Leavenworth a mighty lively place. An immense expedition, for that date, was outfitting for Utah where territorial affairs had reached an intolerable condition by recurring and growing disorders since the massacre of Captain [John W.] Gunnison and his party four years before. Colonel Albert Sidney Johnston was to go in command of this little army.[4] Fort Leavenworth was to the plains, at that time, what New York City is to the Atlantic—the greatest port. Everything started from here. The mails were sent out once a month with an escort and a double set of fast-trotting mules. Trains of great wagons, each carrying from four to eight tons of supplies and drawn by from five to eight yokes of oxen, were dispatched from Westport or Leavenworth across the interminable wastes of prairie and mountain to Santa Fe and the important stations in New Mexico, Texas and the Northwestern Territories. There was a forest of smoke stacks of steamboats along the levee. The galloping of ubiquitous wagon masters in every direction, the turmoil of toiling stevedores unloading boats and loading wagons, and cracking whips of "Bull-whackers," the breaking of fresh horses, the drill of troops of cavalry and companies of infantry newly organized from the recruits recently arrived—all these activities and sounds mingled with military calls of bugle and drum to make an interesting and animated spectacle, a sort of frontier opera of titanic proportions.

General [William S.] Harney, distinguished as an Indian fighter in Florida and on the frontier, was in command of the Post. Tall and soldierly with not an ounce of superfluous weight, prompt and ready to consider any detail, his great experience rendered him remarkably well fitted for his position. The General had the reputation of having at his command an original and exhaustless vocabulary of cumulative and energizing profanity. I never heard any of it myself but did hear a story about him in illustration of this accomplishment. When the old dragoon revolver was first made, a dozen of them were sent to his regiment for trial. A dozen men were selected to carry and use them. When the men were assembled to receive them at the Colonel's headquarters, he [Harney] said to them mildly, "My men, I have selected you on account of your intelligence and

---

[4]The United States had a continuing problem with the Mormons who successfully practiced their independent religion in the promised land of the Utah territory. In 1853 a survey expedition under Capt. John W. Gunnison was attacked by the Indians with the loss of eight soldiers. Even though the Mormons had nothing to do with the "Gunnison Massacre" they were blamed for it. Relations continued to exacerbate as non-Mormon judges were appointed to oversee the territorial courts. In order to awe the Mormons with federal power, an expedition of about 1,500 officers and men under Col. Albert Sidney Johnston was dispatched to the Utah territory in the late fall of 1857. Despite bad weather and Mormon raids on their supplies, the military force survived and marched into Salt Lake City on 26 June 1858 without bloodshed.

steadiness to test this new arm," and then went on to explain to them its action and use, showing that each pistol had two cylinders, both of which were kept loaded so that when the one in the pistol had been exhausted it could be removed and replaced by the extra one in a moment. Now said the Colonel (warmly):

No man can be such a blankety blank fool as not to see the importance of not losing this extra cylinder, for if lost you will have only six shots and when they are gone you will be at the mercy of your enemy and if you have lost it I hope to God he'll kill you, and if he don't by the blankety blank blank I will, but I expect to hear that they are all lost before you ever get a chance to use them and if I do, (furiously), the very first one that is lost the blankety blank idiot that lost it will wish that all the blank blank Indians in Florida had him instead of me, blank blank him. Now go and lose them, blankety blank.

Captain Alfred Pleasanton was Acting Assistant Adjutant General to General Harney and seemed to like headquarter's duty.

I had the pleasure of meeting my old friends of Carlisle, Captain and Mrs. [Charles H.] Tyler, who were going with the 2d Dragoons to Utah. With them was Mrs. Stanley, awaiting the return of Captain [David S.] Stanley, who was out on the plains, up the Arkansas, somewhere, with the 1st Cavalry under [Col. Edwin V.] Sumner fighting the Cheyennes. Other old friends were found here, among whom were, Captain W.[William] S. Hancock, [Charles G.] Sawtelle, [George A.] Gordon, Doctors [John M.] Cuyler and [John J.] Milhau.

By the 9th of September we were ready to move. Lieut. Colonel [Daniel T.] Chandler, 3d Infantry, was in command of our column; Major [James H.] Carleton, of the mounted troops; and Captain W.[William] T. H. Brooks, 3d Infantry, of the infantry portion. We had an enormous supply train for New Mexico and our own mule train carrying our baggage, camp equipage and supplies. There were a dozen married officers who had private ambulances for their wives. These ambulances were marvels of strength and perfect in their appliances and adaptations to the uses of a family. They were thoroughly weatherproof and could be converted into sleeping chambers in rough weather. Major [Electus] Backus, 3d Infantry, and Lieut. Orren Chapman, 1st Dragoons, accompanied our expedition. After our packing was completed we made our adieu to the friends to be left behind and drew out without any order of march to Salt Creek, three miles west of the Fort and formed a regular camp. Our regulations for camp and for the march were promulgated and order was established. Mounted guards patrolled around the outskirts of our immense herd of oxen, which covered several hundred acres when grazing. The men were given their first lessons in picketing their horses. [Lt. Joseph G.] Tilford, [Lt. George] Jackson of the Rifles, [Lt. Richard S. C.] Lord of the 1st Dragoons, and myself each commanded a mounted troop of about 62 men. Captain [Lafayette B.] Wood, Lieuts. [Alexander N.] Shipley, [John McL.] Hildt, and [Thomas W.] Walker, all of the 3d Infantry, commanded the companies of infantry. Our Surgeons were Doctors J. C. McKee, and [Pascal A.] Quinan.

Sawtelle and Gordon came out from the Fort in the evening to help us let go of civilization. The following morning, Lieut. J. E. B. Stuart of the 1st Cavalry, on his way from Sumner's command to Fort Leavenworth, stopped and breakfasted with us. We listened with eager interest to his narration of the fights, hardships and fatigues that the 1st Cavalry had experienced during their campaign against the Cheyennes. Stuart had been severely wounded in the combat on Solomon's Fork about six weeks before. I never saw him afterward except on the field of battle command-ing Southern Cavalry.

On the 10th we made our first organized march to the "Stranger" creek, ten miles. Our trains, when extended on the road, occupied half the distance. This was a day of hard work as is invariably the case with the first day in all extended military movements. It was my first tour as Officer of the Guard and I had a busy night. Just at dusk a beautiful, dark bay horse with black legs came galloping from the plains directly into my camp and was caught. He had the appearance of being highly bred— beautiful head, splendid nostrils and fine ears—and there were old saddle marks on his back. With him was a thoroughbred setter dog. These animals had evidently belonged to some sportsman but there was nothing to show that they had been recently used and they had probably wandered a long distance—perhaps Indians had got their master. I appropriated the horse, and the dog adopted me as master at once and afterward always slept at my feet. I named the horse "Stranger" and the dog "Sport." We remained at this camp on the 11th and Captain Stanley called in passing from Sumner's returning expedition into the Fort.

The ensuing night about eight o'clock, Walker, who was Officer of the Guard, was brought into camp on a stretcher bleeding from a broken head. Colonel Chandler sent for me and asked me to take the guard again as there was trouble with about thirty mutinous drunken men who had been arrested for disorderly conduct. The Colonel told me to use my own judgement. I found the prisoners turbulent and refractory, and defying the guard which was uncertain what to do. The trouble was incited by half-a-dozen very bad men of the infantry, who were fresh recruits enlisted in New York and totally undisciplined. The leader was a big ugly ruffian who had struck Walker and nearly killed him. The guard were men from the Carlisle depot, well drilled and disciplined, on whom I could rely. The mutineers were yelling loud enough to be heard all over camp. They had not yet undertaken to escape, but seemed determined to raise a general riot. I did not draw my saber, but used the free scabbard with the saber in it. In less that two minutes we had half a dozen down, and tied, and all of the prisoners seated on the ground in a circle with sentinels around them with everything quiet, and this was the last trouble of this kind we had.

On the 12th we made twenty miles to "Hickory Point" where we found fine grass and good wood but muddy water. This had been a battle ground of "the free state party" the year before, which might at this distance of time be regarded as the first picket shot of the war which followed four years later.[5]

There were three essentials to the welfare of a column crossing the plains: wood, water, and grass at the camping places. None of them was too plenty, often one and sometimes two would be missing, and for fifty miles on the "dry route" all were lacking. "The dry route" was across a big bend of the Arkansas River, and in taking it to save a long distance, it was necessary to carry along water for the camp, the "bois des vaches" or dried "buffalo chips" being gathered for fuel. These would make a fire like peat.

---

[5] Averell is referring to the bloody civil war in Kansas, a microcosm of the national war which would follow seven years later. While in camp on Grasshopper Creek (13 September 1857), Averell wrote to his brother Oscar:

We have a very strong command, some six hundred, and the Infantry that are with us are a perfect rabble and it takes all our time to keep things in order. One of them at 'the Stranger' (creek) struck an officer. . . . I was detailed as Officer of the Guard and . . . the result of our intercourse was that two of them were laid out cold and quick for half an hour or so, and I bent my sabre some over their heads—and had no more trouble after that. I have the reputation of killing at first sight now—Our camp last night was at 'Hickory Point' where a battle was fought between the free state men and pro-slavery party two years ago—This is the most beautiful country I ever laid my eyes on and it will eventually be the garden of the States.

As it is not likely that any people will ever again cross the plains with a wagon train and as but few are living who ever experienced that mode of travel, I may be pardoned for mentioning minor incidents and chronicling details of our experiences which would be omitted were not those days forever gone and already nearly forgotten. We were generally up with the dawn and, breakfast soon over, the advance moved out upon the road followed by the train which steadily unwound from its corrals. If the conditions were favorable we halted for an hour or more in the middle of the march for the day, unsaddled and grazed the horses, while we had a light lunch of a biscuit, bit of bacon and half an onion. Of all vegetables the potato and onion are the most essential on the march. We generally reached camp from two to four o'clock in the afternoon and had our dinners toward six o'clock. Where antelope abounded on the plains and ducks or fish in the river, we went in quest of them after reaching camp. We found the old fashioned "Dutch oven" the best cooking utensil in existence for general purposes. A round hole a little larger than the oven was dug in the ground with a little side trench for a draft, and in and over this hole the fire was built to cook the dinner. A favorite dish for breakfast was baked beans, made by first parboiling the beans and then placing them in the oven the previous night in quantity sufficient to half fill it and then sticking several small prisms of bacon into the beans and filling the oven with water. The cover was put on and the oven set in the hole, surrounded and heaped over with coals. In the morning a solid mass would be found in the oven, which, when sliced and dressed with a little salt and red pepper, was very palatable and satisfying with hot biscuits and coffee.

We always had one essential to the enjoyment of a meal not to be found of equal quality anywhere else in the world, that is, a natural and unfailing appetite. Chapman, who set out from Leavenworth an invalid in an ambulance, soon got into the saddle, became hearty and strong, and gained thirteen pounds crossing the plains. If some of the weary and surfeited club men of the East, who long for an appetite, would try six or seven hundred miles of prairie, leisurely, leaving all luxuries and fancy drinks behind, they would be liable to find something novel to them in life.

On the 14th of September at "Indianola" we met the 1st Cavalry under Colonel Sumner coming in from the Cheyenne expedition. They

were the most bronzed and ragged crowd of white men I had ever seen.[6]
They were fast approaching the Indian in complexion and costume.
Among the officers I saw my old Carlisle friends, Captain McIntosh and
Lieut. Lomax. The latter was wearing the remnants of a straw hat the
crown of which had entirely disappeared permitting his long black hair to
stream out over the sides. Naked toes were seen protruding from the
wreck of cavalry boots and their clothing, excepting their overcoats,
which were mostly kept rolled, was an affair of shreds and tatters. The
main thing was all there however—the ability to fight. They had humiliated the powerful and defiant Cheyenne tribe on their own chosen battle
grounds.

Colonel Sumner looked the ideal cavalry Colonel, grizzled; erect,
sleepless and always on duty. I never heard of his being "stumped" but
once by a subordinate and that was by Lieut. Orren Chapman, who was
now with us. Some years before Chapman was serving at a Post commanded by Colonel Sumner, who always appeared in uniform, coat buttoned to throat, at reveille to receive the reports of his officers. One
morning Chapman did not appear and the Colonel sent his orderly for
him. Chapman came forth in a hurry, buttoning his coat as he hastened
along, approached the Colonel and saluted. Said the commanding officer,
"Mr. Chapman, you were absent from reveille."

"Yes," replied the Lieutenant, "I slept over it."

---

[6]The Cheyenne expedition was one of two military expeditions out of Fort Leavenworth in 1857
against the Plains Indians. Colonel Edwin V. Sumner was in charge with orders to capture all
Cheyennes who had committed depredations against whites and to secure a promise against future
depredations. The best description of this expedition is from the letters of Eugene Bandel originally
written to his parents in German. Bandel wrote:

You should see us in our prairie outfits; don't imagine a uniform. Every man is wearing a broad-
rimmed hat, each of a different color; white trousers of rough material; a woolen shirt of red,
green, blue, or brown—in short, of any and every color, usually open in front and worn like a
coat; the shoes (we still have shoes, though who knows how soon we may have to wear
moccasins) with the uppers slashed wherever they might chafe in marching. Even the arms are of
different kinds. The bayonets of the privates are with the baggage; my sword, too, is in the
wagon, for there is no such thing as hand-to-hand combat with the Indians. Every man carries a
long hunting knife in his belt, and some a five or six-shot revolver. A gun over the shoulder
completes the soldier. In this respect there is no distinction between officer and private.

(Eugene Bandel, *Frontier Life in the Army, 1854-1861*, pp. 123-4.)

"No excuse, sir," said the Colonel.

"I did not offer it as an excuse, Colonel, but as a reason."

"It's no reason, sir," said the irascible Colonel.

"Well, it's a fact by G—d," was the nettled reply of Chapman.

After a moment's hesitation the Colonel said, "Well, sir, don't let it occur again."

We reached the "Kaw" (Kansas) river on the 15th, about eighty miles from Leavenworth, and were two days and nights crossing that stream by means of a rope ferry. Here Captain W. S. Hancock of the Quartermaster's Department came out from the Fort with a pair of horses and a buggy to bring us our mail and take back our letters. He was a very fine-looking man, in the prime of life and of most pleasant and affable manners. He occupied my tent while he remained. I remember that he wore a suit of soft, brown velveteen. His visit renewed our pangs of leaving the States. During our delay Jackson, Hildt, Walker and myself drove down to Topeka to procure some additional vegetables. There were, according to my recollection, but thirteen houses in the place, although streets and avenues were staked off and named.

Our junior Surgeon, Quinan, or "Peruvian Bark" as we called him, shortened into "P. B." for convenience, was a decidedly objectionable person to all of us, being an opium fiend and glaringly neglectful of his wife who seemed a very worthy lady. The commanding officer kindly sent her back to Leavenworth from this point and if P. B. had fallen into the river no one would have mourned his loss. It seems necessary to mention this incident as it relieved us from subsequent grief on one occasion afterward concerning this "Medico" who came to be a burden.

Our march was without special incident until we reached Council Grove where we saw buffalo for the first time and met the Santa Fe mail coming in. There was something very impressive to me about this mail. A dark spot appears on the Western horizon, coming rapidly toward us and steadily growing in size. A little nearer and soon a cloud and trail of dust is discerned out of which is coming a small, swaying coach, drawn by three pairs of fast-trotting mules under the lash of an outrider, the outfit followed by a herd of eight or ten mules driven by another mounted man. Soon the voices of the drivers, the cracking whips, and the muffled rattle of the wheels are heard. Here they come with all the fascination of a speed many times greater than ours. "Whoa! whoa!" Down spring the wiry and wary drivers, each bearing two six shooters on his belt. A touch of a string or two and six mules spring from the harness and in a quarter of a minute are rolling on the grass and kicking their heels in the air. The strong little coach covered with dust, its boot, water proof and full of mail bags, and with two or three rifles strapped to the sides, has come over seven hundred miles, sixty-five miles mountain roads and the remainder treeless prairie, and with an escort only to the Cimarron. Its obvious indifference to the perils of the plains and indomitable purpose to go through at all speed is an eloquent manifestation of an unseen but invincible power which is understood and respected even by thè Indian. The legend of its life is emblazened in large letters on each door of the coach "U.S. Mail." The great flying Post Office cars of today are respectable; this Santa Fe Mail was heroic.

At Cotton Wood we rested a day, as wood, water and grass were plentiful and it was desirable to exercise our men at target practice before entering a region where it might be useful. Buffalo appeared in numerous herds grazing northward. Being Officer of the Guard I was prevented joining in the chase with several officers who returned empty-handed and with their horses so fatigued that orders were issued that there should be no chasing of buffalo without special permission.

On the morning of the 26th, my company had the advance and Major Carleton was riding with me. I had a little five-shooter with which I could shoot well at twelve paces, but the Major said it was good for nothing with buffalo. He was quite right but I did not know it and the result of the discussion was the Major wagered me a basket of wine to be had at Fort Union that I could not stop a buffalo with it, much less kill one. We were passing a spot called "Little Turkey Creek" in an itinerary for the reason, possibly, that there was no creek there and no turkeys could have ever been seen about it. There were some water holes, however, to mark the place in the prairie monotony. Shortly there appeared a small herd of seven buffalo coming from our left in a lumbering gallop to cross the trail in front of the column. To a side view the buffalo appears of the contour of a huge animated ham with his shaggy, heavy head on the big end. His powerful forelegs are short and columnar to sustain his immense weight, his hind legs being comparatively long, small and slender. He turns about on his forelegs.

As the herd was running it would cross our course about a half a mile in front and the Major could not resist the temptation, so he said to me, "Take after those fellows, Averell, and see if you can stop one with that pistol." I was riding "Stranger" who was already prancing and eager for the chase. The buffalo crossed the road as I arrived and turned to the right in pursuit. My first shot was premature and passed near my horse's head. It was an enormous bull in rear of the herd and I saw at once if I hit him with a shot from that pistol he probably wouldn't know it, so I raced up on his left with the idea of hitting his backbone. One's arm when riding a running horse must perforce rise and fall with the horse and a leveled pistol describes a considerable arc up and down. The expert buffalo hunter would follow directly behind the buffalo until he was ready and the ground favorable when his trained horse at the signal of spur and rein leaped close along the left side and the hunter reached down almost touching the buffalo behind the foreleg with the muzzle of his pistol, fired a shot which penetrated the vital parts, the horse wheeled promptly to the left to avoid the turn of the wounded and ferocious beast which was then left alone. If he blew blood from his nostrils the shot was fatal, if not then another was given him. I was not an expert and had a toy pistol. Aiming carefully for the ridge along the loin I fired, and the beast stopped and turned on me. His aspect was terrible but it was easy to keep out of his way for his left hind leg was broken midway between the gambrel joint and the foot. Having aimed at the backbone with a "drop," the shot had struck the small bone of the leg and broken it.

Down came an orderly with "the Major's compliments and requests that the Lieutenant will not kill the buffalo until the command has passed and the ladies had an opportunity to see him." To this was returned, "My compliments to Major Carleton and I will spare the life of the buffalo until the column has passed." I could not have killed that buffalo with a wagon load of such pistols. By teasing the buffalo he was incited to hobble down to within a hundred yards of the trail, and the command and the ladies enjoyed a free and unique show. The Major said: "It was hardly fair to select the smallest bone in the buffalo to break." I had great credit for the shot until dinner time when my conscience compelled me to own up that I had not seen nor thought of the bone before firing but had aimed at the back bone, four or five feet above. After the command had passed I finished the buffalo with a minie rifle ball in the curl of his forehead and cut out his tongue as a trophy. We began to enjoy buffalo meat and especially the marrow bones. The buffalo cow was alone killed for meat.

We frequently passed pairie-dog towns, some of them quite extensive. My dog "Sport" was forever vainly trying to catch one. It was even difficult to shoot them. The saucy little fellows would sit on the edge of their holes and chatter or bark until they detected danger when no flash could be quicker than their disappearance.

On the 28th I was left behind to await the death of one of our best men, Sergeant Cline, who was dying of cholera morbus—and to bury him. He was conscious for an hour or more and I sat by him and read some prayers for him while some of my guard, out of sight and hearing on the bank of Chavis creek, were digging his grave. I read the service at the grave and a volley was fired above it. A fire was built over the grave to prevent the wolves disturbing it. There was a legend about this place. A Mexican trader, named Chavis, from Santa Fe, came into the States once upon a time and was followed by ruffians who on his return fell upon him here and robbed and murdered him.

We overtook the Command at "Big Cow creek" which during the night rose ten feet and stopped the Santa Fe mail going west. Two years before, Captain Richardson's camp was burned out here. The great perils of the prairie were a prairie fire and a stampede. The latter was the more dreaded. It was a panic among animals which if not stopped instantly might not be controlled, and a command left without animals two or three hundred miles from help was badly wrecked. It might be caused by a wolf, by running buffalo, or by Indians. The remedy was, on the first intimation, for every man to run to his horse and stand on the picket pin so that it could not be pulled up and to draw the horse to him with his lariat and quiet him, taking a loop about his nose, and for teamsters to go to their mules and attract their attention with the whip or with feed. We had two or three starts of this sort but succeeded in subduing them immediately.

On the 30th of September we passed those notable objects called "Plumb Buttes." They were two protrusions of indurated argillaceous sand which could be seen at the distance of a day's march, appearing like a pair of small haystacks. We camped at the bend of the Arkansas 272 miles from Fort Leavenworth. So we had averaged about thirteen miles per day. We had laid over four days, so that our marches averaged really sixteen miles a day. The effect was very noticeable in the infantry. The first week they had straggled a good deal and required a rear guard to prevent them seeking the wagons for a ride. Now in the morning it was a pleasure to see them swing out of camp with elastic route step, moving as a body without a straggler and keeping it up without fatigue until a halt was made, when pipes were lighted and songs, laughter and all the indications betokening good health and spirits could be heard.

At this camp we were astonished to find another camp near by. We found a party of officers, some with their families, going into the States— some on leave, others on recruiting service. Among them were Capt. and Bvt. Col. Andrew Porter and wife, Capt. [John G.] Walker and Lieut. Roger Jones, of the Rifles; Capt. [Josiah H.] Carlisle, 2d Arty; Major McRae [Nathaniel C. Macrae] and wife, of the 8th Infantry; Captain [Augustus A.] Gibson and Lieuts. DeLagnel [Julius A. de'Lagnel], W.[William] D. Whipple and [John R.] Smead. Colonel Porter was Captain of "F" Co. Regt. Mtd. Rifles, to which I had been assigned, and therefore I felt an uncommon interest in meeting him. As I was on guard that night I could not go to see him, and he and Captain Walker came down to see me and spent an hour or two. Colonel Porter had won his brevet in the Mexican War when a brevet was esteemed a high honor, and my first impression of him was fully confirmed in after years. He was a handsome, well-proportioned man, slightly inclined to be stout without being so; a fine head crowned with luxuriant hair; clear, strong eyes, beaming with intelligence; and with courtly manners in which formality and good humor were charmingly mingled. He was about the truest friend, bravest gentleman and purest man I ever knew. I shall have to chronicle many reminiscences of him hereafter and of Whipple and of Roger Jones. At Walnut creek, Lieut. Craig turned back on account of the serious illness of his wife.

We turned into "Dry Route" four miles beyond "Pawnee Fork," and I had an opportunity to mark the place by killing a badger which was about the hardest thing to kill on the plains. After turning up the Arkansas near the ruins of Fort Atkinson,[7] we came upon a territory of rattlesnakes and killed great numbers and happily escaped any injury to man or beast.

Dr. Quinan promised us another funeral this day and was not expected to survive the night, but he was yet alive when the command moved the following morning, and I was left with a guard and three days' rations to await his death and to attend to his burial. This was the most doleful of duties. The doctor had become greatly emaciated and had the appearance already of a cadaver lying upon his bed in a tent. A wagon and

---

[7]Fort Atkinson, built in 1850, was abandoned three years later due to the lack of proper building materials. See Robert M. Utley, *Frontiersmen in Blue: the United States Army and the Indian, 1848-1865*, pp. 66-68.

an ambulance had been left with me to carry the camp equipage when the doctor should no longer need it. His breathing could scarcely be detected and his hands were cold and clammy. I waited three weary hours on the bank of the Arkansas with an occasional visit to the doctor's bedside. No motion, no change. He would reply to no questions and manifested no sense of hearing, feeling or seeing. Opium had claimed him at last.

The command had long passed away out of sight and no living thing was visible. On one side of us was the wide, shallow river with prairie beyond, on the other, at a little distance, sage brush and sand hills. I selected a point for his grave where the work would be easy and after waiting another mortal hour concluded to set the men to work. But before doing so thought I would take one more look at the dying man. On seeing him without apparent change and having failed in all my efforts to rouse him or make him talk, it occurred to me to try an experiment. After carefully instructing the Sergeant, I returned to the bedside. Presently the knowing Sergeant entered and saluting said with a tone of apparent trep- idation, "Lieutenant, Indians are prowling on the sand hills." I directed him to have the men to load and cap their pieces and prepare for a fight. When the Sergeant had got beyond the word "Indians," Quinan had turned slightly, and as I gave my orders he raised slowly, and as the Sergeant hurriedly went out he bounded from the bed exclaiming, "Oh my God, where is my double-barrelled shot gun?" and while jumping into his clothing by my direction, he kept up the cries of a groveling coward, "Oh what shall we do? Let us get into a wagon and run it into the middle of the river and then they can't get at us." I said that would only prolong our misery, that our only chance was to hitch up, put him in the ambulance and fight our way through to the command. The Sergeant and men understood the matter thoroughly and acted their parts with a real- ism that I was afraid would kill the doctor with fright. We got his bed into the ambulance with him upon it and the wagon loaded in less time than it required to tell about it. And then we took the road with some- thing of the speed of the Santa Fe mail while the men kept up a desultory fire for a mile or two. Precaution had been taken to remove the caps from the doctor's shot gun, and a man rode with him to tell him how things were progressing as he dared not look out.

We reached camp, twenty miles, about 5 P.M., and the wagon and ambulance were sent where they belonged and I repaired to my camp where I found Majors Carleton and Brooks and all of our young fellows in front of my tent taking their comfort with pipes and discussing the demise of Quinan. They agreed while it was a sad thing to happen to bury a man amid such desolation, yet there was a certain fitness about it as related to this victim of opium. After I had become settled, one of them asked me about his death and how long he had lived. I told them he had not died. Then in astonishment they wanted to know what had happened, and when they had been told they were inclined to believe that I was guying them, and Dr. McKee and two or three others who had thought it their duty to take a last look in the morning went over to the hospital to see—half ashamed and doubtful if they were not "sold" anyhow. When they came back it was my opportunity to deliver a lecture on the proper treatment of opium fiends for my friend Dr. McKee, and they called me "Doctor" for some time. Quinan lived to be tried by a court-martial a year or two later and to be dismissed from the service.[8]

The influence of fright upon men and animals is sometimes amazing. I have seen a broken-down horse that could not be persuaded by any urging to get up nor to make the slightest effort to move, lying with an obstinacy which nothing could overcome, finally abandoned by a moving column, and a short time after, that same abandoned horse would come racing into camp with head and tail up and snorting under the impulse of terror. I saw officers and men do things at the first Battle of Bull Run that they would not themselves have remembered nor acknowledged afterward and probably never did the like again. At fires I have seen things of the same sort. Under the sudden impulsion of fear the reason seems completely unseated and the excited imagination arouses an energy so prodigious as to seem supernatural.

We did a great deal of hunting and fishing along the Arkansas. Buffalo were so plentiful that on some days the landscape in every direction seemed alive with them as far as one could see. One day after reaching camp we lost twelve oxen stampeded by them. Deer and antelope were seen every day. Jackson was our best hunter for antelope and we were indebted to him for several good dinners. A quarter of baked or roasted antelope was just about enough for four of us.

On the 9th of October, Jackson wounded a deer on Choteau Island and it escaped to our side of the river when Dr. McKee knocked it over with a charge of buckshot, but as it lay kicking McKee fired the other

---

[8]Dr. Pascal A. Quinan was permitted to resign from the service on 7 July 1862. The man would survive for more than thirty years after the incident Averell describes. Quinan died on 30 June 1889.

barrel when the deer jumped up and ran into the river to cross. The doctor called out to me, as I was nearest to the point where he left our side, to go for him. The water was nearly knee deep and the bottom rough. Drawing my six-shooter, which I had only used since discovering the weakness of my little pistol, I dashed into the river and was fast gaining on the deer when my horse sprang into a large hole, at least ten feet deep, turning a half somersault, carrying me under and hitting my head with one of his feet in his struggles to get out. A few minutes later I found myself being carried ashore by Sergeant McCleave and two or three men who had fished me out. My pistol was presumably at the bottom of the hole and the deer was visibly nearing the other side of the river.

Thirty-one years later, when on a visit of inspection to the California Soldiers Home near Napa, the Commandant, Captain William McCleave, U.S.A. (retired), stood at the entrance to receive me. The driver as I alighted thought it proper to say to the Commandant, "This is General Averell."

The Captain replied, "I know General Averell better than anyone in California; I knew him when he was a boy."

I asked him where and he said, "Don't you remember being almost drowned once in the Arkansas River?"

"Oh yes," said I, "and probably would have been but for a young Sergeant who pulled me out."

The Commandant, a soldierly man with streaks of gray in his hair, said with hesitating voice and moistened eye, "We were both younger then, General, and I was that Sergeant."

There was one feeling or sentiment about camp life that I have never forgotten. The position of our tents was of course dictated to some extent by the position of our command, but within proper limits we selected the most agreeable spot with reference to the local features. The tents once pitched, the immediate surroundings—trees, rocks, moss and flowers—entered into the make-up of our home and we adjusted ourselves to it as little children accord themselves to a playhouse. And when we broke camp in the morning and the tents were struck, there was a brief, faint sense of desolation as we gave the spot a parting glance.

We had a sensation in the loss of an officer one day among the buffalo. Lieutenant Richard Lord rode the most powerful horse I ever saw in the cavalry service—over seventeen hands high and well proportioned. In running buffalo the horse became frightened and ran away in a north-easterly direction until he and his rider were out of sight. We waited an hour or more and then followed him with a small party several miles, getting no sight of him and losing his trail in the buffalo tracks. We had no Indian or scouts accustomed to trailing, and darkness coming on we returned to camp and built a large bonfire, keeping it up all night. At daylight we fired volleys of small arms. We had a conference in the morning and concluded that if he had not been disabled, he would be certain that he was north of the Santa Fe trail and when the sun rose he would go due south to strike it, and I took twenty-five men and returned on the route. So many men were taken in order that a long skirmish line might be formed if necessary to search the prairie. Our surmise proved true after going ten miles and our eyes were gladdened with the sight of a solitary horseman coming westward who was our friend. His horse had run about twenty-five miles passing through landscapes of buffalo, in spite of all efforts of his rider to check him. Finally Lord concluded to take the risk of jumping off while hanging on to the reins. He threw the snaffle rein off the horse's head and carried the end to his left hand, sprang to the ground and hung on for dear life and stopped the horse. He remained at that place all night, bothered occasionally by wolves which seeing an animal fastened were disposed to attack him. When the sun rose he mounted and directed his course southward until he struck our trail.

About the 14th of October, near the ruins of Bent's Fort, we saw the first signs of Indians. The next day my company had the advance and about midday the first Indian appeared. He came forth with shy, hesitating footsteps from a thicket on the bank of the river to our left. He had no blanket, his loins and hips were covered with a light mud-discolored cotton fabric wound about him, the light red color of his skin was deepened in his face with some pigment, and his long, straight, black hair parted in the middle fell in luxuriant confusion down his back and upon his shoulders and partly screened his face. He wore leggins of skin and moccasins and carried a bow and quiver of arrows diagonally across his back strung to a strap of hide across his shoulder. The first, curious quick impression he made on me has never been forgotten nor was it ever repeated. It shaped itself into a question that arose to my mind, "What on earth is this creature doing here?" I had seen buffalo, antelope and other animals on the plains and they all seemed to be at home and to harmonize with nature. But here was a man wandering in the habitat of wild beasts with no shelter, no smoke of fire visible. No home but that of the wild animals under the sky. It was my first recognition of the savage condition. He was a Cheyenne and was sent to the commanding officer who had an interpreter who could speak Mexican and enough of the Indian dialects to sustain common intercourse.

About three P.M. of that day Pike's Peak gleaming with snow could be seen due west like a white cloud on the horizon. It afforded us our first glimpse of the Rockies. That evening many Cheyennes came into our camp and had a big talk. They were a portion of the tribe which had escaped the chastisement of the 1st Cavalry under Sumner. They were all beggars and wanted coffee and sugar especially. They also wanted the doctor to give them medicine for their sick. One of these latter was a girl, emaciated and covered with sores. She sat on the ground with her head resting upon her knees between her hands. Her only garment was a dirty tattered skirt of heavy cotton stuff like bagging. Her skin had an ashen hue. She had two remarkable features which had survived: namely brilliant, burning black eyes and a profusion of matted black hair which fell upon the ground as she sat. They said she was a captive whom they had purchased of the Kiowas. She had been unable to walk for some days and had been subsisting on the tuna plucked from the prickly pear through which she had been dragged by a pony harnessed between two poles, like shafts, upon the rear of which a rude basketlike litter had been woven. Her name was "Gregoria." The doctor said she might not live long. She could speak only a few Indian words. Negotiations were opened which resulted in her purchase for one bucket of sugar and another bucket of "hardtack." She was turned over to our camp women, of whom we had half a dozen or more, with directions to bathe her thoroughly and supply her with necessary clothing, but they were enjoined not to cut her hair. The doctor directed her medical treatment and in a few days she began to improve.

Of Bent's old Fort nothing was left but broken-down ruined walls of house, corral and garden overgrown with weeds. It had been established early in the century by Bent as a trading post. He married an Indian woman and had three children, two sons and a daughter, whom he sent to the States to be educated. The daughter returned to him and cared for his home after her mother had died and on one occasion saved his life. His sons after their return soon abandoned their home and lapsed into barbarism. One evening the daughter discovered persons skulking outside the garden walls who proved to be her brothers gunning for the old man —so goes the legend. The new Fort, which we had passed two days before we reached the old Fort, was about 150 feet by 75, built of sandstone found in great abundance and of convenient dimensions in the immediate vicinity. Its site was well chosen on a bluff about forty yards from the river which here runs narrow and deep below at the foot of a natural wall thirty feet high. It did not seem to be completed, the Indians having presented to Bent the moving alternative of leaving himself or his scalp. The Cheyennes had already drawn on the inner walls a pictographic history of Sumner's fight with them. They would admit of having lost only ten Indians.

We crossed the Arkansas on the 17th of October just below Bent's old Fort and had five days' marches, camping at "Timpus River," "Orchard Spring," "Hole in the Rock," and "Hole in the Prairie" before we reached the Raton mountains. The character of the country became more rolling and broken, the wood and water plentiful and the grass luxuriant. The chiefs of the Cheyennes—Prairie Wolf, Great Bear and White Antelope—travelled along with us and hung about our camp for two or three days expressing great friendship for us. They said their tribe was composed of two divisions and that the Laramie part or sub-tribe had committed the depredations for which they had been punished by the 1st Cavalry. They mourned the loss of their lodges and winter stores and were going to leave their women and children up the Purgatory river while the men went after buffalo. Our interpreter for talks with them was called John—half Mexican and half Cheyenne. Wild geese and ducks made the sky clamorous with their flight and tracks of deer were frequent.

We laid over the 24th to rest our animals before crossing the range. Our camp at "Orchard Spring" had been in a shallow valley and the next morning my company had the advance. As we came up out of the valley we saw two snowy clouds ahead shining like silver, but as we neared the plain above, there was gradually revealed a most impressive view of the "Spanish Peaks." Exclamations of surprise, wonder and admiration broke forth from the men in the column. Certainly I had never before seen anything so sublime in mountain scenery. The peaks appeared so near that we expected to pass them before night, but after four days more of marches they seemed higher but no nearer.

The mountain camp, contrasted with the prairie, delighted our men beyond measure. Plenty of wood, abundance of pure spring water and, near the foot, valleys of grass. The sublimity and splendor of the mountain views were indescribable, but it was not until we had climbed the pass some distance that one of the finest mountain spectacles, I think the finest in the Rocky Mountains, was enjoyed. Looking toward the north from a point well up the Raton Range, we saw in the middle ground to the left both Spanish Peaks, their summits separated by thirty miles but seeming within one-fourth that distance of each other. In the morning sunlight, the cones shone against a pure cloudless sky like frosted silver which ran in lanceolated streaks a little way down their sides where they were lost in tender purples with dashes here and there of vermillion tints which seemed ever changing, and these purples deepened into indigo in the shadowy abysses below. In the foreground down below us were mountains, which seemed children of the pair, clad in warm browns and deep greens. To the right stretched the prairie far away to the distant eastern horizon, traversed by the Arkansas and its tributaries, which were plainly indicated by their fringes of cottonwood. To the left center, beyond the middle ground, towered "Pike's Peak," and to the right of it farther on, "Long's Peak" reared his summit above a long escarpment of tumultuous mountains stretching from the foothills of the Spanish Peaks far away to the "Sangre de Christo" range which formed the northern horizon in the dim distance. Here were brought under the same *coup d'oeil* two immense magnitudes, each enhancing the other, the supreme height of the peaks with the illimitable horizontal breadth of prairie. Such conditions with such objects cannot be found elsewhere on the continent.

It was a trying day going over the range. The cavalry preceded the column and made the passage in one day to get the horses to grass. The train assisted by the infantry came over with some distress and only one accident in two days, and we were all encamped on the Cimarron on the 28th. Two days more brought us to Fort Union, New Mexico, 723 miles from Fort Leavenworth. We had made the journey in fifty-two days. Now it can be traversed by railway in as many hours. Then along six hundred miles of the route not a sign of a human habitation was to be seen. Now that country has been surveyed and divided into sections and quarter sections, and as I now ride through it in a palace car on a summer day and look out for the old trail and the camping places I can see nothing but broad fields of waving corn and grain, and farm houses and barns between the thriving towns. Countless windmills lifting the water from beneath the ground and young growing forests diversify the plains which we once thought uninhabitable. And all this is but one subordinate feature of the mighty transformations which have characterized American development within my memory.

[4]

New Mexico

A t this period, 1857, popular knowledge of our Territories was quite limited and indefinite. The reports of U.S. Engineers who had run boundary lines, or of officers of the army in charge of exploring expeditions, had afforded interesting, but fragmentary glimpses of the wonderful topography of these vast regions which had been under the dominion of the Government of the United States only about nine years. The Territories had become distinguished in the minds of eastern people to a small extent by their chief natural features; as Utah, by its Great Salt Lake; Colorado, by its peaks and parks; New Mexico, by the valley of the Rio Grande; and Arizona, by the *cañon* of the Colorado. But knowledge of the mountains, wildernesses, valleys and deserts stretching far away northward to the British possessions was yet more meager and conjectural. All definite information of their inhabitants was confined to the Territorial governments that had been established since their acquisition from Mexico, and to the expeditionary forces and military posts which maintained governmental authority. It was impossible to appreciate the immensity of the areas of the four territories—Colorado, Utah, New Mexico and Arizona—which are grouped about the intersection of the 37th parallel of latitude with the 32d meridian west of Washington. We can now only approach a conception of the extent of their aggregated areas by an effort to realize that it is equal to the sum total of the areas of all the seventeen states touching the Atlantic from Maine to Florida and including Vermont, Pennsylvania and West Virginia. The area of New

Mexico alone is greater than the united areas of New York, Pennsylvania, New Jersey, Delaware and Maryland.

The principal topographical feature of New Mexico is the Rio Grande which enters it from Colorado on the north and running along the backbone of the Rocky Mountains, like a half-developed spinal cord in embryo, leaves it at El Paso on the south. As the Nile to lower Egypt, so is the Rio Grande to the habitable portion of New Mexico. Agriculture waits upon its waters which are drained away by unnumbered *acequias* to irrigate its fertile but thirsty soil. The Mexicans, for protection and defense against twenty thousand savages, lived in towns from Taos to El Paso. The principal tribes of Indians were the Navajos in the northwestern part of the territory, the Gila Apaches in the southwest and Mescalero Apaches in the southeast. Outside and near its boundaries and ever ready for savage incursions were the Kiowas, Comanches and Apaches of the plains on the east and the Pi-Utes to the northwest. The most interesting population was that of the seven scattered Pueblos, numbering about eight thousand souls. Their ancient and time-worn towns were monuments of peaceful industry amid the wrackful desolation surrounding them.

To maintain the civil government in New Mexico and to keep its communcations open with the States, the military forces employed were the Regiment of Mounted Riflemen and the 3d and 8th Infantry. These were distributed among a dozen or more Posts and Cantonments, the principal ones being Taos, Fort Union, Berguin, Fort Marcy, Albuquerque, Las Lunas, Fort Craig, Fort Thorn, Fort Filmore and Fort Bliss along the Rio Grande, Fort Defiance 180 miles west of Albuquerque over the mountains as a flank defence, Fort Stanton on the southeast, and Fort Buchanan on the southwest. These Posts were generally garrisoned with one company of Mounted Riflemen and one or two of Infantry. In the scope of its duties on the frontier, along with the "Fifties," the "company," as it was then known, received a consideration quite equal to that accorded to a regiment thirty years later. The Indians were more numerous then, but not so well armed as they became a generation later. The gigantic schemes of land robbery and for converting enormous appropriations into private fortunes had not then become a regular business. "For forty years the encroaching white people had never kept a Treaty, and the Indians had never broken one," was the saying of General Harney, but the difficulties resulting had not been extensive. They were sporadic and

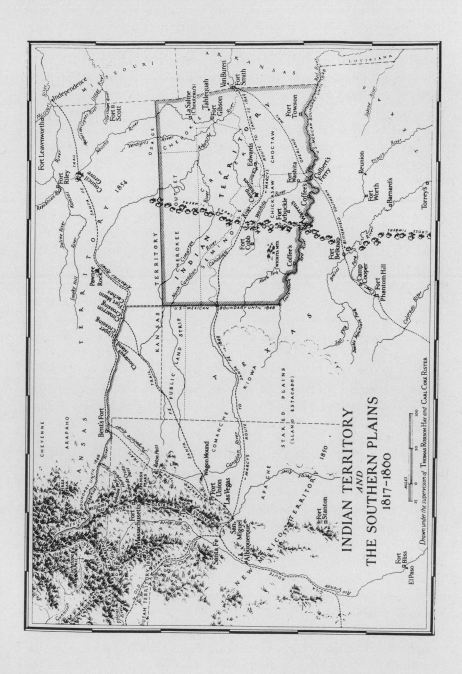

INDIAN TERRITORY
AND
THE SOUTHERN PLAINS
1817–1860

Drawn under the supervision of Thomas Robson Hay and Carl Coke Rister

trivial compared with the despairing struggles of tribes forcibly torn away from the ancient habitats of their race and driven into rocky and forbidding deserts to carry out the wickedness of conscienceless land grabbers which became a systemized industry after the Civil War.

The military headquarters of the department of New Mexico were at Santa Fe and Brigadier General [John] Garland was in command. I remember that Major W.[William] A. Nichols was his Assistant Adjutant General, Major [Langdon C.] Easton his Quartermaster General and Dr. [David C.] De Leon his Surgeon General. The headquarters of the regiment of Mounted Riflemen were at Fort Union. Our arrival at that Post Oct. 31, 1857, with several hundred recruits and heavy trains of supplies was an event. Many officers galloped out miles to meet us and the garrison was full of joyous excitement. Those were the most blessed moments of army life—the meetings. For the first time I saw my picturesque Colonel, W.[William] W. Loring, who had left an arm at the Belen Gate, City of Mexico. His erect soldierly figure of medium height, bright black eyes full of expression, straight black hair, mustache, and imperial, easy courtesy and fine conversational ability, altogether made an agreeable and lasting impression upon me. Strange to say, I never saw him again until after a quarter of a century had filled his life with military experiences of the war for the Union and of a decade as Major General in the Egyptian Army. We greatly enjoyed the hospitality of our friends, Captain Llewellyn Jones and Lieutenants Julian May, W.[William] B. Lane, [Christopher H.] McNally and [Hyatt C.] Ransom of the Rifles, who lived in quarters, and we found it almost novel to dine at a table and sit on chairs again.

At the end of a week the assignment of men and horses had been made to the different companies of my regiment. My camp was broken and I set out with a detachment of about 200 men for the Posts on the Rio Grande as far down as Fort Bliss. Lieutenants Richard Lord of the 1st Dragoons and [John McL.] Hildt of 3d Infantry were with me. I was charged also with the transportation and safe delivery of $250,000 in gold coin to the quartermaster at Santa Fe. The young captive girl who had been acquired from the Cheyennes was to be taken to the Indian Agency at Santa Fe as no one knew where, or to whom, she belonged. She had regained good health, strength and form to a remarkable extent and seemed disposed to sprightly talk, but no one could understand her words except a few common to both Indians and Mexicans. The first snow fell on the 7th of November and so deep that it retarded our march, but as we had abundant supplies and good tents we enjoyed the route which passed through forests of pine and piñon, picturesque gorges and rugged *cañons*.

Las Vegas is distinguished in my memory as the first Mexican town I ever saw. It was then a dirty hamlet of adobe and jacal habitations, alive with yelping dogs and swarthy blanketed "greasers," and our first impressions of the natives were not such as to make us hilarious about our future social prospects in New Mexico. We stopped an hour at the ranch of Dr. Boise, an American noted for his hospitality and high character. Regarding the Americans who had become established in trade at different points in the territory or engaged in government employment, it was well learned in time that they were not Ishmaelites, but men of strong adventure who had found social life in the East too vapid and weak to satisfy the natural pioneer craving. A man who was not equipped with a good character for truth and honesty and with steady nerves might occasionally flit about the frontier for a while in those days, but if he undertook to settle down he was liable to discover at any moment that the climate was unfavorable. The chaff of humanity might float through and about the frontier, but only sound grain could take root and flourish. Among the men well known and widely esteemed in the territory at that time were Dr. Boise, of Las Vegas; Moore and Reese, at Tecolota; St. Vrain, Socorro; Weber, Fort Defiance; Sumowski, Fort Craig; McGroirty, Fort Filmore; and McGoffin, Fort Bliss.

The third night we encamped at San José where our first impressions of Mexicans, which we had received at Las Vegas, were pleasantly modified by making the acquaintance of an admirable representative of the *gentes finos* class in the person and family of Don Antonia José Sena. The stately courtesy of our reception, the earnest assurances that his house and all within it was ours, and that he and his family kissed our hands, was more than entertaining; it was a hereditary perfection of social art which excited the imagination and set one dreaming of Old Spain far away back through the smoky glaze of her history and mystic legends when the prodigious pride and extravagance of her grandees brought forth magnificent heroes and exalted saints. What a marvelous vitality of race traits where Castillian manners have survived a transplantation of three centuries from Alhambra to Adobe!

Some of the memories of that first short journey in New Mexico are yet vivid. It was my first separate and independent command. My companions were the best of fellows and the men seasoned by a march of two months were in good health and spirits. The morning of the fifth day was the brightest I can remember. Two feet of snow had fallen quietly and the mountains and valleys were white and silent. The sky above was a clear and speckless blue. A heavy rime had covered every trunk, branch, leaf and needle of the forest with gems which gleamed with irridescent splendor in the morning sunlight. The horsemen preceded the infantry and train to break the road and from many points we could see the winding column following us, passing through prismatic rifts of light and color. The forenoon was a revel of light and life and to it the shades of evening brought us a worthy contrast as we descended into the valley of the Pecos River.

Here we found ourselves in the presence of an extensive and ancient spectacle of death. Upon an elevated *mesa* which commanded the valley were the ruins of a structure which was as old as the hills when the Spaniards came three centuries before. Here were broken and disordered fragments of adobe ruins mingled with huge stones which had formed parts of walls. It was known as the ruins of the Pecos Church. The outlines of the *estufa*, or sacred chamber, about forty feet across could be partly discerned. Here on the low altar the sacred fire had been watched and not allowed to languish since the world was young. The legend ran that the mighty Montezuma, the Brother of God, had first brought the fire and decreed that it should not go out until the white man came from the east. When, at last, the white man came, the faithful vigil of the priests was broken and the fire was carried to another pueblo, Jemez.

We encamped in the snow near the ranch of "Jim Pidgeon," a stray and funny Frenchman, twenty-one miles from Santa Fe. The following morning, with the escort of a Sergeant and twelve men and with an army wagon carrying $250,000 and the rescued captive girl, I proceeded to Santa Fe while the command under Lieutenant Lord took a road to the South West to strike the Rio Grande below the city. It was bitter cold when we reached the plaza in the city of the Holy Faith. I reported to Major Nichols and turned over the money to Major Easton, but the Indian Agent refused to receive or care for the Mexican girl, alleging the want of money as an excuse, so there was nothing to do but to carry her on down the Rio Grande until some suitable place could be found wherein she might be domiciled. After my detachment was cared for, I went to El Fonda, or the city Hotel, where I found Captains Llewellyn Jones, McLain [George McLane], [Andrew J.] Lindsay and W.[Washington] L. Elliott of the Rifles and Mrs. Elliott, the latter my old friends of Carlisle.

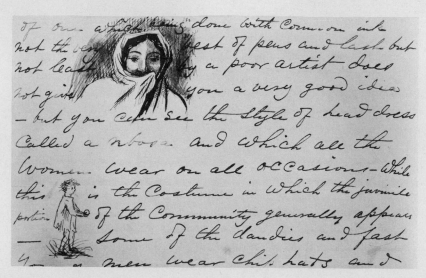

Sketches of New Mexican woman and child by Averell in a letter to his father. Fort Craig, New Mexico, February 7, 1858.

". . . you can see the style of head dress called a rebosa and which all the women wear on all occasions—while this is the costume in which the juvenile portion of the community generally appears—Some of the dandies and fast young men wear chip hats and a shirt in addition to their national costume which is a pair of breeches and a blanket."

I was grievously disappointed with the appearance of Santa Fe. So much of expeditionary force had been expended by the government to acquire this great Territory, and here was its capital of jacal and adobe boxes, none of them over ten feet high, except the church on the plaza and the hotel. The streets were dirty, dog-haunted lanes, which took their chances for width and direction among the houses. These flat habitations were not susceptible of any finish or embellishment—not even white-wash. I could not regard it seriously as a city and felt incredulous about its alleged antiquity. There was a total absence of commercial or social activity on the streets—not a vehicle, except the army wagon, to be seen. Perhaps the frequent and tottering little *burro* with his big ears and big load should not be omitted. The appearance of the citizens was not exhilarating on this wintry day. The sinister, dusky men wrapped in coarse blankets and smoking shuck *cigarrillos*, the women with their limp skirts and limpsy gait casting venturous glances with a single eye from the folds of their *rebozos*, and the clamorous and furtive curs afforded all the indications of outdoor life.[1]

General Garland, a tall old hero of the Mexican War, and who personally resembled the typical "Sir Anthony Absolute," entertained me graciously at dinner with some of his staff and I had a fine opportunity to learn something of the territory, the character and tendencies of its semi-barbarous and savage population and of the slender network of military occupation stretched over this formidable region. A heavy concert of the 3d Infantry band followed the dinner, but some of the younger men soon carried me off to a fandango, or "*baile*." It was at the house of "Carmelita" whose fame as an *arpista* had extended beyond the limits of the Territory. After disposing of our cloaks in the vestibule we entered a larger room beyond with a hard smooth floor and seats arranged around the sides. At one end upon a slightly raised platform sat musicians with harps, violins and guitars—two or three of each. The room was well filled with people of both sexes. When the music began the dancing responded at the first vibration and at once the floor became alive with a waving, gliding, turning throng of couples, and I realized for the first time that there was an element or a quality in their music and dancing as foreign and untranslatable as certain similar elements in their language.

A fandango can no more be described than it can be painted. The life and motion defy us. It was not difficult to imagine that one might trace certain prominent characteristics to the constituents of the blended blood

---

[1]In December 1857 Averell wrote to his father describing his trip across the plains, military life, and his first impression of the people and scenery of New Mexico.

This is a queer country indeed—the surface formation is very strange to me—like scenes in theaters—very little wood and water and curious looking mountains towering into the clouds with snow on their summits though it is summer at their base—at some places you can see them over topping each other way into the distance till it is difficult to tell whether it is mountains or clouds you are looking at and then at sunrise when we were passing the Spanish Peaks they seemed like colossal mountains of changeable satin or silk and we were surprised at their being fifty miles away when they looked about an hours gallop. It is a queer people here too—houses, dogs, dinners, everything is queer & strange. A kind of Indian summer laziness seems to pervade everything and everybody and this influence soon extends to anyone who comes to live here—no matter how much energy they bring with them—they push around for a while, get a house, and then sit down in its shade to loiter away an easy life. Their wants are few—a blanket at night and a little 'Chili' tortillas for food. Houses are built of mud and the customs and habits of the east are preserved in all their primitive purity—chairs are unknown and women sit on the mats and smoke *cigarrillos*—but every Mexican is polite and their manners are very easy. . . . Like Spaniards, Mexican men and women have their price—what would be infidelity and want of virtue in the States is not spoken or thought of as at all out of the way here.

of the Mexican: that the perfect time, the simplest element of music, and the inspirational fervor, came from the Indian; the graceful, stately, almost reverential manners from the Goth; and the sensuous, leopard-like motion from the Moor. Given such blood and life, in a climate at least resistance, in willowy forms with flashing black eyes, gleaming white teeth and glowing lips, with bits of color floating among the draperies, and vibrate a throng of such forms with resistless, ravishing music, and the result is a fandango. The women are mostly young, below twenty, and all smoked *cigarrillos* which each very deftly made for herself, the wrapper being the inside silken husk of corn. The handling of the *cigarrillos* even when dancing, furnished as many opportunities for the display of airs and graces as any señorita of Madrid might find with a fan. No introductions were required and one danced with whom he would. When a dance was finished it was *de rigeur* to take the señorita to the refreshment room and regale her with sweetmeats and a glass of wine.

The next day passed quickly in visits with army people with whom anything only two months from the States was fresh and welcome. Among them were Captain Llewellyn Jones and his interesting family who were soon to follow me down the Rio Grande on their way to Fort Bliss. My friend [George] Jackson was to join this company. The Captain's two daughters had shared the fortunes of the regiment from infancy, and had, as little children, been often given a ride on the saddle bow by officers on the march. They have now, nearly forty years later, the becoming, silvered hair of grandmothers. In '61 I had the honor of assisting at the wedding of the younger in Washington to Captain Roger Jones of the Rifles, who was afterward Inspector General of the Army. The elder daughter was already the wife of Captain (afterward General) Innis Palmer also of the Rifles.

First Lieutenant Orren Chapman of the 1st Dragoons, who had crossed the plains with us, was here awaiting opportunity to join his company in Arizona. He was an extraordinary man in his irrepressible spirits and power to entertain. He seemed never to admit a serious view of life, which lasted him only until Jan. 6, 1859. In '58 at Albuquerque when thought to be dying he sent for Major [Daniel H.] Rucker, the Quartermaster, who came at once and asked what he could do for him. Chapman said, "I want a sign painted and put up over my door."

"All right," said Rucker, "What sign do you want?"

"Dying done here by old Chap," was the faint but cheerful reply.

On the 15th I got away from Santa Fe and following the Rio Grande

made a continuous and rapid descent for a dozen miles. Below Gonzales'
Ranch I met company "G" of the Rifles with its Captain, [Thomas G.]
Rhett, and 1st Lieutenant Alfred Gibbs. There was a mutual curiosity in
the brief acquaintance which ensued as we had never met before and had
been hearing of each other ever since I was assigned to the regiment.
Although we were about six years in the same regiment, the thirty minutes of our interview on the road covered the intercourse of our lives. I
never saw Rhett again. He became a Confederate General,[2] and the next
time I saw Gibbs he was at head of a regiment of Union Cavalry in the
Shenandoah Valley, Virginia.

On the following day we passed down the beautiful and interesting
portion of the great valley where could be seen broken relics of pottery but
no inscriptions nor legends to tell of their origin, or who had used them.
The temperature was delightful and the landscapes were the joy and at the
same time the despair of an artist. The topographical details were novel
and picturesque. Sand hills and slopes wrought into shapes almost grotesque, interspersed with mesas or tracts of table land with precipitous
sides, and behind this fantastic middle ground, bluffs shouldered up into
the foothills of rocky, mountainous ranges whose dizzy summits softened
into changeable purples which in the distance were lost in the sky. We
passed by Algadones and Bernalillo and through some stretches that
seemed transferred from Palestine—flat-roofed, white-washed houses;
vineyards and fields where oxen at work were fastened together by a yoke
across their heads in front of their horns and attached to an awkward
lumbering cart with solid wooden wheels and guided by a blanketed
native with a long goad; women bearing *ollas* of water upon their heads.
Ours was the part of the Roman soldiery although as devoid of their
costumes as of their customs.

Six miles below Bernalillo we reached camp at San Dia overlooked by
its melon-shaped mountain 13,000 feet high. This was a compact pueblo,
quite neat in its appearance and surrounded with a broad and thorough
agriculture.

Here an incident occurred in which our Mexican captive girl experienced a curious restoration of memory. She had never been able to speak

---

[2]The highest rank held by Rhett in both the antebellum United States Army and the Civil War
Confederate Army was major. In this rank he served as a paymaster in the American army and an
assistant adjutant general in the Confederate.

any intelligible words excepting a few of those common to both Mexicans and Indians. My servant who had been into the pueblo to purchase some chickens, eggs, etc., brought me among his change a small Mexican coin of the value of three or four cents which was tossed to the girl sitting on the ground by a fire not far from our own. She picked it up and gazing at it a moment suddenly started up and ran to us exclaiming, "Mirez! uno quarto, uno quarto," and she instantly began talking volubly in Mexican Spanish and afterward she told her story. The years that had flown since her capture had not been counted but we conjectured they might have been eight or ten.

A long time ago when she was a little barefooted girl, she was playing in the vineyard with her little brother when the dreadful Apaches came and killed her father and mother and all the people but her and her little brother whom they carried away. And they travelled a great way in strange lands where there were no trees but sometimes many wild buffalo and many horses. She knew not how long she lived and wandered with the Apaches, but one time she was sold to the Indians called Kiowas with whom she wandered and lived several more winters, and then she belonged to the Cheyennes. She could not tell how, whether sold or captured. She was hurt, she knew, and was carried rapidly on a pole litter dragged along by a pony in great haste far away when the Indians were fighting, and she had nothing to eat except the tuna picked off the prickly pear, and then the fighting was over and they came to the big river again. Then they were frightened by many soldiers coming again, but when they saw that they had many wagons, so many, they knew the soldiers were not coming to fight and they came near; and she was so sick she could not walk any more and they brought her to the soldiers; and they took her away from the Indians and the rest we knew. But she did not know where her home had been.

Some amusing incidents occurred here. We had purchased some wood of the pueblo, which was called for from the house tops by the governor of the place, and it was brought forth in many little bundles and piled up in camp. Among those who came out with it was a likely young buck in a gay blanket who, like all Indians, loitered about the camp to satisfy a childish curiosity. He attracted our attention and in conversation we learned that he was a son of a chief. This noble young Aztec dandy took a fancy to the Mexican girl and made a proposition to us for her purchase and we at once entered into a haggle about the price. The girl overhearing the bartering talk was at first downcast; but perceiving a want of sincerity on my part perhaps, she brightened up and looked her best; and it was curious to see how this poor outcast of the desert assumed with ready ease and grace the airs of an accomplished coquette. This aptitude seems born in a woman. The Indian offered me his blanket and I told him to ask the girl. She gave him a pouting look of reproach ending in a half smile which revealed her beautiful teeth and told him in substance that he could not value her very highly if he thought a blanket would buy her. He then returned to me and increased his offer adding a cow, and so the trade progressed, each time the girl fascinating him more and more deeply until he had offered pretty much everything he possessed of cows, sheep, goats and other personal property, and if he had owned the pueblo I believe that girl would have enticed him to give it, but it suddenly dawned on him through the amusement and laughter he was creating that his passionate affection was being trifled with and he desisted.

A little later he took another fancy, and this time to Dick Lord's high cavalry boots for which he offered his embroidered and embellished moccasins. Lord let him try one on. With hard pulling he got his foot into it and strutted about admiring it immensely. His bare foot, unused to other confinement than that of the close fitting but soft and yielding moccasin, soon began to swell and to become uncomfortable. The Indian slyly tried to pull it off. Then he tried in earnest. Lord offered him the other boot and demanded the other moccasin but the Indian now quite frightened struggled in every way he could to get the boot off his rapidly swelling foot but finally, giving it up, begged us to have it drawn. A giant Dutchman who was cooking at a campfire in the rear was called and told to draw the boot. He solidly seized it and began to pull, which naturally drew the Indian along the ground until he seized a friendly mesquite bush and hung on for dear life. Something had to give way. The mesquite has deep and long gnarled roots which make it impracticable to pull out of the ground—at least by a Dutchman however gigantic. For a minute or two there was a painful tug of war and the boot came off and the Indian catching up his moccasin and blanket started on a run for the pueblo, and the screams of laughter of that Mexican girl which followed him were such as to make one doubt that she had ever known the sorrows of captivity among savages.

Albuquerque was reached the next day and some of my men were assigned to the garrison at that place. The town seemed to me quite as large as Santa Fe and with more life. We met Dr. De Leon, Captain John

D. Wilkins, Major Rucker, the Quartermaster and Lieutenant J.[John] W. Alley. Captain W. L. Elliott and wife were also here, having preceded me from Santa Fe. The temperature was most enjoyable, and the social attractions of the place, without a theatre or any public amusement other than the *baile*, seemed never to languish. The nightly entertainments of two sisters called "The Gracchi" were the most notable in those days. After two days rest we set out with the remaining detachments for Forts Craig, Thorn and Filmore, crossed the Rio Grande to the west side and camped that night near the pueblo of Isleta.

Here I accepted an invitation to dine at the Governor's to gratify a curiosity as to the domestic life in a pueblo and enjoyed a unique entertainment. Sitting upon a *colchón* or mat in a room about twelve feet square, carpeted with *jerga*, with a table about the size and height of an ordinary chair before me, my dinner was served one dish at a time by the daughter of the Governor who was called the Princess and known as the prettiest girl in New Mexico. She was of medium size with a well-rounded figure of graceful proportions and had fine black straight hair, dark eyes, regular features with a small and pretty mouth and a ruddy complexion. She remained standing during the repast receiving the dishes from a *peon* at the door. Some delicious *vino del pais* was given me. One wine had a light sapphire tint and a flavor like tokay azul. The Princess had a light noiseless step and her motions possessed dignity and grace, but her attention seemed fixed upon the dinner. I do not forget that the first two or three dishes were some form of chili, one of them being chili verdi and hotter than I could well bear on my tongue. Afterward came various things, tortillas, frijoles, eggs, onions, mutton; but everything was "chili Colorado," and a curious sandwich of finely chopped spiced meats rolled in a fine silken corn husk shaped like an elongated croquette. There was a little fireplace in the corner of the room in which some small sticks of piñon and mesquite, stood on end, were burning just enough to secure good ventilation. When the dinner was finished the old Governor came in and offered me *cigarrillos* but permitted me to use my pipe instead. Then the Governor and daughter seated themselves, both smoking *cigarrillos*, and we sustained a curious and limited effort at conversation. It is wonderful how many ideas people without a well understood common language can exchange. The Princess's dress was a beautiful, varicolored blanket fastened on the shoulders with brooches of elongated, polished agates and her hair was plaited down her back and set off with shining silver discs. Around her waist was a belt similarly embellished. For the first time I observed that peculiar dress of the ankles made by winding wide strips of buckskin many times around them from the middle of the calf down to the moccasin over the top of which the winding was tapered down and arranged to fit the instep neatly. It was figured out afterwards with my friends that my pueblo host and his daughter had regarded and treated me as an exalted personage who must dine in solitude.

Our march down the Rio Grande valley was a continuous diversion. The delicious climate of itself made mere existence a pleasure, but to divert us at every step we advanced were the glorious mountains on either hand and far enough away on one or the other side to appear delectable, the fringes and basques of cottonwood along the river, and the vineyards near the towns with the novel and picturesque methods and conditions of life, as one after another came into vision in masses and separated into details as we approached and receded into gathering distance as we passed, made every day's journey a high and exhilarating entertainment.

At Las Lunas we were hospitably greeted by Captain George Sykes whose company was stationed there. During the Civil War by the sheer unaided force of merit, he developed into one of the most efficient and reliable general officers of the Union Army. Here I met Horace Randall, 1st Dragoons, on his way to the States from Arizona. At Limitar, near which we encamped one night, a respectable Mexican woman named Barbarita became interested in our Mexican girl and won her confidence and consent to abide with her, promising me that she should not become a peon, or slave, but live as one of her family and so, with some joy at finding rest and some natural regrets at parting from those who had befriended her, the poor girl bade us "adios" with commingled smiles and tears.

The *raison d'être* of villages unsupported by country in this valley became fully apparent as we passed them. In addition to the necessity for defense against savage incursions, it could be seen in the necessity for irrigation upon which all agriculture depended. The maintenance of an *acequia madre*, or mother canal, with all the distributing *acequias* required at times a large amount of convenient and reliable labor such as no open country could supply. Each village had a *Major Domo* who had the authority to turn out the population *en masse* when required.

About twenty miles below Socorro, the principal village south of Albuquerque, we reached the *Bosque Bonita*, an extensive and beautiful woodland of large trees, covering a wide and long stretch of bottom land, which was noted from Santa Fe to Mexico. Here was our last camp before reaching my destination. The next day, the 25th of November 1857, lacking only two days of three months from Carlisle, my preliminary experiences to actual army service ended at Fort Craig. West Point, the cavalry school of practice, and crossing the plains were all introductory chapters to a real army service which was now to begin. And what a life confronted me! A long weary waiting to become a gray-haired Captain, or garrulous and grizzled Major, or mayhap with luck and longevity a wrinkled, wise and wakeful Lieutenant Colonel who might eventually command a Post and have a choice of quarters. No one's most daring dreams ever soared to the heights of a Colonel's eagle. Here after a day's rest, the last of my companions of the long journey from civilization, Lieutenants Lord and Hildt, left me and proceeded on their way.

5

Fort Craig

Fort Craig was an imposing object in this country of small houses. It was simply an enclosure of a rectangular area of about six acres with a massive adobe wall ten feet high, and occupied a high table land which on the east terminated at a short distance on the Rio Grande in a precipitous bluff a hundred feet above the river. From its western end the ground ascended in gentle slopes to the bold serrated ranges ten to fifteen miles away. The sally port and guard house were in the middle of the western end and within the eastern end were enclosed the corrals and stables for the cavalry horses and the animals and wagons of the Quartermaster. Along and within the north side were two buildings each ninety feet long with a high, roofed veranda along their fronts. Each building had extensions to the rear on its flanks to the wall of the fort, containing dining rooms, kitchens, store rooms and servants' quarters. Each building contained two sets of quarters and each set was divided by a broad hall while in rear a dividing wall made a separate rear court yard and small garden for each. On the opposite or south side of the plaza were two similar buildings for the two companies of the garrison. The hospital was in the northeast corner, the sutler's store in the southeast and the quartermaster and commissary stores between. The structures were as massive and high as the strength of materials would admit and the finish as perfect as possible. Of course the roofs were flat. The long porticoes were sustained by simple rude Doric columns fashioned from piñon or pine trees brought from the mountains, and the buildings were separated by intervals equal to their front length so that the general effect as viewed from

123

the sally port had a Grecian simplicity and breadth that in this country of mean, pell-mell mud buildings might justly be considered grand.

Water for the Fort was drawn from the river in water wagons up a ramp way and wood was plentiful along the river banks. On the opposite side of the river was a wide bosque which extended three or four miles up and down the valley. The finest grama grass grazing abounded on the slopes to the westward and two miles up the river began an extensive wide bottom which reached up to Bosque Bonita and afforded a bountiful crop of hay for winter forage. There were enough deer to invite hunting, and duck and other water fowl were plentiful in the season. The site was well chosen for observation and defence. To the eastward, over the river, the view extended across the Jornada del Muerte from fifteen to twenty miles taking in the dim outlines of the Morgollon and Oscuro mountains. To the south some fifteen or twenty miles, the view terminated in a lofty independent range which ended on the left bank of the river in a marvellously perfect profile of an upturned human face whose expression underwent wonderful and fascinating changes as the evening shades slowly stole after the departing sunlight up the bold breast of the mountain. Each prominent feature—the chin, lips, nose, brow—was daily gilded with sunset glows ere it was shrouded and buried in night. This was old "Fray Cristobal," whose sublime good night we never failed to witness. In this vast silent landscape he was good company.

The garrison consisted of company "F," Regiment of Mounted Riflemen, and a company of the 3d Infantry commanded by 1st Lieutenant Alexander McRae, R.M.R., and Lieutenant M.[Matthew] L. Davis, 3d Infantry, respectively. The Post was commanded by Lieutenant Colonel [Daniel T.] Chandler, 3d Infantry, and the Surgeon. was Dr. Glover Perin. These were all the officers. The Captain of my company, "F," Bvt. Lieutenant Col. Andrew Porter, was in Europe on leave of absence and my 1st Lieutenant, Gordon Granger, was on recruiting service. When I relieved McRae from the command of the company there were left four officers at the Post and only one of them, the Surgeon, was married. Mrs. Perin had been Miss Page of Cincinnati, and a most lovely and accomplished lady was she who had given up all the delights and charms of the life of a social belle to join the army. And the great pleasure, the unique gratification of furnishing to a little garrison the only ray of precious social sunshine it possessed, day in and day out as the long weary months wore by, with her worthy husband and sweet little girl children, seemed to satisfy her completely. Not a repining word nor a murmur of regret was ever heard.

McRae and Davis were of the classes of '51 and '52 at West Point and both from North Carolina. Already distinguished for gallantry in Indian engagements they were, besides being efficient and experienced officers on duty, most desirable companions in garrison life. Their future careers, widely different, led both to their death in '62, five years later. McRae's fate, after a tour of recruiting service and other duty, brought him back to this same Post to command a battery in General Canby's mixed forces which were endeavoring to check a Confederate invasion from Texas at this point on February 21, 1862, and when his frightened canoneers abandoned their pieces McRae calmly drew his revolver and leaning upon a gun made every shot count until he was killed. Davis joined in the secession of his State and died near Raleigh in '62.

Sumowski the Sutler was a rare old Polish gentleman of noble family who with [Charles] Radziminski had been exiled and had come to this country where they enlisted in the 2d Dragoons. Sumowski served three enlistments of five years each, two of them as Orderly Sergeant of Captain Pike Graham's company. Commissions were offered these young gentlemen and while Radziminski accepted, Sumowski declined, saying he preferred being the first Sergeant in the regiment rather than the lowest officer. Once when Graham's command was surrounded and cut off by Indians in Florida, a volunteer was called for, to go as a courier for reinforcements. Two volunteer couriers in succession were killed and a third was called for from Graham's company. Sumowski presented himself for the service and when asked why he did so replied that he would not ask any soldier to do what he could not himself undertake. He was gone so long that it was believed that he had shared the fate of his predecessors, but on the morning of the fourth day when hope had well nigh died out, an unusual commotion was discerned among the beleaguering savages, and presently the sound of a distant bugle was heard which was repeated again and again nearer at hand. The Indians broke away sullenly from the direction of the sound and soon there appeared gleaming through the everglades the guidons of a squadron of Dragoons with Sumowski guiding it to the rescue. It was said that officers of that regiment returning from a furlough never failed, after paying their respects to the Colonel and other officers, to go and shake hands with Sumowski.

When a soldier he never drank any strong drink but once, and then it was by order. The 2d Dragoons had been for some time dismounted much to their humiliation and disgust, and when the order came to remount the regiment at Natchitoches, the grim old Colonel Twiggs issued a verbal order that any man found sober in camp the ensuing night should be put in the guard house. That was the only occasion Sumowski had ever got drunk. He was attacked with pulmonary consumption and was wasting away. So at the end of his third enlistment he went to St. Louis to die. Mr. Robert Campbell, one of those rare, great-hearted merchant princes who were developed on the frontier in the first half of the century, said to Sumowski, "Go as Sutler to some post in New Mexico; I will furnish and deliver your store of goods, repay me at your convenience and take three drinks of pure whisky made into a toddy every day, one just before each meal." Sumowski was constrained to believe this better than certain death, the sutlership was secured, and when I found him at Fort Craig in '57 he had repaid Mr. Campbell and had acquired a snug capital of his own and his health had been restored.

My company had seventy-seven men present for duty who were with half a dozen exceptions fine, healthy, dutiful soldiers and their horses and equipments were in good condition. The Sergeants were young men and ideal soldiers. It occupied me a few days in settling myself in quarters and inspecting everything before really taking hold of the reins. To our delight Captain Llewellyn Jones arrived with his company from Santa Fe on his way to Fort Bliss at El Paso and tarried with us for a few days. His family and Lieutenant W. H. Jackson, my old comrade of Carlisle and the plains, were with him and we were comparatively gay. Jackson of course quartered with me. We dined at midday, and on the afternoon of the 7th of December an hour after dinner while Jackson and I were taking our smoke siesta, Colonel Chandler hastily entered looking very pale and agitated, as he was afflicted with some trouble of the heart, and said a Mexican from a point on the other side of the river three miles below had just come in with the report that a band of Indians were at his ranch and had killed one of his cattle upon which they were feasting and that the women were unprotected. He desired me to take a party of mounted men and go down and see about it. He did not credit the report, but it must be investigated.

My company's horses were grazing on the slopes a mile away or more but those of Captain Jones were in the corral and Jackson offered me a mount. While Jackson went to the corral to have the required horses saddled, I ran to the company quarters and turned out the Orderly

Sergeant and a dozen men with their arms. In fifteen minutes we were in the saddle and trotting down the river along the road to Fort Thorn. Jackson insisted on accompanying me. We came opposite a large jacal ranch pointed out by the Mexican three miles below and before crossing halted a moment and had the men cap their rifles and revolvers. The ford was good, excepting about thirty yards in the middle which we found no difficulty in swimming, holding up the rifles. Fortunately there were no doors or windows in the river side of the ranch so that our arrival was unobserved. So soon as the men were across we moved quickly around to the opposite side of the ranch where there was an entrance and there were some rifles and bows standing beside the door. I sprang down with my Orderly Sergeant, Hugh McQuade, and seized them in a moment and handed them to two or three of my men to carry.

While this was doing, a dozen Indians with their chief came rushing out of the doorway to be held up with the rifles and revolvers of my men who were formed in a semicircle in front of the entrance. We had the dead drop on them and they were silent and quiet. They had about a hundred braided lariats, showing that they were after horses—perhaps our herd. I explained to them as well as I could that they must go with me to the Fort. Then they were stubborn and had to be urged and pushed away from the building and gathered in a squad with my men surrounding them. Jackson was on one side with two men and I on the other. We had not gone ten yards when the chief gave a peculiar yell and the Indians stooping down flew out between our horses and scattered like a covey of partridges. I called to my men to fire and hunt them down and fired at the chief myself, hitting him in the side and back with the same little fiveshooter that I had carried on the plains. My horse began to rear and plunge with fright and I sprang off his back and slipping the reins over the cantle let him go.

The chief ran around the ranch by the north end and I by the south and met him on the river side when I fired again hitting him in the thigh. As I cocked my pistol the fourth time, the lever which revolved the chamber was broken by a protruding bullet preventing movement. Then I ran to the Indian to strike him with it upon the head. He met me aggressively and seized my uplifted right wrist with his left hand and my left elbow with his right and turned me around into the hollow of his left arm drawing my right arm under my left, all in one quick motion, and then releasing the hold of his right hand brought it around and tried to catch hold of my free left arm in which he failed, and instead I caught his right by the wrist, but he pulled it down to his waist and drew out a belt knife. We were about the same height, he the heavier. I was young and strong and had never been seriously injured. We tore up about a square rod of the ground in our struggle. I realized that if ever I lost hold of his right wrist my life would go. I was frequently off my feet and, notwithstanding my disadvantage in the hold, I kept the Indian busy. I thought of a great many things: one was, if he was hit in the shooting, why didn't he weaken? He did not pause an instant for breath, as most wrestlers do, while my breath was giving out. He was native to this rarified air and I was unused to it. It was an age. We breathed in each other's face. Nearly all my strength went to the grip of my left hand to keep the knife away.

Just then I heard Jackson's voice, "Steady Averell, I'm going to shoot." Oh, welcome sound! but the Indian heard it too and used me as a shield keeping his head down. Then I could hear the tread of Jackson's horse almost upon us, a revolver was thrust under my left arm, there was a report and the Indian let go and sank to the ground. Jackson had placed the muzzle of his revolver almost against the right forearm of the savage when he fired, and the arm being bent the ball passed through below and above the elbow.

Considering the chief settled we turned our attention to the remaining Indians so soon as I could get my breath. They had scattered in every direction and the men were after them. There were only five bodies found although some were fired at in the river and others reached the bushes along the bank. When no more were to be found we returned for the chief but he had disappeared. Several cowardly Mexicans turned up from hiding places, all armed, and the chief of the Indian band was hunted for in vain until some one called our attention to a small closed door in the end of the ranch which opened into a storeroom. It was tried and found secured on the inside, and when broken open the Indian was discovered. Three or four Mexicans entered, bravely enough now, and after a hard struggle dragged him forth. He seated himself on the ground and looking up at me said sullenly, "Tirez corrajo!" A Mexican offered me a large revolver and begged me to shoot the Indian. I said, "No, he is a brave man, I would rather kill you." He was placed upon a horse and started with two men for the Fort.

My horse was caught and we continued the search for some time and then returned to the Post which we found in great excitement. My Indian had arrived and, dripping with blood, was standing before the commanding officer who was questioning him in front of his quarters. My firing had been heard and the garrison was under arms. My horses had been driven in and saddled. The arrival of the wounded chief had allayed all apprehension about my party but yet such an unusual event naturally created commotion. During my brief absence Captain Richard S. Ewell, 1st Dragoons, (afterward the Confederate General) and my old friend Lieutenant Orren Chapman had arrived with an escort on their way to Fort Buchanan, and after I had dismounted and reported, Ewell came forward greeting me and putting his hand on my head said, "Young man, there is a Brevet hanging over your head, I have been scouting for Indians all my life without any luck and here you are a fortnight in the country and make a strike in sight of your Post."

The Surgeon dressed the wounds and set the broken arm of the Indian, and in a fortnight he was walking around the Post with, of course, the watchful eyes of a rifleman upon him. He was a chief all the while. He would not go near the men's quarters but would come to mine, and I entertained him as much as possible with pictorial papers and such little talk as we could have in the few words we both understood. I took him to the Sutler's and made him some presents of things he fancied. Women's fashion plates attracted his attention more than any other kind of pictures. He would hold them sideways and upside down with curiosity. A month later he was taken by a passing military wagon train to Fort Union whence he was sent to his tribe. He was a Kiowa and had come fully 200 miles away from his home range with his party, and it was firmly believed that an attempt would have been made on our corral, or on our herd when grazing, had not information of their arrival at the ranch below reached us in time to frustrate the scheme.

That particular Indian had an unusual destiny shaped for him which was afterward made known to me by a singular chance. In 1863 a party of Indian chiefs came to Washington to see the Great Father, President Lincoln, and this Kiowa chief was among them. They remained in the East two months or more, a part of the time in New York City where Mr. P. T. Barnum, the great showman, entertained them for a fortnight at the 5th Avenue Hotel, N.Y. City, and gave them a reception twice a day during their stay, at his museum at the corner of Broadway and Ann streets, where throngs of people who were admitted at the usual price shook hands with them. When the Indians discovered or became aware that Barnum was exhibiting them as a matter of business, the reception ceased, and they returned to Washington where the Kiowa chief was taken ill of typhoid fever and after a fortnight's illness died. He was attended during his illness by Dr. [Socrates N.] Sherman, a volunteer Surgeon of Ogdensburg, N.Y., who afterward became medical director of my cavalry division. The Surgeon observed the Indian's scars and on inquiry about them was told of the little fight on the Rio Grande and afterward informed me of his observations. The Indian was buried in the Congressional cemetery.

I was awakened early by my Orderly Sergeant the morning after the Indian affair with a report which had just reached the Post that a party of Indians had attacked a ranch two miles up the river on the opposite side. Taking the Sergeant and twenty men I crossed the river and soon met a Mexican youth who had started the report but now denied it. We scoured the country up and down for miles without seeing any trace of Indians, excepting the crosses which Mexicans had already stuck up over the places where Indians had fallen the day before. Captain Jones' company proceeded on the way to Fort Bliss, and Captain Ewell and "old Chap" delighted us with their visit until next day.

Colonel Chandler had brought out a billiard table in sections and we had great interest setting it up in a small building in the northwest corner of the Fort. No billiard palace ever had greater attractions for the votaries of the game than had ours for us. Its ceiling was lined with white cotton sheeting tacked to the *vegas* and at one end was a platform with chairs for the audience which never exceeded two persons unless when Mrs. Perin would occasionally honor us with her presence. I was always fond of billiards but never enjoyed the game anywhere in my life so well as at Fort Craig. Two Mexican gentlemen recently from the city of Mexico, Armendarez, had taken possession of an immense estate which adjoined the government reservation, and they occasionally visited us and enlivened our billiards, as they were excellent players.

There were in my company about half a dozen of the typical characters then common to the army who looked upon the guard house as their permanent residence, the occasion of this predilection being drunkenness. After looking about a little I had a guard house delivery of my men who were ordered to be sent to me individually after being bathed, shaved and dressed for inspection. The oldest prisoner was a bugler over fifty years of age, an innocent old Norwegian named Lindahl who could play "Home Sweet Home" on the cavalry trumpet, but he must have an unmitigated wallowing drunk after every pay day and the native *aguardiente* with which he produced it left him a helpless wreck after each debauch. With the old fellow I made a bargain and exacted his promise that he would come to me after every pay day and I would give him an order on the Sutler for what he required of the best whisky and that he would drink no other. This worked well and the old man got his order regularly and after two or three days absence would return and report for duty in good condition. A harder case was that of an educated Englishman, a graduate of Oxford, about forty years old. He was a determined, sullen drunkard and such a thing as human sympathy was unknown to him. It required some time to make him listen, with his inner ear, and to awaken hope and a sense of duty, but at last he yielded and I furnished him an object in life. He should teach an evening school in the company as several of the men had no education whatever. Blackboards were made of clothing boxes and school books were sent for to the States. It was an interesting entertainment two months later to look in on his school.

The next important drunkard was one who was technically known in the recruiting regulations as "an idle dependent of respectable connections," a tall, fine looking American, about twenty-five years old of good family and with a good academic education and who was an excellent and rapid penman, had read considerably, and was a fair musician. There was a link twisted in his life, which after I had gained his confidence was revealed to me. The alternative was presented; he must let me help him to be a self-respecting soldier or I would take the earliest opportunity to get rid of him. He was worse than useless, he was an incubus, he might become useful to himself and to others and do the duty he had enlisted to perform. He surrendered without reserve and I received his promise that whenever he felt there was danger of his yielding to temptation he should come and see me at once and that he must regard me and the doctor as his best friends and if he really needed the drink he should have it. He never came for a drink. I made him company clerk and librarian and I shall have more to say of him.

My company fund arising from savings of rations amounted to about $1,500 and was steadily growing. A well-chosen little library of 250 volumes was procured from the States and the mechanics of the company built and furnished a library room. The book cases had doors with diamond-shaped stained glass windows, the glass being bits of varicolored fabrics. Magazines and weekly newspapers were taken and the men greatly enjoyed their library. Regular hours for drill and target practice, mounted and on foot, were established. A special drill for Indian fighting was taught and the company soon grew so expert that from a marching column of twos, sets of fours could be formed, the men dismounted and thrown one hundred yards in any direction, deployed inside of one min- ute. Races for both men and horses were held every Saturday. For these the men and horses were classified according to speed. Prizes were offered from the company fund of $10, $5, and $2.50, and the men learned how to put themselves and their horses in condition and they would wager their own money on their skill, pluck and judgement. These were about the happiest days of my army life. There was no longer use for the guard house.

General Garland and his staff came down from Santa Fe about the middle of December on his way to Fort Bliss to spend the holidays with his daughter, Mrs. Longstreet, wife of Captain and Brevet Major James Longstreet, 8th Infantry (afterward a distinguished Confederate General). I was detailed to escort him with twenty men. We went by the way of Forts Thorn and Filmore taking six days for the journey of 180 miles. It was a jolly week at El Paso with dinners, fandangos and races. I found my classmate Lazelle and my old chum Jackson at Fort Bliss. We went over the river to attend *bailes* in Chihuahua. There we saw Mexican ladies of fair complexion, pure Castilians, who were far more refined, graceful and better dressed than any we had seen at Santa Fe or Albuquerque. Their surroundings were also far superior—better houses with more luxurious furniture. Only in one thing there was no difference, they all smoked *cigarrillos.* General Garland ordered a general court-martial to convene while we were there to try such prisoners as might be brought before it. I was detailed as a member of the court and having no full-dress uniform with me was obliged to borrow Major Longstreet's. He was then a stout, jolly man of about 36 and I at 25 had not altogether lost my West Point form, so to make his coat fit me it was necessary to button it over a small pillow which occasioned some amusement. There were no cases of impor- tance brought before the court.

Shortly after my return from El Paso official intelligence was received from Santa Fe that 300 Kiowa warriors were on the Pecos bent on a raid to Val Verde, as our location was known to Mexicans, to avenge the death of their warriors who had fallen on the 7th of December. Captain Trevitt with his company from Albuquerque and Lieutenants Lane Lawrence, and Baker with a company of Rifles from Stanton were ordered out to inter- cept them. We kept on the alert turning out frequently under arms to be ready for any emergency.

About this time we were deeply interested in the news from Utah where our limited force under Colonel Albert Sidney Johnston was in a critical position at a great distance from Fort Leavenworth, his base of supplies. Captain R. B. Marcy, 5th Infantry, came down to the Rio Grande for cavalry and battery horses and draught mules and returned about the middle of February with an escort of one company of Infantry and twenty-five mounted Riflemen. When information was received in March that the Mormons intended intercepting Marcy on his return to Utah, his escort was increased by two companies of Infantry from Albuquerque and one company of Rifles from Fort Union with two months' rations all under Colonel Loring, who sent messengers to overtake Marcy and have him await reinforcement. There was a very unsettled feeling throughout New Mexico during this period and all the posts were held in readiness for orders at any moment. The Adjutancy of the Rifles was offered to me about this time but I preferred to command a company.

There was nothing doing in New Mexico at this time to show the slightest *raison d'être* for any army, no mining nor manufactures. There was a necessity for the protection of civil courts but the justice there found was a vain, illusory thing. It gave employment to a judge who travelled the circuit with a retinue of lawyers. No verdict against a criminal was ever obtained or expected from a Mexican jury. As an educational function of government the jury was a failure. It had been in use nine years and no improving results were yet perceptible. There was a total absence of schools. The climate was supreme in its domination of the enterprise, habits, dress and morals of the people. But little was required to sustain life and that was acquired with the least labor. Peonage, or Mexican slavery, was maintained. The population at this time with individual exceptions was not half civilized.

Lieutenant Davis, Mr. Sumowski and myself went in the latter part of January '58 to attend the wedding of a worthy Sergeant, whose time had expired, to the daughter of the most prominent Mexican family in Socorro. We drove up in an ambulance with a small escort taking along some saddled horses. Crossing a bleak stretch of bottom land with an uneven surface of sand hillocks covered with sage and mesquite brush, we noticed at a little distance from the road on our left a shred of cloth. Nothing escapes the eye of men habitually on their guard when travelling in such a country. We sent a man to examine it who returned at once with the report that the body of a woman was lying behind the hillock. We went to investigate and found a body, which the men recognized as that of a young Mexican woman who had been working for our company laundresses and had started for Socorro only two days before with a Mexican who was going there with a cart. She had a few hard-earned dollars when she left—nothing was now found. Her throat had been cut and not much pains taken to hide the body. We could not arouse enough interest in the matter in Socorro to have the body buried, and we were obliged to employ persons to have it done, and when it was asked if some one would not set about hunting up the murderer and bring him to justice the eternal "*Quien saba, señor*" was the only response.

The wedding took place in the evening with a great show of candles and vestments and was followed by a fandango. There was an improvisatore who twanged a guitar and reeled off typical verses while the dancing was going on. There were *dulces y vino del pais abundante* of course. The banquet came after midnight with viands varied in every way except in the common element chili. One would think that a family esteeming itself *gente fino* would have embraced opportunities during nine years of American occupation of the country to catch on to the simplest civilized ways of eating. The natural curiosity and ambition of women should have led to the discovery of the improved methods, manners and styles of an invader who had come to stay. There were fifty people at the banquet and the principal table furniture selected for the occasion was washbasins, some white and some figured, with large iron spoons such as one sees in a kitchen. Being persons of high consideration, we had basins of silver. The combined novelties of the ceremonies, costumes, language, manners, music, dancing, food and wine made a deep and unfading impression on my memory which, however, has ever since seemed like a dream.

When we set out to go to the little "fonda" or hotel of Socorro where we were to lodge, we were escorted by youths bearing torches and preceded by musicians and dancing couples. We occupied a large room carpeted with *gerga* and having one large bedstead at one end and *colchones* at the other. Davis and myself occupied the bed and Sumowski the mattresses. It would doubtless not be advisable to chronicle, even if our youth and inexperience excused the facts, but that candor which is necessary to a truthful and complete history of this Mexican wedding compels the statement, that Davis and I were amazed to find ourselves the next morning lying in opposite directions on the bed and could not account for it until Sumowski explained that we had differed on going to bed as to which end was the head and, being unable to agree as to that important matter, had amicably arranged that each should occupy the bed according to his individual views.

The fiesta attending the wedding continued through the next day and night. During the morning there were races around the plaza and through the town, firing of guns by Mexicans dressed as vaqueros mounted on fleet mustangs and some of them accompanied with girls riding behind them. There seemed no order, regularity or point in their exercises, simply a noisy, racing crowd from one end of the town to the other, a desultory fusilade and then race and fire again, as objectless as the pasture play of a lot of spring lambs in a pasture and not more intelligible. Toward evening the entire wedding party drove and rode to Limetar seven miles above as the guests of Don Louis Armijo who resided at the home of his late father the Mexican General Armijo. The banquet and fandango at the house of Don Louis were in better form than those of the previous night and we were all lodged in the long and wide *sala* in which we had danced and dined. *Colchones* were spread along each side and curtains hung between the two rows. Don Louis showed us the solid silver bedstead with its rich curtains and counterpane of silk with lace trimmings and priceless linens which had been used by his father. The ex-sergeant who was married had established and developed a fine ranch between Fort Craig and Socorro, and he and his bride secured a transfer of the Mexican girl who had been left at Barbaritas to their own home where she would rank as first maid of honor. Don Louis Armijo was the only Mexican in the valley at that time, excepting the Armandarez and St. Vrain, who dressed in American fashion and was fully civilized. He had a pretty victoria and a fine pair with American harness which was a curiosity to the natives for three hundred miles up and down the river. Vicente St. Vrain, son of the St. Vrain who became the owner of some of the vast concessions in Colorado and New Mexico acquired under the treaty of Guadaloup Hidalgo, was at the wedding with his wife. But he could hardly be called a Mexican as he had received his education in the States and had spent much of his life outside of New Mexico.

The great want of this country is water. The soil is marvelously fertile where water for irrigation is available. All that we used at Fort Craig was hauled from the river in water wagons. One day hunting toward the western mountains, I came upon a clear running stream four or five yards wide and six inches deep. Following it down, it gradually diminished in volume until within three miles of the Rio Grande it disappeared altogether. From the vanishing point toward the river its course underground was marked for most of the way to the river with small green bushes. Its little shallow, narrow valley struck the river three miles below the Fort. Near its mouth was a mound or a circular elevation a hundred feet in diameter and fifteen feet high in its center. Upon digging a little about this mound pieces of pottery were found with the same marks as were to be seen upon that now in use at the pueblos. Here had once been a pueblo which had been abandoned after the stream which supplied it with water had failed to reach it. The source had partially failed or the air had become more arid and absorbed it.

We built a little dam where the stream ran strongest and thence cut a narrow ditch to the Fort following the contour lines of the surface in such manner as to secure a uniform flow. We coaxed it along the ditch the day it was completed as far as possible but could not get it to the Fort. About ten o'clock the following night there was an alarm signal made by the sentinel on the east side of the garrison the cause of which upon investigation turned out to be a stream of water which had stolen into the Fort like a thief in the night, on the west end, had passed through the plaza and had attacked the adobe wall at the east end. The entire garrison became water worshipers and turned out to welcome the tiny stream. Although the ditch was no wider than a spade, yet from the limited surface exposed this living stream was lifted into the air during the heat of the day at the rate of about forty gallons a minute.

No matter how high the temperature out of doors, or how great the exercise, no perspiration ever appeared on the skin. Its evaporation and immediate absorption by the air prevented the distress, which would have been experienced in such a torrid heat at the level of the sea, by lowering the temperature upon the skin. Some interesting calculations and deductions, not pertinent here, although infinitely reminiscent, could be made of the amount of water given to the atmosphere daily by the Rio Grande in its descent from an elevation of 7,000 feet at Santa Fe to 3,700 at El Paso through an exposure of 400 miles. Without the loss it has thus experienced, it would rival the Missouri in volume and the *Jornada del Muerte* would be a lake instead of a desert. Those who peopled the hundreds of pueblos which once stood in this valley, and that are now dead and buried in ruins that yield no record, were probably surrounded by climatic conditions quite different from the present and far more favorable to human life. The sun worship must have originated when light and heat were far more precious and rare than they are now in this country.

Sometimes our garrison was not visited by the paymaster and paid regularly every two months, and when it was much needed, our Sutler, Sumowski, would pay off the men and take the receipted pay rolls as his vouchers. In the spring of 1858 he had not sufficient coin to render this service and desired to go to El Paso to obtain it. The commanding officer gave me authority to accompany him with an escort. We determined to take the shortest route, that by the *Jornada del Muerte*, which would save us two or three days of travel. This was across a burning desert ninety miles without water. It was a dead, level, arid waste which began just across the river from Fort Craig and was from twenty to fifty miles wide. Its dim eastern boundaries could be seen from the Fort in the Oscuro mountains.

The general course of the Rio Grande in the sixty miles below Val Verde leads it but twenty miles to the westward as if to avoid the certain death of the *Jornada* which there awaits every other living thing excepting lizards, horned frogs and the branchless cactus. Within the bend which the river makes to avoid the desert, broken ranges and peaks protrude as a lofty barrier to protect the river from the burning thirst of the desert that would instantly swallow it up. Brave old *"Fray Cristobal,"* with his back braced against the barren silence of the "Journey of Death," and his triumphant face uplifted 3,000 feet toward the heavenly blue, smiles daily at sunset upon the slowly dwindling current of the oldest river in the world. *Fray Cristobal* saw it in its mighty youth when it lashed mountain slopes and devoured *mesas*, while yet the polar tides were fashioning a valley for the future Mississippi. These protruding mountains furnished convenient lurking places for the watchful Apache who from some height discovering unwary or unprotected travellers across the barren plain could descend and strike them with assured certainty of success. We concluded to enter the *Jornada* at night to avoid the heat of the first day and also any hostile observation from the mountains. An ambulance drawn by four mules driven by Sumowski's Mexican servant José was to carry us, and a wagon drawn by six selected mules was to transport an armed escort of a Corporal and six men with about fifty gallons of water and three days' cooked rations.

As the last rosy glow of sunset fell upon the brow of *"Fray Cristobal,"* we crossed the river on the 7th of April 1858 and entered the desert. The road was a well-marked straight lane through the cactus which grew of all sizes from a few inches to the ten to twenty feet of the *gigantes*. The latter was not frequent, the average height being five or six feet. These had generally turban tops. There was a half moon which relieved the profound and awful silence of that other terrible dread on such a road—darkness. The shadows of the top-heavy cactus slightly swaying in the light wind presented a weird, fanciful appearance of life and movement to our eyes when waking suddenly from an occasional nap and before we remembered where we were, and the glaring white bones of animals which often could be seen by the wayside lent a high light to this dark and dismal picture of desolation. We were not exempt from a certain nervous strain which did not promote conversation. The wheels made but little noise and the foot falls of the animals seemed deadened. Washers had been fixed on the axles which prevented the sound of their chucking in the boxes of the wheels, which peculiar sound can be heard a great distance in a still night.

We drove at a steady trot for four hours which seemed very long. Then a halt was made long enough to give the animals a light drink from a bucket, and then on again until about three o'clock in the morning, when a rest was taken, the animals unharnessed and given a chance to roll and cool off, not, however, without the security of a lariat. When they were cooled and watered and fed which afforded us a rest of two hours, we set out again and drove steadily, with a few halts for a drink of water, with alternating gaits of walk and trot until 11 o'clock when we rested for four hours during the intense heat of the day. One mule could go no farther and a "spike team" was made up of the five remaining to the wagon. We reached the river about 8 o'clock that night having done the ninety miles in twenty-five hours.

The following day we reached Fort Filmore and arrived at Fort Bliss, El Paso, on the 10th. In this delightful, balmy climate we spent three days. Major Longstreet had received permission to apply for a leave of absence of six months and an extension of six months. Life here was a steady, tranquil siesta, and these were the last days I ever spent with my friend W. L. Jackson. He was the most charming of men as a comrade and companion. Full of perfect health, cheerful spirits and an even temper hard to ruffle, fond of horses and all manly exercises, a remarkable shot with rifle or pistol, a graceful easy dancer, high minded and generous, he was my ideal of a gentleman and a cavalry man. The fortunes or misfortunes and fatalities of the Civil War separated us and he became a Brigadier General of cavalry in the Confederate Army. I rejoice that he has survived. He is now the co-proprietor with his distinguished brother, Judge Howell Jackson of the U.S. Supreme Court, of the great Belle Meade breeding farm near Nashville, Tennessee.

On our return from El Paso we had two or three thousand dollars in silver in a box in our ambulance and stopped the first night at Fort Filmore forty miles from Fort Bliss. We were united in our inclination to return by the longer route by Fort Thorn rather than again cross the *Jornada del Muerte.* We hoped to reach Fort Thorn on the evening of the 16th of April but fell short about ten miles on account of the deep sand upon the road and went into camp. On our arrival at the Fort next morning we found intense excitement prevailing. A fearful tragedy had just occurred. There was an Indian Agency quite near the Post and around it and under its protection a number of Indians—men, women and children —had been living. At daybreak that morning a party of armed Mexicans from Messilla, a small Mexican town opposite Fort Filmore, had charged into the Indian camp near the Agency and butchered men, women, and children indiscriminately. Upon learning what was going on, 1st Lieutenant W.[William] H. Wood, 3d Infantry, quietly turned out the garrison under arms, consisting of one company of Infantry and one company of the Rifles under Lieutenant [George W.] Howland, and while the rifles were saddling he went out with the Infantry and captured the whole party within half a mile of the Fort as they were retreating with a number of little children whom they had made captives. In a few minutes Howland joined Wood with his Rifles, and the Mexicans, thirty-six in number including their leader, one Juan Ortega, were brought into the garrison, disarmed and placed under a strong guard. Parties were sent out who collected the dead bodies of three women, three men and one boy all of whom were buried in the rear of the garrison cemetery. Three of the wounded, two women and one boy, had been placed in hospital. Upon the first alarm the Indians had fled in every direction seeking shelter and protection. The people at the Agency had been fortunate enough to save a number of lives. Some of the Indians who had escaped under pursuit to the river bottom to hide among the trees and shrubbery were yet unaccounted for and it was feared that some of them had been wounded or killed. One of the women had been pursued and killed within five hundred yards of the Fort to which she was running for refuge. The boy that was killed was a favorite of the garrison, and after killing him the Mexicans had ridden around his body and expended some of their surplus ammunition by shooting his head to pieces.

These Indians were of the Gila Apache tribe which had been at peace and on friendly terms with all about them for several months and had given no cause for this cowardly outrage. It was but a repetition of the horrible massacre perpetrated but a short time before at *Donna Ana.* The Indian women had helped the laundresses of the garrison, and the boys and men were busy with such chores as they could find to do, and they all made use of the rejected parts of beef at the butcher's shambles and were happy and contented. Lieutenant Wood was obliged to exercise immediate watchfulness to prevent the soldiers from putting the Mexican fiends to death. We were all half inclined to think that he had made a mistake in capturing them when he had the chance to wipe them off the face of the earth. Had the enormity of the outrage been fully known to the soldiers when they captured them, there would have been no subsequent proceedings in which these miscreants would have felt any interest, and the government would have been saved some expense.

I started our escort on the road about noon to go to a spring about twelve miles up the river and make camp while we waited for Wood's dispatch about this butchery to the General commanding the Department, which we would carry as far as Fort Craig and would forward from there by courier to Santa Fe. We started about 2 P.M. in the ambulance. The road was over the slopes of the foot hills which here ran down to the river, and during the latter part of the day's journey it was heavy with sand. About 4 o'clock we were slowly ascending one of those sandy slopes when the mules suddenly started and broke wildly out of the road to the right among the sage brush. José succeeded in pulling them to a trembling standstill when there arose from the brush a hundred yards in front about a hundred and fifty Indians in an irregular scattering line. They had arms with bows strung and arrows in their hands and had on their war paint. The mules were frightened and trying to get away. We both jumped out of the ambulance on opposite sides. I had a double-barreled shot gun loaded with buckshot and a heavy revolver. Sumowski had only a revolver. We were both ready. I understood the situation at once. These were Gila Apaches on the war path to avenge the massacre of the morning, and I apprehended that our escort had been wiped out.

It was now touch and go with us. If a shot or an arrow had been fired we had gone up. I immediately stepped forward in advance of the leading mules a little distance toward the Indians and called out, "Jefe! venga se par acá" (Chief, come here), at the same time taking from my pocket the long white envelope containing Wood's dispatch and holding it up. Indians have a great respect for papers. I knew there was not the slightest show for us and therefore there was not any use in being the least distrustful or remaining on guard with my gun. The chief came, soon followed by three or four others. I explained to them with the assistance of José that I was the bearer of a dispatch to the Great White Chief at Santa Fe which would tell him of the murders of their friends, and that the assassins were prisoners, and that the great chief would punish them—told them how badly we felt about it and asked the chief to go himself to the Fort and see our chief there and satisfy himself that the prisoners were secure. I asked him to tell his people that we were their friends and to have them un-string their bows and put up their arrows, which he did. I gave him and a few about him some smoking tobacco which was the most precious thing in the estimation of an Indian. Then at a word from the chief they moved away from the road and out of the way of the mules. We shook hands with the chief, re-entered our ambulance and moved on.

The experience was really uncomfortable at first until I had the chief close to me. Many things might have happened. Had the mules not taken alarm but gone steadily ahead, possibly and quite probably our first knowledge of the presence of Indians would have been an attack which would have ended our lives there and then, and after that our escort would have been followed up and exterminated. We breathed more easily when we reached the spring and found our party safe and also found there the women of the Indians who had been sent to the rear showing that they had expected to fight. The presence of the squaws was a guarantee that we would not be disturbed. We reached Fort Craig on the 19th without further incident and sent on Wood's dispatch without delay.

On April 26th Judge Benedict at Santa Fe issued his warrant for the arrest of the thirty-six Mexican murderers and General Garland sent an order to the commanding officer at Fort Thorn to furnish a military guard to assist the sheriff to convey the prisoners to Socorro when, if upon examination they were committed, they were to be turned over to the commanding officer at Fort Craig for safe keeping until their trial in June. The feeling of the soldiers against the prisoners was extremely bitter for their lives, to say nothing of their comfort, were put in constant jeopardy by the savagery of the Mexicans who, knowing the army would prevent Indian reprisals, seized every opportunity to perpetrate the most brutal and cruel atrocities upon the Indians. Besides, the soldiers knew that no punishment would result from these court proceedings. Consequently, the prisoners were treated by the soldiers with a consideration distin-guished by an unaffected and candid severity. It was generally a curse and a kick, and the kick was apt to come first. Some of them tried to escape, at least it was so reported of three or four by soldiers who were called up to explain the occasion of the discharge of their pieces. The Mexican who had been fired at never returned with the soldier to deny it. We had the prisoners at Fort Craig during the month of May, and it is possible that during that time the survivors may have been penetrated with the notion that they had committed an error. It is certain that there was nothing in the result of the subsequent court proceedings nor in their treatment by the citizens of Socorro to inculcate the idea that they had not done a meritorious deed. The guard which took them to Socorro for trial in June was composed of details from both of the companies at the Post and both Lieutenant Davis and myself accompanied it.

Judge Benedict held the court. The Judge with about a dozen lawyers who traveled with him made the evenings pleasant. They were all bright men, good storytellers and votaries of the old-fashioned game of draw poker. The court in session was something worthy of contemplation. All the forms of empaneling a jury were strictly observed. The public interest reached its climax when the case of our prisoners was closed, and the Judge charged the jury beginning in Spanish with sonorous declamation, "Señores Caballeros—," and a dozen Mexicans arose to their more or less bare feet from the jury benches. Crownless chip hats surmounted the heads of some through which their long, coarse, black hair streamed in wild exhuberance. All wore the *serape*, a coarse blanket from which all color and cleanliness had fled. The *cigarrillo* solaced their arduous mental strain. They could have said unanimously to the prisoners, "Estamos hermanos" (we are brothers), and appearances would have sustained the statement. They were as dark and sinister a lot of rascals as ever cut a throat or stole a mule,—"Señores Caballeros!" And the Judge went on to state in Spanish that there was no doubt that the crime of murder had been committed, it was not denied and there was no defence nor mitigation offered. The horrible atrocity that the prisoners had exhibited in the killing of the women and particularly of the little boy was especially dwelt upon; and that the public safety had been jeopardized by this cowardly and unprovoked crime. The Judge called upon them to do their duty as citizens of the greatest republic on earth, and to show that they themselves were worthy and capable of self-government, and much more of the sort. The Señores Caballeros endured it patiently and shuffled out when it was concluded and returned as soon as they had smoked another *cigarrillo* with a verdict of "not guilty," and the prisoners were discharged. If the prisoners could have come or could have been brought conveniently under the observation of our soldiers again, I fear they would have been saved the trouble of a journey back to Messilla.

We started at once for Fort Craig with our guard in order to prevent any irregularities. At the Molino, half way to the Fort, where we camped, a courier brought me orders to proceed with the effective men of my company at once to Fort Defiance with all possible expedition. So with the Rifles of the detachment I continued on to Fort Craig that night.

6

To Fort Defiance

My order to proceed to Fort Defiance with my company simply called for its available fighting strength and did not contemplate the removal of the company property from Fort Craig. It was occasioned by the threatening and insolent conduct of the Navajo Indians toward the garrison of Fort Defiance, an isolated Military Post in the heart of their country, and about 180 miles west of Albuquerque on the other side of the great divide. It was about 120 miles from Craig up the Rio Grande to Albuquerque, so we had a march of 300 miles before us during the hottest summer weather. It being the 30th of June the exacting duties of muster day delayed the completion of our numerous preparations until the next day when property was stored, records secured, and everything put in shape to leave for months. The heavy uniform jackets and caps were discarded and two blue flannel shirts and a felt hat were purchased from the Sutler for each man which gave them real comfort and greater freedom of action.

With three Sergeants, three Corporals, and fifty men all mounted on the best horses and with two wagons, each drawn by six mules, for transporting forage and rations, I set out early in the morning of the 2d of July and made the march to Fort Defiance in eleven marching days with ease and with the loss of only one man from sunstroke. The heat fell upon us in burning waves up the valley and our marches were made early in the morning and late in the afternoon, the midday being spent in the shade of some convenient bosque. A halt was made in the afternoon of the second day when the soldier fell under the sunstroke, and he was placed in the shade of a tree where every effort was made to revive him by dashing water upon him and giving him brandy, but he lived only about an hour. We buried him upon the summit of a foothill at sunset and no human ears but our own heard the three little volleys of the Corporal's guard fired over his grave. This was the differential of glory.

On arriving at Isleta on the west side of the river and opposite Albuquerque, orders were received requiring me to await dispatches for Major W.[William] T. H. Brooks, 3d Infantry, commanding Fort Defiance. Leaving my men in camp on the west side, I crossed the river in a skiff and swimming my horse to the old town and called on Colonel [Benjamin L.] Bonneville whom I then saw for the first time. He was in command of this Post and two months later was to succeed General Garland in command of the Department. His army career had been rendered somewhat famous by his capture by the "Indians" while on an exploring expedition in the "Far West" in 1831. The journal of his adventures, during the five years he was lost and dropped from the rolls as a Captain, was written up and amplified by Washington Irving.[1] I found him a stout, robust old gentleman inclined to the ready conversation and bonhomie characteristics of his race. Those who ever saw him still remember his colloquial habit of beginning every sentence with the phrase, "I tell you sir." At this time there were at this Post Major D. H. Rucker, one of the great Quartermasters of the army, his brother, Dr. Winslow, and Lieutenant [Lawrence W.] O'Bannon. After a pleasant dinner with Major Rucker and family and a game of chess with O'Bannon, I recrossed the river in a skiff and slept in camp.

The next day I repaired to the town again and waited all day for the dispatches to be carried to Major Brooks. Other troops, it was expected, would be ordered to Defiance besides my company and it is not the easiest thing in the world to prescribe a plan of operations in such a wild country with uncertain and partly unknown wants at one end of a long line, and vague information and scant supplies at the other. Throughout all the vast regions of the West, wherever any portion had been penetrated by the army, careful itineraries had been made of distances, topography, wood,

---

[1]Washington Irving immortalized and romanticized Bonneville's life in his book, *The Adventures of Captain Bonneville, U.S.A. in the Rocky Mountains and the Far West* (1837).

water and grass. From the one furnished me of the route to Fort Defiance, it could be seen that the first day's march up the sandy western slopes of the valley would be the most difficult, so a very early start was made on the morning of the 7th of July. The day proved oppressively hot. Anyone may now ride comfortably over the route in a palace car upon the Atlantic and Pacific Railway, but the memories of a journey made before a railway had crossed the Missouri River may not be devoid of interest.

Our first camp was at "Sheep Spring," twenty-seven miles from the Rio Grande. Its water was welcome after our weary march through the hot, deep sand from dawn until sunset. The spring bubbled from beneath the finest example of a fan-shaped deposit of slate I ever saw. Its section across its axis occupied about half a quadrant in extent. It was upon the border of an empty lake whose water-worn shorelines were as distinct as though it had been abandoned but a year. Islands whose tops slightly inclined in the same general plane were sparsely covered with shrubs but the bottom with many yawning cracks sustained only a trifling vegetal growth of grease wood. The lake had been from ten to fifteen miles wide and perhaps twice as long before its bed had been tilted and emptied by the successive upheavels which made the Rocky Mountains. The story of the life and death of the lake was told by the fan-shaped slate. Here was a graphic explanation of the general desolation of this region in which thirty or forty pueblo cities had perished leaving no record but obscure mounds and broken pottery.

We traversed ten miles of the lake bottom the next day and passed the ancient pueblos of Laguna. Here the sight of a neat house with a gable roof was a surprising reminder of things we had not seen nor heard since leaving the States. It was the house of Revd. Mr. Gorman, a Baptist missionary, and we halted and dismounted long enough to permit me to pay my respects to the good man and his family. Here were the neatness and comfort of a white-man's home and its refreshing little dooryard with green sod and shrubbery contrasted with the shadeless squalor of the vermin-haunted pueblo hard by. Here the Gospel touched the heathen. It was a brave little gleam of that kindly light which has persisted through eighteen centuries. Well-grown naked children of the heathen with long, matted hair were scampering out over the broken and crumbling walls to gaze at the soldiers. The bronzed and hardy Riflemen gathered around the missionary's little home for a moment and caressed it, so to speak, with kindly eyes and drew a few breaths of the air which surrounded it.

Not far above Laguna our road passed along and over a curious, black, rough flow of hardened lava underneath which was running a stream of water. The water was a dirty, brick red where it left the lava and was called "Argua Colorado," farther up across a break in the lava this water appeared yellow and was named the "Argua Amarillo," while above at the upper end of the lava before the mountain stream disappeared beneath it the water was dark and clear and known as the "Argua Azul." As we steadily ascended the long, wrinkled slopes toward the distant summit of Campbell's Pass, clusters of cedar and piñon began to appear, increasing in size and numbers until nearer the top considerable areas were covered with dense growths of these evergreen trees. The temperature became less oppressive and we greatly enjoyed the pure, rarified air and the expanding views behind and around us. The snorting horses admonished us to halt frequently a few minutes to enable them to get enough breath. At the divide we had yet fifty-five miles to travel down the western slopes to reach Fort Defiance.

Thirteen miles beyond the summit we halted at the "Ojo del Oso" or "Big Bear Spring"—the finest spring in New Mexico. Its clear, cold water flows in a perennial stream. This was a favorite resort for Indians and we began to keep a sharp lookout for them. Toward the evening of the 13th of July we arrived within sight of the Fort. As we came nearer we could see many mounted Indians, singly and in groups, riding swiftly in various directions. They drew away to the right and left as we approached and presently officers from the Fort came galloping out to meet us; and on our arrival within it, the entire garrison turned out and greeted us with welcoming cheers. The Indians had recently become so insolent and offensive that the garrison had been kept in a nervous condition of apprehension that an attack was impending. My company had been expected but not so soon in such very warm weather. My men and horses were in better condition for active service than when we started from Craig. There are many useful secrets regarding the conduct of a long march which are revealed only by experience.

The garrison at the time of my arrival consisted of one company "I" Mounted Riflemen, Captain George McLane and 1st Lieutenant and Brevet Captain J. P. Hatch; and two companies of the 3d Infantry, 1st Lieutenant William D. Whipple and 2d Lieutenants T.[Thomas] W. Walker and William Dickinson, all under the command of Captain and Brevet Major W. T. H. Brooks, 3d Infantry, the Surgeon of the Post being Dr. J. C. McKee, my comrade and messmate across the plains the previous year.

The attitude and conduct of the Navajos at this critical juncture is well described in the following report of Major Brooks to the Department Commander, viz:

Headquarters, Fort Defiance, July 15, 1858.

Sir:

For the full understanding of our relations with the Navajos, I propose to relate in their order the events of the past week. Up till the 7th instant, our relations continued as reported on the first of the month. On the 7th instant I established the haycamp at the pond on the other end of the *cañon*. The next morning two of the men came in and reported the camp had been fired into by Indians with arrows during the night. I immediately proceeded to the camp and found that eight arrows had been fired, one of them killing a dog, and three others entering the tents, one of them going into the bed of the man *said* to have been on Post. Nothing could be discovered as to the number of Indians engaged.

As no particular damage beyond the insult was done, and as an Indian had been fired upon by a sentinel in the garrison, to scare him away from a target where he was picking up old bullets and balls, I made no complaint of the matter to Sarcillo Largo and some other chiefs who were in the garrison, a few days afterwards merely cautioning them that it might be a dangerous experiment to try again.

On Monday, an Indian came into the garrison and hung around for three or four hours, trying to sell a couple of blankets, or more likely, waiting the opportunity that finally presented itself. Having sold a blanket to a camp woman and within thirty yards of the door of my quarters, he saw my servant boy, Jim (a slave), coming towards him and pass in rear of the camp women's quarters; as Jim was about to pass him, the Indian jumped upon his horse and as soon as Jim's back was turned he fired an arrow which passed under the boy's shoulder blade into the lungs. The Indian immediately put whip to his horse and left over the hill. The boy, strange to say, never uttered a word or exclamation, but attempted to pull the arrow out, in doing which he broke it off near the head.

The head of the arrow remains in the body, the doctor being unable to extract it. The boy is still alive, but there is no doubt he is mortally wounded. I think this act may be characterized as one of greater atrocity than that committed in 1854 and reported by Major Kendrick in his letters of October 8th of that year.[2] The boy maintains, and all believe his statement, that he never did anything to the Indian, did not speak to him, and thinks he never saw him before. The next day I sent for Sarcillo Largo and demanded that the assassin should be

---

[2]This story is concerned with an incident which occurred in October 1854, when a Navajo killed a soldier. The Indian agent, Henry L. Dodge and Major Henry L. Kendrick demanded the return of the guilty brave. After much argument the man was turned over with an arrow in his groin, and the military quickly hanged him on the spot.

given up to us. He at first wavered and said perhaps the boy would not die. I told him it made no difference, the Indian shot to kill and he must be given up. After various pretexts he said that he was then on his way to Zuñi, that on his return he would attend to it, and that he would send after him. On my expressing dissatisfaction with so much delay, he provokingly replied that I ought not to be in such a hurry, that it was six weeks since I had killed Mamelito's cattle and I had done nothing yet towards paying for them. I gave him well to understand that I would not pay for his cattle nor would I allow it to be of the slightest effect for shooting the boy. In the conversation I had tried to picture to him the consequences of a war to his people and that it would certainly be made on them did they not give up the murderer. On leaving he asked if we would send to Laguna Negra to receive the Indian when they had caught him; I told him I would. But none of us felt any hope or confidence that he would do anything in the business. It is thought the Indian is not what is called a *pelado* but a man of independence and hence the hesitancy of the rich or influential men of the tribe to take any steps that might commit them with their own people.

Two hours after Sarcillo Largo left the garrison, Lieutenant Averell with his company arrived, giving us a surprise not the less agreeable because it was unlooked for, and from the conduct of the Indians I think they could hardly have been aware of his approach.

I sent Lieutenant Averell with his company yesterday as a guard to the hay party at La Joyoa for which duty I had previously detailed Captain McLain and his company. I have commenced haying full early but the season admits of it earlier than usual. The crops of hay may not be as heavy as some other years, but if we do not get two crops in some places we hope to make up the loss of hay by the grazing the grounds will yield. The hay secured, we have a force at once ready to take the field.

I received by the hands of Lieutenant Averell special orders No. 60 and your communication of the 24th ultimo. Until the effect produced by the arrival of Lieutenant Averell on the Navajos is known I shall not ask for any more reinforcements. In the meantime I will continue with all expedition our haying and make such preparation as lies within us for taking the field.

We have at the Post only four months' provisions after this month, for the garrison proper, an additional supply will be necessary with the arrival of more troops.

If a campaign becomes necessary and I can see no alternative, I would respectfully call attention to Major Kendrick's suggestions as communicated in his letters of October and November 1854. In addition I would respectfully suggest that if possible the Utahs be encouraged to repeat their expeditions into the country for they appear to have inspired the Navajos with a dread not to be gotten over. I have been asked by Sarcillo Largo what I would do in case the Utahs would come this far into their country as they have threatened. I replied I would not interfere and would act with whichever tribe showed itself to be our best friend. I do not think it would be at all practicable to attempt to urge war against a particular band of the nation and not with all as Major Kendrick seemed to think might be necessary.

July 16th. The boy Jim died this morning. I have delayed the mail thus late with the double purpose of receiving the mail from Albuquerque and of knowing the fate of the boy. The mail is not in. Our requisitions for cartridges for the rifles have not been filled, the train which is on the way may have ammunition for us. With the exception of rifle cartridges (new pattern), there is a good supply of ammunition at the Post for the command now here.

Although I have said I would not at present ask for more reinforcement, yet it would add to our confidence in ourselves to know that a supporting force was as near to us as the Rio Grande to rely upon in case of actual hostilities.

> Very respectfully,
> W. T. H. Brooks,
> Captain 3d Infantry and Brevet Major,
> Commanding Post.

Headquarters Department New Mexico,
Santa Fe, August 1, 1858.

7

The Navajo and His Country

The understanding and possible enjoyment of the reader of any sort of historical chronicle are greatly facilitated by a knowledge of the threatre of action. I shall not pretend to write a history of the Navajo War of 1858, but it may happen that in pursuing my reminiscences through a few months of arduous and painful experience in hunting Navajos through "infamous hills and sandy, perilous wilds" a considerable part of the substance and summary of that conflict may be unfolded. The wonderful and ceaseless activities, attended with hardships and privations, of that little but heroic band of American soldiers who thrashed and subdued the most powerful and warlike tribe of Indians then on the continent, are worthy of historical record, but my faltering chronicle will be prevented the dignity of such consideration for the reason that I shall have to rely almost entirely upon my memory which during the succeeding years has been overwhelmed with the deep and voluminous impressions of the great Civil War and its results. Yet my confidence in those memories of earlier years is not shaken; for now, after nearly four decades have flown, they arise clearly through the confused recollections of later times like a strong and legible palimpsest.

The region wherein lies the habitat of the Navajo is an elevated, wrinkled, rarified sort of desolation on the Pacific slopes of the Rocky mountains. Its scant water, where there is enough to run, finds the Colorado River chiefly through the San Juan and Little Colorado. Its general arrangement of mountains shows an original tendency to ranges from four to eight hundred feet high and running parallel to the great divide. In the slight elongation, or stretching, which attended their successive elevations, they were broken transversely in many places and some of these great fissures, worn down by the weather of ages to the level of their bases, were converted into passable canyons. The western side of the ranges generally show fractured strata at an angle of 45°. The occasional buckles in the ranges, caused by a more general and undulating uplifting of the great continental range, created eccentricities whose manifestations are bold knobs, bluffs, lofty pinnacles, and cul-de-sacs of hills with precipitous escarpments sometimes enclosing lakes and ponds. The valleys between the ranges are generally destitute of any vegetal growth excepting grass, but the summits and sides of the hills and ranges are commonly quite thickly wooded with piñon and cedar. The most remarkable canyon is the "Canyon de Chelly" about fifty miles northwest of Fort Defiance; and the most notable lake is Laguna Negra about twenty miles to the northeast.

The Navajos occupied one hundred miles square lying in the northwest corner of New Mexico and lapping over the corners of Arizona, Utah and Colorado which cluster about the intersection of the 37th parallel with the 32d meridian west of Washington. The Navajos were occupying this country south of the San Juan when they first became known to history. They numbered from 17,000 to 20,000 souls and were the most powerful tribe then known and could assemble from 2,000 to 4,000 formidable warriors at any time within two days. They were well armed with bows and arrows and lances, and about ten percent of their number, with rifles. The principal chief of the tribe at that time was Sarcillo Largo (Big Ears) and other subordinate chiefs of subtribes were Sandoval, Manuelito, Nah-kish-lah-nee, Herrero, Ca-e-tah-no and Armijo. The Nation, as it was most often called, was rich in herds of horses and flocks of sheep and had also fields of corn, wheat and barley. From time immemorial they have made beautiful blankets of wool of brilliant and pleasing colors, chiefly red, blue and yellow on black and white grounds in strange zigzag and complicated figures. These blankets are waterproof, heavy and warm and will last through the roughest wear and usage of three or four generations.

The men are tall and muscular and some of them of noble appearance. Their faces, especially in profile, resemble the ancient Jewish type without the beard, the nose aquiline and the mouth well-shaped without the coarse thick lips common to some other tribes. The women are well formed with oval faces, inclined when young to the big-baby expression, rounded limbs without being stout, small hands and feet, and they are reputed neat and cleanly. The sexes are also distinguished by their dress, as are those of birds by their plumage. The men wear blankets of the gayest colors while those of the women are of broad black and narrow white stripes, running up and down when worn, with a few lines of red and blue. The leggins of the women are of buckskin or sheepskin wound many times around the calf and ankles above the moccasins like those of their sisters in the pueblos. Their hair is arranged in plaits or braids hanging down the back and sometimes, with the *ricos*, the braids are ornamented with thin silver discs diminishing in size from that of a silver dollar at the neck to that of a dime at the end of the braid. The blanket when worn leaves the neck, shoulders and arms exposed which are adorned with numerous strings of beads of chalchihuitl and other bits of stones regarded as precious. The chiefs had generally four wives who were treated with equal respect and they ate with their husband and it was said their voices were heard in the councils. Whatever labor was required to be done was performed by peons or slaves who had been captured in war.

Fort Defiance was located at the eastern mouth of Canyon Bonita which passes through a long range about four hundred feet in height. The Canyon has a crescent shape so that on entering it on either side of the range one cannot see throughout its length although it is less than a mile. A rivulet flows through it and furnished water to the Fort which was no doubt the controlling reason for the selection of this site that otherwise has several objectionable features. From its elevated surroundings which have the shape of a horse shoe with the opening towards Albuquerque, the Fort could be commanded on all sides except from the opening by a plunging rifle fire at long range. The barren rocky ridge about eighty feet high on the eastern side of the Fort prevented all view in that direction. Shortly after my arrival a block-house was built upon it which became useful as an outpost and lookout. The higher, densely wooded, main ridge or mountain on the west, through which ran the Canyon, was connected by a spur to the northward of the Fort, with the rocky ledge on the east. It was a cul-de-sac in which a Military Post having been built was quite appropriately named Fort Defiance. It not only ostensibly defied the Navajos, but it also defied every accepted principle of the military art which should have controlled its site and construction. And it was not a Fort when completed, but simply a rectangle three hundred yards long and two hundred wide enclosed with small log houses and without stockades or other defensive works. The officers' quarters along the north side were double log cabins each twelve feet square with flat dirt roofs and a detached kitchen in the rear. The men's quarters were elongated log houses around the east and south sides while the store houses and shops still longer and more spacious occupied the west side. The laundresses' cabins were outside the store houses. That important feature of every frontier garrison, the Sutler's store, stood outside the northwest corner and was a large, double log house, one part devoted to a trading store, the other being used as an officers' club. In those days, which now seem ancient, the army on the frontier was expected to build its own forts and cantonments and would have as soon looked for manna from the heavens as for any special appropriation for such purposes. Every nail and every pane of glass was counted and accounted for. As scouting, fighting, escorting mails and trains occupied most of its time, the army then had little use for spacious and comfortable quarters; and so, without second thought, Fort Defiance was built where the conveniences of good water, fuel, build-materials, and fighting Indians would be most readily combined.

After forty years it is difficult for the survivors of that period to forget the changes they have witnessed and recall the rough frontier life with its tragic vicissitudes in which they participated; and to those who have been born since the frontier disappeared, it is quite impossible to imagine the conditions and exigencies which then controlled the life and operations of the army. It must be understood that amid the clashing and warring elements of savagery that were ever ready to rend each other, to maintain any sort of security for life, property and commerce, it was a supreme necessity that the army should dominate with undisputed sway, without reference to a feeble civil authority which was generally remote, sometimes unfriendly and always slow. Hence, when an atrocious and unprovoked murder was committed like that reported by Major Brooks, the hard necessity for an application of force could not be escaped.

The intense interest and satisfaction of the meeting with my old friends and comrades after long months of separation by hundreds of miles cannot be described. The first night sufficed only to break the seal of our individual silences and solitudes. To let loose the long pent experiences of our separate lives and again commingle our hopes and fears had to be continued at our next meeting.

The day after my arrival I was sent to La Joya, eleven miles to the northward, to guard a haying party. The country was beautiful with abrupt and unexpected mountains, pretty plains and slopes and inviting *rincóns*. Only streams of water and a civilization worthy of its charming landscapes were wanting to make it a real Utopia. We had a lovely camp near a spring and far enough away from cover to be safe from night attack. Small "A" tents were furnished for the men. Our camp was generally in the form of an equilateral triangle, the picket line of the horses inside the line of company tents filling one side and my own tent being in the opposite angle with the tents of the Sergeants between me and the line, the 1st Sergeant in the center. There were probably, as we ascertained, about 2,000 Indians around us within four miles, but as long as their women and flocks and herds were with them, peace was guaranteed.

Hundreds of Indians would come about our camp in the day time, but were all sent away before sunset with injunctions not to come within sight of the camp at night as they would be fired upon if they did. My standing order, strictly observed, was that no soldier should ever be without his arms day or night. No matter what happened he must never have to seek his weapons. They were slung to him when eating and sleeping— they were never laid down whatever he was doing. When Indians are not using their bows or are not prepared to use them, the string is loose, the loop at one end being slipped out of the notch in the bow. When it is strung the Indian with half a dozen arrows in his left hand can shoot them as fast as an expert can fire a revolver, and at sixty yards they do not miss. They are especially to be dreaded at night for the arrows make no noise, and when driven into man or beast cannot commonly be removed without leaving the head behind in the body. Indians coming into or around my camp were not allowed to have their bows strung or arrows in their hands and my men were ever on the alert. When Indians began to come in, one of my men would quietly loiter out, one for each dozen Indians, and lie down where he could keep them in view and every motion be watched. Nothing escaped the eyes of the Indian; he saw every slightest thing although looking as indifferent as a cat. It makes no difference about odds in numbers in their favor with Indians, if they can see a lot of dead certainties against them they will never attack.

I occasionally visited the Fort with an escort of two to four men. One day in returning to my camp an Indian well mounted was observed following us at a little distance. Upon halting and showing the hand uplifted and palm to the front, the Indian would return the signal; but on turning to approach him he would scamper up the slopes to the timber.

After repeating this two or three times we went on to camp where we had not long been when the Indian who had followed us appeared and turned out to be a squaw, the daughter of Nah-kish-lah-nee, to whom I had made some presents at the Sutler's store in the garrison. She always rode about with a retinue of followers some of whom had now joined her. She was persuaded to dismount and come near my tent and sit down where she was given something to eat. Her name was Ah-tlan-tiz-pa, or was so pronounced, and she was undoubtedly the prettiest Navajo woman in the country. I mention her because she remained friendly to us and afterward rendered valuable service. Like my Kiowa chief had been, she was more interested in women's fashion plates than any other form of art that could be shown. She gave us valuable information concerning the country.

My company remained here some time after the haying party had finished its work, on account of the grazing, and the officers of the Post rode out to see me about every day sometimes staying over night. Sarcillo Largo paid me frequent visits, generally with warriors and squaws accompanying him. He once brought me some native tobacco plant, a wild weed with a yellow flower. At the foot of the western slopes of the mountains in certain places could be found very fine garnets, some of which I secured as souvenirs and afterward regretted that I had been so easily contented, for it was found that when properly cut they were as beautiful as the ruby. Of all places in the world, one would think our camp at La Joya the last one in which to read *Little Dorrit*, but for that reason perhaps I enjoyed it the more on a second reading. Books have strange wanderings and *Little Dorrit* will never find a welcome in an odder place than a camp among the Navajos. Irving's *Life of Washington* was the next old friend that drifted my way. But Irving had the wings of the morning any way westward and had flown to the Pacific slopes of the Rockies in his *Astoria* and *Adventures of Bonneville*.

No white men having seen the Laguna Negra and it being desirable to know something of the way to it, I was asked by the commanding officer to obtain the information. Taking a Sergeant and twenty men on the 24th of July, I got quickly over the nine miles to the lake from a description of the trail given me by the Indian girl. The lake, dark and deep with an area as I recollect of about fifty acres, was surrounded at a little distance from it by bold mountains. In the valley about it were cornfields and grazing. It was a secluded stronghold for flocks and herds. Its approaches could be easily defended. Our coming was not discovered until we were within an hundred yards of the lake where there was an extended camp of several hundred Indians. There was an immediate commotion, but we dismounted and I left my men standing to horse with their rifles in their hands capped and ready for action and revolvers handy while I without stopping an instant walked at once down among the Indians at the foot of a little slope and shook hands with the nearest ones who appeared to be leading men. Sitting down upon a rock, I took out my pipe and tobacco and gave some to the chiefs and talked with them—all that it was possible—about the fish in the lake and the grazing and everything in sight, until the place and all its surroundings were impressed on my memory. Then bidding them a cheerful and easy good bye with a handshake, I returned to my men and we mounted and got back to camp, when I at once made an accurate map of all the country observed, which, as will be seen, served an important purpose afterward.

Whatever little there was of a social character among these Indians was exhibited in all its varieties and phases about my camp at La Joya. It was about my only opportunity to observe them before hostilities began. They were always on horseback, only the slaves went on foot. The calf of the leg was not much developed except in the slave. Individuals and parties were often passing my camp in various directions. Sometimes a whole family or subtribe would camp near us for a night or two. To see the chief stop on some slight elevation which would give him a view of his surroundings, seat himself to witness the camping operations of his people, the care of his flock and herd, the wives and slaves the while preparing food, the spread of blankets with here and there bits of bright color, the docile, bearded goats stalking in and about with dignity or springing aside with agility to avoid a kick or a blow, mounted youngsters galloping outside the herds to prevent straying, women crouching about the little curling smokes of the camp—all this spectacle was easily transferred by imagination into old patriarchal pictures. It seemed to me when I thought of the story of morose and implacable old Saul pursuing David in the wilderness of En-Gedi—when the young man captured his blanket in a cave, or when the old king pitched in the hill of Hachilah and lay sleeping with his spear stuck in the ground at his bolster and his people lay round about him and the devoted David to prove his loyalty took the spear and canteen from his bolster—I say when that conjured scene appeared with this about me, that Saul seemed very like a jealous and irreconcilable old Navajo chief and that Saul's people in their equipments, customs and environment furnished strong prototypes for this lost tribe. Utterly lost, for they knew not and had not record or legend of who they were or whence they came. They lived as their fathers had lived.

Their young men came and played games near our camp to entertain us. One, which I think would prove difficult to our athletic clubs of the East, was played with a lance and a wooden wheel about a foot in diameter with a two-inch hole burned through its center. An Indian standing at the end of a straight course would cast the wheel to roll swiftly along the course while another Indian with the spear, starting a little in advance, would run with it and thrust the spear through the hole without knocking down the wheel.

Their archery was amazing. A quarter of a dollar set loosely in the end of a split stick at sixty yards was quickly knocked out without disturbing the stick. Many astonishing feats of this kind were performed on horseback. It was curious to see a dozen Indians, after having shot away their quivers of arrows, all run and gather them up, each his own, without the slightest hesitation, when to us on a careful examination no difference between them appeared to our eyes. It required great strength to draw their bows which were covered on the convex side with sinew fixed to it like bark to a withe. No one, not even an Indian, could draw it with an arrow and hold it bent to take aim. The Indian always did it in one motion, and aim was taken during that motion, so that he let go the string the instant it had reached the limit of tension. He wore a broad wristlet of heavy hide or leather around his left wrist to prevent injury from the string when it flew home. My men reciprocated the intention of the Indians to impress us with their marksmanship by practicing one day with their rifles off hand at a blanket rigged on a bush to represent an Indian in height, size and shape, having an Indian stand along side of it as a model until it was finished. Out of twenty snap shots at 200 yards, nine went through the figure. At that distance their arrows were not reliable or fatal.

My company returned to the Fort on the 31st of July, and during the lull that came before the storm, we kept up our drills; and a good lookout guarded haying parties and occasionally took the ladies out for an airing with sufficient escort to ensure safety, until about the 10th of August when Captain [George] McLane with a part of his company as an escort started for the Rio Grande with the ladies of the garrison.

On the 19th of August, Major Brooks, Dr. McKee, Mr. Weber and I started for Zuni to engage a number of spies and guides for service against the Navajos, with a part of my company as an escort. The sixty miles were easily made in two days over a trail worn deep with centuries of use. Major Brooks and Weber rode in an ambulance and the doctor and I were mounted. About half way we stopped to look at some ancient stone walls five or six feet high, thirty feet long and eighteen inches wide. The cement between the stones was as hard as the stones. These were not over one-and-a-half inches thick and each course was doubled before breaking joints. There is no history or legend concerning the builders, but they were probably outworks to some city.

A good view of the broad valley of the Rio Colorado Chiquito opened out when we were yet three miles from the city of Zuni. It would have been considered a plain but for the course of the river which was indicated by an irregular fringe of trees that bordered it and led us to observe the gentle slopes on either side. To the right and left in the valley we noticed towers about twenty-five feet high, at intervals of half a mile, and from the top of the nearest one there immediately went up a slender smoke which was repeated from one to another on the left, in which direction we beheld the famed Pueblo standing on a slight elevation beyond the stream. We of a new nation whose birth was witnessed by men yet living were approaching a city whose beginning is lost in forgotten fables. The capital of the ancient Cibola was visited and explored by Spaniards a century before the Mayflower landed. It excites the imagination and begets a feeling of awe. And yet this is modern Zuni. For uncounted centuries the ruins of a more ancient Zuni have been crumbling above the debris of a still more ancient town upon a mesa a thousand feet high, several miles from this place. Throughout this land are mesas on whose summits are found ruins of ancient stone walls and rooms which supplement a legend of the flood which may be heard in all the pueblos. The glow of the setting sun that fell upon the place added enchantments of high lights and pronounced shadows to its mysteries and produced commingled and blended effects of fortress, tower and terrace. Its solitude was impressive.

We traversed a breadth of cornfields and pitched our camp within five hundred yards of the town. A squad of Pueblo Indians visited us and we acquainted them with our character and desire to see the Governor. An *Alguacil* or sheriff soon came to see us, and the Major made known to him through our interpreter that we had important business with the Governor, and entertained him with food and our old-fashioned army toddy judiciously weakened, and gave him some smoking tobacco. Being a little fatigued with our day's ride we did not visit the Pueblo until the next day. On the morrow some sort of officials came and conducted us to the city. As we came near, it appeared a sort of honey comb of rectangular structures of adobe piled up to the height of four or five stories, each tier in ascending leaving a terrace upon the roof of the story beneath from ten to fifteen feet wide. The hill or elevation some thirty feet in height, upon which the town was built, was itself composed of the debris of houses which had preceded those in view. As the wear of time had destroyed structures and tiers, others had been superadded. It was evident that two or three of the basement stories had been swallowed up by the falling detritus of ages. The exterior slopes of the foundation were cultivated up to the walls and laid out in curious little garden plats, some of them not larger than a dining table for six persons. These miniature gardens were each surrounded by a tiny wall about four inches high and an inch thick made of hard cement. In these toy-like enclosures were growing varieties of the red pepper or chili verdi and chili colorado.

We entered the town by means of ladders to the roof of the first story and thence through a narrow way, which ordinarily was closed, to an interior room where we were presented to the Governor to whom we stated the object of our visit. The promise of arms being furnished to those who should be sent to assist us against the Navajos and the prospect of booty in horses and sheep had evidently more weight with the Governor than the consideration of pay. The Governor must advise the *Cacique* and a council was necessary before an answer could be given. During the delay which would be caused by these proceedings we went about the interior plaza and examined the avocations of the inhabitants. It was said that the town contained 3,000 people, but we could not believe there were more than 1,500 to 2,000 present.

The manufacture of pottery was most interesting. The mixing and kneading of the clay and the shaping of it into *ollas* and *tenajas* and the formation of grotesque and fanciful little vessels bearing a rude resemblance to animals was fascinating, but the most marvellous part of it was the marking of them with the curious figures they bear which was done rapidly and without copy or model as a ready penman would write his language. Yet the figures did not vary perceptibly from those which may be found on broken pottery dug from the ruins of a nameless and forgotten pueblo. And the meaning of the figures, if they had any, was as unknown to them as their origin. Having no written language, there is nothing to prevent changes in that which they speak, and that there have been great changes is evidenced by the fact that all the pueblos differ in their spoken language, some to such an extent as to render them unable to talk to each other without using the Mexican which is somewhat common to all. The people possess very little curiosity and are orderly and busy. The making of war implements and hideous head adornments for warriors attracted our attention, and it required an effort not to betray an amusement at the serious earnestness of the artisans at work upon them. To describe the many domestic industries—the making of baskets and curious mats, dance ornaments and toys for children, the grinding of corn and the preparation of food—would occupy too much time and space. A number of eagles were kept in cages about the place and I remember well the steady, piercing gaze and flash of their eyes. A single wing feather is the coveted head adornment of a warrior who has killed an enemy in battle. But the most striking sight was that of two or three albinos— natives with white hair and eye brows, white skins and weak, white eyes with the faintest shades of a milky blue and saffron yellow under pink lids.

In the evening, by request of the Governor, we were presented to the *Caçique*, who is the highest authority in all affairs of church and state and a Priest of Montezuma. We found ourselves in the presence of a venerable Indian whose appearance at once inspired respect and whose attitude, dress and manner of natural dignity and authority was a full expression of the elevated character of his office. The strong features of his face, devoid of any suggestion of the grovelling, brutal expression common to the savage, fixed our attention. The dark, iron-gray hair which fell at full length surrounded with a band of white feathers; the gold pendants in the ears and strings of beads and chalchihuitl about the neck; the voluminous blanket, in which were interwoven strange figures, which fell from his square shoulders; and the embellished moccasins below his embroidered leggins altogether made up a presentment comporting well with his ancient and mysterious office. Although it was apparent that he was dressed for an important ceremony, yet he bore himself with the ease of an habitual usage. We were at once conducted with about a dozen of the principal men who surrounded the *Caçique* to an underground room called the *estufa*. It was about thirty feet long by eighteen or twenty feet wide and full of shadows, the only light being that of a little flame upon a low altar at the farther end which was built of some solid material and in the gloom reminded me of a blacksmith's forge. Two figures, one on either side, stood watching the light. We followed the *Caçique* across the *jerga* carpet toward the light and lent ourselves to the arrangement of all in a semicircle or horseshoe-shaped figure with the open side toward the altar. Then all sat down upon the floor facing inwards except the Priest who remained standing facing the light and casting his long shadow across the circle and the room to the wall beyond.

The scene to us was in the nature of a surprise. The powerful impression which its weirdness and silence wrought upon us was deepened by its unexpectedness. After a motionless silence of two or three awful minutes, the Priest extended his arms slightly to the right and left with open palms to the front and with a low, deep voice pronounced an invocation or prayer. Then he received from one of the figures a large pipe and seated himself to complete our circle. The other watcher with a long white splinter lighted at the flame, held it to the pipe; and the Priest drew a long inspiration and then emitted from his lips a jet of smoke directly upward and another downward, then one to the right hand and another to the left, and passed the pipe to the next on his right, and so on it was handed around the circle, each person making the smoke take the same directions until the pipe was returned to the Priest. As the interpreter afterward explained, the first upward direction of the smoke was an act of recognition and submission made to Him whose name is never spoken, as the Father of All; the second direction, of recognition and dependence made to Earth, the Mother of all living things; and the directions to the right and left, a recognition of the brotherhood and mutual dependence of mankind. It did not escape my notice that it was in itself a sign of the cross.

I have seen thousands prostrate in silent submission to the uplifted Host in a cathedral and heard divine service in a pine forest with a reverent audience of pioneer families; I have heard the songs of Zion mingling with moaning billows on the ocean, and witnessed the efforts of all creeds and faiths to satisfy that inborn longing of every human heart to seek the Creator; but never have I paid more reverent attention to religious worship anywhere than to that of these children of memory in their *estufa*. The sacred fire on the altar had never been extinguished. They believe that it was lighted by Montezuma, the brother and equal of Him whose name is unspoken and whose eye is the Sun where Montezuma now abides, but that he will surely come again when the dead shall be raised and mankind judged and that he will then reign in eternal peace and glory. They believe that he now manifests himself to his children in Light and they adore it. Their religious devotion is a part of their daily lives and enters into all they do. Their Faith and Obedience are perfect. What a wonderful and mysterious meeting of extremes! The end of all scientific research in its ultimate and simplest terms found in Matter, Force and Motion, an eternal Trinity, indissoluble even in thought, manifested in Light, here found an object of worship by a benighted race from the beginning. Their religion is pure pantheism. They name the medium or mediator between themselves and the unknown, Montezuma. When the ceremonies of the *estufa* were concluded, the *Caçique* spoke regarding our mission; and without changing our positions, the subject was thoroughly discussed and everything was arranged to our satisfaction, and the next day we set out on our return to Fort Defiance.

8

Ready!

On our return from Zuni my company was taken through Canyon Bonita to the open country on the west side on account of the excellent grazing to be found there for my horses. My communications with the Fort were easily kept up through the canyon, yet there was a slight feeling of isolation as it was impossible to leave my company for a moment on account of the extreme tension of our relations with the Navajos. We were constantly on the alert and ready for any emergency. My camp was in the triangular form, and in the nighttime the sentinels' orders were to fire at any one discovered approaching it from any direction except that of the Fort. Signals had been adopted by which we would be advised of the coming of messengers or friends through the canyon. On the 27th of August a small party of spies and guides arrived at the Post from Zuni with the promise of a larger party later on. These resulted from our visit to that place.

About midnight of the 29th I was awakened from a sound sleep on the ground in my tent by a singular noise like that which would be made by trying to strike a match on the canvas. It was a bright moonlight which afforded sufficient light through the canvas to enable me to see all about my tent. It first occurred to me that the noise might be caused by the scratching of a twig of a bush moved by the wind or by a stalk of dry grass. But it was repeated so steadily and with such force that I raised myself and took my revolver in one hand and raised the tent wall with the other. A human face near the ground appeared, and I heard the peculiar hissing sound, "Tscieu," which Mexicans make to invoke silence. It was the Indian girl Ah-tlan-tis-pah. She was trembling with excitement and quickly creeping into the tent arose to her knees saying, *"Quidado! Quidado! Teniente,"* and rapidly told me that there had been a fight at Ojo del Oso (Big Bear Spring, forty-two miles from the Fort on the road to Albuquerque) and that several Indians had been killed and hurt and that *"el Capitano Americano"* had been shot in the side with a bullet and warning me to look out, the Indians might attack me before morning. I conjectured that this must refer to Captain McLane who had been sent to escort a train going to Albuquerque with the ladies of the garrison and to meet the outcoming mail, some days before. The girl was so positive and earnest that I should be on my guard, crying, *"Quidado! Quidado! Sin Falta,"* that I went out, called the Sergeant, had the horses saddled and put the men on the *Qui vive.* On returning to my tent I found the girl was gone. The sentinels on post within ten paces of my tent had not seen her come nor go. How she had made her way by them through the grass without being seen or heard it was impossible to guess, especially as she had never before been in that camp.

There was a comet of surpassing splendor visible about this time which we were told filled the Indians with fearful forebodings of war and disaster. It was a most impressive object and during that night and many following ones we had many opportunities to observe it.

At dawn the next morning I moved through the canyon to the Post, where I found that Captain McLane had just been brought in with a gunshot wound in the side, the ball having glanced off a rib. He had had a lively fight with Navajos at Big Bear Spring the day before in which six or eight Indians had been killed. The officers were astonished on my arrival to hear me immediately ask about McLane's wound, and more so when I told them the news had reached me several hours before and that it was the occasion of my coming in. My company was immediately sent to scout the road toward Albuquerque on account of the expected trains. We met three trains at the Puerco River and waited on their movements until they were safely near the Fort and then went on to Bear Spring to see if there was any aftermath of a fight left for us. We saw ten Indians with whom shots were exchanged at long range, and after trying in vain to get nearer to them scouted on to Bacon or Carrissa Spring where I met Colonel D. S. Miles coming out with company "A" of the Rifles with Captain W. L. Elliot and 1st Lieutenant W. B. Lane, and Lieutenant Hildt with "C" company of the 3d Infantry. On our way to the Fort, Colonel Miles directed the burning of the wheat fields at Bear Springs. We reached Fort Defiance on the 2d of September. The following reports of Colonel Miles to the Adjutant General of the Army and Adjutant General of the Department will best give the status on September 3d and 8th, 1858.

Head Quarters, Navajo Expedition, Fort Defiance, Sept. 3, 1858.
Colonel:

I have the honor to report in obedience to Department order, special, No. 73, present series.

I arrived at this post on yesterday afternoon in command of "A" Company Mounted Rifles. Captain Elliot and Lieutenant Lane and 59 rank and file, and "C" Company 3d Infantry, 2d Lieutenant Hildt and 65 rank and file.

On the 29th ultimo, Captain McLane, Mounted Rifles, while passing Bear Spring was attacked by a party of Navajos. He reports he killed six or eight and was wounded in the right side himself, which will disable him for the next twenty days. This fight has precipitated matters and makes war inevitable. I shall commence operations in the field on the 8th instant, with 310 rank and file, leaving at this post under Bvt. Major Brooks, 3d Infantry, a force of 120 rank and file. These Indians, it is stated, can bring from 1,500 to 2,000 warriors into the field,—report says they have assembled at Cañon de Chey. I shall march to meet them wherever they may be found. I am Sir,

Respectfully,
Your obedient servant,
D. S. Miles,
Lieutenant Colonel 3d Infantry,
Navajo Expedition.

To
Colonel S. Cooper, Adjutant General,
Washington City, D. C.

Head Quarters, Navajo Expedition, Fort Defiance, N.M., Sept. 8, 1858.
Major:

Today was completed the block house on the hill east of this fort as its defence, and the necessary preparations for taking the field. In the several conferences I have had with the Navajos, they were informed that this was the last day I would talk with them. Two days since, Sarcillo Largo came in and said he now was convinced we were in earnest and that he would then say what he never had before, that the murderer should be brought in, that the chiefs and head men were after him in every direction. Sandoval is here and expresses much concern at the near prospect of war, occasionally he would come in and say the murderer had been seen near Bear Spring, another time he was in a cave near Laguna Negrita, at another time in some other place. This morning with much parade he was led through the garrison stating in his great haste that the murderer was caught near Chausen yesterday afternoon. After a while Sarcillo Largo and a few came in to say that the murderer when captured was desperately wounded and had died last night, and requested a wagon to bring the dead body in. I told Major Brooks as Commander of the Post he should not give the wagon, but might send a mule to pack this dead body; he did so, and after some delay on the part of the Indians, the dead body was delivered to the Major, who called in the attending Surgeon and all who knew the murderer to identify him. Every individual witness the moment he saw the body pronounced it unhesitatingly an impostor—that it was not the murderer. Sarcillo Largo with many chiefs and some hundred followers are waiting my presence to go into council with them. I shall decline to do so as their attempted deception makes them unworthy of further conference, but I send word to them by Major Brooks their falsehood is exposed and I will have nothing more to say to them. The result I will state when the council adjourns.

My order No. 4, will inform you on tomorrow morning, I declare war and march against these Indians to find them where I can, for not a guide or spy with me knows the country, some were here twenty-five years ago, one about seven years since. I have a Zuni Indian as a guide who may be serviceable. In connection with this I regret to state Major Kendrick has not left at the post a single map or sketch of his explorations, nor is there any person here that has been over the country farther than Laguna Negra. My march will be like an exploration of an unknown region.

I must state my conviction that Captain McLane's fight at Bear Spring, which I deemed premature, has not in any degree hastened or advanced the attack I intended making tomorrow on these Indians, their duplicity is sufficient evidence that they never intended to deliver up the murderer, and I or no other commanding officer after he was ready (such were the threats and state in which this affair stood) could hesitate to attack at once. The regret is now that he had not done them more injury and suffered less himself.

I earnestly request that Major [Electus] Backus and command be placed in position as soon as possible, that he be ordered to march on Tunni-chey and from there to Chusen where he will halt and communicate with me as I wish to establish there or at Cañon de Chey a depot for him to operate around until all the Navajos are driven south and out of that almost impregnable fastness. If my requisitions are promptly complied with I shall be able to supply him from here with pack mules from my column without delaying its defensive operations in the neighborhood as there are many planting grounds and villages within one or two days march of this vicinity where pack mules could be spared while acting against them. I take for granted by this time Captain Lindsey with Howland's company and his company of the 8th are enroute, guarding the train, if he is not, I hope and pray you will have him dispatched at once. Every scout will require repair, men get disabled, when our horses break down. The arrival of the train, if the requisitions of Captain [John P.] Hatch, A.A.G. [Assistant Adjutant General], have been filled, has the means to keep us in order and filling up the ranks to replace disabled men, enabling me to keep constantly in the field, for I feel confident no one, two or three scouts with as many battles will end this war. The wear and tear will be great; immediate measures should be adopted to keep me supplied with reinforcements, and Quartermaster's stores, mules, horses and mule shoes, clothing, particularly shoes, and to let loose on these Indians all the surrounding tribes and inhabitants, particularly the Utahs and Mexicans, the two they seem to dread the most. I should think it advisable to send me a Battalion of five or six companies of Mexican volunteers, under Colonel St. Vrain (if possible), at the earliest date. I want also, immediately, a Mexican interpreter and guides that know the country. A guide I have on the Gila by the name of Antonia, I was told he has been a captive among the Navajos, must have known the country and speak their language, he resides at Limitar. Major Brooks has returned from the council; he delivered my message. The chiefs stoutly asserted the dead body delivered was the murderer, but very many here know to the contrary and believe they recognize the body of a Mexican captive boy who has frequently visited the garrison. The attending physician says he was shot, perhaps, *early in the morning*, and no doubt rests in my mind but they have committed the double crime to shield the real murderer.

Enclosed you will receive copies of orders Nos. 3 and 4.

I am, Major,

> Very respectfully,
> Your obedient servant,
> D. S. Miles,
> Lieutenant Colonel 3d Infantry,
> Commanding Navajo Expedition.

To
Major W. A. Nichols,
Assistant Adjutant General,
Santa Fe, N. M.

Colonel D. S. Miles had been graduated from the Military Academy in 1824 and had seen a great deal of service in Florida, Texas, the Mexican War and in New Mexico. He was at this date about fifty-four years old, nearly six feet in height, but with a considerable stoop in his shoulders. Spare in flesh, he was surprisingly vigorous in action. With grizzled hair and beard he displayed the social habits of a man of forty. He was a great talker and sometimes gave his vivid imagination a loose rein. Undaunted in the face of hardships and privations and ready to accept any responsibility, he was nevertheless a strict constructionist of orders. He came to Defiance with a reputation for being a great Indian fighter and in the previous year had been distinguished as Commander of the Gila expedition against the Gila Apaches. Assuming the direction of our military affairs with quick intelligence, he hastened forward our preparations to take the field. It occurred to some of us then that perhaps he dignified the

Indian a little too much in his intercourse, but we did not care so long as there was a chance for a campaign. When we heard that the Indians had caught and killed the murderer and were going to bring his body into the Fort, I remember there was a feeling of disappointment among the younger officers who had indulged in expectations of a great and active campaign which would realize their dreams of the glory of honorable mention in general orders from the Headquarters of the army, or mayhap, of having their names on a marble at West Point where they would contribute to the legendary lore of future generations of cadets.

The Indians played the tragedy without a fault of word or action and with a naturalness of general effect and personal expression which revealed a true conception of human nature and a careful study of the "business" of the play. The prelude was an expression of submission by the chiefs to our demand for the murderer and of an earnest determination to acquiesce in any terms that would restore our confidence and good will. Then came the reports of the chase of the murderer from point to point until the climax of his capture, after he had been desperately wounded, was reached. This effect was heightened by the formal and gloomy entrance of the chiefs with the tidings that the murderer had died of his wounds thus preventing them the satisfaction of delivering him to us alive. Then interest was sustained by the arrival of messengers reporting the approach of the chiefs with the dead body. We all went out on the parade grounds and saw the body unbound from the pack mule and laid on the ground—still and limp. It was a finely formed man a little above thirty years old. A coarse cotton cloth was wound about his loins and his long hair hung in disordered locks over his neck and shoulders. There was a large bullet hole but slightly stained with blood through the arch above the left eye. The face was otherwise undisfigured and calm. The recumbent figure with the loin covering, the long hair and the suggestion of blood, surrounded with sinister Hebraic faces, brought to my mind a quick unspeakable hint of a similar scene which has been recalled by the Christian world on every Good Friday throughout eighteen centuries. This innocent creature had been sacrificed to save the Navajo nation from the punishment of war. He must have known his fate for at least an instant—when he saw the gun aimed at his head. His sacrifice was useless.

When we had recovered from the momentary shock of this sudden and appalling tragedy, the chiefs had fled and the opportunity for a quick and merited retribution was gone forever. The instant the brutal deception was revealed we should have seized the chiefs and held them in the guard house until all our demands were complied with and two murderers had been hanged. Yet there was an afterthought—long after—that might tend to soften the hard and hideous character of the tragedy. These Indians, with long extended but undying heredity, knew and practiced no other rule or method of balancing accounts between individuals or nations except the Levitical law—"Eye for eye and a tooth for a tooth"—and may have considered that the offering up of a fresh dead Indian ought to balance our account of a dead Negro. And the astuteness which they exhibited in the attempted deception showed them equal even to discrimination with regard to rank and station, that the killing of their slave should stand against the murder of our slave.

All negotiations were now at an end and our preparations, which had not been suspended since Colonel Miles' arrival, were very nearly completed for our first expedition. We had "A", "F" and "I" Companies of the Rifles, three companies of Infantry and some Mexican spies and guides under Don Blas Lucero, an aggregate of 430. To those of us who had never served with more than one company in the field this seemed quite an army. Orders had flown from Headquarters since the 3d, and No. 4, which had been issued on the 4th of September, consisted of four letter cap pages of instructions how to march, fight and camp, and covered all the exigencies of the expedition day and night. The Army of the Potomac, even in its youth, did not require so voluminous an order to move it. But while our force for the field was a mere fragment—310 men—the known strength of the enemy of 1,500 to 2,000 warriors that we were liable to meet, and the numerous and varied perils and difficulties we must certainly encounter made these instructions and admonitions eminently proper. With five small companies we were going into a region which even the bad lands of Dakota do not equal in roughness and difficulties, an undertaking in the like of which thirty years later it was thought necessary to employ as many regiments.

The practice of packing, with the training of pack-mules, was our chief occupation for a few hours each day. The most convenient pack for an officer was made with empty champagne baskets covered with strong tent canvas cut in one piece and strongly sewed on so that when complete the pair would have the character of saddlebags which when laid across the pack saddle would bring the baskets squarely on the sides of the mule so that above and between them the roll of blankets and camp outfit could be securely placed. The number and variety of things that could be got into a pack was marvellous. The Mexicans were the most dexterous packers.

They were likewise the most merciless. All the contrary and combined ways of a mule were familiar to them and they would tackle the wildest kicker with a swift directness and complete success that confounded the mule and amazed us. When wars are all over what will be done with the mule?

Colonel Miles had ordered me to give an exhibition drill of my company in Indian fighting and the other mounted companies to witness it and to adopt it. It proved satisfactory then and afterward. Indians no longer came near the Post, but they could often be seen hovering about at a distance and doubtless the keen eyes of their lookouts upon the heights in the vicinity were constantly upon us. Major Brooks and 2d Lieutenant Dickinson with Company "G" 3d Indantry, filled up to a hundred men, were to remain at the Fort as a garrison. From our spies we learned that the Navajos had said that the Canyon de Chelly could not be taken from squaws and that they would collect their people there if they failed else-where, and defy us. Therefore it was determined to make the Canyon our first objective point. On the eighth the Indians diverted themselves with firing at our pickets around the Fort, but this afforded our men some excellent practice at long range and satisfied two or three Indians of the danger of such diversion. The following is copy of order No. 4, viz:

Headquarters, Navajo Expedition, Fort Defiance, N.M., Sept. 4, 1858
Order)
No. 4)
    1.   The campaign we are about commencing against a numerous, wily foe, requires of the troops the utmost vigilance to prevent surprise or avoid ambus-cade. On every occasion the troops must be ready to attack or resist one, with prompt obedience to the orders given without hesitation, with daring, and with the utmost coolness. The following rules and order of march are published for the government of all and will be read to each company that every soldier may per-fectly understand what is required of him to perform. A strict compliance will be exacted.
    2.   The order of march will be as follows; Captain Lucero, guides and spies in advance, followed by two companies of Mounted Rifles, the two infantry companies, the pack mules, servants and led horses and beef cattle, the rear guard to be a mounted company. Each mounted company to alternate daily, the infan-try companies will do the same. The pack-mules will follow the infantry com-panies in the same order of march as the companies, two mules to be led by one soldier and each company train to be under the superintendence of a noncommis-sioned officer, the senior noncommissioned officer of the train to have charge of the whole to see the mules are kept closed, in case of attack to resist, if a battle ensues to corral and slowly follow the direction of the troops.

3.   In case there is an attack in front the guides and spies will hold to their position, the leading mounted company will deploy to the right, the second mounted company to the left, and the two infantry companies will advance and deploy, the commander of the rear infantry company will detach a noncommissioned officer and ten men to hold the front of the packs, the rear mounted company to act as a reserve and the commander to give general directions to the pack train. Should there be an attack in the rear the reverse of this disposition will be made, the troops will countermarch, the front now rear mounted company will be the reserve. Should a battle occur officers commanding companies must hold their companies in order not losing their organization and under perfect control companies in line of march must not depart from it at every attack in front or near by small squads of the enemy but await orders. Nor will the mounted troops chase single or small parties of Indians. When engaged, officers must be careful not to fire where there is a possibility of wounding our own men. There will be no firing on the line of march except at an enemy, without permission or knowledge of the commanding officer. The encampments will be as far as practicable in the same order as that of march, each company having company guards to herd their horses and mules and to guard at night when picketted. There will be an officer of the day and general guard detailed daily to mount at retreat, for *piquetts* for the camp the number to be ordered according to circumstances. The relief of three to be placed together at one post occasionally to walk but mostly to lie concealed and to be moved after dark from the position taken first. This guard will be considered relieved after daylight in the morning and will join their companies, all fires or candles in tents will be extinguished after dark nor re-lit until after daylight.

4.   If there is an attack or an alarm at night the companies will form under arms, the companies attacked will vigorously repel it, the balance of the companies remain fast to await orders. Should the alarm be from stampede of the horses and mules, part of the infantry companies and the whole of the mounted companies will secure them, always having their arms in hand.

5.   No bugle will be sounded on the march except from Headquarters when it will be immediately answered. In battle the utmost attention must be observed to the bugle signals. The usual signals in camp will be given by word of mouth.

6.   At retreat a minute inspection of arms and ammunition will be made by every company commander.

7.   One hour and a half will be allowed from reveille to the general when all will march a signal or sound will be given at the proper time for the mules to be brought in to be packed. Horses will graze to the last moment before saddling.

8.   During the march a halt will be made every hour when all men straggling will close up.

9.   The Captains of mounted companies will each detail one intelligent, well-mounted private to report to the commanding officer at the commencement of the daily march (the same one will be preferred). These men may be used in transmitting verbal orders. A bugler from the second mounted company in line

will also report to the commanding officer at the same time. The infantry commanders will detail as a pioneer party for Headquarters, two men each from their companies: they will not be subject to company duty except in battle.

10.   Officers commanding companies are requested to march with and encamp near them.

11.   During the continuance of battle, plunder will not be permitted; after its close, horses and sheep will be collected, the latter to be preserved; of the former to select the best and most serviceable, the balance to be shot. In passing corn and wheat fields the troops are permitted to use as much of either as they want.

12.   Officers commanding mounted companies will make their men dismount in ascending or descending steep hills or ravines.

13.   As there might be a probability of companies being separated temporarily from their packs, officers commanding companies will be careful to see at the commencement of the daily march that one day's ration cooked is in their men's haversacks.

By order of Lieutenant Colonel D. S. Miles,
Thomas W. Walker, 2d Lieutenant, 3d Infantry,
Adjutant Expedition.

9

Canyon de Chelly

September 8, 1858. From this date onward events crowded on each other in rapid succession. Offensive operations began. The Indians under apprehension of active hostilities had withdrawn their flocks and herds to a distance of forty or fifty miles from the Post in every direction and with their system of signals could keep themselves informed of the strength and direction of all our movements and remove their animals to more remote and inaccessible regions if necessary. They were at home at all points; they had the freedom of birds in all their movements. Their only impedimenta were their flocks and their women and children. The women and children guided by signals would drive their animals a day or two in advance of any expedition we might make. Our impedimenta were the pack mules. We could move no great distance without them. Occasionally we left them in charge of the Infantry while the Mounted Riflemen made a dash of two or three days, but under the most favorable conditions the packs would interfere with our freedom of action.

Captain W. L. Elliot, being senior officer of the Rifles on duty, had command of the three companies "A", "I" and "F", the company commanders being 1st Lieutenant and Brevet Captain J. P. Hatch, 1st Lieutenant W. B. Lane and 2d Lieutenant W. W. Averell. 1st Lieutenant W. D. Whipple and 2d Lieutenant J. McL. Hildt commanded the two Infantry companies. The Staff of Colonel Miles was 2d Lieutenant T. W. Walker, 3d Infantry, Acting Assistant Adjutant General, and Assistant Surgeon J. C. McKee. Captain Elliot camped with me on the night of the 8th in the first frost of the season. Frost and loose horses disturbed our rest

177

during the night, but the sun rose brightly on the morning of the 9th and we were all packed and ready to move by 8:30. After our grizzly old chief had delivered his final exhortation to the pack-mule train, we set out under the guidance of a Zuni Indian.

Our first day's march was not an inspiring success. The guides led us about twelve miles northwest from the western mouth of Canyon Bonita by a circuitous route to what was known as Ewell's Camp where we found ourselves within about forty-five minutes ride of the Fort. During the day distant horsemen could occasionally be seen disappearing at points from our observation, but no resistance to our progress was anywhere offered. Our campground was full of such enormous gopher holes that we feared some of our animals would come to the grief of broken legs. After dark the Zuni guide and two Mexican spies set out to discover something of the enemy. The Zuni discovered nothing that we did not already know and the Mexicans lost their horses. The pickets awakened the camp two or three times by firing at prowling Indians. Without fires or lights and with these occasional disturbances our rest was very much broken.

At 6:30 on the 10th we were on the march into a mountainous country heavily timbered with pine and some oak. After crossing a rocky ravine we passed through five or six miles of a beautiful forest of pines growing on gentle slopes with here and there grassy glades. About 9 o'clock, while halting for our pack train to close up, Don Blas Lucero came back with a Navajo who had just been taken prisoner. Colonel Miles ascertained from him that the dead Indian that the Navajos had brought into the Fort as the body of the murderer was a slave that they had killed to deceive us. In addition to this, and which was of greater interest to us, he said that the Navajos were expecting us at Canyon de Chelly. In the middle of the afternoon our little army emerged from the forest upon a large plain where the surface was generally whitened with gypsum but with some grass occurring on scattered areas. Here we encamped far enough away from cover to be safe from any but long-range fire. About 5 o'clock an Indian rode upon the summit of a little eminence half a mile off and stood as immovable as an equestrian statue, observing us at his leisure. Four sharp shooters tried to hit him without success. We were not annoyed by picket firing during the ensuing night. It was my turn for rear guard duty on the 11th and I soon found that patience and pack mules do not travel the same road.

A march of seven miles brought us to the head of a ravine through which we descended to some small cornfields and huts where fires were still burning in their front. Indians had evidently but just left the place in great haste. One buck was overtaken with a shot which killed him. Our course had been due west about twelve miles. Turning to the northward on a deep, well worn, dry trail which ran through a thick growth of piñon, two miles brought us out upon the verge of a broad, elevated landscape of solid rock with only a stunted shrub here and there to emphasize the complete desolation—no life, no thoroughfare, except for birds of long flight. Its general level as far as the eye could reach was broken by rough ledges and jagged projecting masses. We came presently near the brink of a frightful abyss forty miles long and two hundred and fifty yards wide. Its bottom we could not yet see.

This was the wonderful Canyon de Chelly into which no white man had ever penetrated. Its sides were vertical, but sometimes broken by fissures and rifts in the red sandstone. Its general course was from east to west. We were informed of but three entrances, one at the head, another at its mouth and a third by a side canyon which broke out of the main chasm seventeen miles above the mouth. We had been guided to the last point. There were quite a number of scattered Indians to be seen mounted or sure-footed, fleet horses, to the right and left of our column, and signal smokes were rising in every direction from point to point. In the side canyon, through which we were about to descend into de Chelly, the action of the elements since the mountains were brought forth had broken off fragments from the edges and sides which had formed a rough ramp at the base. The Infantry picked their way down the crest of this precipitous and rugged debris, followed by the Rifles in single file leading their horses. It was a slow, painful and often perilous path and the most difficult part of the undertaking was getting the pack mules down. The rear guard waited two hours upon the slow and laborious motions of the column, meanwhile standing off the Indians who were gathering with increasing boldness about the entrance. With our rifles it was easy to keep them at a distance in the open, but so soon as we were lost to their sight by our descent they were emboldened to prowl along the edges and fire down upon us. Some of our best shots, with finger on the trigger and eye on the brink above, made them shy by killing one and wounding some others. It was found at once that our men were not at such a disadvantage as we at first glance had apprehended they might be. They were in the shadows below with very little relief to bring them into clear view as targets, while an Indian on the edge above could be distinctly seen from below against the clear sky. We had reason to believe also that a bullet fired upward was not deflected by different densities of the air so readily as when fired downward. Our casualties in the side canyon were limited to the animals which were injured by falling, only one mule being shot. There were places in the descent where the declivity was 45° and crevices through which some of the pack mules could not pass without rearrangement of their loads. As we went down and down, sliding and tumbling, the temperature fell slightly, although 1st Lieutenant Lane of the Rifles remarked later on in the main canyon amid the spattering of bullets from above that it was a "D—d hot place."

When at last we had reached the bottom of the main canyon, we found ourselves a thousand feet below the general surface. The width was not uniform but averaged 250 yards at this point. Where the course of the canyon was parallel with the planes of fracture in the rock, the walls were vertical and straight, but where its direction was at an angle with the fracture, the sides were broken into gothic or fantastic shapes. A shallow stream called the "Rio de Chelly" of slightly brakish water from five to ten yards wide ran westward toward the San Juan. Near the junction of the side canyon, which we had descended, with de Chelly, the bottom ground was comparatively extensive, and from its center arose a column of red sandstone the circumference of whose base was over a hundred yards and its top on a level with the summit of the canyon walls. We pleased our chief by naming it "Miles Column."

The leading companies of Rifles turned to the left and dashed down the canyon several miles, killing one Indian and capturing an old subchief with two squaws and some children, while the Infantry and rear guard followed rapidly, subjected to a desultory fire from the Indians who had gathered along the southern edge above us. By keeping near the wall on our left, the Indians above had difficulty in getting vertical shots without exposing themselves to the view of our sharp shooters. There were but few places where a front or rear fire could be delivered and they were well covered by our alert marksmen. The tumult of voices of men and mules, the prolonged reverberations from side to side which made every shot seem a volley, the strange gigantic shapes of the towering rocks, the lowering gloom of the profound depths, the keen sense of discovery at every step, and the business and diversions of a strife for life of riflemen—all these things, I say, made up an uncommon, almost unearthly scene, the intense sensations of which after nearly forty years remain still fresh in my memory. The Indians in the canyon made no stand but fled before the Riflemen. The frequent angles in its course prevented long-range firing.

Night fell upon our command while we were yet several miles from the mouth of the canyon. We must camp within it and the Indians were now gathering and increasing their annoyance. The height of the sides had been gradually lessening as we advanced toward its mouth which weakened our cover without increasing the enemy's exposure. Fortunately for our chances of rest with the comfort of whole skins, it occurred to someone to utilize the old Indian prisoner. It was ascertained from him that his son was a young chief of the savages on the rocks above, and by direction of Colonel Miles he called out to his son that if our camp was fired upon during the night he, the father, would be hanged in the morning.

We were agreeably surprised to find green corn and ripe peaches growing in the vicinity of our camp. There were excavations high up in the cliffs which it was supposed had at some remote period in the past been used as dwellings, but they were inaccessible to our inspection. There were also some ancient inscriptions. The impression upon us in that camp at night was like that of a colossal open grave. Looking out of the gloomy shadows below, there was no vision except a starry belt of heavens above. It was a situation to bring a man and his senses mighty close together. If awfulness be a desirable functional characteristic of a prison, combined with health and comfort, the Canyon de Chelly would of itself furnish the highest and deepest ideal for such an institution.

We were not troubled during the night but soon after starting in the morning the annoyance of bullets whistling overhead and spatting the rocks unpleasantly near us began. The precipices on either hand had now run down to a height not exceeding two or three hundred feet and had become irregular and broken, affording the enemy some cover, but luckily at one place it was of such a character as to afford one of our infantry companies, Whipple's, an opportunity to climb to the summit, where it kept pace with the command in the canyon and covered its march to the mouth from which we emerged about 10 A.M. on the 12th of September. Not far away from the canyon we went into bivouac near some cornfields belonging to Nah-kish-lah-nee who soon displayed a flag of truce upon an eminence not far away. The Adjutant, Lieutenant Walker, and our interpreter went out to it and received the chief's message, which was that he wanted to know why we were there eating up his corn as the murderer was not there and he wanted peace. Colonel Miles returned the answer that we had no talk for anyone until the murderer was brought in.

From the captives it had been learned that over the hills about twelve miles south there were lakes and large herds and flocks and many Indians. At 12 o'clock that night it was ordered that Captain Elliott go with the Mounted Rifles to scout the region indicated. Lieutenant Lane awakened me when they were nearly ready, and we were soon in the saddle and on our way to the rendezvous which was an old stone house half a mile from camp. So soon as "A" and "I" companies had joined mine we set out with a Navajo prisoner for a guide and with the Mexican spies. It was a clear, starlight night but we traveled very slowly on account of the ignorance of the guide and the indistinctness of the trail which was very tortuous and hilly. At 3 A.M. the spies went ahead while we waited. They did not return 'til day was breaking, and after three hours hard riding until after sunrise, we came to a great plain where in several directions mounted Indians could be seen riding rapidly in small circles which is one of their modes of telegraphing. Some sixty Indians could be seen gathered upon a little hill in the distance who fled at our approach, and with the utmost effort we could only capture 5,000 sheep and goats which we drove to Laguna Colorado where we met Colonel Miles with the remainder of the command. The Colonel had released two squaws and three children in the morning as they encumbered our march. Then we proceeded in a broiling sun to recross a range of sand hills to some fine cornfields but where there was no water except what was found by digging holes.

During our slow march with the drove of sheep and goats, a considerable number of mounted Indians threatened us on both flanks; and as we were too tired to pay much attention to them, they became emboldened and would dash down more closely and fire at us. There were two well-mounted braves who became particularly saucy. Having got tired of their capers, I directed Sergeant Cosgrove of my company, who was the best rifleshot in the whole command and rode a good "quarter horse," and Corporal Mayhew, who was also an expert shot and well-mounted, to see what they could do with the two Indians. They were both light riders and good hunters. Drifting outward from the right flank almost imperceptibly and with an appearance of careless fatigue, they drew nearer and nearer to the two Indians and farther away from the flank. But after a while the Indians observed their movement and began to edge away. The Sergeant and the Corporal in an instant were going at a quarter-racing gait and rapidly closed the distance between them and the Indians. For over half a mile they ran and had got within a hundred yards of the Indians when Cosgrove went like a shot off his horse, which the Corporal held, and down on his knee. There was a little puff of smoke and one of the Indians tumbled before the sound of the shot reached us. The Sergeant brought in the Indian's horse and traps.

Many Indians hovered around camp at night, and we set our pickets with care and arranged our dispositions in case of attack. About 3 A.M. we were awakened by cries of distress. The Indians had crept up on the pickets and fired arrows into them, mortally wounding one soldier and seriously wounding three others. We assembled at the points agreed upon for defence, and I went to the tent of Captain Elliott, commanding the Rifles to be ready to receive and execute orders. As I approached his tent, a figure appeared dimly in the darkness at the corner of it and I heard the click made by the cocking of a gun. I called out, "Elliott," in order to warn him and a voice from the figure exclaimed, "My God! Averell is that you? I was going to shoot you thinking you were an Indian." The Captain's nerves were terribly shocked by the narrow escape he had from a serious mistake. We deployed a line around the camp, the men lying down in order to see more easily any figures against the sky, and although there was considerable firing the remainder of the night, yet we had no further casualties.

We left this place a little after 6 A.M. and traveled southeast through the most desolate, torrid region imaginable for a dozen miles—no vegetation whatever and the topography chiefly of hard, round, red sand hills. Here was a dead spot surely on the earth. We passed through a fallen forest of petrified trees, some entire and retaining the original color of their bark. Limbs broken off showed beautiful lines and colorings of agate. My company was in advance and Walker, the Adjutant, who could generally see more things than anyone else discovered a large flock of sheep with his glass a mile to the westward of our trail and I was sent to capture it. There was an appearance of a large flock on some low hills in that direction but it turned out to be an assemblage of drift or elongated boulders about the size and color of sheep and their distribution over the surface was such as to give the appearance of a grazing flock at a distance.

I had not gone far before Lieutenant Lane with a bugler followed and recalled me at the same time, telling his bugler to go to the left up to the trail and there await the closing up of the command. When my company arrived at the trail, we halted and dismounted; and the sun was so burning hot that we were glad to get under our horses to enjoy the slight relief furnished by their shade. When the column was closed up, Lane came forward and called for his bugler, Fisher, by name. But Fisher was not about. We moved on, striking a piñon forest within two or three hundred yards. This was the opening of a narrow valley which, with the low hills on either side, was thickly wooded. We had not penetrated it more than a hundred yards when we came upon the body of bugler Fisher lying upon his face dead. He was naked except his hands and feet, the gloves and socks not having been removed. These Indians never strip the extremities of the dead. He had been struck in the mouth and in the back with spears and pierced with two arrows and had made no noise. His horse, arms, saber and bugle were gone, not a vestige left. There were plenty of moccasin tracks about. We buried him near where he fell.

Whipple's and Hildt's companies of Infantry were ordered to the front and furnished flankers on the summit of the low, wooded hills to the right and left, and we moved forward again. The Infantry soon scattered large numbers of Indians concealed on the crest, doubtless with the intention of attacking us. Whipple and Hildt were two of the finest officers to have in an Indian or any other fight that I ever knew. Both tireless, cool, quick and skillful. After passing the hills we turned eastward and arrived at the upper cornfields of Pueblo Colorado about 3 P.M. With our wounded and a great flock of sheep, our progress was tedious and slow. We were learning a few Indian tricks. One was that we could not be in camp anywhere an hour, generally less time, before groups of Indians would gather upon the higher points in the vicinity to observe us. Now, the moment our camp was chosen, pickets were at once sent to such prominent points without being seen if possible and to lie concealed, making low screens with sage brush, and never to fire without being able to show blood on the ground or other competent evidence of efficient work. This after awhile enabled the savages to restrain their curiosity within reasonable limits and prevented them studying points for night attacks upon us. There was firing upon our camp all night at Pueblo Colorado but at too long range to effect any damage, and our pickets could show results the next morning.

The next day was tedious, as the Indians were gathering in larger numbers and were showing a disposition to ambush and surprise us if possible. As it was my tour as rear guard, I gave them something to think about at the start. Whenever we left camp in the daytime, although not an Indian might be visible at the time we quitted it, yet our rear guard would not be half a mile away before mounted Navajos would gather in the abandoned camp like wolves about a dead buffalo on the prairie. This morning I left ten riflemen concealed in a screen of bushes on the campground; and when the rear guard had gone half a mile from it, the usual Indian rally took place. We lingered then to see if our men would require assistance and to take back their horses to meet them. When the riflemen opened on the gathering savages, no hornet's nest ever created a quicker dispersion. One was killed and several were wounded and helped away by their flying friends.

The fortitude of a wounded Indian was astonishing. If on the ground, another Indian mounted would ride to his head and swing his horse around so that the wounded Indian could seize the horse's tail which he would involve in a hold with the end of his blanket, sometimes with a single hand, and the horseman would gallop away, dragging the disabled Indian on this blanket sledge. I have been within ten yards of such a performance upon fairly smooth ground when a fallen disabled buck by a call brought a mounted one within reach when he caught the horse's tail and an end of his blanket together in his right hand closed the blanket around his body with his left and in five seconds the horseman was away drawing the fallen man swiftly along on his back and right side.

It was a weary day of twelve hours in the saddle in an atmosphere of blinding dust raised by 5,000 sheep with whose incessant bleating our ears were worn to the point of distraction. The Navajos harassed our flanks and rear all the day long but were kept beyond arrow range by our riflemen and infantry who were constantly improving in their practice. When we reached Fort Defiance after 6 o'clock we had marched only twenty-eight miles, but they were longer and more wearying than fifty miles would have seemed without the tedious impedimenta of the sheep.

The net results of our seven days' scout, in tangible things that could be counted, were six Indians killed, two or three captured with half a dozen squaws and children, and over five thousand sheep and a few horses. The wounded, estimated upon our observations and upon a reasonable ratio to the killed, could not have been less than thirty. Per contra, our casualties had been one bugler and one Private of the Rifles killed, and one Sergeant and one Private of the Rifles and one Private of the 3d Infantry wounded. These owed their safe return to the Fort with their lives to the skill and zeal of our gallant young Surgeon, McKee. We had learned some valuable lessons in the art of hunting and fighting savages and in taking care of ourselves and animals. We had also acquired a knowledge of an important section of the enemy's country which was of great service to our later expeditions. It simply enraged the Navajo and promised to unite the fighting men of the nation in an effort of vengeance.

We found the mail from the States awaiting our return. It had arrived from Albuquerque under the escort of Captain Wiltard's company of the 8th Infantry and the precious letters which it brought, although a month old, made us forget the wily, truculent Navajos, the nightly attacks, the daily pursuit, the forbidding deserts, even the Canyon de Chelly—all these fresh and hideous memories vanished for a little while to give place to the peaceful scenes of civilized life which came to soothe and enthrall us under the magic charm of news from home.

10

Las Collittas and Laguna Negra

September 15, 1858. Three or four days rest were found necessary for shoeing horses, repairing and replenishing packs, and for general recuperation, as our available forces were not yet sufficient to have two scouting columns equipped and ready to operate alternately in the field without intermittent delays. As there was no room in the Fort for my men and horses, I camped with my company outside at a little distance but not so far away but that I could accept the daily hospitality of dinner at Captain McLane's, Major Brooks' and Lieutenant Whipple's where nearly all the officers were usually met. We revelled in the luxuries of dessicated vegetable soup, canned fish and oysters, with mountain mutton as the *pièce de résistance*. With the keen appetites which never failed us, we enjoyed the canned oysters fully as well as ever we had the fresh half-shelled ones at Baltimore.

We were gratified with the news which Captain Willard had brought that more troops had been ordered to join us, for it was plain to be seen that we had undertaken a task which would require a much larger force to perform efficiently than was now in the country. On the night of the 19th Major Brooks set forth with his company under Lieutenant Dickinson, and Hildt's of the 3d Infantry, and my company "F" of the Rifles to take a turn at the Navajos by striking them at the cornfields at the Collittas where was also a rich grazing section.

We had already learned thus early that it was hopeless to undertake to bring the Navajos to a fight without a surprise, not possible to effect in the daytime. They could communicate intelligence with such rapidity by

signals and disappear with their movable property and families so promptly and completely on the approach of danger, that if one were ready to
believe in general appearances alone he would say after a few scouts that
the country was practically uninhabited. And subsequent events proved
that the only successes we ever had against these Indians were achieved by
night marches.

We started quietly at 10:30 P.M. in a southerly direction from
Defiance and after a march of fifteen miles came to a halt within a mile of
the point where we expected to strike the enemy and waited for the dawn.
When we could see, we swept down the broad valley in fine style but saw
not an Indian. Our expectations had not been very strong, for the fertility
and importance of this place so near the Fort must have assured the
Indians of an early visitation. We bivouacked in the cornfields, to the
delight of our horses, and opened their *caches* where their green corn was
sweating in the ear unhusked, and our men fared sumptuously that day
which we idled away, for it was useless to move.

Any doubt of the presence of Indians in the country which our morning's experience might have raised was removed at night. Our camp was
selected in a convenient semicircular *rincon* in the edge of a low *mesa*, and
around the brink of this our pickets were placed where they were well
covered from hostile observation and fire and could best observe anything
approaching over the upper table land. Muskets loaded with buck and
ball were used by the pickets. At a hundred yards they would cover a considerable space, far more than that occupied by one man. The pickets were
carefully instructed not to fire without being able to show evidence of its
effectiveness in the morning. At 10 P.M. the savages opened on us at long
range without drawing the fire of the pickets, but wounded a few horses
slightly.

The inexperienced and amiable Lieutenant [William] Dickinson
afforded us a little amusement at the instance of Hildt. Dickinson was an
agreeable young gentleman who had just been appointed from civil life, as
one might know from his being so nearsighted as to be unable to distinguish persons at ten paces, which made it necessary for him to wear glasses at all times. Nothing but a dense ignorance or complete indifference to
the requirements of the service could have permitted the appointment of
such a helpless young man as an officer in a regiment on the frontier.[1] Of

---

[1]Despite Averell's description as a "helpless young man," Lt. Dickinson was breveted a major on
21 July 1861 for gallant and meritorious service in the First Battle of Manassas.

course, Hildt and myself having been engaged in a campaign of a week regarded ourselves as old Indian fighters who were not to be surprised at a little thing like a night attack on our camp. But the Indians came nearer and the bullets occasionally battered the rocks near which we were lying wrapped in our blankets. We were as anxious as it was necessary to be, but there was nothing to do unless our pickets were pressed and they had not yet opened fire. After the rocks about us had been struck with a few shots, Dickinson became uneasy and inquired of Hildt what made the peculiar noise.

"Bullets," said Hildt, "are you hit?"

"No sir," replied Dickinson, "I think not."

"Well now, you'd better be sure," remarked Hildt. "Men are sometimes struck and don't know it and are found dead afterward; better get up and shake yourself," and Dickinson actually took the advice.

The Indians finally succeeded in drawing the fire of our pickets, but when they had received it we were troubled no more that night. The next morning we found a saddled horse near by with blood on the pommel and stirrup and on the ground in several places, and a moccasin, a number of arrows and other things indicating that buck and ball had been effective. There is hardly any noise that man can produce that is more startling than gun shots fired into a camp in a still night, and yet, with reliable pickets properly armed and posted, the camp will become quite used to it and even sleep.

At 6:30 the next morning we were wending our way down the Collittas Canyon expecting a warm reception but saw only one Indian. We entered the Canyon Chenilla three hours after starting and followed its course for six miles when we struck a heavy, fresh trail of horses and sheep which we followed rapidly an hour when it was found that the canyon came to an end in another from which there was no outlet. We tried first the right hand branch for a mile and then the left, and although we could see plainly that the Indians had driven their herds and flocks through these branches, we could find no outlet. They had forced the drove over ground that was impassable to our horses and pack mules and had left blood on the jagged rocks in some places.

We returned under fire most of the way to the mouth of the Canyon which had proved an empty pocket and on reaching the Collittas Canyon tried the effect of a double on the last camp. Taking ten riflemen and Don Blas Lucero with five Mexican spies, I made a dash for the cornfields and came so near getting two Indians that they abandoned their horses, saddles and lances. We had no trouble that night and were glad to sleep after thirty-two miles of fruitless scouting.

Early on the 22d we took an easterly course and crossed the Albuquerque road about seventeen miles from Fort Defiance and then a northerly direction which led us by some fine lagunas, but without finding any Indians. Went into camp at 3 P.M., and Major Brooks with myself and some guides went carefully forward a mile and a half when we were brought to a halt by a gesture of one of the guides in advance. Stealing back toward us, he called out, "Muchos caballadas, Señores!" Dismounting, we made our way to the front availing ourselves of the screen the bushes afforded. An immense valley stretching to the northward appeared below us with cornfields, small lagunas and several small herds of horses. The slopes falling into the valley from the height on which we stood were not difficult but were long, and the distance from their foot to the nearest cornfield was not less than four miles. On the right of the valley was a mountain chain wherein our glasses revealed numerous ravines and canyons. We studied it well and returned to camp taking care to make no smoke that would reveal our presence.

At 3 A.M. we were in the saddle and got to the slopes and down them before it was light enough to see a mile away. My company with the spies and guides took a rapid gait, but the unavoidable dust we raised, and which could not be avoided at any gait, was soon seen by the enemy and at once little clouds of dust moving from many points toward the mountains showed that we were too late. Don Blas Lucero with his Mexicans made a gallant but ineffectual attempt to cut out a herd of horses two miles beyond. That we did not start earlier was due to the advice of Blas Lucero to which our fatigue rendered it easy for us to yield, and our start would have been quite early enough had not the guides delayed us nearly an hour in finding a trail down the slopes.

We remained near the ponds and cornfields until next morning enjoying the rest and forage. The Indians annoyed the Mexican camp during the night but left us free from disturbance. In the morning they appeared in considerable numbers out of rifle shot and indulged in yells and gestures which were intended to be offensive. Our men were forbidden to waste any ammunition upon them, but a few of our best marksmen put themselves in unnoticeable positions ready for use. Emboldened by our indifference, the saucy braves ventured nearer. It was a perfectly open plain without any cover away from the cornfields. We were saddled early always. When the Indians had come as close as they would, they kept their horses in constant motion to avoid our marksmen for whom they had a profound respect. A dozen riflemen quietly got ready to mount, and as many on the ground at the word let the howling savages have it. It was interesting to observe the result. Simultaneously with the flash of the rifles, every horse of the Navajos seemed to spring and plunge, a few riders seemed to lose their seats and two or three were dismounted momentarily, but the greatest number clung to their horses' necks and all scattered and fled like scared antelope with some of our mounted men in pursuit for a short distance.

They kept out of reach during the day while we were returning to the Post quite dissatisfied with the result of our five days' scout. We had added some valuable information to our knowledge of the country, had wounded a few Indians, perhaps killed two or three, and captured four horses, two saddles, two lances, and a yellow dog which followed us from the cornfields and should not be omitted of mention. Reaching the Post on the evening of the 24th, we found that the forces had been augmented by the arrival of Captain [Andrew] Lindsay with his company "H" of the Rifles who had come with Captain Elliott and Lieutenant [George L.] Willard, returning from their escort duty on the Albuquerque road.

On September 24th, the same day of the return of Major Brooks' scout to the Collittas and eastward, another scouting column started northward for Laguna Negra under the leadership of 1st Lieutenant (Brevet Captain) J. P. Hatch with "I" company of the Rifles and 1st Lieutenant W. D. Whipple with company "B" 3d Infantry. This was an important point which had not yet been threatened or visited except by myself and a small party while at the hay camp at La Joya in July. It was also a strong place, easily defended. Hatch and Whipple were the ideal men for the work of getting there. They left at 10 A.M. with 116 rank and file and a Zuni guide, and our prayers went with them for Laguna Negra was a place which, if they could reach without discovery, a fight could not be avoided by the Indians. The chances were altogether against a surprise. The barking of a dog, the error of a guide, the clank of a saber or the clatter of iron-shod hoofs in a rocky canyon—so many things could warn the savage ever on the watch.

Taking the road to La Joya, they branched off it onto the trail mapped on my visit in July; and after a march of twenty-seven miles, the toil of which was doubled by the constant strain of the care with which it was made, they struck a band of Navajos at daylight. The Indians made a few quick, frantic efforts to escape that are intuitive to surprised animals and then realized that a fight was not only imminent but on. There were two situations in which an Indian of those days could be relied on to fight —whenever you or he were cornered. Then he was dangerous. Hatch gave him no time to remover from his surprise. There was some fighting and a duel between 1st Sergeant McGrath of the Rifles and the chief of the band, who stood his ground and fought well until his last round was gone before the Sergeant downed him with a shot that disabled him. Six Indians dead on the ground and two wounded, fifty horses captured, with a lot of buffalo skins, blankets and camping traps were the results.

Toward evening the next day our anxiety at the Fort was relieved by the arrival of a Zuni Indian courier from Hatch with the news of his good success, and he with his tired command came in about dark. This was one of the most brilliant and effective blows which had been thus far delivered. The qualities of Indian savagery, pure and simple, was illustrated in the Laguna Negra fight by one of our Zunis quietly and cooly cutting off the head of a squaw to get the string of chalchihuitl about her neck without breaking the string.

We had now explored the country in three general directions with many zigzags and knew its topographical features fairly well from thirty to fifty miles. There were no flocks and herds within forty miles of the Fort in any direction, and we must go beyond that limit to find them; but it was necessary to have more troops for such extended expeditions. While reinforcements were assembling from points hundreds of miles distant, it was important to keep the savages occupied to prevent their concentration on our single line of communication one hundred and eighty miles long; therefore, during the next three days we were busily occupied in getting our troops in readiness for a longer scout, while Lieutenant Hildt was sent with his company to guard the heavy ox-train toward Albuquerque for supplies.

[11]

Chusca Valley

Our preparations were completed for a more extensive and if possible a more energetic scout than any we had yet made and the column set out on the 29th of September. It consisted of "A", "I", "H", and "F" companies of the Rifles commanded respectively by Captains Elliott, McLane and Lindsay and 2d Lieutenant Averell; companies "B" 3d Infantry and "K" 8th Infantry commanded by 1st Lieutenants William D. Whipple and Willard respectively; and Don Blas Lucero with his Mexicans making an aggregate of 293 soldiers and twenty-two guides and spies. Colonel Miles was in command and a very important and judicious change had been made in his staff by the appointment of 1st Lieutenant William B. Lane of the Rifles as Adjutant.

Lane was a long, lithe Kentuckian, physically contructed on approved bluegrass lines as to bone and muscle, but without the proneness to aggressive colloquial eloquence common to his fellow statesmen. With a good American face, deep-set earnest blue eyes, a firm mouth partly concealed by a well-trimmed beard and mustache, he made himself felt and understood with few words. He was an ideal cavalry man who was able to perform personally and efficiently everything that duty would require of a soldier and all his efforts and ideas tended to the highest fighting efficiency, which he regarded as the proper normal condition of a soldier. Colonel Miles had the energy and willingness to assume any responsibility, but needed near him a man like Lane with sound judge-

193

ment and who enjoyed the confidence of everyone, in order that misdirection and eccentricity might be prevented. The Colonel had among other singular habits that of wearing two hats at the same time, one above the other. They were of some sort of grass or straw and broad brimmed. More comfort may have been obtained by their combination than would have been enjoyed by the use of one singly, but their bizarre appearance upon his head forced a certain distinction and notice even among Indians.

We left the Fort at 7 A.M. feeling fresh and in good spirits and took an E.N.E. course up broken and irregular slopes for twelve miles and then descended through a rough and rugged country six miles farther which brought us within four miles of the lagunas and cornfields of Chusca Valley. Here Elliott and McLane were detached with their companies and twelve guides to go to the left and enter the valley at a point north of the trail we were following, and I was ordered with my company and four Mexicans to bear off to the right and enter the valley at a point south of the trail and make a converging dash with Elliott at the cornfields. When I had entered the valley and was within three miles of the lagunas near which were the cornfields, a number of Indians with a small *caballada* and a flock of sheep were descried by their dust making their way with all speed toward the mountains beyond.

Realizing that should I undertake the chase with my entire company, a number of my horses would be broken down, ten of the fleetest were ordered to the front and the remainder were directed to follow at a steady trot. With the ten I took a rapid gallop toward a point where, if reached in time, the flying herd could be intercepted. My horse "Stranger" was eager for the chase and hard to hold down to a speed which the others could keep. The ground was a fair rolling dry plain with little herbage, but now and then there were colonies of gopher holes for which we had to keep a sharp lookout, for, at our gait, to step in one of these would be the ruin of a horse and the loss of a man. My selected ten men were light riders and as well up to the business in hand as any that ever followed a trail. The Indians had fully two miles the start and in a semicircle in rear of their herd, with swinging lariats and wild whoops and yells, swept their frightened animals like a prairie fire toward the mountains. For some time they tried to drive a flock of sheep, and the distance between them and the pursuing rifles had been reduced to less than a mile before the sheep were abandoned and they went on with the horses alone. The leading horses of the *caballeros* could be seen clearly with their manes and tails leveled in the swift passing air while those in rear were blanketed with a low cloud of dust which partly hid them and the howling savages behind them from view. Soon, we noticed the mountains were nearer and the canyons opening wider. Without the sheep, the Indians were not losing distance and would escape us. Our paths converged. We had covered seven miles at a trying pace. My horse had plenty of go left but the others were about at their best. However, we must get within touch after such a run, so I called on them for their last effort; and even the horses seemed to understand that we had to get there; and we did, in time to cut nine horses out of the herd and get in a few shots at the Indians. In the final burst one of my horses fell dead and his rider was thrown several paces ahead but not seriously injured. We brought our captured horses and a thousand sheep back to the laguna near which Colonel Miles had established camp. Elliott came in about dark, driving another flock of a thousand sheep and reported having killed two Indians and wounded four. Colonel Miles in his official report said, "On the hill I was marching I could plainly witness the operations of these gallant officers and see the Indians and herds flying before them."

We enjoyed our sleep that night without disturbance. We had learned another trick of use in picketing. A mule possesses an inherent antipathy to an Indian and keener faculties for detecting his presence or approach than any other animal excepting a thoroughbred dog. The mule manifests his knowledge of the approach of an Indian by a quick and decided display of restiveness, straining at his lariat and always facing, with his long ears cocked, toward the coming Indian. In the night he discovers the Indian by both scent and sound and tests the strength of whatever holds him from running away. So our men on picket learned to fasten a mule securely in rear of their position, out of sight of the enemy, and then to watch the mule. An Indian might creep up against the wind on a picket without discovery by a man with the keenest senses, but he could not get within a hundred yards of a mule without being announced.

There was a scarcity of water in the ponds and it had been spoiled by the rush of animals into it, so that we moved camp in the morning a mile or more northward where there was a fine lake which Colonel Miles named for our Mexican chief guide, "Lake Lucero," and corn was carried, from the fields we left, upon the pack mules for the use of the animals. The horses required rest after their terrible race of the previous day.

Our Zuni guide said that to the eastward over the high mountains was a large lake where all the escaped herds of the day before would first stop for rest. The Colonel ordered a night march and Captain Lindsay to conduct it, Lieutenant Lane the Adjutant going in command of Lindsay's company "H." This was McLane's company "I" and my company "F" and Lucero with twelve guides, 126 men in all made up the detachment. We started at 10 P.M. on a night march I shall never forget. It was made mostly in single file. The trail for ten miles was a combination of spiral and zigzag mountain paths, and it was so dark that one had to keep almost in touch with the horse in front to avoid losing the way. My company being in the rear necessarily suffered from the constant extensions and contractions of the slender column which took place from the frequent delays in front. Much of the way we led our horses. We could not see the length of a horse sometimes and we were occasionally torn with bushes and projecting rocks to say nothing of our anxiety when the man in front would get out of sight and hearing after passing some difficult point. We must have passed along the brinks of precipitous places at times for loosened stones could be heard tearing through trees far below us. There would be halts now and then, and we would wait until ready to drop asleep when there would be heard a faint rustle of movement far ahead which would increase with the quickening tread of horses' feet as it approached until the horse in front would suddenly move on to keep the continuity unbroken, and so on with intermittent halts and starts where the trail was difficult. In some places, for quite a distance, the trail ran over ridges of smooth rock and was perfectly invisible to our eyes. At such points a dusky guide would remain to indicate the direction.

We did not reach the laguna until 3 o'clock in the morning, having traversed fifteen miles with an accumulation of fatigue that one would not ordinarily get in thirty miles of rough riding. We found the lake dried up and abandoned. The trail we had followed showed evidence of the recent passage of a large number of animals and we continued upon it. About daybreak we came to a deep canyon down into which the trail, nearly a mile in length, wound and twisted through crevices and down steps where a horse would have to be urged and pushed in plunges of three or four feet in depth and pulled down declivities of forty-five degrees. Horseshoes were torn off and often horses fell, but down we went.

Captain Jack Lindsay was generally considered one of the most indolent men in the regiment. His chronic attitude and occupation was a lounge with a pipe and a book. It must be a promising diversion that could draw him away from his *dolce far niente*. But here he came out strong and undertook what made even the guides tremble. The sight of a smoke and the sound of barking dogs in the valley below decided him and he gave the order to Lane who was in advance to go ahead and accompanied him. How they got down I don't know, but my company jumped, slid and fell by turns until the bottom was reached. When Lindsay and Lane were nearly down, they met three mounted Indians about to ascend the trail who immediately turned at a gallop to alarm their friends in the valley. Realizing that every chance would be lost without a sudden rush, Lindsay started on with Lane and the first dozen men who reached the bottom at a gallop after the flying Indians, leaving word for Captain McLane and myself to follow as quickly as possible. As soon as McLane's company was down, away went he at a gallop, and it seemed an age before the rear of my column reached the valley when we mounted and followed. We could hear nothing for three or four miles but could easily keep the trail as it was now broad daylight and the sight of abandoned Indian camp belongings hastily scattered along the way showed that for once we had found them unawares.

After going nearly five miles I could hear firing and that guided me, as well as a broad trail, to a canyon in which I found a lot of stock and plenty of Indians who fired upon us from the cover to which they ran. Putting my Indian drill into practice, a part of my men drove them along the hillsides and through rocky thickets while the remainder drove out a thousand sheep and ten horses. On coming out we met Lindsay with the other companies and guides with three thousand sheep and sixty horses that they had captured. In the onset Lindsay and Lane had, after a hard gallop of five miles, followed the Indians across the valley to a canyon, dashed through them and cut off their stock, but finding the Indians very numerous, they seized upon a wooded knoll in the middle of the canyon to hold it under a hot fire until assistance should arrive, sending back a small party to guide McLane to the place.

When McLane had arrived at a full gallop by fours, he dismounted his men and cleared the canyon of Indians on both sides, and the sheep and horses were collected and driven out. It was McLane's firing that guided me to the other canyon, across which the sound came, as no guides were sent back to show me the way; and it was fortunate that it so happened, else my little fight and the resultant captures would have been missed. The Indians gathered rapidly on the tops of the main canyon where it was impossible to reach them and our men were unnecessarily exposed to their fire which determined Captain Lindsay to collect and take care of what we had. One Sergeant of company "H" was shot down and two Privates of the same company were among the missing. By Captain

Lindsay's direction I deployed my company and ran it over the ridge where the missing men were last seen but could not find them. While looking for them we saw five mounted Indians coming in single file along a narrow valley behind the ridge; and giving the signal to lie down, my men awaited the word. When the Indians were opposite us at the distance of about four hundred yards, I gave the command and two of them fell out of their saddles—one dead and the other squirming.

This was Kay-a-tana's band to whom the *casus belli*, the unsurrendered murderer, belonged and Blas Lucero said they were all there. Without the surprise we should have had some trouble here. Had time been allowed them to get their flocks and herds a little out of the way and to assemble their men for the defense of the canyon, it would have been a more difficult affair. As it was, the damaged trees on the knoll, which had been held by McLane and Lane, showed that their fire had been warm. Eight Indians were known to be killed and many wounded. Their encampment and property, consisting chiefly of blankets, buffalo robes, corn, etc., such as could not be handily carried away, were burned; and four thousand sheep and seventy horses were driven away.

We marched about fifteen miles in a W.S.W. direction, very slowly with our incumbrances and suffering from want of water. At about 2 o'clock P.M. word was brought back from the advance that there were two small water holes ahead. Guards were placed around them until the men had an opportunity to get a drink, and then the horses were watered with great care to prevent their getting their feet into the holes. A tin quart cup of water failed to satisfy my thirst and the memory of it is fresher than was the water. We reached the "Point of Rocks" on the Albuquerque road before sunset and stopped for the night. There was plenty of water but little grazing, and there was little rest for us as the threatening appearance of Indians about our camp demanded the constant vigilance of the entire force. We had no pack mules with us, consequently little or no food and no shelter except that which our blankets afforded. Lane camped with me and was inspired by long suffering to look through his saddle bags when lo! he found a little package of tea which a provident and prophetic wife had put there for just such an occasion. How we did enjoy it from a tin cup! With some fresh mutton chops broiled on the end of a stick and a hard biscuit or two, we dined like lords, calling the tea as we passed it back and forth by the names of the most delicious wines we had ever tasted. We had been in the saddle about twenty hours with little to eat or drink, and we slept well in spite of night attacks, it may be believed. There was no grazing at this place; consequently, we left it before sunrise with my company in advance, and after going three miles to the Puerco stopped to graze, and again three miles farther on to allow our horses to feed on the cornfields for two hours.

Seventeen miles from Fort Defiance, Colonel Miles with the remainder of the command joined us, and we camped with Whipple and Willard to relieve us of picket duty about twelve miles from the Post, Colonel Miles going on with Elliott and his company. We followed them the next day. The results of this short campaign were the killing of ten Indians, the wounding of many, the capture of Kay-a-tana's camp material, eighty horses and 6,500 sheep. Our loss was two men killed, one Sergeant wounded and one horse killed. We found on our arrival October 2, a farther increase of our forces by the coming of 1st Lieutenant [George W.] Howland with company "C" of the Rifles with the mails from Albuquerque.

12

Navajo Vengeance

I n the scout we had just made, we approached the limit of endurance and much repairing was required. The captured flocks had become burdensome. On the 3d of October, Major Brooks with his company and Willard's of the Infantry, and Elliott's and Howland's of the Rifles were sent to drive the sheep and ponies to the Rio Grande. The pickets were now troubled nightly with great persistence by the Indians; and on this night, although there was evidence that Indians had been wounded in front of the pickets, a Sergeant in charge of one of them had been shot with an arrow. It seemed that the immense losses of herds that the Navajos had sustained had let loose their owners and their followers with desperate purposes of revenge.

My camp was about 1,500 yards south of the Fort and a little south of the Canyon Bonita. It was only a bivouac without shelter. On the 5th about noon I had been up to the Headquarters on foot and was returning to my camp. My men were lying about their fires, and the horses picketed out, grazing, about 250 yards beyond them under a guard of a Corporal and six men. When about 300 yards from my camp, my attention was attracted to the base of the wooded mountain west of my bivouac by the sight of many mounted men riding nimbly down the ravines. The low foothills intervened between the mountain and the camp of my company so that this movement could not be seen by my men, but from my position I could see behind the foothills. There seemed to be two or three hundred mounted men in a great hurry. A moment's reflection convinced me they were Indians and running toward my camp I called to the men,

"Turn out and run to your horses! Every man to his horse!" They ran swiftly and reached their horses as about two hundred Navajos came over the foothills swinging blankets and lances and whooping and yelling in the most frightful manner. They swept down over my horses and men and for a moment it seemed to me all must go. But my men holding their horses with one hand used their revolvers with the other and made quite a racket of firing. The Indians passed over like a vivid, howling wave and with them was borne away my horse "Stranger" and the horses of everyone of my noncommissioned officers, six of the best horses besides my own.

Their plan, well devised, had been to stampede the herd, which would have been a success but for my opportune notice of their approach. Had my men been obliged to lose one second in looking for their arms, their horses would have been lost anyhow, but by their having them constantly upon their persons or in their hands, they reached their horses in time. The noncommissioned officers were all paying attention to the men instead of their own horses and in firing at the Indians. The Indians had nearly passed by the time I had reached the horses. There were three Indians killed dead enough to lie still, and I saw others on the ground who escaped. One on the ground called to a mounted Indian who quickly turned and rode close by the fallen one who seized his horse's tail and twisted it and the end of his blanket in his hand, and turning himself on it the mounted Indian galloped away dragging the other along the ground.

Another band, still larger, simultaneously appeared to the eastward, coming up out of a ravine ready to assist the attacking party. My company was saddled as quickly as possible, and mounting the best horse left and followed by twenty men, I chased the Indians about six miles without my hat. An Indian riding my horse "Stranger" on bare back and with lariat twisted in his mouth would wait for us, slapping his thigh and yelling at us, until we would get within three hundred yards of him when he would get out of our reach. Sergeant Cosgrove tried to hit him with a shot from his rifle but failed. That Indian had as much reason to be happy as I had to be miserable for I felt the loss keenly and never saw "Stranger" again. The men had run to their picket pins, stood upon them and pulled their horses toward them with their lariats; and some who had attempted to hold my horse and the Sergeants' horses said that the Indians cut the lariats between their hands and the horses. The attacking party did not fight at all, their entire purpose was to stampede the horses. I was profoundly thankful that they had not succeeded as it would have been a humiliation and loss from which it would have been hard to recover.

The reports of the spies and guides and experienced Indian fighters were that, as soon as the flocks and herds had been driven to places of safety with the women and children, we would not have to look for Navajo warriors. This consideration had instigated the territorial and departmental authorities to send another column into the Navajo country under Major Electus Backus, 3d Infantry with companies "E", "G" and "R" Mounted Riflemen under Captains [Thomas] Duncan and [Robert M.] Morris, commanded by Major C. [Charles] F. Ruff, and company "D" 3d Infantry under Lieutenant [Henry B.] Schroeder; companies "B" and "I" 8th Infantry were commanded by [Isaac V. D.] Reeves and [James] Longstreet; along with them were also one officer and twenty-five men of "E" company, 8th Infantry. Doctors [William W.] Anderson and [James T.] Ghiselin were also ordered in about October 1, 1858. Our various small operations were deferred until the return of Major Brooks.

We were expecting a train from the Rio Grande with ammunition, and it was supposed to be escorted by Howland and Hildt; but after the bold attack of the Navajos on my camp so near the Fort, uneasiness was felt regarding it, and on the 8th of October, Captain Lindsay was ordered to proceed on the Albuquerque road with his company and mine and meet the train and return with it. We started rather late and marched twenty-four miles, and as it being stormy and rainy we went into camp near some cornfields but well away from cover. Our picket lines to which the horses were tied were stretched along the ground and the corn fodder brought and piled along and upon them. Our picket guards were put out about two hundred yards, and peeled rods were set up to indicate to the camp their direction in the darkness. The men occupied the ground on each side the horse lines, and Captain Lindsay and myself were sheltered under a small "A" tent outside the middle of one side and near a huge solitary rock about the size of an omnibus, which must be there yet.

About 11 o'clock at night the picket in rear of our tent fired upon some prowling Indians. My dog "Sport", always sleeping at my feet, had been growling for several minutes before, and he never failed to detect the approach of Indians at night. Notwithstanding my chidings, the dog grew more violent, and I got up and taking my revolver went out to see if all was right. I walked a little way toward the picket which was firing, stooping down so as to be able to see anything moving against the cloudy sky which was only lighter than the ground. I turned about to return, thinking it best to let the men, who were quite awake and ready, turn out and form a circle on the ground around our horses in case attack was impending. Just as I turned, bang went a gun in the bushes behind me and a burning sensation was felt in my left thigh together with a blow which almost knocked my leg from under me. I realized that I was hit and put my hands on the wound to see if the femoral artery had been cut. It bled very freely but there was no jet. Calling to the Sergeant of Company "F," I directed the night formation, and reliefs taking direction by the picket sticks went out towards the pickets to support them in case of necessity. The other pickets opened but the Indians found us so thoroughly on the alert that they desisted from further disturbance.

When all was quiet, Sergeant McQuade came to me and said, "Lieutenant, I am afraid that one of our men is hard hit."

"Why do you think so?" I asked.

"I heard that peculiar ugh! a man makes when he's badly hurt," explained the Sergeant, "when that firing was going on."

"Well Sergeant, I should not be surprised," I told him. "Bring the Hospital Steward to me."

Blankets were thrown over our little tent to prevent a light being seen, a stump of candle was lighted, and my wound was dressed as well as possible. The ball had passed entirely through the middle of the thigh inside the bone but very close to it and had carried in some shreds of my underclothing. Lindsay was in great distress and wanted to start with me for the Fort at once, but was persuaded to wait 'til morning. The pain was considerable and the blood could not be staunched. At break of day along came Howland and Hildt with their train, and I was placed in a wagon and driven to the Fort where we arrived about 6 P.M. very tired. Dr. J. C. McKee took me into his quarters.

A wound that cripples a strong, sound man is a most serious event in his life. Its effects are complex in that his mental and moral natures must yield to modifications coincident with the physical alterations that ensue. He that was self-reliant and independent must now lean on others. He could once lend his strength and now he must always borrow. A few threads in the Gobelin web of life and character are snapped, the pattern changes, contracts here, extends there and sometimes becomes awry and distorted. The most serious and immediate result is the enforced restraint. It is so hard to quit work. Other changes follow in time—some soon, others late.

For three days the Surgeon hardly left my side. The wound at the entrance and exit of the ball presented the end of a black cylinder about two inches in diameter showing the limits of the contusion. This of course extended through the thigh involving the bone on one side of the path of the ball and the femoral artery on the other. If the latter should giveaway, the most skillful surgeon could not be too near at hand to prevent a fatal result. Fortunately, a wounded man who receives proper attention does not fully realize the situation; and singularly enough while enduring the greatest suffering, like men going to assured and certain death, he will notice the most trivial things and trifling incidents with a keen and complete attention. The conduct of my dog "Sport" was curious. He would lie by my bedside and watch all that was going on with close attention and seemed to manifest an appreciation of the Surgeon's work, but at any expression of distress or pain by me would spring to his feet with an eager look of inquiry and walk about as though it would afford him great satisfaction to find the person or thing that was hurting me.

An unaccountable incident occurred while the Surgeon was making his first examination and before I had been in the garrison an hour. We were in the rear room of McKee's double cabin when the back door opened and in glided the Indian girl who had warned me of danger on the night following McLane's fight at Big Bear Spring. She threw herself on her face on the ground and remained motionless. The guards about the Fort had orders to fire on any Indian coming within range; but she, as I was soon informed, had ridden boldly in at a full gallop. The unaccountable things about the incident were, first, how she could have known I was wounded and, second, how could she have known where I had been taken. None of our people had seen her since the war began. The Indians who attacked our camp when I was wounded could have been the only ones to inform her of that, and from the high hill west of the Fort any Indian could have seen me taken from the wagon in which I was brought. However she knew these things, there she was, and it was not until after repeated assurances that I was alive and not fatally hurt that she partly raised herself and crept toward my bed. She exhibited fright and horror, and by signs and the motions that are made in shooting an arrow and firing a gun, accompanied with a hissing sound for the arrow and a *click* for the gun, she assured herself how the wound had been given. Then by motions like those made in breaking a stick, she asked if the bone was broken. Arrangements were made by Hildt by which she could enter the garrison without becoming a target for the practice of picket guards; and so, to borrow the idiom of our ancient friend J. Fenimore Cooper, the Indian maiden occasionally brought the breezy vigor of the piñon-clad mountains and the ruddy glow of savage life, unfettered by any conventionalities, into the quiet dead and alive cabin of the wounded paleface.

My friend Hildt of the 3d started a ranche for ourselves in a few days, the front room of which became quite a club room for our kind friends who were forbidden by the Surgeon to come any nearer to me. The Colonel commanding gratified me by assigning 1st Lieutenant Lane to the command of my company. There was no officer of the Rifles whom I would have preferred to him, and although he was not under the slightest obligation to do so, he would drop in and tell me all about the men and horses and what was doing every day when he was not absent on a scout.

The campaign went on, or rather, the series of scouts of four or five days duration were continued. Major Brooks with two companies of Rifles and three of Infantry fortunately found a force of one hundred Indians ready for a fight near Bacon Spring on the 10th and killed and wounded twenty-five and pursued them as long as he could find them and then made a vigorous swing through the Chusca Valley to Laguna Negra and back to the Fort. Captains Elliott and McLane struck the Navajos again for 1,500 sheep and four horses in the Chusca Valley. Major Backus was on the way to Jemez with the second column against the Navajos where he was to be joined by a hundred Ute Indians on the 15th. It was also rumored that the ladies of the garrison with confidence renewed by the increased strength of our forces had determined to rejoin us here.

On the 15th the greatest show ever seen in the Navajo country arrived. It was made up of 160 Zunis the most of them mounted and all armed and equipped in the most amazing costumes, masks of animal faces and horns and feathers on their heads and hideous shields in their hands. Our Colonel's double headgear became comparatively an unnoticeable simplicity. I could not go out to see them but Lane and others would drop in often and report some new hideousness—some uglier display of truculent savagery. These were the allies for whose services Major Brooks had negotiated by Zuni. Had their capacity for destruction commensurated with the ferocious aspect they affected to present, we could have annihilated the Navajos without employing a soldier. But alas and alack! their appearance was deceiving. They would never fight unless supported and protected by soldiers. They would maintain large fires when in camp during the night or day, the light or smoke of which could be seen for miles around, and orders were as idle as the wind. But they could steal horses. All Indians exhibited upon occasion the results of a careful culture and a perfected heredity as horse thieves. Captain Lindsay on the first night after his arrival at Fort Defiance lost a valuable horse which had been picketed near his tent for greater security in the interior of his camp, with self-confident guards all around. The lariat had been cut near the

picket pin and the horse taken out of camp without disturbing or alarming anybody. There were evidences of the work of Navajos and the manner
in which it was done pointed out by our Zuni friends next morning. The
Zunis could steal horses from Navajos. They brought us a rumor that the
Navajos were going to burn our haystacks that night and attack the Fort.
While such a thing seemed incredible, measures were taken to secure the
stacks from incendiary fires.

Next morning the daylight, the most precious thing in the world
and always waited for and greeted with joy by invalids, was yet dim in my
cabin when sounds of an unusual disturbance outside reached my ears.
There were quick bugle calls and hurrying feet. My faithful man, Peter
Kinney, ran out to ascertain the cause and soon returned with the report
that the Navajos were attacking our guards at the other end of the canyon.
I had my bed pushed alongside the front window which was opened.
Through the intervals between the quarters on the other side of the garrison, the Mounted Rifles could be seen going toward the canyon at a
gallop and a detachment of Infantry running up on the ridge on the east
side of the Fort. For sometime no one could be seen to tell me what was
the condition of affairs. Shouting voices and distant shots could be heard.
Reverberating through the canyon, rifle shots sounded like a battery. A
second quest for news by my man brought back the report that the herd
under guard of fifteen mounted Riflemen in front and ten Infantry men in
rear, which had started through Canyon Bonita toward the grazing
grounds beyond, had been attacked by the Navajos and that Lieutenant
Lane with company "F," dismounted, had started at a double-quick at the
first alarm followed by Lieutenants Willard and Hildt with their
companies of Infantry.

It was a beautiful, clear Sunday morning and the sun was soon above
the eastern ridge and flooding the grounds with a blaze of light. The same
warm glow at that very moment was falling upon countless church spires
in the east, spires that were trembling with the vibrations of church-
going bells, and freshly dressed and fragrant throngs were wending their
autumnal-tinted ways to an inspiration of music and eloquence laden with
the message "On earth peace, good will toward men." And here, out of
the wild canyon roaring with the shots and yells of war-painted devils,
soon came bronzed men with burning eyes gently bearing by my window
to the hospital the writhing forms of brave soldiers with arrows buried
deep in their bodies. The stories of the strife which followed were that the
guard of the herd had been suddenly charged by three hundred mounted

Navajos who had been concealed in ambush, that the fifteen Riflemen had performed their duty nobly, although one-third of their number were killed and wounded, and had saved all the company horses in their charge, excepting three, and the Quartermaster's herd and all the sheep and cattle, but that sixty-two mules had been lost. Lindsay, McLane and Howland had quickly passed to the front with their mounted riflemen and scoured the country for miles until the trail was lost by the scattering of the Indians. The Zunis were fortunately camped near the point of attack and took a creditable and lively part with the guard in repelling the onset. The Navajos had tried to throw one of the wounded guards on a horse, but another rifleman shot one of the Indians, wounded another badly, drove off the party engaged in the attempt, seized his wounded comrade, put him on his horse and triumphantly rode off under a cloud of arrows.

13

Pueblo Colorado

T he next day after the attack on our herds, October 18th, Colonel Miles set out with "F", "H" and "I" companies of the Rifles, "C" of the 3d Infantry, and "K" of the 8th and the Zunis, with eight days' rations, to scout in the direction of Pueblo Colorado. The principal approaches into the garrison were barricaded as we seemed liable to attack at any time.

We were three days looking anxiously for Whipple's return from escort duty on the Albuquerque road, and our nervousness was not relieved until the 21st when he arrived by way of Zuni, which direction he had taken in order to relieve the extreme distress of a party of emigrants who were on their way to California and had been broken up by a frightful disaster. They had undertaken to go by Beale's route to California but had been stopped by impassable mountains and deserts, where they suffered from want of water. But worst of all they had been attacked by the Mojaves, their men nearly all killed and their teams and cattle run off. The survivors started back toward the Rio Grande over a hundred miles distant, without shelter, destitute of food, and the cactus and mesquite soon tore the women's clothing to shreds. They became scattered and lost, and some were crazed with suffering and fright. It was meeting some of these which had taken Whipple out of his way to the rescue of all he could find. Six of them were brought to the Fort by him and others sent to Albuquerque.

How this helpless emigrant train could have been permitted by the Territorial authorities to undertake a journey over a route never before travelled by an emigrant, or anyone else except an exploring party, and with no guard nor guide excepting an illustrated Congressional Report, is beyond comprehension. For nearly three hundred miles they must have travelled under observation of Territorial officials who should have informed the government at Santa Fe of their progress and purposes. It was the highest criminal negligence to permit them to attempt to pass through a country adjacent to that in which we were carrying on a destructive war and which should have been regarded, by any consideration of the indefiniteness of boundaries, as within the theatre of hostilities. The want of common sense and the prevalence of red tape which generally afflicted the half-fledged thing called a Department or Territorial Government in those days furnish the only explanation of their atrocious stupidity.

The season was advancing and rain storms swept over the camps and our unsheltered horses. What was counted a straw floated in on the cold wind toward the last of October which showed a new set in the blast of hostilities. Juan Armijo, a Navajo who was half Mexican and wholly rascal and who had been employed as an interpreter, came in to see if we were not satisfied. The guard house became his home without any ceremony.

On the 23d of October came a welcome arrival to Fort Defiance: Major [William K.] Van Bokkelen of the Quartermaster Department, and family, Major O.[Oliver] L. Shepherd, 3d Infantry, and Lieutenants [Henry C.] McNeill and [Ira W.] Claflin of the Rifles and Dr. Ghiselin, and with them Mrs. Brooks, to join her husband. With them came also recruits for the Rifles and Infantry. Then we received a mail and newspapers from the States. The Navajo War was just getting into the newspapers and those gentlemen who were conducting it, old and young, were eager to see what the papers had as news and whether their names, if mentioned, had been spelled correctly.

Colonel Miles returned after a five days' active and widely extended scout empty-handed, with the exception of a hundred horses captured or stolen by the Zunis. But there was no peace for the wicked Navajos. Howland was immediately sent out with his company and Don Blas Lucero's Mexicans in the direction of the Collitas and returned after a day's absence with twenty-one prisoners, mostly women and children but having one valuable acquisition among them in the person of Torribio, a chief among the Navajos. Torribio had a fine son about a dozen years old whom he gave to Captain Hatch, who had his hair cut off and dressed him in a suit of clothing like a white boy. The natural Indian traits of the lad were more conspicuous in his new suit than before. The first night after being dressed he disappeared and search was made with lanterns everywhere it was thought possible for him to be, even in the wells, and at last he was found curled up with his new clothing on the warm ashes of the kitchen fireplace in an outhouse. He made a lariat of a clothesline and amused himself by lassoing Major Van Bokkelen's little children and throwing them down, nearly choking them to death, for which Lieutenant Hildt, who rescued them, boxed the little Indian's ears. A few minutes after I saw the little savage with a sharp stone the size of his fist tied in a sling, following Hildt around stealthily, and warned Hildt, who turned and caught him in time to avoid a serious injury. Captain Hatch at once got rid of his prize. Torribio and Juan were employed as guides and spies. They seemed to have no objection to help us fight their own people, for a consideration, and Torribio was at once sent out as a spy while another scouting party of four companies of rifles, "A", "F", "H" and "I," with "C" and "K" of the 3d and 8th Infantry respectively, was made ready for another scout. On the 27th of October some Navajos approached the Fort with a flag of truce asking for peace but received from the Colonel the usual reply, "No peace until the murderer is given up."

While Major Shepherd and Howland went to the Collitas to cut the corn and Major Brooks went on the road toward Albuquerque to meet a train, Lane and Whipple kindly helped me to kill time with chess, that most excellent of all instrumentalities for that purpose. The newspapers had been publishing the wonderful exhibitions of Paul Morphy and others in playing a number of games simultaneously and blindfolded, and having abundance of time—in fact all of it not required for eating and sleeping—on my hands, I undertook the blindfold game. Trying with patient friends sitting in the front room of our cabin while I was in the rear one, it was not found difficult to run from a dozen moves in the first attempt to thirty or forty, whatever number was necessary to finish a game. After a very short time the effort became easy and my friends declared I could play a stronger game blindfolded than with open eyes. Then two games at once were tried with fair success, but I do not believe that more than one should be attempted for beneficial mental exercise. The grim old Colonel would come in occasionally and play a game of picquet with me. The Colonel required management sometimes, as do most men who possess untiring energy and a liability to eccentric and ill-considered action, and the officers who were all loyal to their commander and devoted to duty relied occasionally upon me to dissuade him from some of his fanciful projects. As I had his confidence and friendship, he would generally listen to me. I wish to God I had been with him an hour on that terrible night before his surrender of Harpers Ferry in 1862.

Nineteen days after my wounding, I got on crutches made by a company carpenter and soon satisfied myself that my strength was nearly all gone, but the renewed use of my muscles led to its rapid restoration.

It was manifested in many ways that there was a growing disposition among the Navajos to sue for peace. On the 29th a tall young Navajo approached the Post very cautiously with a white flag. When brought in he proved to be a son of the old man we had captured in the Canyon de Chelly. Colonel Miles invited all the officers to the powwow which took place between him and the Indian. It was conducted through Juan and a frontier trader who was thoroughly expert in Mexican and Indian *palabres*. The Colonel sat in one corner of the room and the officers on the right and left. The Indian stood in front of the Colonel at a distance of three or four paces. He was a graceful, athletic man of 25 years, about six feet in height, with fine features, and stood erect with bowed head which he never lifted until near the close of the interview. His attitude was a natural expression of dignity and submission. No Roman orator ever wore his toga with more ease and grace than did this savage his splendid blanket. When it transpired that he was the son of our old captive, the Colonel quietly gave an order to the officer of the day to have the old man brought from the guard house, and when this was done the old Navajo stood with his old blanket folded across his breast behind his son who did not know what had happened. The old man gave no sign by eye or other feature that he knew his son was in front of him.

The son pleaded eloquently for peace for his people. He argued that the whole Navajo nation should not be held responsible for the act of the murderer, because he was a powerful man in a subtribe over which the nation could exercise no control. That his people should not be required to do something impossible to be done. That they could not punish him if they wanted to do so. That now no one could enforce the will of all the chiefs, for he had run far away to another tribe and the whole nation could not get him without a war which they could not carry on at so great a distance without leaving their own country defenceless. They had been punished unjustly and severely, many innocent men had been killed and some women had been murdered and robbed by our allies the Zunis. Their flocks and herds had been taken and many families made destitute, their cornfields destroyed, and the women and children were hiding and starving in the mountains, afraid to build a fire, afraid of the light of day. Their suffering for an offence they could not prevent nor punish had been very great. With peace they would find it hard to live through the winter, without it they would die. He himself had suffered much, his father was dead and even his body could not be found; and his father's family, now dependent on him, was shivering and hungry in the mountains. All this and more went through two tongues to reach our ears.

The Colonel was gifted with an exhuberant imagination and possessed creative ability in the direction of hyperboles, metaphors, etc., and when speaking about the Great White Father, his attributes and power, he "lifted the limit" and exalted his horn over the blessings of civilization and the operation of law. It did not occur to him to draw an illustration from the fact that thirty-six Mexicans had murdered several innocent Indian women and children under the protection of a Military Post and had gone scot free from punishment under the operation of the law in New Mexico within a few months past. When he came to the statement of his own personal and official power and said, "I will restore your father to his family,"—the words went through the interpreters and when Juan had said "family," the Indian started a step forward and said, "Oh no! no! none but the Great Spirit can do that,—" Colonel Miles said, "Turn where you stand and see!" suiting to his words an action of the hand.

The young man hestiated a moment when the words reached his ear through Juan's tongue. It did really seem he might think it a trifling with the gravity of his mission and his personal dignity, but he turned his head in an obliging way half around, stopped an instant, saw his father, and in a moment the stoicism of both was gone and they were hugging each other with exclamations and caresses which betrayed intense joy. As the young Indian turned from his father toward the Colonel again, his attitude and face were a study of battling emotions which held the spectators spellbound. Colonel Miles followed up his coup by saying he was going to permit him to take his father home with him. When this was interpreted to him we were all watching him closely. When the last word fell from the lips of Juan, the Indian's face convulsed and he eyed the Colonel a second, then sprang forward, throwing himself down at his feet and embracing his knees, cried in excited tones, "Leh! Leh!" with an action and accent which thrilled everyone present. The old man his father was also deeply agitated but maintained his self-control. I have seen

Salvini as Sampson rescuing his infirm father from the Philistines before an audience trembling with emotion, but in all the range of histrionic art handled by the masters, I have never seen that simple little scene approached in its intensity and strength of expression.[1] They departed together very happy and loaded with presents from those who had witnessed the incident.

These manifestations did not prevent Colonel Miles from setting out on the following day with "A," "F," "H" and "I" companies of the Mounted Riflemen and "C" and "K" of the 3d and 8th Infantry on a fifteen days' scout in which he met Major Backus with his column and made a second visit to the Canyon de Chelly. Major Ruff of the Rifles also joined Miles' column. The results as reported were ten Indians killed and some wounded while our loss was twenty-five horses and twenty mules.

During the absence of the column, Captain Trevitt of the 3d with his company and Major Theophilus Holmes arrived at the Post. The sad news of my friend Van Camp's death in an Indian fight in Texas came by the mail which Trevitt brought, and also the direful news of Steptoe's fight with the Klamath Indians in Oregon wherein Captain Taylor and Lieutenant Gaston were killed.[2] Major Holmes was an agreeable and entertaining old gentleman and very strong at chess. Our next meeting was during the Seven Days' Battles near Richmond in '62 when I had the fortune to give the advance of his corps a slight check with my cavalry the day before the battle at Charles City Court House.[3] Lieutenant Lane contrived some very comfortable shelters for the men by excavating square holes three feet deep of the size of a wall tent. The ground was dry and easily cut like cheese. Over this excavation a wall tent was pitched, steps cut to descend into it, and a neat little fireplace cut in the back wall over

---

[1]Tommaso Salvini (1829-1915) was an Italian-born tragedian who offered a wide repertoire in both England and the United States. His greatest role was Othello.

[2]Lieutenant Cornelius Van Camp had died with an arrow in his heart on 1 October 1858, when he and a group of Indian scouts had become cut off while pursuing a retreating band of Comanches. Lieutenant William Gaston and Capt. Oliver H. P. Taylor were killed in the action described on page 68. For further information on both actions see Utley, *Frontiersmen in Blue*, pp. 130 ff; 200.

[3]Averell is referring to the Battle of Savage's Station (June 29, 1862). A disorganized Confederate attack occurred against the Union Army which was withdrawing towards the James River. The Confederates did not launch their attack until the late afternoon by which time the Union Army had left their original positions. General Thomas J. Jackson's failure to get into position until 3 A.M. the next day probably saved the Union rear guard from a disastrous defeat. On the following day Lee's army attacked again in the Battle of Charles City Court House, more commonly known as the Battle of White Oak Swamp.

which a chimney was built outside the tent. As wood was plenty and but little required to keep the tent warm, these quarters were preferred to those built of logs. My strength had returned so that I was able to get about a little to camp and to the Sutler's store.

In a command which now amounted to above a dozen companies there was a variety of talent and there were enough men with theatrical experience to get up a theatre. A large storage building was fitted up with a stage, scenery, orchestra and seats for three or four hundred persons. Officers occupied the boxes and the veritability of these was not left in doubt for they were constructed of the empty clothing and shoe boxes slightly modified. Such plays as "The Maniac Lover" and "The Irish Tutor" with songs, dances and specialties made up the entertainment. Among the men who assumed feminine parts there was a handsome, beardless little Sergeant of McLane's company named Blackwood with a remarkably musical contralto voice. With profound secrecy the Sergeant was brought to my quarters where I prepared him for a new role and had rehearsals to be sure of him. In a proscenium clothing box my roommate Hildt, who was the only one in my confidence, and I awaited the presentation. There were generally two pieces with songs and specialties between. When the first piece had been concluded and the curtain rose on the entr'acte there appeared a good looking Navajo squaw coming down the center in perfect costume, jet black braided hair with discs and spangles, a streak of red paint where the hair was parted, red cheeks, strings of chalchihuitl and coral about the neck, the regular squaw blanket with belt, the buckskin-bound ankles and moccasins. Nothing was wanting as she came down with her pigeon-toe walk timidly toward the footlights and the orchestra struck up the "Tombigbee River." Whispered questions were asked in the audience: "What is that squaw doing there?" "Is she lost?" etc., etc.

Then she began without a flutter her song which ran:

> When your columns are rushing at the flushing of morn
> And your rifles are flashing through the tall Indian corn
> When our warriors are flying or yelling or dying
>
> You never think of the Navajo squaw.
>   Tu-i-tshan-dah, - Tu-i-tshan-dah,
> You never think of the Navajo squaw.
>
> When your bugles are sounding and you're bounding away,
> She is hieing and shying from the light of day,

See her signal smokes curling—her warriors whirling!
While you never think of the Navajo squaw.
    Tu-i-tshan-dah, - Tu-i-tshan-dah,
You never think of the Navajo squaw.

To the hills she has fled for her friends are all dead,
And her flocks to the white men are gone
There she is listening—her dark eye glistening
List! the wind to you brings her low moan,
    Tu-i-tshan-dah, - Tu-i-tshan-dah,
You never think of the Navajo squaw.

The makeup was so perfect and the pathos which little Blackwood threw into the refrain, "Tu-i-tshan-dah," which means, "Oh! woe is me," was so effective that the audience listened in silent surprise until the singer began to pigeon-toe walk up the stage and the curtain was falling when they broke out into loud applause and demanded an encore. The only apology possible for this reminiscence is its necessity to a truthful picture of our desolation at a remote and beleaguered Post.

During my leisure time, which was all that was measured by the clock, I made a bird's-eye-view sketch of the Canyon de Chelly from memory at the point where we had entered it which is given elsewhere. It was recognized by the officers who had been in the expedition. Some studies of Indians also filled the time agreeably as well as the answering of many letters which my mishaps had drawn forth from friends in the army whose sympathy was comforting.

There came in with Major Backus' column, Captains [Thomas] Duncan and [Robert M.] Morris and Lieutenants [Joseph G.] Tilford and [Herbert M.] Enos of the Rifles, and Lieutenants Schroeder, [Milton] Cogswell, [Henry M.] Lazelle and [John R.] Cooke of the Infantry, so that we had altogether over thirty officers at the Fort. Some had not met since leaving West Point as with Lazelle and myself. He was one of the most charming companions with an active, well-stored mind and a philosophical temperament. Cogswell had been one of our instructors at West Point for whom cadets had the highest regard. Captain Duncan had come across the plains with Dr. McKee, Hildt and myself a year before and we were not long in flushing game for his chief fad—hunting. As remarked before, the country around Defiance was as utterly destitute of game as the Sahara—there were even no snails there. When Duncan's company was going into camp after its arrival, the Captain shouldered the "old guide," as he called his rifle, and started forth to hunt. There were some fifteen or twenty officers in the club room at the Sutler's exchanging experiences, when in the course of an hour, Captain Duncan walked up to the door, threw down a coon he had shot, set down the "old guide," and called for a glass of ale.

After quaffing a beaker of this refreshment, he wiped his lips with satisfaction and turning toward us remarked, "You gentlemen all say there is no game about here. I believe it's because there is no hunter about here. Now I've been out with the 'old guide' not more than half an hour and have got a coon already. It's all in the hunting gentlemen, I tell you, it's all in the hunting."

Just then the tall First Sergeant, McGrath, of McLane's company came up to the door, saluted the Captain, who turning his head said, "What is it, Sergeant?"

The Sergeant replied: "If the Captain please, we would be glad to have the skin of that coon, the company brought him up from Texas and he was a great pet, and—"

The Captain interrupted, "Take it along Sergeant. Take it away," and the Sergeant picked up the dead coon and walked away.

There was a silence as deep as a grave until the Sergeant got out of hearing when about fifteen or twenty officers arose and remarked, more or less simultaneously and with increasing vehemence: "Coon!" "All in the hunting!" "Old guide!" "Coon!" "Plenty of game!" "Pet coon!" and continued to make these remarks, at the same time drawing nearer to the Captain who raised his hands in supplication and with an expression of face which might be called "hunted to death" and color symptoms of approaching apoplexy.

So soon as he could make himself heard he said, "Gentlemen, hold up now. I'll make a strict bargain with you." Silence was secured and he went on, "It is a basket of wine on me now and the same on any one of you who shall ever say coon to me again." This was considered fair and was accepted, and Weber was ordered to bring in the wine.

[14]

Peace

Behold their valiant ones shall cry without:
the messengers shall weep bitterly.

On November 16th Armijo, an influential chief, came into Fort Defiance under a flag of truce and had a long talk with Colonel Miles about peace, and these conferences continued three or four days. It was not at all improbable that the approach of the column under Major Backus toward Fort Defiance, where it arrived on the 17th of November, had convinced the Navajos of the determination of the government to destroy their nation.

Their condition was sufficiently serious to check and suppress the vengeful impulses of the most hot-headed and blood-thirsty chiefs among them. Winter was at hand. Their retreats for winter shelter were untenable. They had been despoiled greatly of food and flocks, hence came the cry of their people for peace. Sarcillo Largo and all the principal chiefs came in on the 20th and sued for peace. On that day a truce of thirty days was granted to the Navajos on condition that they bring in all captives and that they elect one chief whose authority should extend over the whole nation and that all subchiefs should obey him. And that they surrender the murderer as soon as they could catch him.

Reports were required of every officer who had ever had a separate command for even ten minutes, and now those who had left stations and their wives elsewhere in the territory began to beat the bars of restraint and show anxiety to get away. My friend Lane was the first to escape on

219

the 21st of November with Major [Cary H.] Fry the Paymaster. Lane had received intelligence sometime before that a daughter had begun life at Fort Stanton while her father was running the chances of ending his own among the Navajos, and then he would often comb his mustache and express his belief, with certain emphatic embellishments, that he would never see that daughter until she was grown up and married. So Lane was entrusted with despatches to the Headquarters of the Department.

At the end of the month, 1st Lieutenant Gordon Granger arrived in a snow storm. Granger was a strong character, unconventional to the limit of patience sometimes, but generous, brave and tender hearted. If there was any place where angels were reported as fearing to tread, Granger was bound to hunt it up and stalk over it with jingling spurs and clanking sabre. One time, years before, when the country was first occupied, it was a legend that in Socorro there was a blood-thirsty Don, who insulted officers of the army whenever they came in town and that it was dangerous to encounter him, and that Granger going in one day with an orderly met the desperado. Granger was an excellent shot at birds and his orderly carried his shot gun loaded with buck and ball. The Mexican bully took especial pains to attract Granger's attention while making some terribly offensive remarks about *Los Gringos*. Granger could speak Mexican fluently and approaching the Greaser spat in his face whereupon he was challenged to immediate combat.

"All right," said Granger. "You'll not have long to wait." The Mexican wore a gay sash or scarf about his waist and Granger told him, "I will cut that sash of yours in two."

The matter was arranged and settled right then and there on the plaza. Granger having the choice named shotguns. The Mexican took his distance when his weapon had been brought, and when the word was given, Granger cut the sash in two with buck and ball at the first fire— and the Mexican also.

On the evening of December 7 there was a symposium in our quarters and pretty much all the officers of the garrison were there. We had stories and songs and a collation. I could get about very well on crutches and had occasion to go to the back door to order something from the kitchen in rear. In opening it with my left hand I let go of my crutch a moment and unwittingly lifted it from the floor by the hold under the arm, and at the next step my weight came upon my leg and the thigh bone snapped like a clay pipestem and I fell. Lieutenant John Cooke who stood nearest me was the last person, except my man Peter Kinney, that I remember seeing until next day. The hurt of the wound had been great, but the pain of the compound oblique fracture was greater than I could bear, and the Surgeons and attendants had great trouble with me during the night. Anderson, Ghiselin and McKee were all personal friends and, fortunately for me, the most skilful surgeons. After five days sleepless torture with an inclined plane machine, McKee went into a carpenter's shop and made a special straight splint reaching from my foot up under my arm, and I fell asleep while it was being applied. Now in order to prevent any movement, the end of the splint which projected beyond my foot was tied to the bed post at the foot of the bed on the left and for ten days I was not permitted to turn or move.

At noon one day during this time, my attendant had gone to dinner after heaping some fresh wood on the fire. In a short time the fat piñon sticks all ablaze rolled off the fire onto the floor. The chimney was built of sticks and plastered upon the inside with mud. The sticks of the chimney took fire which quickly mounted to the ceiling of dry piñon vegas laid side by side, and under these it rapidly spread and the whole room over-head was aflame. I could not move and had no knife in reach with which my fastenings could be cut. A pitcher of water and a glass was within reach, and I made ineffectual attempts at first to extinguish the fire by throwing water from the glass. Then finding it impossible to release my foot, I covered myself as well as possible with a blanket and tucked in the sheets as far as I could reach. Of course I had exhausted myself in unheard calls for help. In a few minutes fire began to fall all over the room and on my bed, and the thick black smoke descending threatened suffocation. Then I wetted my handkerchief in the water and spread it over my face and waited with the hope that the fire would find its way out of the cabin and be noticed before I should perish. It seemed a long while, and it was becoming scorching hot and difficult to breathe, when there came a violent rush through the front room and into mine and the bed was picked up and carried out with me upon it. So ended a disagreeable experience. I was removed to the quarters of my friend, Captain J. P. Hatch.

News soon arrived that Colonel Bonneville, the Department Commander, was on his way to Fort Defiance, and Captain Gordon Granger left on the 18th of December to meet him and escort him to the Post. He arrived on the 21st with the Indian Agent, Collins. Colonel Miles nor any other officer was invited to attend the council of Bonneville and the Agent with the Navajo Chiefs, and Colonel Miles and his command were ignored out of existence when in a general order issued on the 25th by the Department Commander announcing the conclusion of a treaty of peace, the principal officers commended were those who had been performing staff duty at Santa Fe during the War.

On Christmas day, very appropriately, the announcement of the restoration of peace and good will was made. Presents were given to the Indians, and the relaxation of the strain of keeping a hostile attitude was very agreeable to all. The dispersion of the troops immediately began, "F" and "I" of the Rifles going to Fort Craig, "A" to Stanton, "C" to Filmore, "E" to Berguin and "G" and "H" to Union. The snow was now about four feet deep and the weather bitterly cold. There was a sadness felt at the departure of my friends one after another that could not be enlivened. Some of them I never saw again. The all involving and fateful Civil War wrought great changes with our relative rank and army relations, and some of us met in opposing armies. Only half-a-dozen of the whole number at Fort Defiance in '58 are now living. Dr. McKee is one of the survivors and to him under the Providence of God my restoration to health was due. And Whipple of the 3d was a light of my life in those dark days. He was one of the most accomplished and gentle comrades I ever knew in garrison life and one of the most fearless, cool, efficient and cheerful officers I ever saw in battle. Lieutenant Whipple became steadily distinguished during the Civil War by his fidelity, zeal and wisdom as an Adjutant General to prominent commanders and finally as Chief of Staff to that noblest American of them all, General George H. Thomas.

Dr. McKee's capital operations and above all his marvellous ability in the establishment and administration of immense hospitals during the Civil War are among the important matters of its medical and surgical history. Nineteen years after our parting at Fort Defiance, I went one glorious morning up on the Savannah at the Port of Spain to take breakfast with the Surgeon General of the Island of Trinidad. He showed me through his tropical garden while breakfast was preparing and gave me a glimpse of his fine library. With a sweep of his hand he said, "I could replace everything here excepting these," and he took down a volume of the Medical Records of our War and opening it at random continued, "There! see how thoroughly that case is reported, with photographs before the operation and after recovery—lower jaw carried away, tongue hanging down, lovely case, new jaw built up, complete restoration, nothing like it." I asked who was the operating surgeon and after examination he replied: "Dr. J. Cooper McKee." And sure enough it was my old friend, and I was proud of his work and fame.

Guerro, the newly elected chief, was the eloquent young Indian to whom Colonel Miles had restored his father over two months before, and he now frequently visited the Post. After making his acquaintance and giving him several small presents, I persuaded him to sell me his blanket, the same that he wore when he appeared before Colonel Miles and which, barring accidents of fire, will last through the next century. My restoration was slow, and it was fifty-three days before I could sit up. Major Backus, who had been left in command of the Fort, was in feeble health and made application for a leave of absence to go to the States to which he received a favorable response on February 2, 1859. By this time I was able to get out of doors again on my crutches, and as the weather had been for some time quite mild and clear it was determined that I should accompany the Major to the Rio Grande.

On the 8th day of February I turned my eyes for the last time on Fort Defiance, the scene of so much suffering and so many privations and trials. Weak and dependent, it wrung my heart to leave my friends Whipple, McKee and others behind, but parting with comrades endeared by the strongest ties that can bind men to each other was an ever recurring incident of army life. We had an ambulance which had been lined with blankets for the journey of 180 miles to Albuquerque, drawn by four mules, and two wagons for an escort of a Sergeant and ten men and the mail and baggage. A wide sack of two buffalo skins with the hair inside had been made for me into which I could be slipped at night and a flap at the mouth could be buttoned down over my head and face in case of extremely cold weather. The day was fine and the road tolerably good. I remember there was thin ice in the tracks of animals along the way and that my dog "Sport," who had been vainly chasing prairie dogs over a year, excited everyone by his success at last in catching one. We went eighteen miles the first day and got off early next morning, and notwithstanding the amount of snow upon the ground increased as we ascended, we made twenty-four miles to Big Bear Springs.

During the night a frightful storm of snow and rain came on and our "A" tents threatened to leave us every moment in the high wind. The Major was taken very ill. The storm increased to a tempest of blinding snow and we started on without breakfast in the morning. The Major was helpless and howling as loud as his infirmities would permit. The leading mules could not be seen by the drivers. Men were out knee deep in snow ahead to keep us in the road which could not be seen and had to be sounded and felt for. About 1 o'clock P.M. we reached Carrissa Spring but found it frozen—all solid ice. We drove ahead with mules plunging in the constantly deepening and drifting snow, the wind frequently driving us off the road. In spite of all precautions, snow was driven into the ambulance so as to cover us several inches in depth, and the cold was rendered more penetrating by the biting wind. The gallant struggle of our escort to reach the summit was over about 3 P.M. when we descended on the eastern slope four or five miles and encamped in a thick piñon wood of young trees. The men quickly cut a roadway into it and cleared a camping place piling up the brush around it to protect us from the wind and to corral the mules. The thermometer marked 20° below zero and the men drove the mules around the fires to keep them from lying down and freezing.

Poor Major Backus seemed growing hourly worse, and under the belief that he was dying, he sent his watch and other valuables in to me to take to his wife in Detroit. He was afflicted with excessive hypochondria and the Surgeon had given me a small box of pills, one of which was to be administered to quiet him in any violent attack. Our little tents adjoined and I could not help knowing the extent of his tantrums and realized that the time had arrived to use a pill. So calling my good man Kinney, I gave him the box with directions to give one to the Major, who, after a little while, became perfectly quiet and sank into a profound slumber to the great relief of the little camp. A little later I reminded my man to return me the box of pills that they might be convenient when needed again.

"Faith, Sir, and I gave them to the Major Sir!" said he.

"What, all of them?" I enquired with alarm.

"Why, yes Sir, of course, and they've done him a power of good, Sir."

Here was another kind of trouble on hand. Calling the Sergeant I told him what had happened and that to save the Major's life he must have some strong coffee made quickly and given to him and that he must be aroused and kept awake at all hazards. Snow had been melted to furnish water for men and animals.

If the mules should live through the night we could get out of this, but if they were to freeze with two helpless men to be carried fifty-eight miles to the nearest habitation, the situation would become serious. How circumstances will alter cases! A little while before, the Major's vehement plaints and goans had distressed the whole camp, and now, after two or three hours wrestle with his profound coma, we hailed with pleasure the first manifestations of returning consciousness, and when he began to resist and rave at the men at work upon him, we were delighted. Poor Kinney, who had been broken hearted with the apprehension that his mistake might kill the Major and had labored unceasingly to restore him, came into my tent and reported with tears of joy in his eyes, "Thank God Sir, the old gentleman can shware [swear] again. He's all right now Sir."

In my buffalo sack, unable to move, I had a fine opportunity to consider the contrasts presented along here in my own experience. Exactly eight months before to a day, I was riding by this spot healthy, strong and hopeful at the head of a company of gallant Riflemen—riding into the unknown. Now I was being carried out, without my company, a cripple in a sack. A hypochondriacal old Major going home to die represented the result of the highest expectation of rank and happiness there was before a young army officer anyhow in those days. But the exigencies of the present moment left little time for gloomy reflections.

The morning light revealed one mule frozen to death and all the rest trying to arrive at the same conclusion. Major Backus declared he could go no farther but must die there. However, I ordered the mules hitched up making one "spike-team" and told the Major he could probably die in the ambulance as easily as there on the ground and had the Sergeant and Kinney put him in, notwithstanding his contrary orders and protestations, and then had myself picked up and put in. Then began some of the hardest mule whipping ever seen for a few miles down the slope until we worked our way out of the deep snow and the sun came up and the wind went down and things began to brighten. We made twenty-five miles that day with mules nearly broken down but the Major improving. The day following we reached Cuvera, a small Mexican and Indian town, with the mules given out entirely. Selecting the best mules for our ambulance, on the sixth day we pushed on to sheep springs, and on the seventh day out reached Albuquerque with Major Backus able to sit up. Here were found several friends some who had preceded me from Fort Defiance.

After two or three days' rest I was taken down to Fort Craig by pleasant stages, the weather being delightful. Gordon Granger took care of me and the comforts and spaciousness of the quarters compared with those I had left at Fort Defiance, together with the sight of my company again, afforded me great satisfaction. The Sergeant who had married in Socorro brought his wife and Gregoria, the whilom Mexican captive, down to see me one afternoon, all on horseback. The girl was so grown and improved that she could not have been recognized as the little emaciated wreck I had first seen on the Arkansas. We had many visitors at Craig during the month I remained there gathering strength for the journey homeward. Major [John S.] Simonson, Colonel Reeves, Major Van Bokkelen, Major Cary H. Fry, Major [Theophilus H.] Holmes, [George B.] Cosby, Du Bois and others, whose names are no longer to be found in the Army Register. Among the travellers who stopped at the Post for rest and refreshment was the venerable Father Macheboeuf.[1] This famous Priest journeyed everywhere through the Rocky Mountains from Mexico to the British possessions alone. With his saddle mule and saddlebags he was welcome at all Military Posts and traversed with safety all Indian tribes. A learned and holy missionary, without scrip or purse, this devout peacemaker carried with him a section of the blessed kingdom to illuminate his lonely pathway.

The evening before I left for the States, the clerk of the company with his glee club serenaded me with some excellent songs, one of which was original and dedicated to me as a farewell. The contrasted conditions of my finding and leaving this man at Fort Craig is one of my little consolations. The Sergeant asked permission for the men to come across the parade ground to see me off, and the touch of their earnest eyes as they said good-bye remains in my memory. They are all gone where good soldiers finally go. The 1st Sergeant, Hugh McQuade, fell mortally wounded at the first battle of Bull Run, as a Captain in the 38th New York Volunteers; the 2d Sergeant became a 1st Lieutenant and Adjutant of a New Mexican Regiment; the 3d Sergeant, a Lieutenant Colonel in the Confederate service; and the 4th Sergeant, a Major in a Union Cavalry Regiment. The company clerk, of whom I have spoken, ascended during the war through all the commissioned grades to that of Brigadier General of volunteers.

Leaving Fort Craig for the last time March 30, 1859, my journey up the river to Albuquerque was without noteworthy incident except the meeting of officers at different points. Major McComb and Lieutenant William H. Bell at Sabinal, and George Sykes, Whistler and Freedley at Las Lamas. At Albuquerque I enjoyed for a week the hospitality of my old friend Lieutenant M. L. Davis of the 3d. While there in his quarters at

---

[1]Joseph Projectus Machebery (1812-1889) was a French Catholic priest who came to the American missions in 1839. As a missionary he preached to and worked with the Indians in Ohio, Rocky Mountain Arizona and New Mexico.

Albuquerque there was an interesting incident not often witnessed even in those days.

After dinner one evening, shots and loud voices were heard in the town and soon a noncommissioned officer of Davis' company came running in asking him to come to the company. I awaited his return an hour or more. He came back flushed and excited and explained that eight or ten American women who had been rescued from the emigrant disaster beyond Zuni and brought back to Albuquerque, had been furnished lodgings in a house engaged by the Quartermaster for that purpose and that the officers' wives and families had given them sewing and laundry work to do until their future could be provided for, and they were nice respectable wives and daughters of western farmers, that they had lived comfortably without molestation until that evening a party of Mexican toughs under the influence of *aguardiente* had forced their way into their quarters and assumed a consideration such as would be accorded to Mexican women. The American women had informed a passing soldier who ran to his company and the men had become uncontrollable. They wished to impress on the Greaser element that an American woman was sacred and to do this effectively had tied lariats about the necks of the offenders and dragged them through the streets to the corral. Then, their American blood being up, they went hunting for Greasers through the town and it was [illegible] to stop the boiling at this point that the officers had found it difficult to do.

At Santa Fe I found many old friends several of whom were met at dinner with Colonel Bonneville. The Colonel was in good spirits and his ancient French *savoir vivre* was aroused to the point of giving us experiences of his army life years before any of us were born. There were Cogswell, Roger Jones, Gibson, O'Bannon, Trevitt and Craig whom I can recall. An army wagon was modified by placing elliptical springs under the box and this was my palace car across the prairies, Zumowski's Mexican boy José attending me as far as Leavenworth.

I expected to return to the territory within a year and left my faithful dog, my little library and a collection of choice traps at Fort Craig, which I never saw again. My next visit to the country was made twenty-eight years later when the ascent of Campbell's Pass was made in a palace car. There was a town with street lamps at Big Bear Spring and a railway station on the spot where I was wounded in the night of October 8, 1859.

15

Homeward

That vague but natural restlessness which attacks people who are about to die or to make a long journey afflicted me from the moment my leave of absence was received at Santa Fe; but while awaiting the readiness and convenience of my companions for the journey, an excellent specific was found for my impatience in the social entertainments of my friends and in some interesting and absorbing contests at chess with Lieutenant Roger Jones of the Rifles, since Inspector General of the Army, who was by long odds the best player I ever met. Of twelve games I plumed myself highly on winning three. In my crippled condition the alluring fandango was of no use to me. I was fortunate in having for fellow travellers Colonel Miles and his family; Major Backus, somewhat improved in health; Major Gibson; Captain Fred Myers of the Quartermaster's Department; Captain Trevitt of the 3d Infantry; and Lieutenants William D. Whipple, 3d Infantry and William Craig, 8th Infantry. It was a curious illustration of the effects of slow promotion in those days that Major Backus, although he had been promoted to a Lieutenant Colonelcy in the last January, yet, his nine years use of the rank of Major had made the title so much a part of his name, those who knew him could not readily drop it and even when using his new title sometimes surprised themselves by using both and calling him "Colonel Major Backus."

At last we bade farewell to the ancient city of the Holy Faith and passed all the points with but momentary notice which had aroused in us such deep interest when we entered the country. Our mental vision stretched across the great plains to which we were hastening and over which our wagons would soon be rolling at the unusual speed of thirty miles a day. We noted little and remembered nothing by the way. There was but one incident that is left in my memory of the route west of the Arkansas River. At the present writing, cyclones and blizzards which destroy towns and obstruct travel have become so common an occurrence that the mention of one would not add an attraction to any story intended to be interesting; but the one I remember differed from the modern meteorological disturbance in the point of view from which it was observed. My observatory was an army wagon bounding over the prairie drawn by six runaway mules. A black, hurrying, unexpected cloud rushing from the northwest, bursting upon our train of wagons on the road in torrents of rain and hail, balls of fire ricochetting along the ground and making terrific explosions, blinding flashes of lightning, deafening thunder claps, a dozen army wagons following the lively and eccentric stampede of the frightened and uncontrollable mules which drew them, made up the incident which lasted fifteen or twenty minutes. Providentially, the storm had struck us where the prairie was smooth and the mishaps were few and trifling, but the sensations experienced were sufficiently acute to keep a man wide awake while it lasted.

At Cow Creek we committed an error which in a "tender foot" would have been pardoned but in old campaigners it merited the humiliating inconvenience which resulted. We violated the long-established maxim of the plains: "Always cross a stream before going into camp." The creek was dry, only pools of water appearing in its bed, which was about a hundred feet wide and ten to fifteen feet deep with vertical banks of hard prairie alluvium. It was late on our arrival; and as the crossing was difficult owing to the steep ways down and up the banks, we went into camp on the west side. The night was clear and pleasant, but we heard the water running in the creek before morning and at sunrise it was bank full, and we were obliged to wait during the next day and night before we were able to cross. The flood had come from the mountains hundreds of miles away where a heavy rain storm had fallen and the water was now on its return journey to the sea.

During the day of waiting there approached a spectacle which will never more be seen in this country. The head of an hegira of people from the eastward, men, women and children in and on all sorts of conveyances, wagons, carriages, buggies and carts drawn by horses, mules and cattle, bringing all manner of household goods and furniture, farming stock and implements, cows and sheep in droves, geese and chickens in coops, dogs running on the outskirts or loitering in the shade of the wagons, and now and then a cat sleeping securely on top of a bundle of bedding. Some matronly women on horseback with infants in their arms and often another young one astride behind them, younger women in riding habits and gauntlets, boys urging forward precious milch cows which made furtive efforts to graze by the wayside—this was the astonishing living stream that broke into our eastern horizon and steadily approached until it was checked by the obstacle which held us bound to our camp. Their hail was answered across the creek and a few young men swam over to see us. They were going to Pike's Peak and their destiny was to create and equip the State of Colorado to which we and our fellows had broken and blazed the way. We were returning from our work to rest awhile—some of us forever. They, the unwitting State builders, were going to replenish and subdue that mountainous region to civilization and were so eager to get on they did not want to stop at the creek. A party borrowed the box of one of our wagons which was lined with corrugated metal for boat service and with infinite labor unloaded our wagon and their own and transferred their goods across the creek, restored our box and reloaded it, by which time the waters in the creek had subsided so that a fording could be made. I remember a grandmother with her scant gray hair combed smoothly back, bravely coming over in one of the little boat loads wherein conspicuous was a kitchen safe with a tin front in which were punched figures of cornucopias. I hope it proved a good omen of comfort and plenty in the climate they were seeking.

Meantime the living flood was swollen and many acres were covered with their camps on the eastern side. Their numerous little fires and moving lanterns, the hum of voices, the mingled sounds of laughter and song—the unexpectedness of the spectacle altogether, so far out on the plains, produced in us a surprising sensation which it is impossible to forget. While it was coming, another scene was enacting behind us about a mile distant which also will never be repeated on this continent. A dozen Mexican hunters were riding swiftly around a herd of a few hundred buffalo and killing them with lances. But few escaped and the ground was soon covered with bodies from which the hides were stripped and the carcasses left to the wolves. For two or three days we met and passed detachments of the great throng of emigrants all moving steadily westward with the illumination of hope, confidence and expectation on their faces. They looked upon us with the deepest interest and liveliest curiosity and would stop us on the way, or gather about our camps, and ask numberless questions which we answered with patience and pleasure.

At our camp near the "Big Bend of the Arkansas," I had myself carried to a little camp of a single family nearby which attracted my attention. There were the stalwart father and healthy, hearty mother, both past middle life, two well-grown sturdy sons, and three daughters, early and late in their 'teens. All their effects were carried in a great covered wagon drawn by four strong horses and there were three or four saddle horses and ponies. They had turned off the well-worn trail a little distance toward the river where the grass was good and the water not far away; the men were busy looking after the animals while the girls had set up some sticks in a tripod from which a pot was hung over a fire already kindled, and the mother was seated on a chair with busy needle mending some garment. Their camp had nothing of the harmony with nature around it that a gypsy home exhibits, for the chair and other things and the manner of using them showed their brief camping experience. I met a ready welcome and we were soon acquainted briefly with each other's experiences.

They were farmers from Illinois and I refrained from making the mistake of telling them they should have remained there, but after learning their plans and the make-up of their outfit, gave them such information as I had of the country and advised them how to provide against many discomforts and dangers. Generally, it was not to look for mines that I advised them, but for land near running water where grass grew and there to establish such a home as they could and to save their corn and plant it and then those who found gold would bring it to them for their corn. The good mother called the father and boys and bade them listen to advice that would keep them together in safety and comfort and at the same time bring the gold to their hand. There were so many things I could tell them about a ranche and the application of irrigation, and the questions they desired to ask seemed so endless in number that it was difficult to leave them, and our parting was like that of friends of years instead of hours.

Leavenworth did not long detain us, and Captain Myers and Lieutenant Craig accompanied me on a steamboat down the Missouri to St. Louis. They were ideal companions for an invalid. Craig was graduated from the Academy in 1853 and had seen a good deal of frontier service. He was original and impetuous in action and sententious and pithy in conversation. In one of his scouts against Kiowas and Comanches he had astonished the Department by capturing four hundred horses and mules *with Infantry*. As Adjutant of Colonel St. Vrains' Battalion of New Mexican Volunteers in 1855, that distinguished beneficiary of the Treaty of Guadeloup Hidalgo formed a strong friendship for Craig and bestowed upon him an immense tract of land in Colorado embracing the great Las Animas Grant, the proving and perfecting of the titles to which and its settlement afterward employed the best years of Craig's life. Without any habit of or passion for gambling, he had in New Mexico the reputation of having phenomenal and invincible good luck at all games of chance, which had become so well known that a monte bank would close on his approach.

A little incident occurred on the steamboat coming down the Missouri which sustained his reputation and afforded amusement to many astonished passengers. On the deck in front of the cabin a man with what was called a "lay out" or "sweat cloth," with the aid of two or three stool-pigeons, was fleecing a crowd of forty or fifty people. We were seated near by and observing the alluring ways of the gang for some time when suddenly Craig arose and made his way through the crowd to the table and put down a half eagle which won. He left it and its winnings on the cloth for a few bets when the gambler declared the bank closed. Then Craig asked him the value of his lay out and the sharper said twenty dollars. Craig took up his money leaving twenty dollars against the outfit and offered to throw the dice for it, which was accepted, and again he won. Taking up the cloth he carefully folded the dice, boxes and counters within it, closely observed by the passengers, and then stepping to the side of the boat threw the bundle overboard and resumed his seat and the conversation as if it had been a usual and ordinary interruption.

At the old Planters' House in St. Louis I found several army friends, among them Major Longstreet as full of life and jollity as ever. No man living then, even with a prescience of the tremendous national struggle that was impending, would have dreamed that Longstreet would become a great commander upon whose word and action the most awful and mighty events of its history would depend. That was the last time I saw him before the war, a hearty, robust man overflowing with good spirits and the life of every social reunion. When next we met, years after the war, in the office of the Rebellion Records of which his own operations formed a prominent part, the strains of herculean effort and the trials of heartbreaking disaster had left deep impressions on his features no longer responsive to mirthful emotions, to which his whitening hair lent a harmonious significance.

The restful quiet of my home, happily found unbroken and surrounded with the friends of my youth yet living to express their affectionate interest, after my two years' incessant work at the cavalry school followed by a year and a half of arduous service on the frontier, was infinitely welcome. But I was a cripple and for a long time—not until the summer of 1860—could I lay aside even one of my crutches. However, a cripple, when once accustomed to the restraints of his disability, unconsciously furnishes an opportunity for the soothing influences of philosophy, and the enjoyments that would escape a sound and active man are not denied him. And if his sphere of activity be contracted, so perhaps will he be spared the memory of many little regretful mistakes of life. At my home and at the homes of old friends and at a few watering places in the country and by the seaside, which were then all accessible to people of moderate means, the seasons of 1859 and '60 passed quickly and pleasantly away.

It may be noteworthy that at that time Saratoga was a pleasant shady village with one spring—the Ocean House at Newport was the chief dependence of visitors for shelter and comfort—the "White Sulphur" and "Old Sweet" springs of Virginia and Old Point Comfort were par excellence great social resorts. All the places which now broider the Atlantic coast from Maine to Florida with extravagant and eccentric architectural creations were then undiscovered. Even Coney Island with its ephemeral population of a hundred thousand or more was then represented by one old ramshackle tavern in a clump of shade trees and a few heaps of oyster and clam shells. Bathing suits were not needed there in 1860. Avon Springs in the Genesee Valley of New York state was then a popular summering place with half a dozen spacious and comfortable hotels where fine people came from New York, Philadelphia, Baltimore, Washington and other Southern cities and from St. Louis, Chicago, Detroit, Cincinnati, Cleveland and other Western towns with their carriages and servants for reasonable recreation and good health. The modern millionaire was unknown. Anglo-mania had not yet afflicted society. There were plenty of refined and cultivated Americans to be met in our summerings. Bedizened social aggression was an impossibility.

At that time Mr. James Wadsworth, afterward General of volunteers, was living on his large estate near Geneseo and the hospitalities which his friends enjoyed in a generous country manner were pleasant and memorable. He was a brave, broad-minded, observant and vigorous country gentleman of the loftiest patriotism who gave his life to his country when he fell with his face toward the enemy on the bloody field of Spotsylvania. Two of his sons, Craig and James, were also distinguished for their active and meritorious service during the war.

When the summer of 1860 was over and gone and the friendly throngs of gentlefolk had departed on their homeward journeys, the sequestered resorts which they had enlivened with captivating and unassuming social charms had known them for the last time. Alas! Avon is now but a lonely sanitarium and all other similar resorts of that period have since been transformed into vanity-fairs or have become desolate. The *dies irae* of many time-honored institutions and social conditions was about to open the day of wrath. American society was soon to be shattered by a revolution, invaded by shoddy, and the worship of the demoralizing old god Mammon was to pervade the land. The old army was not to escape the general calamity. All its venerated customs of service and its immutable regulations, its mathematical tactics and rigid discipline, its cherished history and sacred legends, its unyielding *esprit de corps* and guiding maxims—all those attributes and characteristics which had made it the proud bulwark of the nation—the old army, I say, was to be swallowed up and diffused in an immeasurable solution of untrained humanity wherein its proportion to the other ingredients was to be as less than one to one hundred. We have seen what of it survived—what leavened the resultant mighty host.

16

Going to the War

I t is the purpose of this narrative to refer to the political conditions of the country which preceded the war only in their relations to the officers of the army. For years the controversies of the press and the debates in Congress had been watched by them with keen attention, and the growing acrimony and passion of the agitation, with recurrent outbursts of violence and bloodshed, had been regarded by them as a state of things that would be controlled or quelled in due time. The sentiment of loyalty to the flag and love for the nation was universally and unquestionably dominant in the minds and hearts of the army until the winter of 1860-61. Not until the thought of secession and disunion had become an organized threat did officers of Southern birth begin to examine their own minds and purposes. Then began the straining and tightening of the social tie, which was the strongest thing in the South. Its fibers were drawn from the strong and unique character which had become inherent and hereditary in eight generations of men sustained by the degradation of human labor. Their habits, manners, customs and modes of thought had assumed the stability and permanency of race characteristics. They had ceased to be conscious of an habitual disrespect of law and an inordinate readiness to an extravagant display of personal responsibility and, in some respects, of an arrogance illy concealed by a stilted courtliness of manner.

Fortunately for the social reputation of the South, there were numerous lofty exceptions to the common home aspects of Southern society which were made by exceptional education elsewhere, and it was from these splendid examples of a curbed, cultivated, refined and chivalrous manhood that the South was judged by the outside world. I had seen a few young men of good Southern families come to the West Point Academy who on acquaintance made one wonder how they found their way there. The social tie which bound the South together vibrated with the quick emotions of an impulsive people and was stronger than any government. It was sacredly enshrined in their hearts under the misnomer of State loyalty. The misconception of states rights and all dreams of international relations between States vanished in the smoke of the first disunion gun. Socially, the whole South was one.

Enmeshed by birth and ardent living associations within this transcendant social influence, under whatever name, an unprejudiced mind may imagine how and why many Southern officers, believing in the inherent and inalienable right and probable success of secession, yielded at last and forsook the flag of the Union—some early, many late, but early or late, the tears and anguish of most of them attested the strength of the force which broke their allegiance.

A brief consideration of the conduct of these officers, who were most nearly my contemporaries at the Academy, will afford a fair typical view of the general effect upon the army of the attempted secession of the Southern states.

In the seven classes, from 1852 to 1858 inclusive, there were graduated 289 men with a majority of whom I had personal acquaintance and all of whom I knew by name. Of this number 19 had died before the breaking out of the Civil War. Some had been killed in action with hostile Indians, and others had died of wounds, disease or accidents. Nearly all those living in 1861 took an active part in the war.

Seventy-five of them joined their fortunes with the Southern Confederacy and nearly one-third of these had lost their lives when the Confederacy expired. Ten of the seventy-five were all Northern men by birth and also by appointment, excepting three who were appointed "At Large." Twenty Southern men by birth and appointment, of the same seven classes, remained in the United States Army and all distinguished themselves by their zeal, ability and gallantry, some conspicuously by courting wounds and death in hottest battle, like [William R.] Terrill, [Benjamin] F. Davis, [William P.] Sanders and [Samuel S.] Carroll. [1]

There was at the beginning of the war an attempt made to prejudice

---

[1] Terrill was from Virginia; Davis was born in Alabama but appointed to West Point from Mississippi; Sanders was a Kentuckian; and Carroll had been born and raised in Washington, D.C.

the Northern people against West Point upon the false and senseless allegation that a national spirit of patriotism was not properly nourished at
the Military Academy. That there were twenty Southern men who were
not controlled by the powerful and ineradicable social influences of the
South renders admissable the presumption that some superior and dominating principle had been inculcated during their academic career. Had
they never come to West Point, their lot had remained with the South.
That ten Northern young men yielded to the example of esteemed officers
of rank and to the insidious fascinations of the quasi-chivalry which
diverted and deluded Southern people at the opening of the war proved
the weakness of the ten and at the same time demonstrated the strength of
the temptation which the twenty Southerners had resisted.

One hundred and ninety-two of the seven classes mentioned survived
the war; seventy-five lost their lives in the Union Army and twenty-two
in the Confederate. The abler and most highly esteemed officers of the
army who joined the Confederacy most deeply realized the appalling
gravity of the crisis and lingered to the last before announcing their
decision. All who left the service received little consideration and no
sympathy in the North, for the idea of a dismemberment of the Union
filled the Northern mind with such abhorrence that everything favoring
it, or which was even indifferent to it, was anathematized.

The North, generally contented with the economic emancipation
which had found at the Fifth Census 28,666 slaves in the North, and had
since then quietly swept slavery from every Northern state except Vermont, which had none, and had extended long and widening rifts of free
labor across western Virginia and Kentucky to Tennessee, entertained no
general desire nor purpose to accelerate the expansion of the area of free
labor and shorten the path to total abolition of slavery by the employment
of other forces than those which had already operated so steadily, successfully and peacefully. In the South, the dominant social and political
leaders had for a long time realized that in separation or secession was to
be found the only security of their social structure. As no united people
can exist without patriotic sentiment, so, when allegiance to our Union of
States had been renounced, at once a new government and a new flag received the passionate fealty of a resolute people, and Southern society was
resolved into a furious vortex into which was drawn every force available
for war. Yet be it remembered that a large majority of the officers who
went South did not go until all hope of averting separation or war had
fled, and some of them remained true to the flag after hostilities had

commenced and even fought for it until they could relinquish their commissions without jeopardizing the honor or safety of their commands.

Of several such instances, the following letter received by me from Lieutenant Richard K. Meade, Jr., of the Engineers, is an illustration. He was a most accomplished officer, an excellent scholar, and a lovable gentleman. He was a Virginian and a son of Hon. R. K. Meade, once United States Minister to Brazil. He served faithfully until the gallant Major Anderson and his command were safe and did not resign until May 1, 1861. He died in July, 1862, at Petersburgh, Virginia.

Fort Sumpter, Feb. 12, 1861.

Dear Averell:

We are still preserving the *"status quo,"* which means according to the S. C. translation, that we must wait till they have finished constructing all their batteries and bombproofs directly under the very muzzles of our guns for the purpose of attacking us. They have now constructed two batteries, (one bombproof of iron), on Morris' Island bearing on us, one at Fort Johnson, and on Sullivan's Island, besides Fort Moultrie. They have also a battery constructed behind the houses, (as we learn by report.)

I cannot give you the condition of our own works, as this letter has to run the gauntlet of the Charleston Post Office. Suffice it to say, we are *ready*. We have been for twelve days past, and are still procuring fresh meat and vegetables from the city. They are brought from the city to Fort Johnson where we receive them to avoid a collision unnecessarily. Hayne has returned from Washington with the President's refusal to give up the Fort, and we are anxiously awaiting the *next step*. We fully appreciate the extreme difficulty and delicacy of our position, but our duty points to but one course.

I can write no more at present as the boat is about to leave with the mail. Snyder is here and begs to be remembered to you.

Truly your friend,
R. K. Meade, Jr.

This letter besides revealing the upright and honorable character of Lieutenant Meade also throws a clear and bright light upon the scene so dramatically setting in Charleston harbor wherein by fortuitous but fortunate circumstances the newly fledged and impatient Southern Confederacy was led two months later to fire upon Fort Sumter and its famishing garrison of patriots, thereby lighting the torch of war, the first malignant flash of which inflamed and united the whole North.

The subsequent career of the few officers who were guilty of treacherous conduct in surrendering United States troops or property, or who were recreant to their trusts in leaving unsettled public accounts, ended in ignominious oblivion. They suffered the living death. Their names are generally omitted from the histories.

In February 1861 I was yet a 2d Lieutenant in the Regiment of Mounted Riflemen and on sick leave. I had been on crutches for eighteen months from my wound received in the campaign against the Navajo Indians in 1858, but had so far recovered as to be able to walk with a cane, and apprehending that I might be overlooked or forgotten in the preparations for the coming war, I left my home on the 25th of February for Washington to see Mr. Lincoln inaugurated and to show myself ready, in case of necessity, for any service that might be required. The public mind was distracted with the wildest apprehensions about the safety of the Capital, and even of the life of the President elect, who had arrived in Washington on the morning of the 23d, after running an alleged gauntlet of conspiring assassins on the way. Washington was crowded with people, very few of whom seemed wholly sane. Everyone was feverishly asking or imparting the latest news. Securing rooms on New York Avenue, I visited some of the principal hotels, which were thronged with excited men from every state North and South collected in groups discussing the crisis. There were no loud voices nor outcries. Intense brooding apprehension possessed all thinking men. Washington, I imagined, had a little the aspect of Herculaneum listening to the throes of Vesuvius. Very soon I met several army men one after another; and confirming the proverb of misery's love of company, we gathered together and exchanged hopes and fears. The chiefest and last lingering hope among us was that no gun would be fired and that some miraculous thing would come out of the Peace Congress or the Crittenden proposition or from some source by which the terrible strain of the situation might be relieved.

The next day several of us went, as by a common, despairing, impulsive effort for comfort, to visit the tomb of Washington. On our return I made a brief call at Fort Adams and had an interview with Lieutenant G. W. P. Custis Lee, the eldest son of Colonel Robert E. Lee. Very like his father in personal appearance and innate dignity of manner, it was an agreeable surprise to find him quite ready to speak on the supreme question which engrossed all men's minds at that moment. He exhibited the deepest emotion in stating his attitude and his last remark was, "Averell, that Arlington estate over the river is mine. I would give it in a moment and all I have on earth if the Union could be preserved in peace, but I must go with my State," and I left him leaning his elbows on the mantle-piece with his face buried in his hands, agitated with profound grief.

The inauguration was at hand and the air was charged with alarming rumors of intended efforts to prevent it and to assassinate Mr. Lincoln. On the 1st of March I called on General Scott. Never was I so impressed with the personal grandeur of any man as I was with that of the old hero on that occasion. Grand as a Colossus in repose, thoughtful as Angelo's Moses, and as calm as a lofty mountain brow towering above the storm, unworried and unwearied, his whole expression was comprised in the word *ready*. He received me graciously and after making particular inquiries about my health and strength he asked me many questions about the temper and sentiments of the Northern people as well as of the feelings and purposes of the army officers whom I had recently seen. Regarding the inauguration he said, "Mr. Lincoln will be inaugurated without any disturbance; every point is covered." I told him the object of my visit and he kindly said, "Wait a little, my young friend. We will see; there may be need of you." The visit was a consolation to me—the comforting "shadow of a great rock in a weary land."

One of my visits of obligation as well as of pleasure was to pay my respects to the wife of the President-elect at her hotel. About her were three or four young ladies, one of whom was Miss Cameron, a daughter of the Senator from Pennsylvania, but none was there who was competent to defend and protect her from the curious and intrusive crowd whose presence and talk would soon transform entertainment into bedlam.

Four years before I had witnessed the inauguration of Mr. Buchanan without anxiety and with all the exhilarating satisfaction which a moving pageant with its banners and music brings to untroubled youth. Now, as Mr. Buchanan was yielding his great office to Mr. Lincoln, the maturing experience of four years and the infirmities of a wound upon me, and with the vivid realization of impending peril to the nation oppressing my mind and heart, my emotions seemed [illegible] with every word and movement by a hair-trigger. The delivery of the inaugural address gave me the first opportunity to see and hear Mr. Lincoln at the first supreme moment of his life. He stood out, separate from the prominent and distinguished men who thronged the eastern front of the Senate chamber of the Capitol, upon the massive projecting balastrade which encloses the southern flank of the flight of steps to the portico. As he took his position with easy deliberation in front of and above a countless multitude of silent, attentive men, his tall figure in strong relief against the vast marble whiteness behind him appeared distinct, picturesque and solemn.

The intensity of the people's interest in the man and his words from the outset to end of his address was something to be felt but impossible to describe. Thrills of emotion swept over the sea of upturned faces as his mighty theme unfolded, exalted, illuminated and permeated with the ideas of an American nationality that would constitutionally defend and maintain itself. His frequent earnest emphasis, reinforced with striking attitude and forcible action, made him for the purpose of the hour seem to be American patriotism personified. It would be a most fitting memorial of that occasion if a bronze statue of Mr. Lincoln with something in it suggestive of his life and action when delivering his first inaugural could be placed on that very spot.

There are few living who can remember the rare, old, well-settled and well-occupied society of Washington in that period. The superb and graceful reign of Miss Harriet Lane in the White House had been gently and harmoniously extended and blended with during the four years which were now at an end. The retirement of Miss Lane was soon followed by the complete social wreck of the old capital. During the trying month of March 1861, when the fate of the Republic hung upon the lanyard of a loaded gun, there were several social events, in every one of which there was a risk of an ending like that of the historic ball in Belgium's capital when "sounds of revelry by night" were brought to a sudden close. There was a wedding at the Navy Yard and a grand ball at the Arsenal, which was punctuated by the disappearance of the dashing Colonel Magruder the next day across the "Long Bridge." And then the Carroll family, highly distinguished for its generations of lovely women and brave men, gave one of the last and most memorable balls of that lurid season. At all of these I met many of my comrades of the army. Among them I remember Griffin, Fitz Lee, Lomax, Ramseur, Sprigg Carroll, Frank Wheaton, Torbert, Lawrence Williams, Turnbull, Sullivan, Elderkin, Armistead and Gordon Granger.

Senator and Mrs. John J. Crittenden were then living at the National Hotel as was also Mrs. Chancellor Walworth, a friend of my cadet days. A son of Senator Crittenden was the Lieutenant Colonel of my regiment, the Rifles, and Granger and myself were made to feel quite at home in their quarters. Two or three evenings after the inauguration we were visiting them when a band of music began a serenade under the windows and a multitude of people filled the street with loud calls for the Senator which took the noble old gentleman to the window from which he delivered one of those eloquent and patriotic addresses for which he was famed. It rang throughout the country for several days afterward.

On one evening I had an interview, memorable to me, with Hon. Stephen A. Douglas at his house, which was accorded to me by the grace of his wife. Mrs. Douglas, it is remembered, had enjoyed, as Miss Ada Coutts, the national distinction of being the belle *par excellence* of Washington society. The "Little Giant," as Judge Douglas was called by his admiring friends in Illinois, sat under the warm glow of his library lamp and I listened to his brilliant conversation and pithy comments upon the situation with great pleasure. When I asked him his opinion of the results should South Carolina fire upon Fort Sumter he answered instantly, "An army of two hundred thousand men."

With my member of Congress and fellow townsman, General Robert B. Van Valkenburgh, afterward our Minister to Japan, I visited the Senate and House and met many remarkable men who seemed keyed up to the high tension of the times in their speech and action. Among the eminent men I met and admired were Governor [Solamon P.] Chase of Ohio, Secretary of the Treasury, and Governor [William H.] Seward, the Secretary of State. The reputed greatness of these two Statesmen was never diminished by the near acquaintance I afterward enjoyed.

Of the military men I met, Major Don Carlos Buell, with whom I became intimately acquainted, struck me as possessing the largest grasp of the situation and the best estimate of the military means that would be required to preserve the Nation.

Danger differentiates men as the magnet attracts and separates the particles of magnetic iron ore from the grosser materials which surround them. At this time the hazardous exposure of the White House and Treasury became glaringly notable, when, at once, a body of volunteers were quietly segregated from the panicky throng which filled Washington and assembled under General Jim Lane, a Senator of Kansas, and Captain James E. Jones of Steuben County, New York. Their proffered services as guards were accepted and they were mustered into the United States Service and furnished arms and ammunition. A young man named D. S. Gordon was Orderly Sergeant of the Guards. He was afterwards distinguished in many actions and became Colonel 6th U.S. Cavalry.

In the rough experiences of the frontier life, where "the drop" originated, many of these volunteers had learned to shoot with rapidity and precision. They were men with steady eyes and reliable nerves, like their leaders. Captain Jones, my fellow townsman, was a tall, muscular man about thirty-two years of age, with kindling gray eyes which often twinkled with the quaint humor of his anecdotes and stories, but those who ever met their rare glitter in anger never wished to refresh their remembrance of them. He came of a race of men remarkable for dauntless courage and strength upon which the pioneers confidently relied in hours of danger. The Captain bore a strong resemblance to President Lincoln in person and character. He had been in charge of a Government Land Office in Kansas during her most "bleeding" years. This original force was established in the White House and Treasury and kept ward and watch on every approach day and night. They accommodated and accustomed themselves to the surroundings daily in a curious way of their own which Captain Jones called "drills." The people who at a respectful distance entertained themselves with criticisms upon the doings of this democratic and ununiformed guard little dreamed that it could have extinguished and eliminated from the show business, any company of equal force of those pretty tactical athletes, which daily had delighted them, in much less time than would be required to count them. It would have been a rash lot of lunatics, tired of life, who had undertaken to do any unlawful thing in or about the premises they were guarding.

Southern officers began to disappear from the city and the distress of our parting was acute and trying. We are prepared for most of the agonies of life by the education of sympathetic observation or by experience, but this was a new, supreme, untried, cursed grief, for which there was no consolation except the blessed sense and privilege of doing our duty. At last came the news, like the sound of the trumpet of the last great day, on the 12th of April, and men and women came forth from their houses with halting steps, pallid faces and compressed lips, sat silent on their door steps, with clenched hands, and some with their eyes closed—*South Carolina was firing on the flag of the United States upon Fort Sumter.*

17

A Long and Perilous Ride

On the morning of the 16th of April I presented at the War Department the following letter:

Washington, D.C.,
April 16, 1861.

Colonel:

I have the honor to report myself at this place on leave of absence for the benefit of my health. My leave expires on the 12th of June next and although the restoration of strength to my wounded limb is not complete, a sense of duty to the United States Government, now that it is in danger, impels me to forego the benefits which might arise by availing myself of the unexpired time. I therefore respectfully request that I may be considered ready for duty.

I am, Colonel,
Very respectfully,
Your obedient servant,
William W. Averell,

2d Lieutenant, R. M. R.
Colonel E. D. Townsend,
Assistant Adjutant-General.

After handing in my report I went to the office of General Scott to inform him of the action I had taken, fearing the information, being of an unimportant character, might not reach him through the Adjutant-General's office and I might be overlooked and obliged to remain idle. While waiting alone a few minutes in the General's anteroom, Colonel

Robert E. Lee arrived.[1] It was the last time I ever saw him. He was wearing an officer's overcoat as the morning was quite chilly. We shook hands and exchanged some inquiries and remarks about health and the weather. I saw that he was greatly troubled. He did not stand still but kept slightly lifting one foot and then the other as if they were cold. His impassible face did not conceal an expression of keen distress. About his eyes there was an appearance of long loss of sleep. No words were needed to tell me what troubled him. Remembering my brief interview with his son, Custis Lee, it was awfully plain to me that something portentious to his life and to the country was under consideration between him and his revered chief whose confidence and affectionate regard he had enjoyed during and since the Mexican War, when he and McClellan were the trusted engineers of his glorious campaign to the Mexican capital. There was a poignant sense of peril and of bereavement in the realization of this personal crisis in the life of a man for whom I had such an unbounded admiration. When I came out from my brief audience with the General in chief, I stopped and said, "Good bye, Colonel Lee." He started, extended his hand and his voice dropped almost to a whisper as he said, "Good bye, Mr. Averell."

It is possibly not well remembered how the regular army was scattered at that crisis—the dismay of the government when the treachery of Twiggs in Texas had involved a large portion of our forces there in a disgraceful surrender and had tied up a number of fine officers with paroles under which they chafed hopelessly for months while their more fortunate comrades were winning honors and promotion on the battlefield.[2]

There was still in that section a force under Colonel W.[William] H. Emory, consisting of the First Cavalry, First Infantry and a part of a battery, which had not been involved in Twiggs' treason, nor disturbed

---

[1]Robert E. Lee was at home in Arlington on 16 April 1861. On the following day he received a message from General Scott requesting a meeting on the 18th. Before this meeting, Lee discussed the military situation with Francis P. Blair, Sr., who advised Lee the nation wanted to make him the commander of the federal armies. Lee told Blair that he had carefully considered the situation and had decided to stay with Virginia. Upon meeting with Scott, Lee immediately informed him of his decision to resign. The question remains if Scott ever formally offered the position of commanding general to Lee. For further information see Douglas S. Freeman, *R. E. Lee: A Biography*, Vol. 1, pp. 435 ff.

[2]David E. Twiggs (1790-1862), old and perhaps senile at the beginning of the Civil War, was in charge of the Department of Texas. In February 1861 he surrendered all the Union posts, forces and supplies in Texas to the force of Texas Rangers under Ben McCulloch. He was dismissed from federal service on 1 March 1861 and was appointed major general in the Confederate Army three weeks later. He commanded the district of Louisiana but died little more than a year later.

by orders from Washington up to the middle of April, but now they were dangerously isolated by the intervening turbulence of secession in Missouri and Arkansas, and the War Department, at length aroused to the necessity of prompt action, determined to make an effort to save that brigade. Neither the mails nor the telegraph could be used to carry orders in that direction, and the only safe means of communication must be through a trusty personal messenger. There were a number of active officers in Washington at that time, yet amid such confusion and uncertainty of opinions and purposes and so many astounding instances of defection, it is not surprising that the authorities hesitated in the selection of a messenger upon whose discretion and fidelity the fate of so important a portion of our very small military establishment might depend.

It was on the evening of the same day I reported for duty that I was in the lobby of "Willards" when Majors Irwin McDowell and Fitz-John Porter and Captain J. B. Fry, all of the staff in the Adjutant-General's Department, dropped in, casually as it appeared, and Captain Fry asked me to play a game of billiards. While engaged in the game, the Captain quietly asked where I lodged and requested me to go to my room when the game should be finished and he would follow me. Complying with his request I was soon joined by the three officers who then broached the object of their visit. They wished to know if I was able and willing to undertake a long journey involving an unknown amount of fatigue and danger. This was what I had been anxiously waiting for and I asked them to try me. After being assured of my physical ability, they requested me to call at the War Department; and my visitors took leave without further explanation but enjoined silence about their visit or its object.

A sense of responsibility involved in mystery is not somniferous and the night that followed was long and feverish. When morning came I lost no time in reporting at the War Department, where I was received by Major Fitz-John Porter. My papers were ready and were as follows:

> To Lieutenant William W. Averell,
> Mounted Riflemen,
> Washington City.
> Head Quarters of the Army,
> Washington, April 17, 1861.

Sir:

    You will, by the order of the General-in-Chief, proceed at once to Fort Arbuckle and deliver the accompanying letter to Colonel W. H. Emory, or the senior officer present, receive from him communications for the government and return to this city.

> I am, Sir,
> Very respectfully,
> Your obedient servant,
> E. D. Townsend,
> Assistant Adjutant-General.

This was in the handwriting of Major Porter, excepting the signature, and on the back of it was endorsed in the same hand as follows:

> Head Quarters of the Army,
> Washington, April 17, 1861.

The General-in-Chief directs the quartermaster at Fort Smith to extend every facility to Lieutenant Averell, to enable him to execute his orders with promptitude.

> (Signed) F. J. Porter,
> Assistant Adjutant-General.

I was required to read and memorize the instructions to Colonel Emory to provide for the contingency of a necessity for their destruction. They were in brief that he should assemble his command and take it, with all public property that could be transported, to Fort Leavenworth by the most secure and expeditious route.

Fort Arbuckle was three hundred miles West of Fort Smith which was in Arkansas on the border of the Indian Territory. I also received additional verbal instructions providing for such contingencies as might possibly occur in the course of my hazardous and uncertain mission. Major Porter then went over the maps with me, and as he knew the country well, gave me some valuable advice and information, besides a deal of encouragement by his kind and friendly manner.

Providing myself with a good suit of butternut clothing, my black overcoat and a slouched hat, with a common carpetbag to match the outfit, and without a "good bye" even to my brother, I left Washington at 2.45 P.M. on the 17th, took the Western train on the Baltimore and Ohio Railroad at the Relay, and reached Harpers Ferry about sunset. While the train stopped here, I saw Lieutenant Roger Jones of my regiment who commanded the detachment guarding the Arsenal. He apprehended an attack by the Virginians, and aware of the inefficiency of his force to defend the public property, had already made his arrangements to

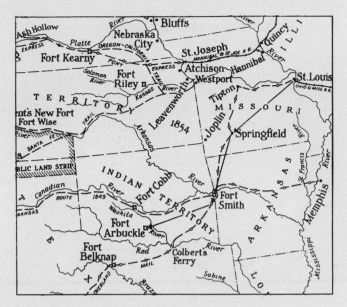

Averell's route to Fort Arbuckle.

destroy it and retire into Maryland with his command. All along the route
hence to Cincinnati and St. Louis the wildest excitement prevailed. The
railroad stations and telegraph offices were crowded with eager inquirers
for the latest news, while in every city, town and village, the rolling
drums and waving banners announced that the Nation was aroused and
arming for the great conflict. By the time I reached St. Louis the news of
the seizure of Harpers Ferry and the riot in Baltimore had added fresh fuel
to the patriotic fire of the West.[3]

Carefully avoiding all demonstrations and discussions, I left
St. Louis on the morning of the 20th and arrived in Rolla, one hundred
and fifteen miles distant, at 5 o'clock in the afternoon. At a tavern, the
office of the Southern stagecoach lines, I learned that I would be obliged
to wait over Sunday with other passengers, among whom was a prominent
Missouri judge and an embryonic rebel general. As these were times when
travellers were liable to be impertinently questioned as to the whence,

---

[3]On 19 April 1861 a Massachusetts infantry regiment and Pennsylvania militia unit was
attacked in Baltimore while transferring trains. The soldiers fired into the mob which was throwing
rocks at them. The troops managed to board the train to take them to Washington, D.C., but four
soldiers and twelve civilians had been killed.

whither and wherefore of their movements, I composed an innocent little narrative to meet the apprehended emergency: "I belonged to a strong secessionist family of St. Louis and had a sister married to one of the United States officers at Fort Smith. In view of the threatened troubles in Arkansas, I was going to escort her back home." As I knew all the officers of that Post and had acted as groomsman to one of them some years before, I took the liberty of imagining myself a brother to that estimable lady and felt so happy in the thought that I could have faced the most searching examination without flinching.

Nevertheless, I felt so awkward in my masquerade and so disturbed with the responsibility of my position that I avoided observation and conversation as much as possible, and that Sunday was the longest and most lonesome day I ever experienced. When I had eaten and slept as much as nature would bear and dawdled about the wretched premises until I became desperate, it occurred to me to ask the landlady for a book wherewith to while away the weary hours that yet remained on my hands. She stared at me some moments before she realized the meaning of so unusual a request, then, shouldering her baby, she climbed up on a chair and fumbling among the dirt and rubbish on the top of a cupboard exca-vated therefrom a ragged volume, which she gave me with the injunction to use it carefully as it was the only book they had in the house. On exam-ination of my prize I found it was an old cookery book, whose appetizing recipes might have amused the fancy of a hungry man, but I was sated in that direction and was glad to turn from the contemplation of imaginary puddings, pies, doughnuts, etc., to something which promised more congenial entertainment.

The landlady's younger sister, whose whole mind seemed to be concentrated on the arrangement of her voluminous hair, remarking my interest in the cookery book, shrewdly suspected that I might have other literary accomplishments, and therefore requested me to write a letter to her mother in St. Louis. I joyfully embraced the opportunity, and with pen in hand, listened deferentially to the amiable family twaddle which my curly-headed dictator thought proper to entertain her distant parent withal. I wrote conscientiously what I could remember of it and filled in the gaps with geography, astronomy, politics, poetry and cookery recipes *ad libitum*. I should like to have seen the old lady when she read that letter.

But the longest day must end at last, and I got off from Rolla next morning about 5 o'clock with five other passengers in the coach. There were three hundred miles of rough staging before me, and I was not so robust and tough as I would have wished. Changing at Harrisons and Waynesville, we reached Dentons at sundown, having made about fifty miles. Here we met a coach going northward filled with passengers, among whom there were three or four ladies. There was a deal of excited talk at supper but it passed without a quarrel, and we continued our route sixteen miles further to Lebanon, where I passed the night amid bed bugs and drunken secessionists.

Except the suffering from aching bones and weary limbs, I was rather pleased with my experience so far. Exhaling their alcoholic and political excitement in wild talk, boasting and profanity, people seemed to be too much occupied with themselves to scrutinize others closely, and provided a stranger acquiesced but moderately in oaths and whiskey, he was all right and might pass unquestioned.

The next night I slept on the same bed with the rebel general Rains at Springfield.[4] He kindly enlightened me on military matters for an hour or so, and confidentially imparted to me his program or scheme of the intended campaign in Missouri. His Honor, the Judge, was more inclined to joviality and at intervals entertained us with a favorite song, "Oh ain't you mighty glad you've got out of the wilderness." As I was then just going in, I didn't help with the chorus much, but I have been willing to sing it since with unction.

As Springfield I took an affectionate leave of my two friends and pursued my journey thence to Fayetteville in company with an old woman who was going to see her son tried for murder. She was a type of the frontier matron, tall, athletic and full of strong practical sense. Her stories of the vicissitudes and terrors of border life were graphic and interesting, and she was going to the trial like an old lioness to defend her whelp. For a change I occasionally sat with the driver and assisted him with the mails when we stopped at Post Offices. My officiousness got me into an embarrassment at one point. A fair postmistress, expecting a visit from her brother, mistook me for that long lost relative. I was confounded and abashed at the warmth of her greeting, assisted as she was by half a dozen boys and girls, who seized my hands and coat tails, vociferating,

[4]James E. Rains, a Tennessee district attorney, had enlisted as a private in the Eleventh Tennessee Infantry and was elected colonel of the regiment on 10 May 1861. "Judge" Rains was not promoted to brigadier general until 4 November 1862.

"How d'ye do, Uncle John?" It was with some difficulty that I checked this torrent of joy and convinced the amiable family of their mistake.

My experiences that night at Cassville were of quite a different character. At the tavern I was assigned to a room where a man had been robbed and nearly murdered the previous night. I took my pistol to bed with me and soon fell asleep, in spite of the unpleasant associations. Some time after, I was awakened by footsteps on the stair and a light flashing through the crack of the door. Cocking my pistol, I challenged the comer and was answered by the landlord, who told me that he was under the necessity of putting another man in that bed with me. That being the custom of the country I had no right to object, but under the circumstances I preferred to leave the bed entirely to the stranger, and took the floor with overcoat and blanket, where I passed the rest of the night with one eye open.

The next day our program was varied by a drunken driver, who let his team run away and smash up the stage. We were consoled by observing that the driver's head was so seriously damaged as to incapacitate him from further mischief for the time. Meanwhile, I procured a lumber wagon to which (with aid of a farmer) I attached the fractious horses, loaded up the mails, the old woman and the drunken driver and thus drove into Bentonville. After a dinner of bacon and greens, and change of driver and vehicle, we continued our journey to Fayetteville.

On starting, I took a complacent inventory of my personality— slouched hat, unshaved and weather-beaten face, butternut suit and pantaloons stuffed into the tops of my dirty boots—and I thought I might travel all over Arkansas without exciting a suspicion against citizenship. However, when within four or five miles of Fayetteville, just as we were entering a wood, we saw four mounted men approaching. As they met us, one rode in front of our leaders and brought them to a sudden stop, while the others closed around the coach, with pistol holsters suggestively unbuttoned. I was up with the driver and the foremost man checked his horse opposite me on the left side of the coach and addressed me sharply, "Look here, stranger. Where di you come from, where are you goin', and what's your business?" In my overcoat pocket I held my pistol, cocked, in my right hand, and was well aware there must be no knuckling in such an encounter, so I answered, as one "to the manner born," "I am from any place else but this, and I am going to get out of here as soon as I can, and if anybody happens to ask you what my business is you can tell him you don't know." The driver, who did not seem altogether at his ease, here gave a knowing wink and said emphatically, "All right here on the goose." This was quite satisfactory, and the ruffians drew off and suffered us to resume our journey.

When we were out of sight, the driver puffed like a man who has been holding his breath. "Stranger," said he, "I just thought you was gone up. They were four of the cussedest cutthroats in Arkansas, and the man you talked with was head devil. He has killed a half-a-dozen men about here and is a terror to the whole region." This circumstance impressed me with the futility of my defensive preparations, for my only firearm was the insignificant pocket five-shooter that I had carried across the plains and in my first Indian fight.

At length we entered Fayetteville, and I recognized the court house where the murder trials were going on by the dirty crowd in front and the number of horses tied to the fence enclosing it. We drew up in front of the Prendergrast Hotel and were received by a great big lazy landlord in his shirt sleeves and carrying a fat baby in his arms. Our old woman passenger at once began inquiring about her son. The crowd from the barroom gathered about the driver to ask the news, to scrutinize the waybill and cross-question him about his passengers. Being faint from exhaustion, I at once secured a room and threw myself upon the bed to rest. Presently, the landlord brought in a drink I had ordered and with a serious countenance said, "This is a pretty hard set around here and they are a little curious about you and I advise you to come out and show yourself. They are mighty jealous about strangers, and if you don't come out and satisfy them in some way, there may be trouble." "But," said he as he turned to go out, "be careful and on your guard, I don't want any trouble here."

The old woman in the stage had given me the cheering information that a fruit-tree agent from New York State had recently been robbed near here and had barely escaped from the country with his life. I recognized the necessity of the case, got up at once and walked confidently into the barroom. At a glance it was easy to pick out the leading fellow of the crowd, leaning with his back against the bar and talking to the others gathered around. Walking up to him I said respectfully: "I am going to take a drink, Sir, will you and your friends join me?" He and three or four of the most villainous looking blackguards accepted the invitation; and after drinking, cigars were distributed at my direction, and while lighting them I managed to ask the leading brigand to step outside with me that I wanted to see him. He willingly led the way and we wandered out of earshot, when I told him confidentially I was on my way to Fort Smith on important business for the cause and wanted to know what was doing there. He told me of all that had taken any shape and what was hoped and expected. I informed him that on my return, in a week or ten days, I wished to see him again as I should have, probably, something of importance to say, but now I was tired and wanted rest and requested him to keep his own counsel and not let me be disturbed. The result of this conversation could be observed afterward quite markedly. Lowering faces cleared up and in the approving glances of the encircling crowd I soon saw that I had been tacitly invested with the "freedom of the city" and took advantage of the privilege to gain a long and undisturbed rest of which I stood greatly in need. This was gratefully prolonged until the middle of the following day when the stagecoach started for Fort Smith.

The first ten or twelve miles of the journey were beguiled by the agreeable conversation of a gentleman who had just been tried for murder and the jury had brought in a verdict of "not guilty" that morning. He entertained me with a particular narration of the incidents of the killing of a man, with which his memory had been refreshened by the recent trial, and with other similar incidents of life and death in Arkansas in which he had figured, up to this time, as the survivor.

At Evansville I met the astonishing intelligence that Fort Smith had been captured by a force of secessionists, eight hundred strong, which had come from Little Rock under the command of Colonel Borland.[5] I could not credit the rumor and kept on my way over Boston mountain. The night was pitchy dark and the road like a rugged stairway of rocks. When near the foot on the southern side, we met a coach filled with passengers coming from Fort Smith. Among them were several ladies, whom I thought might be the wives of some of our officers, but it was too dark to recognize faces and I dared not hazard a direct inquiry. They confirmed the news I had heard at Evansville. Fort Smith was now occupied by Colonel Borland with a thousand men. Four days before, the United States garrison under Major [Samuel D.] Sturgis had been summoned to surrender. This they declined, but not being prepared for a siege, had evacuated the post and marched westward.

---

[5]Solon Borland (1808-1864), a physician, was a United States senator from Arkansas from 1848 to 1853. He also served in the Mexican War, and was appointed United States minister to Nicaragua and the other Central American republics in 1853 and 1854. At the beginning of the Civil War, Borland raised a brigade and seized Fort Smith. Later, he raised the Third Arkansas Cavalry and served as its colonel. He was promoted to brigadier general and died near Houston, Texas.

For me, the outlook was dismal enough, and to complicate the situation it commenced raining heavily, slopping the roads and swelling the streams into torrents. While they were changing the mails at Van Buren, I found a livery stable and tried to hire a horse and vehicle to carry me to Telequa, hoping thus to avoid Fort Smith and reach Fort Arbuckle or some western point were I might find troops of Colonel Emory's command. But all the horse-flesh in that region had been impressed by the insurrectionary forces and I concluded to go on to Fort Smith and to trust to fortune. Crossing the Arkansas River on the ferry boat, we reached Fort Smith about nine o'clock on the morning of the 27th of April.

Here was a scene to be remembered rather than described. Just imagine a mob of wild Southern borderers boiling over with political frenzy and unlimited whiskey. Mounted men riding madly, secession flags flying and women displaying them from windows. Horsemen galloped alongside the stage and peered into the windows, making inquiries or shouting like bedlamites. That I got to the St. Charles Hotel without being shot or hanged seemed like a special providence. About the tavern, men were yelling, women screeching and fluttering secession flags, and everybody in a sublime state of glorification except the landlord, whose countenance was downcast and full of trouble. Remarking this and feeling that I must trust someone—at least partially—I told mine host aside that I would like to see him privately a few minutes. He indicated a back door and told me to go out to the stables and he would shortly join me.

When he came I asked him about the situation. He frankly declared it was d—d bad, the country would be ruined and so would he. His son, the hostler and all his available male help had joined the army, leaving him alone to care for everything including seven horses, and he expected them to be impressed every moment. They drank everything he had and paid as suited them, and he didn't know at what moment the crazy devils might clean him out entirely. Regarding the Fort, he informed me that Major [Alexander] Montgomery, the Quartermaster, (who should have furnished me transportation from this point) was then a prisoner in the Fort. At all hazards, some means must be found of following our troops. So I frankly stated my purpose to reach Major Sturgis' command and offered to buy one of his horses for that purpose. He became alarmed and endeavored to dissuade me from the attempt. The streams were up, the bridges had been burned, and I would certainly be arrested and perhaps worse; but he finally agreed to let me have a horse, saddle and bridle for my gold hunting watch and twenty dollars in cash. I had my choice of seven and selected a well-made, bright bay horse, whose only defect was one blind eye. The trade concluded, my steed was made ready, and the landlord agreed to take care of my carpet bag and slyly brought out my black overcoat, in the pocket of which he concealed a small bottle of whiskey as a friendly remembrance.

On account of my wound I had not been in the saddle for over two years and now began to entertain some misgivings in regard to my horsemanship. On mounting I presently became aware that my horse had never been broken to the saddle, and he began shying, rearing and plunging in a manner which drew all eyes upon us and our eccentric performances. I forgot my lame leg and everything else in rage and despair at finding myself thus exhibited before the public, whose observation and inquisition I was most anxious to avoid. After a gymnastic contest of ten or fifteen minutes duration, my colt took the bit in his teeth and started off at full run. Borland's rough riders, who thronged the streets, promptly opened the way, jeering, laughing and shouting encouragement alternately to horse and rider. Dashing across a level common adjoining the town, we charged through a regiment that was drilling. Their cheers and yells of laughter stimulated my Mazeppa to still more frantic speed. The picket guard sped us on our way with profane gibes and loud hilarity. The breaking of a wild colt is one of the favorite amusements of that country. I kept my seat firmly, and the roads being sloppy, muddy and heavy, at the end of about three miles my horse seemed to have reached the conclusion that it didn't pay and began to moderate his pace.

I then began to realize the situation. I was actually clear of Fort Smith and all its embarrassing surroundings and on the right road. The brute's ignorant perversity had solved the question which had sorely puzzled my human wit. Nevertheless, I did not doubt that the comedy of the runaway colt would be inquired into by cooler heads at Fort Smith and that I would be pursued. So I kept on my way by side paths and through open woods to avoid leaving a trail on the muddy highway. After a while I lost the main road and wandered for a long time, still endeavoring to preserve a southwesterly course. After the trouble of getting around a cabin in a clearing whereat there was a group of horsemen whom I at once apprehended might be looking for me, I continued my journey through the woods until at length I came to the Poteau River, which was full from the recent rains. Following it down until I found a place where the roadmarks indicated a ford at low water, I determined to attempt the crossing.

The abutments and charred remains of the burned bridge were within sight—the first picture of the desolation of the Civil War that I remember seeing.

Taking off my overcoat, I threw it across the pommel of the saddle, crossed my stirrups over it and plunged into the roiled and rushing current. My colt, who had behaved soberly enough since his morning's escapade, now finding himself in a new element resumed his juvenilities. He reared, plunged and struggled frantically to return to the shore we had left. I had swam the Rio Grande with a horse and knew how to handle him. He was very obstinate and thoroughly frightened, and nearly drowned me with his wild wrestling. My overcoat went floating down the stream, but I removered my hat which was following it, and getting on the lower side of the horse held his head slightly upstream and so soon as he saw the other shore he swam steadily, but the swift current carried us a quarter of a mile below before we made the land. Although the distance directly across was not over a hundred yards, he was so frightened and exhausted that he could scarcely get up the bank where we landed. My own condition was not much better. My overcoat had gone downstream, and my boots and clothing were filled with water. I lay upon my back and held my feet in the air until the water was partly drained from my boots then mounted again and rode three or four miles to Scullyville.

As there seemed no excitement here of any kind, I rode through unchallenged and a short distance beyond came to where the road forked. The branch running nearly due west led to Fort Arbuckle, about two hundred and fifty miles distant. The other was the overland stage route to California and passed through Fort Washita, located about sixty-five miles to the southeast of Fort Arbuckle. The heavy old trail showed that Sturgis had gone to Fort Washita. So I took the other road for a mile in order to make a false trail, that any pursuers might be delayed, and then crossed over to the other road, and toward evening met an Indian who confirmed my belief as to the direction Sturgis had taken.

At sunset I stopped at Daniel's Station for rest and forage. I here gave five dollars for a soldier's old blue overcoat to replace the black one I had lost in the Poteau. A supper of bacon, corn bread and coffee greatly refreshed me. Determined to lose no time, I waited 'til ten o'clock, when the moon rose, and then went out to saddle my horse. He had been turned loose in a corral and, appreciating his new found liberty, persistently declined being caught again. But the southwestern borderer is brief and peremptory in his dealing with refractory subjects, whether men or animals. My free-born steed was promptly lassoed, wound up to a stake end, to his infinite disgust, bridled and saddled in spite of himself.

The overland route was so well defined that even the night traveler ran no risk of losing his way, but it was awfully lonesome. The Moon's glimmering light over forest and prairie invested commonplace objects with strange and frightful shapes. Howling wolves responded to hooting owls on every side, while other night birds and beasts lent their strange voices to swell the wild chorus, which resembled the music in the opera of "Der Freishutz."

I was not sorry when, about 3 in the morning, I sighted a human habitation. This was Holloway's Station, which consisted of a double log house on one side and a corral on the other. Turning my horse into the corral, I entered the unfastened door of the house and found a woman and several children asleep on the floor before the fire. I aroused the woman and requested a bed. She gave me a bit of candle and directed me to go upstairs in the other cabin, which I did and found a bed made of a hay mattress and a blanket on a bedstead of barrel staves laid across two poles. Pulling off my boots I turned in and slept the sleep of the just, but from my dreadful fatigue, I imagine more like that of the dead. When I awoke the sun was shining through the cracks in the roof of my chamber, and I heard the sound of rough voices below. Getting out of bed quietly, I looked through the wide cracks in the floor and discovered two men, whose villainous countenances were shaded by Texan sombreros, talking earnestly with the woman of the house. Their discourse was evidently about me. They were asking my personal description and whether I was armed.

I lost no time in worrying on my boots, shrunken with their wetting of the previous day, fixed my pistol handily in my right trouser pocket, and then tried to arrange some plan of action to meet the emergency. At this moment a squaw servant-girl announced breakfast and the sombreros followed the woman into a "lean-to" cabin in rear. It then occurred to me that I might push through the roof of staves, climb down the corner of the log cabin, get my horse and escape while the fellows were at breakfast; but remembering that animal's idiosyncracy, I concluded not to attempt it. The next best move was to present myself boldly and join them at breakfast, which I did. They sat at the left side of the table with their hats on, with the woman at the farther end, and answered my morning salutation with a gruff nod. I took a seat next the door and did my best to swallow some of the cornbread, fried bacon and muddy coffee which crowned the rough, clothless board, all the while considering what use might be made of the table cutlery in a close fight. There was no word spoken, and in a few minutes, as if moved by one impulse, the two men rose and went out. That they might have no time for private consultation, I followed them at once. As soon as I cleared the door they faced me, and one asked, in a sharp, arrogant tone, "Stranger, where did you start from yesterday?" Assuming an air of careless frankness I named Fort Smith. Then, cooly, but more respectfully, he inquired where I was going. I said, promptly, to Fort Washita, and then going over the little fiction I had imagined about the married sister, etc., I made particular and friendly inquiries about the roads, stations and distances and expressed the hope that they were going my way.

My story and ingenuous manner would have possibly have made less impression on the fellow had he known that, all the while I talked, my right hand carelessly resting in my pocket had finger on the trigger and thumb on the hammer of my pistol, with intent to shoot him through the head at the first hostile gesture on his part. As it was he seemed to have lost a clue, and after a pause, inquired if I had seen anyone on the road since I had left Fort Smith? In an instant the circumstance of my change of overcoats flashed upon me and I made use of it. "Yes, I remember as I came along last night to have seen a horseman ahead of me in a black overcoat who disappeared in the woods as I approached." They asked how far back it was.

"I can't say exactly, but think it was only a few miles."

"That's the man we're after," said he quickly, "and we believe it's Montgomery from Kansas or some other d—d Yankee spy. He left Fort Smith yesterday morning."

He then went on confidentially to tell me there were four of them in pursuit of the fellow. One was asleep in the cabin and the other had gone on to Riddle's Station to be on the watch. Not caring to prolong the conversation, I engaged my new friends to assist in catching and saddling my horse, feigning myself to be rather green about such matters and warmly admiring their chivalrous expertness. I then took a friendly leave and started off, charged with a confidential message to their comrade and promising to do all I could to aid in capturing the infernal Yankee.

For eight or ten miles the road led through a forest and then entered a prairie about two miles across. On the farther side of this open ground I observed a cabin with smoke issuing from the chimney. Apprehending that the men I had recently parted with might suspect or discover the deception I had put upon them and renew their pursuit, I did not wish to be seen by anyone who might give them information, and therefore desired to avoid this cabin. Dismounting and tying my horse to a sapling, I took a bunch of brush and carefully obliterated my horse's tracks for more than a hundred yards back, then returning to my horse I skirted around the prairie keeping masked in the wood, and finally finding a secluded patch of grass I again dismounted to give my exhausted horse a chance for refreshment, he having found nothing whatever to eat in the last barren corral the previous night. The grass here was nearly knee high and my hungry horse lost no time in breaking his long fast.

Meanwhile I kept close watch on the road, and in course of an hour my fears were realized by seeing my three Texans dashing rapidly across the prairie and following my intended route. They stopped a moment at the cabin and then, pushing on, disappeared in the forest beyond. I was quickly in the saddle purposing to follow their trail until I was in sight of Riddle's then, by making a circuit around the station, to get rid of them entirely. Nevertheless, when I reflected on the possibility of their meeting their comrade returning from his fruitless mission—a chance which would bring the whole party back on me—I realized the necessity of proceeding with the utmost caution. Presently, I met a man on foot, with whom I exchanged salutations, and asked him if he had passed any mounted men ahead. Squaring himself against a tree, he eyed me curiously and replied, "Well, stranger, I did meet three fellows up here, who said they were after a young man with light hair and a blue overcoat on, and I reckon as how you mought be the very man."

I responded with a laugh, "Well, suppose I am, what then?"

"Well, stranger, I don't know what you've been a doin' of, and I go for every man havin' a fair chance; but believe me, if them fellers catches you, you're gone up certain sure. They say you've fooled 'em bad, and they're turribly riled about it." In addition to his friendly warnings he gave me some valuable information about the country and the roads.

I was then about seventy miles southwest of Fort Smith on the road to Fort Washita. There was but one other road to pursue westward and that was thirty-five or forty miles to the northward of the Washita road at this point. The two roads had a conjunction eighteen miles west of Fort Smith where they gradually separated like a "V" until the Forts, Washita and Arbuckle, sixty-five miles apart, were reached. Between these roads the San Bois mountains reared their rocky, serrated ridges, which as their name indicates were destitute of woods. The thick and luxuriant wood-lands which skirted the northern and southern flanks of the range gradu-ally dwindled into stunted and scattered bushes as the slopes were ascended until finally the bald rocky heights forbade further vegetal encroachment. Where the prairie joined the bottom slopes of the moun-tains there were frequent swamps and bogs where the wild, luxuriance of vines and undergrowth rendered the forest almost impenetrable, and frequent and deep winding arroyos were found which would bewilder the most intrepid hunter. The mountains themselves sank into the rolling prairie an hundred and fifty miles west of Fort Smith. There was a cross road near the western end of the mountains but I could not hope to reach that without meeting those who were seeking my life or liberty. The sympathetic pedestrian, who was so well disposed to reduce the apparent-ly dead certainties against me, made a simple and rough draught of the country and roads on the ground with a stick from which it was plain that if I could not circumvent my hunters on the Washita road I must take to the mountains and endeavor to reach the Arbuckle road.

Advancing cautiously for two miles further, I at length caught a glimpse of four horsemen coming toward me with their heads bent in a careful examination of the road as they approached. I at once wheeled to the right and dashed into the wood as rapidly as I could move and pres-ently found my way barred by a deep gully closely thicketed with laurel. Dismounting, I leaped into the arroyo, dragging my horse after me, tearing my way through the vines and bushes to a crevice in the other side up which I climbed pulling out my horse, mounted and was off again. The feat was scarcely accomplished when I was admonished by a demoniac yell that my pursuers had discovered my trail. The gully seemed to detain them longer than it had delayed me and I made the best use of the oppor-tunity. Thereafter my trail was their only guide and I managed to make tracks faster than they could find them. They showed great persistence, nevertheless, and I had traveled six miles toward the mountains before I got out of hearing of their calls and halloos.

I now made up my mind to abandon the Washita road and to cross the mountains to the Arbuckle route. The distance I guessed might be about thirty-five miles without a trail, through a very difficult country. The difficulties of the route had not been overestimated, indeed they could not be conceived by one who had not experienced them. I shall not attempt to picture them, but often during that terrible journey I realized that it might sometimes be easier to die than to live, and had it not been for the orders I was carrying I should have given up the struggle. Climbing in zigzag lines and pulling my horse up steep and lofty ridges with the hope of seeing the prairie land on the north when the summit should be reached, I was doomed many times to be disheartened by a view of another ravine and ridge, deeper and higher, yet to be crossed. A handful of sassafras leaves afforded me the only refreshment I had that day. On the top of one of the ridges where I had seated myself on a rock to recover from the dreadful fatigue and palpitation of the heart which threatened to disable me, and to give my poor horse a breathing spell, I picked a little flower which I placed on the leaf of a small diary which I carried. The dampness which it had brought from the Poteau River prepared the leaf to receive a good impression which yet remains.

This was the point of my lowest depression morally and physically, speaking after the manner of the meteorologists. The sun was declining and there was another ridge which it was a hopeless undertaking to cross before dark, but with a final effort I succeeded in getting my horse to the bottom of the intervening valley where fortunately a small mountain stream of good water with a patch of verdure along its band was found.

For the sake of my terribly jaded horse and to await the arising of the moon this spot was welcome. Stripping off his saddle I tied his bridle to one stirrup and hooking my arm through the other laid down to sleep while my horse grazed at his leisure. I slept profoundly and on awaking found the horse standing over me snorting with terror. On sitting up and looking around, I perceived we were encircled by hundreds of wolves, gnashing their teeth and howling dismally. On realizing my position, I burst into a hysteric laugh and was startled by the echo of my own voice among the rocks and trees. The coyotes are cowardly wretches and were kept at a respectful distance by a few stones distributed among them occasionally. The dreadfully dismal opera of the night birds was opened and until the moon rose I was lonesome. Down in a deep, dark valley the voices of that night had me at their will. Every cry seemed a hint of horror, and all the shades of gloom were expressed in that howling, shrieking menagerie. The dread of the wolves kept my horse from feeding, and when the moon rose I saddled up and resumed my journey. With the stars for my guide I found it easier traveling than by daylight.

About 2 o'clock in the morning I struck the Arbuckle road and my joy was proportioned to the suffering I had experienced in reaching it. I followed westward for an hour or more, but at length perceived the trail was leading me further south than I thought proper and seeing an Indian cabin at hand I stopped to inquire more particularly about the country. Dismounting and fighting my way through a pack of noisy curs, I reached the door, where I knocked loud and long without receiving an answer. Seeing a light within I called and threatened to break open the door. I proceeded to execute my menace and found a squaw with several children crouching together and apparently dumb with terror. I put my inquiries about the Arbuckle road in every dialect that I could recall without eliciting any other response than a negative shake of the head. Giving it up, I traveled on until daybreak, when I tied my horse to a stirrup and set him grazing and slept for several hours.

When I awoke my legs were so numb and stiffened that I was unable to stand until I had rubbed and manipulated them for some time. I led my horse to a brook where a feeling of faintness was dissipated by bathing my face. I then mounted and soon afterward overtook a half-breed Indian with a drove of cattle. He gave me all the information I desired about the roads and added a bit of cold corn bread and bacon which served me for breakfast. After eating, a fresh trail of three or four horses on the road attracted my attention and, turning back to inquire, the half-breed informed me the tracks were made by a party of men from Perryville who were out looking for some one but, being unsuccessful, had returned to town. I took it for granted they had crossed from the Washita road at the western end of the mountains and were now hunting me, and as Perryville was the last town on my route, some distance ahead, I concluded to avoid the place, so I kept on my way cautiously, stopping frequently to rest and graze my horse.

Approaching the town at length I was startled from a reverie, as I was nearing the summit of a little elevation, by my horse suddenly pricking up his ears and stopping short. Looking ahead over the crest, I saw three mounted men coming toward me. I immediately turned out to the right and, passing behind a wooded ridge, hoped to pass the horsemen without attracting attention, and succeeded in getting to the westward of them and would have escaped notice but for the unfortunate coincidence that when they struck my trail, where I had turned out, they halted and looked about just as I was riding over a short open space to reach the broad forest north of Perryville, and they caught sight of me and gave chase. My raw colt, whose rude experiences had already made him a reasonable horse, seemed now to sympathize with the anxiety of his hunted rider, and carried me better than I could have expected. After a short run we passed through a herd of grazing horses, which confused my trail so that my pursuers, not being able to recover it, gave it up. I continued pushing westward at a good pace for six or eight miles, when supposing I had flanked Perryville, I again turned southward to seek the main road.

After another night in the wilderness with the owls and wolves, and many hours of weary and irresolute wandering, owing to my doubts as to whether I had crossed the main road or not, I was most happily guided to a Chickasaw cabin by the crowing of a cock. Here I awakened a very handsome squaw who entertained me hospitably with the best breakfast I ever enjoyed, of bacon, corn bread and milk, while an idiotic boy brought forage for my horse. Taking some of the bread and bacon to provide for future hunger and the boy for a guide over the three miles to the road I was seeking, the morning sun shone not on a happier man. The point where I struck the road to Arbuckle was ten miles west of Perryville, which, I flattered myself, placed me out of reach of my hunters. My next thought was to reach Cochrane's, the Sutler of Fort Arbuckle, who had a ranch about forty miles east of the Fort. It was necessary to handle my horse with great care as he began to show signs of giving out. I rested and grazed him every two or three hours and bathed and rubbed his legs in running water.

Night overtook me before I could reach Cochrane's, and, finding a convenient spot by the side of a brook, I prepared for a bivouac. To keep my horse from wandering, I tied the bridle reins about one foreleg below the knee giving his head a foot and a half play, and, leaving him to graze, I ate my little bite of supper thankfully, and pillowing my head on the saddle, went to sleep. About three o'clock in the morning I was aroused by the wolves, who had gathered in great force and seemed uncommonly demonstrative. The sky, for the first time during my journey, was overcast and a low fog obscured the view of surroundings. I looked around in vain for my horse. At length, attracted by his neighing, I found him some distance off surrounded by coyotes who, perceiving that he was hampered, had begun to attack him, snapping at his legs and haunches, while he hopped about and kicked in self-defence as efficiently as his hobble permitted. He was so thoroughly alarmed that I had the greatest difficulty in catching him. Saddling up at once I took the road again, and sometime after the rising sun had dispersed the fog, I met an old Negro carrier who informed me, to my disgust, that I had missed Cochrane's and was fifteen miles beyond. I then turned and reached the ranch about noon, with my horse completely knocked up.

The Sutler with his Indian wife was at home, and as he was reckoned a true man by Major Fitz-John Porter I felt no hesitation in making myself known to him. He informed me that our troops had left Fort Arbuckle and were concentrated at Fort Washita, about forty miles to the southward. He gave me an excellent dinner, and to replace my own worn-out steed, offered me the pick of five hundred in his corral in which they had been gathered during dinner. About 2 o'clock P.M. I was again in the saddle upon a fleet mare, whose feet seemed scarcely to touch the earth, and accompanied by an Indian guide named Iser. Iser and I rolled rapidly along until late in the afternoon when a furious storm broke over us, dazzling our eyes with lightning flashes and deluging the earth with water. With it came darkness; the Indian lost the way and I lost the Indian, and after wandering for some time struck the Big Blue River. Knowing that my goal lay some distance beyond this stream, I forded it, with a little swimming in the middle, and picketing my mare by a lariat she wore around her neck, I made my couch in the wet grass on the western bank.

When I awoke in the morning my Indian was sitting beside me, having rejoined me in the night. Riding up from the lowlands we saw the Cherokee mission, and there ascertained that Fort Washita was in the hands of the Texans, having been abandoned by our troops on the previous evening, and that Colonel Emory, with his command, was now encamped on the Arbuckle road only six miles distant. With my fleet steed and a good will, those six miles were soon accomplished, and it was with an exhultant heart that I saw my old comrades in arms just forming squadrons for the march while the infantry were already *en route* ahead. The first officer I spoke to was Captain Eugene A. Carr, who did not recognize me but civilly indicated the direction to Colonel Emory's headquarters. The Colonel was in the saddle, looking as grim as a grizzly bear, and only uttered a short growl in response to my courteous "good morning." Only a month before I had enjoyed his most agreeable hospitality at his house in Washington.

"Colonel!" said I. "You don't seem to know me!"

"No, I don't," he replied. "Who are you?"

"I am Lieutenant Averell, with dispatches from Washington, and here they are," at the same time extending the papers toward him.

The Colonel's sour expression changed suddenly to astonishment and he mechanically reached out his hand, but stopped, dropped his reins and lifting his arms, said, "My God! Averell, how did you get here?"

Then several officers came galloping up—Sturgis, Stanly, Carr,

Colonel William H. Emory, commander of Fort Arbuckle. (Courtesy Library of Congress)

Fish, Colburn, Bowman, Prince, Offley and Major Brown of the Pay Department—all staring curiously, as they suspected some demand from the Texans, and not one of them recognized me, not even my classmate, Colburn. It might have been said of me as of the palmer in "Marmion":

> The mother that him bore
> Had she been in the presence there,
> In his wan face and sunburned hair
> She had not known her child.

I had dismounted and sat down on the ground from a feeling of faintness, I remember, and heard someone reading the dispatch aloud and then the question in several voices, "Who brought it?" and the answer, "Averell, of the Rifles."

The next distinct remembrance—I was in Sandy Colburn's strong arms and the doctors were giving me something to drink. Now I was at home under the flag of my country and surrounded by old friends and comrades. My mission, with all its attendant dangers and sufferings, was accomplished. The excitement and sense of responsibility which had hitherto sustained my strength was over also, and for a few days I had to travel in an ambulance. Colburn outfitted me with clothing, and the substitution for my tatters, which adhered to my flesh in spots with dried blood, was effected with something like a surgical operation.

In the ambulance I had leisure to think over my eventful ride, in which, by the ruling of Providence, my mistakes and misfortunes had been the means of safety and success. The freak of an unbroken colt had relieved me from the embarrassment of Fort Smith. The loss of my overcoat in the Poteau had enabled me to deceive my pursuers at Holloway's. The premature start caused by the wolves was the occasion of my missing Cochrane's, and that detention with the delay on the Big Blue saved me that day from the Texans at Fort Washita. With the information and the fresh horse obtained at Cochrane's, I would still have reached Fort Washita that night, had I not been prevented by the storm. Thus in a blind ride of two hundred and sixty miles through a savage country infested with wild beasts and wilder humanity, seeking an object whose movements were as uncertain and unforeseen as my own, I seem to have been led and driven directly upon that object while it was on the wing and where I least expected to find it. "While man proposes, God disposes."

We arrived at Fort Arbuckle on May 3, where we found Sackett, Crittenden, Williams, C. C. Gilbert, Farrand, Hollister and Powell, who, with a small force, had been left in charge of this Post when the main body went to Fort Washita. While entirely unprepared for such a crisis as had arisen and without orders from his government, Colonel Emory's judicious action had thus far anticipated the wishes of the Commander-in-Chief at Washington. Henceforth his way was clear. The trains were loaded to their utmost capacity, and on the 4th of May the flag was lowered with military honors. Fort Arbuckle was abandoned, and we started northward, conducted by the famous Indian guides, Possum and Old Beaver.

Our march was dogged by a party of Texans who prevented the following of some of our supplies. The idea of being pursued chafed both officers and men extremely and there was especial indignation at the hostile demonstrations of Texans who had lived so long under the protection of the army they were now insulting. At the request of some of the officers, I suggested to Colonel Emory the propriety of turning upon these fellows and giving them a brush, or at least coming to some understanding which would relieve us from the irritation and humiliation of having them on our heels. The result of it was that Sturgis was directed to turn back with a squadron of Cavalry, and I being sufficiently rested to resume the saddle accompanied him.

Retracing our route for about two miles, and after passing through some open timber, we came suddenly upon the advance of the Texans, consisting of thirty men. At first sight of us they quickly rushed into a shallow ravine at right angles to the road, dismounted and leveled their rifles at us. While Sturgis was forming line at a gallop, I rode toward the ravine and called out to the commander to come out as I wished to talk with him. Whereupon a lank, typical Texan, with a rifle across his saddle bow, rode out and halted in front of me. I asked, "Who are you and who are these people with you?"

With the utmost *sangfroid*, he shifted a chew of tobacco in his mouth and replied, "I am Captain Johnson and them men are free-born American citizens under my command."

Then, said I, "Bring them out here and surrender."

Without the slightest tremor he said, "Well, stranger, I can't do it."

"Why?"

"'Cause we're free-born American citizens and kin do as we're a mind to and go where we please."

By this time Sturgis joined me and in his impetuous manner said,

"Bring your men up here and surrender—d—d quick."

Captain Johnson replied almost languidly, "Well, I guess not."

Said Sturgis hotly, "I'll wipe you out if you don't."

With a kindling gleam in his eye, Captain Johnson remarked slowly, "There'll be a good many empty saddles yonder," indicating our line with carbines advanced by a slight nod, "before you do."

"Why!" exclaimed Sturgis, "I am ordered to take you and bring you all into camp, and you know d—d well that I'll obey orders; so if you don't surrender the responsibility will be on you; some of us may be hurt, but every mother's son of you will be wiped out in the end."

Captain Johnson, after a moment's mental wrestle with the inevitable, said, "We can't surrender without conditions."

"What conditions?" asked Sturgis.

"Well, we don't want to be hung nor lose our horses and arms," said the imperturbable Texan.

This proposition indicated so just an understanding of their liabilities and deserts that Sturgis withdrew with me a few paces for consultation, the Texan standing fast. They had the dead drop on about half of our force; the distance between our line and the ravine was about one hundred yards and before the Texans could be driven from their cover our men would be exposed to the fire of thirty rifles in steady hands for two or three rounds. It was finally settled by Sturgis giving his word that they should not be hanged and that the disposition of their horses and arms should be left to our commanding officer, and they were taken into camp as prisoners. I believe this was the first armed array of Americans against each other in the war.[6]

This little affair relieved the exasperation of our soldiers to some extent; but notwithstanding the guard detailed for the protection of the captives, two of them were killed during the night, it being reported they were attempting to escape. It was probably some apprehension that a similar fate awaited the entire gang that induced the Colonel to release the remainder on parole the next day, and thereafter we heard nothing more

---

[6]The problem of "firsts" in the Civil War is an interesting one, but one that is almost impossible to prove. Certainly Fort Sumter must be considered an "armed array of Americans against each other in the war." Averell is correct in asserting that this is a very early engagement. Jefferson Davis had signed a bill of the Confederate Congress recognizing a state of war between the United States of America and the Confederate States of America only the day before. The first real battle of the war at Big Bethel, Virginia, occurred over a month later (10 June 1861).

of our pursuers. Further details of the march of our column back to civilization, although full of pleasant incidents of the march and camp, which I like to recall, are not essential to the purpose of my narrative, and partly belong rather to general history.

I left the command at a little hamlet in Kansas called El Dorado, and with Major Brown for a companion we made the journey to Emporia, sixty-five miles, mounted on mules, between 8 A.M. and sunset. I took with me dispatches from Colonel Emory to the government, one announcing the progress of his command, and another recalling his resignation, which he had been persuaded by unwise friends to leave in their hands a month before, to be used only in case Maryland seceded from the Union. Without knowing the status of Maryland, the Colonel desired to stop the resignation or its acceptance if handed in, and he empowered me to act in his behalf.

At Topeka the first newspaper I saw was *Harper's Weekly*, which contained a full-page picture of the burning of the hotel in Washington where I had left my traps, with the quieting assurance that nothing had been saved. When I got back to the Federal city, on the 31st of May, the "War" had become an accepted fact and the serious work of preparation was going on with greater energy, but with less noise than when I left six weeks before. Reporting at once to the Adjutant General's office, I found that the officers who had sent me to the Southwest were all in the field. McDowell was a General over the Potomac and Captain Fry was his Assistant Adjutant General and Major Fitz-John Porter was with General Patterson. No one remembered that I had been sent anywhere or what for, except Captain William D. Whipple who on seeing my dispatches thought them of sufficient importance to advise me to seek the Adjutant General, L.[Lorenzo] Thomas, who was at the house of the Secretary of War, Mr. Simon Cameron, corner of 15th and "I" streets, and accompanied me.

Calling at Mr. Cameron's, I sent in a message to the Adjutant General that Lieutenant Averell with dispatches from the frontier wished to deliver them. The colored servant returned with the word from Colonel Thomas that he was closeted with the Secretary of War and could not see me, but I might send in my dispatches if they were of importance. Under the advice of Captain Whipple I sent them in by the servant and also at his suggestion awaited an answer, as both the Adjutant General and Secretary might wish to see me when they knew that two regiments of regular troops were at once available. The colored servant presently returned with General Thomas' message: "That the dispatches were of no consequence whatever." And with that the door was civilly closed in our faces.

As a man is apt to estimate the value of a service by what it has cost him personally, I must confess I felt a little bewildered at this flat conclusion to my exciting ride, but in the progress of the grand and glorious historic drama which followed, I very soon forgot those who on that occasion seemed to have forgotten me.

18

Mustering Duty

May 31, 1861. From this time on, whatever I shall write may be considered a raid of recollection through events so vast, varied, complex and voluminous that no man may ever make of them a full and complete chronicle. The many-tomed Records of the Rebellion, however carefully and patiently arranged, are, at best, but a mass of dry, unhinged skeletons. Who shall resurrect and reconstruct the hosts in history and let us see their sinews strain again? Who shall measure the enormous energies that were used or wasted, and who can ever know or dare to name the impulses that set them in motion? It needs be one endowed of heaven, like the Jewish prophet of old, who under the hand and in the Spirit of the Lord, repeopled a valley full of dry bones with an exceedingly great army and drew from the four winds the breath to make the slain live again. All that I shall undertake will be to represent a part of my personal memories and impressions of what I saw and heard in that limited portion of the great theatre of action through which the narrow and quite subordinate path of my activities led me. I fancy no one would write without hope, and mine is that a little gleam of light may be thrown upon some of the obscure facts which fell under my personal observation and perchance tend to dissipate or weaken some of the accepted fictions that have been already written about them.

On the evening of my return from the Indian Nation, I dined with Captain W. D. Whipple and met Captain Robert Williams of the Adjutant General's department and Captain Roger Jones of the Inspector General's—all of the class of '51, and as noble and accomplished a trio of staff officers as any army could boast. From them I learned there were 95,000 volunteers and militia already in the field and 21,000 across the Potomac entrenching the approaches to the river, from the aqueduct opposite Georgetown down to Alexandria. Troops, in separate departments, occupied the frontier of Union sentiment from the mouth of the Potomac to the mouth of the Ohio and reserves were assembled to cover Baltimore, Philadelphia and Cincinnati.

Major and Brigadier Generals had been made, but only two, [Irvin] McDowell and [Joseph K.] Mansfield, were from the Army. The President and Secretary of War and every one about them being politicians and statesmen, there was none, except General Scott, to give general direction to military affairs, and now that the Administration and the public press deemed our vital and vulnerable points secure, there began to be heard murmurs which soon grew to open complaints that General Scott was too old and too slow.

The same lack of understanding of the gravity of the situation and administrative blindness to the mighty exigencies of the impending struggle, which encouraged and justified the puerile criticisms of the grand old patriot and warrior, who was saving life, treasure and time in his plans and dispositions of force, now hastened the heedless untowardness of making generals of politicians without the least military experience to carry out the nascent designs of men whose influence seemed potential in the direction of public affairs. Among many memorable illustrations of the early born intents and purposes of the dominant spirits of those portentous days was the making of N.[Nathaniel] P. Banks of Massachusetts a Major General and in proffering to him the office of Quartermaster General of the Army. There was no position of the army requiring greater experience and knowledge than this. He must not only know the bulk, weight and character of everything required to be carried to or with an army in the field, but he must purchase all Quartermaster's supplies by contract or otherwise or make them. Upon his executive ability the efficient equipment and mobility of an army largely and continually depend, and upon his integrity and business capacity, more than upon any other officer, depends the economical maintenance of the army. Banks was a prominent politician who had been a Representative in Congress and Speaker of the House. He was necessarily destitute of the indispensable experience and multifarious knowledge required to properly conduct the great office, yet he was besought during four or five days to accept it, and the newspapers teemed with paragraphs relating the visits of Major General Banks to the different Departments under the escort of distinguished members of the Administration. There were above sixty educated and trained officers of the Quartermaster's Department at that time who would be expected to act as subordinates to the chief and do his legitimate work. It was greatly to the credit of General Banks' discretion and patriotism that he declined the office. Per contra George B. McClellan had been made a Major General and placed in command, with 13,000 men, of the Department of the Ohio, embracing that state and the new state of West Virginia. He had already entered the latter state and, the day before, his proclamation to the citizens thereof had been published, arousing their patriotism and approving their separation from the Old Dominion. He had entered upon his plan for the defeat and destruction of the Confederate forces under [John] Pegram and [Robert S.] Garnett.

Let us pause here for a moment to mark, in the appointments and purposes of these two Generals, Banks and McClellan, the yet unnoted initial steps which led by divergent paths to an irrepressible conflict between *military necessity* and *partisan cupidity*, that afterward filled the army and the country with bitter antagonisms which long survived the war. It was not personal to these two generals, who are mentioned only as types of appointments on the two opposing lines of action mentioned.

Another remark may be properly made here upon a paragraph of McClellan's proclamation promising the people of West Virginia that he would crush any attempt at insurrection on the part of their slaves. This is remarked, not as peculiar to McClellan, but as common to most of our military advances during the earlier months of the war, showing that the emancipation of slavery was not contemplated at all, at the outset. The second phase of the question, which was beginning to perplex us, came at Fortress Monroe two days after McClellan's proclamation. General Benjamin F. Butler of Massachusetts, who was occupying Fortress Monroe, Hampton and Newport News with nine regiments of volunteers and two thousand regrulars, began to agitate the question of treating the slaves who came into his lines as "contraband of war." General Butler, having been a lawyer, developed a talent for raising novel questions of law, growing out of the war, which amounted to genius. His coincident military operations were also original.

At this time General Mansfield with fourteen regiments, some batteries and cavalry, commanded the city of Washington and its neighborhood. Passes were required for people crossing the Potomac and they were signed by an Aide named *"Drake DeKay,"* whose broad, flamboyant signature became historical. General [George] Cadwallader with 5,000 men was at Baltimore. Philadelphia was protected by General [Robert] Patterson with 3,000 men and Major Fitz-John Porter was his chief of staff. Brigadier General [William H.] Keim had ten regiments at Chambersburg, two on the Northern Central Railway, three at Camp Scott and two at Camp Curtin, in all, 16,000 men. This was the situation on the 30th of May. The dispositions of troops and the plans of General Scott, so far as known, were published nearly every day and the names of regiments and their stations given freely.

To my surprise and regret I learned that the gallant old Colonel [William H.] Emory was no longer an officer of the Army, his resignation having been prematurely handed in by an impatient and over officious friend and accepted before my arrival. While distressing myself the following day with a realization of my helplessness to execute the Colonel's important commission, with which he had impressively charged me on parting with him at El Dorado in Kansas, an unexpected and hopeful opening appeared. Colonel Schuyler Hamilton, Military Secretary to the General-in-Chief, came in the evening to take me, *toute a l'heure*, to dinner at General Scott's. Only his military family were present and the old General kindly placed me by his side. I imagine no one who ever saw General Scott at any dinner was left in doubt as to where was the head of the table. His colossal proportions, jove-like head and impressive consideration for his guests and friends, albeit a little autocratic, absorbed and dominated the attention of all. The General had fixed notions regarding his food and wines and, withal, preferred plain, simple dishes. Among his favorites, I remember, was jowl and greens. One of his imperative injunctions, which I learned, and which every member of his staff did not fail to remember, was that knife nor fork should ever touch lettuce; the teeth alone should be first to bruise it.

My opportunity came with the coffee when the General asked me to tell him of my journey and where I had found the troops of Colonel Emory and where I had left them. This I did as briefly as possible and then availed of the chance to speak of Colonel Emory's faithful conduct and of his earnest desire to withdraw his resignation. The General showed a flattering and sympathetic interest in the story, and at its conclusion put his massive arm about my shoulders and after a few words which exalted me above the consideration of all other rewards whatever, for anything meritorious in my conduct, he went on to say, "My young friend, it is fortunate that Colonel Emory, whom I highly esteem, has one here to place his status in its proper light. I cannot restore him to his position, for that is filled, but I can help make him a Lieutenant Colonel of a new regiment." And later on it was done.[1]

The rapidly unfolding prospects of war attracted to Washington, at this time, a throng of the leading men of the world—the keenest intellects in finance, commerce and manufactures—in everything where tremendous activities were expected. New acquaintances were daily made and the imagination excited by the extending conceptions and realizations of the possibilities and probabilities of the impending struggle. Among the men then met, I remember Commodore [Cornelius] Vanderbilt, who was not yet much regarded as a financial colossus and whose distinguishing personal characteristics were a bad high hat, a high, white neck-cloth and a cigar; Mr. Alexander H. Sibly of Detroit, an embodiment of tremendous, systematic human energy, who a year later under authority gathered and handled everything that floated on the Atlantic coast and moved the Army of the Potomac to the Peninsula and supplied it; Mr. Thomas A. Scott of Philadelphia, who possessed similar attributes and abilities with reference to railways; Mr. Harry McGrath of Maryland; Hugh Tyler of New York; Leonard T. Smith of Kansas; Colonel J. H. Puleston of Pennsylvania; and Commodore Garrison of New York and San Francisco. These men moved things. They seemed to comport naturally with obstacles and magnitudes. Among the many journalists whom I met, Henry J. Raymond of the New York *Times* is best remembered. He was so thoroughly American, so completely *en rapport* with current events, and was so gifted with the ability to see straight and think right, and was animated with such an unaffected, loyal, living desire that the best might always be done that it was impossible not to realize and feel the attraction of his glowing personality. I formed for him a friendship which grew and strengthened to the end of his brilliant career.

During this brief interim of duty I visited several times the Virginia side of the Potomac to see the defensive works preparing. The newness of the necessity and the oddity of entrenchments to defend the Capitol of our country against our own people, produced in me a sensation like that of a strange dream, an unreality, something intangible and quite irrational. It was not until the enemy was eventually met on the field and the first hurtling, hissing blast of a cannon ball aimed at us was heard and felt that this sensation ended. In the light of subsequent experiences, the defences

---

[1] Emory eventually rose to the rank of major general on 13 March 1865, the final reward for years of faithful service.

then preparing were trivial, but that they were considered sufficient by both sides at that time was proved by their not being tested by either.

On June 1st a wild sensation thrilled the country and stimulated the war spirit caused by the news of the cavalry dash into Fairfax Court House by Lieutenant Charles H. Tompkins and Lieutenant D.[David] S. Gordon.

I remember well there was also another one the same day, but of a saddening kind when everybody stopped everyone else on the streets to tell each other in regretful tones that "Stephen A. Douglas died at Chicago this morning at 9 o'clock." If whatever is, is not always right, then it would have been well for Douglas to have lived until the war was over, to have lifted his voice on behalf of Lincoln's purposes.

On the 7th of June I received orders to go to Elmira, N.Y., to muster volunteers into the service of the United States. On my way I stopped off at Baltimore with Captain Robert Williams of the Adjutant General's office and called on General N. P. Banks, at Fort McHenry, to whom Captain Williams was reporting for duty. General Banks was at that time the most prepossessing man of the large class of generals appointed from political life. He looked wonderfully wise and was wise enough to say but little and that little in a sonorous, impressive manner. My friend Captain Williams was so impressed that he disclosed his opinion to me, as I took my leave, by the remark, "General Banks is a great man."

I remained at Elmira on mustering duty about twenty days and during that short period saw a great deal of an entirely new and strange sort of life, which was altogether entertaining and frequently astonishing. Regiments and batteries were assembled here to be uniformed and equipped, and, when ready, to be mustered into the United States Service and sent to the front. Here they had their first camping experiences and received some drilling preparation for active service. Wives, daughters and friends accompanied the volunteers to this military rendezvous and the town hummed like a hive of bees day and night with the feverish excitements of preparation, which war bulletins and rumors occasionally aroused to a high intensity that was manifested in impromptu gatherings and speeches. Yet, withal, a general expression of exhilarating cheerfulness prevailed, especially among the women, and every evening brought its entertainments of music, dancing and song. Strangers made acquaintance in a moment and became friends for life and comrades for the war. The most genial and attractive qualities of every character were shown.

Those earliest volunteers were an exceptionally good class of men, the flower of the land, and their officers were men of superior social standing and influence. There were no disorders. My old friend General R. [Robert] B. Van Valkenburgh of Bath, N.Y., was in command and the master spirit in control, ably and actively seconded by his Adjutant, Captain William Rumsey, son of Hon. David Rumsey, who as member of Congress had secured my appointment to the Military Academy ten years before. Colonel C. C. B. Walker of Corning was equal to all occasions as an energetic and resourceful Quartermaster. There were organizing at Elmira during my stay, I remember, the following regiments: 12th New York Volunteers, Colonel [Ezra] Walwrath; 13th, Colonel [Isaac F.] Quinby; 19th, Colonel Clarke; 21st, Colonel W.[William] F. Rogers; 23d, Colonel [Henry C.] Hoffman and Lieutenant Colonel [Nirom M.] Crane; 24th, Colonel [Timothy] Sullivan; 26th, Colonel [William H.] Christian; 27th, Colonel [Henry] W. Slocum and Lieutenant Colonel J.[Joseph] J. Bartlett; 33d, Colonel [Robert F.] Taylor; and 35th, Colonel W.[William] C. Brown. I had infinite satisfaction in finding myself useful to these officers who were eager to learn. Two of the Colonels, Quinby and Slocum, fortunately for all, were old graduates from the Military Academy.

The culmination of the experience of each regiment here was its muster into the service of the United States, and this was an impressive and solemn ceremony. The regiment was in line and as the roll of each company was called the men answered to their names and stepped to the front and then altogether, with uncovered heads and uplifted right hands, repeated the words of the oath of allegiance and obedience, sentence by sentence, after the mustering officer, and then, after the ranks had been thus mustered, the officers advanced in line with the Adjutant and, halting under the colors, removed their hats and completed the obligation, and the thousands of spectators testified by their profound silence their realization that a thousand men had been separated for a time, many of them forever, from their homes. The fortitude of the women did not forsake them until the trains had rolled away with their loved ones and then their pent-up grief found vent in tears and unrestrained lamentations.

The appearance of the volunteer in '61 and of the same man, a veteran soldier in '65, was remarkably different. Whether it was due altogether to modifications effected by service or to the familiarized eye of the observer, it was a fact that the fresh volunteer and his arms seemed dissociated in effect; there was a duality in his ensemble, his arms and equipments were painfully and separately conspicuous from himself and often in his way; they encumbered him, while the arms of the veteran would seem a part of himself, of his personality, harmonious, convenient and appropriate.

Among the state officials who were occupied with the multifarious duties of the volunteer depot, I remember Colonel Elliott F. Shepard, a young gentleman of prepossessing manners, whose ingenuous and amiable conduct and zealous attention to his duties received general commendation.

My duties at Elmira were terminated by the receipt of the following telegram:

Washington, D. C.,
Lieutenant Averell,   July 2, 1861.
Elmira.

You are ordered to report immediately to General McDowell at Arlington, Virginia.

J. B. Fry.

I found the grassy slopes and open woodlands of Arlington occupied with tented troops, and the heedless disregard of fences and shrubbery in and around the camps gave me my first slight realization of the Civil War. Clanking sabres and jingling spurs of aides and orderlies passing to and fro across the stately portico of the mansion, but lately occupied by Colonel Robert E. Lee and his family, shattered all recollections of the broad and unbroken repose which had surrounded it since the British burned the Capitol. Making my way through the jostling throng at the entrance, I found the interior a hive of military industry. My friend Captain J. B. Fry, whom I had not seen since the night before my departure for the Texas frontier, was now as chief of General McDowell's staff, testing the strength of his Adjutant General's office in the work of reducing the fresh and unorganized volunteers to the order of brigades and divisions; the Quartermaster and commissary officers were gathering and expanding their means for supplying the demands for the growing army and the engineers were employed in the preparation of maps. I was immediately assigned as acting Assistant Adjutant General to the Brigade of Regulars under the command of Colonel Andrew Porter, 16th United States Infantry, who had recently been Captain of Company "F" in the Rifles of which I had been 2d Lieutenant. This assignment was in every way agreeable.

Colonel Andrew Porter was an ideal officer who had greatly distinguished himself in the Mexican War. A gentleman of unfailing courtesy
and of unwavering loyalty to his country and to his friends. While exer-
cising a kindly liberality regarding faults of education or inexperience in
others, he was mercilessly intolerant of untruth, infidelity, neglect of
duty or any form of dishonorable conduct. He had challenged and
"winged" an officer in Mexico for speaking disrespectfully of General
Scott in his presence. I found him at the Washington Club which stood at
the corner of Pennsylvania and Vermont avenues and with him I was
delighted to find my man Peter Kinney who had taken care of me in New
Mexico. Porter's brigade was not yet organized. The regulars crossed the
Potomac on the 5th and camp was established.

Colonel Porter commanded the First Brigade, Second Division, of
General McDowell's army of Northeastern Virginia. The brigade, when
organized, consisted of a Battalion of United States Infantry made up of
companies "C" and "G" of the Second; "B", "D", "G" and "E" of the
Third; and "G" of the Eighth, under Major George Sykes: a Battalion of
United States Cavalry consisting of companies "A" and "E" of the First
Cavalry; "B", "E", "G" and "I", Second Cavalry; and "K", Second
Dragoons, under Major Innis Palmer: Eighth New York State Militia;
Colonel [George] Lyons: Fourteenth New York State Militia, Colonel
Wood: Twenty-seventh New York Volunteers, Colonel H. W. Slocum:
the Battalion of United States Marines, Major Reynolds: and [Captain
Charles] Griffin's Battery 5th United States Artillery—of a total strength
of about 3,700. The New York regiments were well uniformed, the
Eighth in gray, the Fourteenth with blue jackets and red trousers, and the
Twenty-seventh as the regular United States Infantry, and the first two
were well drilled. The Marines were fresh recruits but little drilled, but
with excellent officers. Of course the Battery and the United States
Infantry and Cavalry were of the best officered and disciplined troops in
service.

Associated with me upon the staff of Colonel Porter were Lieutenants
C.[Charles] F. Trowbridge and F.[Francis] M. Bache, both of the 16th
United States Infantry and Lieutenant J.[John] B. Howard, Fourteenth
New York State Militia, the latter as Quartermaster. All were agreeable
gentlemen and efficient officers. Colonel David Hunter commanded the
Division, and his chief of staff was my old friend and comrade, 1st
Lieutenant William D. Whipple of the 3d Infantry, and Captain O.[Otis]
H. Tillinghast, Quartermaster.

There was the bustle of preparation everywhere in the direction of supplies of food, clothing, shelter and transportation, including saddle horses for those who were entitled to them, but there were few drills, no reviews, sham battles or other efforts to accustom the troops to tactical movements or evolutions of a line of battle. Colonel Porter's brigade was the only one of that army I ever saw in line or in review. There were doubtless brigades and divisions whose commanders were unknown to them by sight. General McDowell was a massive, robust and rotund man of forty-four years with a Teutonic face emphasized with a drooping German mustache and a bunchy, bristling imperial with which a white helmet surmounted with a glistening metal spike or lance-head completely harmonized. His voice was a hoarse, chest-toned alto. He spoke rapidly but never loudly and his manner seemed more that of a doctrinaire or a professor than that of a soldier. He had been graduated twenty-three years before and had been on staff or bureau duty twenty years of that time. He was agreeable in conversation and talked well and readily on many topics. He seemed very busy at the War Department and spent much of his time in Washington. I do not believe he ever saw all of his army together and, but for the spiked helmet, I would doubt if one-fourth of his army knew him by sight.

When Colonel A. Porter had his brigade out occasionally on the bottom lands below Arlington for drill, its firing attracted troops from neighboring camps who came to look upon it as one goes to a play—to enjoy the pleasures of the imagination. In the next firing the poor fellows heard, imagination was not called upon to furnish living targets. The headquarters of our brigade were near Arlington House and many of the commanders of divisions and brigades were in the habit of calling upon Colonel A. Porter when they visited the headquarters of the army. There were five divisions and thirteen brigades of an aggregate strength of about 35,000. Could they have had two or three months of camp life with constant drills, daily parades, and frequent reviews and sham battles with firing, and some target practice, this army could have gone toward Richmond with a fair prospect of maintaining its advance, but the terms of several regiments of three-months' men were nearing their expiration and the press of the North was clamoring day after day for an advance "On to Richmond."

There was no untrammeled dominant, directing military mind at the head of the administration nor of any of its departments. It may as well be said here that during the first year of the war the Confederacy kept its military forces far in advance of the Union armies in point of drill, discipline and fighting efficiency. Everything was subordinated to the army in the South, while in the North an impatient and capricious public opinion, strongly swayed by political animosities, constrained and thwarted an administration which was incapable of understanding, even if it were willing, to realize that an epoch of *Force* had arrived and that forty or fifty regiments of citizens hastily assembled from the avocations of civil life did not represent the force that was required to go against a hostile array that was controlled from head to foot and front to rear by rigid military principles actuated by officers chosen for their fitness and efficiency.

As a marked illustration of the forecast exhibited by the opposing administrations I will recall an incident which happened on the 8th of July. It is impressed deeply on my memory as it was the occasion of my first meeting a Confederate in uniform. It occurred on that day to Colonel Andrew Porter, my brigade chief, to take a look at the outposts and pickets of the army. Taking a squadron of cavalry as an escort, we set out to the front and rode beyond the outer pickets perhaps a mile when after passing over a gentle eminence we suddenly descried a small column of a dozen or more horsemen approaching along the winding road, not over five hundred yards from us. They carried a white flag which we had never before seen in the war, and their uniforms were gray. Colonel Porter, without halting, turned his head and gave the command, "draw sabres," and a hundred and twenty weapons flashed in the sunlight while every trooper gathered his horse for a charge. When only an hundred paces intervened between the heads of the approaching columns, the officer at the head of the one in gray raised his right hand, palm to the front and came to a halt. Our squadron was then halted and Colonel Porter directed me to ride down and ascertain the character and purpose of the detachment in our front.

On arriving near the strange column I exchanged salutes with a tall, fine looking officer at the head, who said, "Sir, I am Colonel [John G.] Taylor of the Confederate States Army, bearer of dispatches from President Davis of the Confederate States of America to President Lincoln of the United States."

The sudden shock of this announcement and the strange, commingled feelings of amazement, indignation, sorrow and incredulity which these words and their woeful portent aroused in me will never be forgotten. I said, "Sir, you will please dismount your escort and stand to horse until I return."

My order was obeyed, and the message repeated to Colonel Porter, who thereupon dismounted our squadron after returning sabres and told me to request the officer to approach. I did so and the Confederate came on foot to within ten paces of Porter who stood erect in the middle of the road to receive him. After saluting, the Confederate officer repeated his message, "I am Colonel Taylor, etc.,"

Colonel Porter replied, "I know of no President nor Government in this country except that of the United States and I cannot receive any dispatches from you without instructions from the Government. You will go into bivouac where you are and a portion of my command will remain here until instructions are received."

Colonel Taylor then asked, "Does this conclude our official interview?"

Colonel Porter replied, "It does until further orders."

Then to my astonishment, these two men, who had conducted their interview with chilling dignity, walked easily, almost eagerly, toward each other and shook hands, Colonel Taylor saying, "Andrew, old fellow, how do you do?" and Porter, "Tom, how are you?" and the two sat on a bank by the roadside and held a short chat of old times, when they were comrades and chums in the Mexican War, and a flask of old-time Rye Whiskey was produced from Porter's saddle bags and the usual courtesies of a truce were observed.

The dispatches were ordered in by General McDowell who forwarded them to the Government. They contained a proposition relating to the exchange of prisoners, which our government refused to entertain because it would not recognize the enemy as belligerents. And I do not remember, if I ever knew, how many thousands of our captured men afterward needlessly languished in Southern prisons on that account.

Our brigades were not yet fully organized. Major Innis Palmer joined with the regular cavalry companies on the 10th and the 27th New York did not join until the morning of the 16th. The ambulances arrived only on the 13th and the order for packing up surplus camp equipage and supplies was issued the same day. The news of McClellan's victory in West Virginia with the capture of a thousand prisoners, which reached us on that day, the 13th, increased the clamor for an advance on Richmond. The camps were thronged with visitors daily—men, women and children. All sorts of comforts and devices for emergencies were bestowed on the soldiers by their visiting friends, from a white Havelock cap-cover to a pair of slippers. Senator Crittenden of Kentucky with a party of friends paid our headquarters a visit. There were almost as many opinions about the impending war as there were men, and those of influential politicians and editors were as wild and irrational as any, but they received the greatest consideration.

It was a convenience and pleasure to have our headquarters so near those of General McDowell on account of the readiness of official inter-course and the satisfaction and comfort of furnishing a refuge occasionally to Fry, Whipple and Tillinghast, when those overworked gentlemen desired to escape the trials and turmoils of office work for a few moments rest. Day and night were nearly all the same to us. We brooded together over the difficulties and the dreadful risks that were being forced upon us in setting forth with an army so wholly unready for battle. The officers and men were of the best material in the country, but nine-tenths of the rank and file had never fired a gun, even at drill or in sham battle. Our only consolation and hope was the belief that we should find the enemy no better prepared. On the 15th of July the order was issued to be ready to march at 3 P.M. the next day.

19

Bull Run

The 16th of July, 1861, at Arlington Heights, Virginia, was brilliant with summer sunshine, and the faces of thirty-five thousand attractively uniformed and well-fed men were beaming with satisfaction at the prospect of going forth to the first great battle between civilized white men in our country since the War of 1812. The balmy air wafted the music of numerous fine bands and gently unfolded and toyed with bright banners from Arlington down to Alexandria. The gleaming bayonets of columns wending from camps to highways, the glint of field guns and the rumble of their carriage wheels, the loud commands of voice and louder of trumpet, trampling squadrons and galloping aides, wise-looking general officers with imposing staffs—all the concomitants of a freshly panoplied army—excited and fascinated the radiant throngs of lovely women, attired in summer costumes, whose carriages crowded the roads and fields and occupied every point of vantage from which smiles and flowers and precious souvenirs could be bestowed on the departing soldiers.

The scene presented on the grand portico of Arlington House on that day when McDowell came forth arrayed for the field in the uniform of a Brigadier General and otherwise distinguished by his white helmet with the bright lance-head on top, and followed by a well appointed staff, was impressive. There was no affectation of cheerfulness in the little that was said among officers and a certain grave demeanor of spectators revealed a general consciousness that there they beheld the intelligence and power which was to direct the operations of the army, already in motion, together with that sense of the responsibility which was borne by them for its success or misfortune. The General and his staff at once mounted their impatient steeds and set out along the shaded drive, as fine a military group as any soldier would wish to see.

Our brigade was about the last in the order of march on the road to Fairfax Court House. As it turned into the Columbia turnpike there came Colonel Slocum of the 27th New York, whose regiment had not yet joined, to ask me where his place in the column should be. Going toward the Long Bridge with him, a long, scattered, heterogeneous train of vehicles was descried coming over, loaded with hilarious and vociferous volunteers. It had been a two days' task for me to overcome the prejudices of Colonel Porter against the addition of such an absolutely raw regiment to his brigade, an effort I had undertaken at the earnest solicitation of Colonel Slocum on his arrival in Washington. It was upon my oft repeated and only possible argument that a green regiment with a good Colonel was as good as, if not better than, an older regiment with a green Colonel. The men might be awkward, but they would have confidence, and that quality was indispensible at this juncture. It was only that morning that I had secured the order from the War Department on Colonel Porter's application and had delivered it to the Colonel of the 27th in their camp in Franklin Square, which lovely park had been already converted into a desolation. And the regiment had simply impressed into its service all the omnibusses, hacks, buggies, carts and other vehicles it could lay its hands on in Washington, and here it was coming over the Long Bridge on its way to the war. I told Slocum, if he did not want the order revoked, never to let Colonel Porter see that procession. The regiment joined the column after a little while in quite regular shape.

We were finally stretched out along the Columbia turnpike and with numberless halts caused by the untoward and irregular marching of the troops in front and the general inexperience of everybody, we reached camp about 10 o'clock P.M. having marched between eight and nine miles. The troops had moderated their exhilarant transports of the morning and were glad enough to get fires built and some coffee made as soon as possible. Major Reynolds had given the Battalion of Marines a drill at the manual of arms at almost every halt.

July 17th we had reveille at daylight. Colonel [Dixon S.] Miles with the 5th Division of two brigades under Colonels [Louis] Blenker and [Thomas A.] Davies had been passing our camps part of the night, and morning found him not yet gone by us. Even with my little experience it struck me as a strange thing that there should be a necessity for a fatiguing night march of eight regiments and three batteries during the first twenty-four hours, and while we were yet far from the enemy. We waited two hours after Miles' division had passed for the second brigade ([Ambrose E.] Burnside's) of our division to get out of the way.

Senators and members of Congress drove by us in carriages going out to see the expected battle. Soon after getting on the road we began to pass the abandoned camps of the enemy's outposts and saw remnants of abatis which they had constructed to protect themselves from sudden assaults along the road and some small entrenchments, but lately occupied. The quantities of refuse and the worn and dirty appearance of their camps showed an occupation of some considerable time, but there was that lack of policing, apparent to sight and smell, which suggested that the enemy had been expecting to abandon the position daily for some time. These vacant camps of a hostile force hurriedly quitted, with the indications of their cooking and sleeping arrangements and of their sentinel's posts, were as interesting to our men as are the tracks of dangerous game to a hunter. During our frequent halts they would run over the grounds and study the fascinating evidences of recent occupation with the interest of children. We entered Fairfax Court House about noon and had another object lesson of war in the sight of houses that had been pillaged and some burned by troops which had preceded us. That night [Daniel] Tyler's division was on our right and Miles' on our left.

July 18th. After reveille we marched a mile and then halted until afternoon. While waiting, General McDowell passed by in a covered hackney coach, stopping a moment to speak with Colonel Porter. My youthful fancy, I remember, was stimulated by the apparently sure forecast and seeming confidence of a General who could drive about the country in a carriage while his army was in motion toward the enemy, and my memory reverted to similar incidents of the personal conduct of Napoleon in some of his great campaigns, when after setting his Marshals in motion he would be driven in a comfortable carriage to some distant and unthought of point, where at the nick of time he would lay aside his nightcap and robes, don the historic gray surtout and chapeau-bras, mount his horse and calmly survey from a convenient eminence the culmination of his wonderful strategic combinations. This passing vision of our General with the hat of a Kaiser and the suggested Napoleonic traits was impressive, if not awe inspiring, to the mind of a young soldier.

But, alas! we had not the serried and seasoned legions by whose appointed movements the Emperor could regulate his own to an hour. The orders for the march of each of our divisions had been comprehensive and exact, providing for every contingency. Without tents and in "light marching order" and with subsistence trains following at a convenient distance, our men were loaded with kits they would have thrown away a year later. Instead of each soldier depending on his haversack and tin cup for his food and coffee, the camp kettles and utensils of a mess were carried in wagons which seldom arrived in camp on time and were often delayed or lost. The roads were excellent, sufficient in number and favorable in direction, yet our columns were constantly tumbling into each other and impeding the march. Wagons often blocked the way. The men were so unused to carrying their knapsacks and heavy overcoats rolled and strapped upon them, together with their arms, ammunition and equipments, that they were tired out with every day's short movement. Seasoned soldiers would have made the march to Centreville, twenty-one miles, the first day, and made their attack early the next morning, before the reinforcements under [Joseph E.] Johnston could have arrived from the Shenandoah Valley to the enemy in our front. The Army, the Administration and the people were learning a severe lesson.

Our march extended on the 18th to some fields favorable for camps a mile east of Centreville, and before arriving there we were enlivened and enthused by the sound of heavy guns to the southwestward in the direction of Blackburn's Ford, whence the news soon came back to us that Tyler was engaged, and later, after we had encamped, that his demonstration had been successful in developing the strength of the enemy at that point, that [Henry] Ayres with a section of his battery had been in a tight place, but had maintained his fire until his ammunition was exhausted when he had withdrawn it in good order, and that Lieutenant [Lorenzo] Lorain of Ayres' battery had been severely wounded. All this, it was plain to be seen, had its effect upon our men and produced a marked suppression of the noisy hilarity which had been usual in their camps.

Burnside's brigade, which was encamped next to us, toward Centreville, had an excellent band of music and we were frequently entertained with popular airs, but our ears became a trifle weary during the 19th and 20th with the "Mocking Bird," and I have never heard the air since without remembering the two long days we were so unfortunately halted at those camps. Burnside's brigade was formed about a circle every evening, an hour before sunset, and the Chaplain prayed and preached and the band discoursed sacred music, the brigade commander taking a prominent part in the exercises. After the religious services the band reverted to the "Mocking Bird." In our brigade we had regular guard mountings and drills and our cavalry made reconnaissances to ascertain the position of the enemy.

July 20th. At 8 P.M. I went with Colonel Porter to General Mc-Dowell's Headquarters to attend a council of war to which the division and brigade commanders had been summoned. There was a great tent lighted with lanterns and candles with some maps on a large table around which were gathered the commanders while their staff officers waited at a respectful distance outside. Major J.[John] G. Barnard and Captain A. W. Whipple of the Engineers, and Major [Albert J.] Myer, signal officer, and Major W.[William] F. Barry, chief of Artillery, were also called in. Generals Tyler and [Robert C.] Schenck and Colonels [Erasmus D.] Keyes, W.[William] T. Sherman, David Hunter, Burnside, A. Porter, [Samuel P.] Heintzleman, W.[William] B. Franklin, O.[Orlando] B. Willcox, [Oliver O.] Howard, Miles, Blenker, Davies and [Israel B.] Richardson were present. After a discussion lasting over two hours, the council broke up and on the way to camp Colonel Porter told me it was decided to turn the enemy's left and our division was to do the turning.

July 21st. After about two hours sleep we were out and had the brigade ready to march at 2 A.M., 3,700 strong. The chief natural barrier between us and the enemy was Bull Run, a stream with precipitous banks, which runs from northwest to southeast passing west of Centreville at a distance of four miles, by the Warrenton turnpike which crosses the stream over a stone bridge. Another smaller stream called Cub Run flows from north to south crossing the turnpike three-fourths of a mile west of Centreville and joining Bull Run at a point three miles to the south west. The enemy on the west, or right bank, of Bull Run defended all its crossings by earth works and field artillery. Nearly a mile above the stone bridge was a practicable ford opposite the enemy's left, and still two miles farther up, beyond the enemy's left, the stream could be easily crossed at an undefended ford. The plan, in a word, was to hold Blackburn's Ford southwest of Centreville, in force, and make demonstrations at that and other points up to and including the stone bridge, while our division after crossing Cub Run should turn to the right and follow a circuitous road through the woods to the upper ford, cross it, and turning downstream clear away the defence of the lower ford and let Heintzleman's division across; then, facing westward with that division, go for the enemy. The

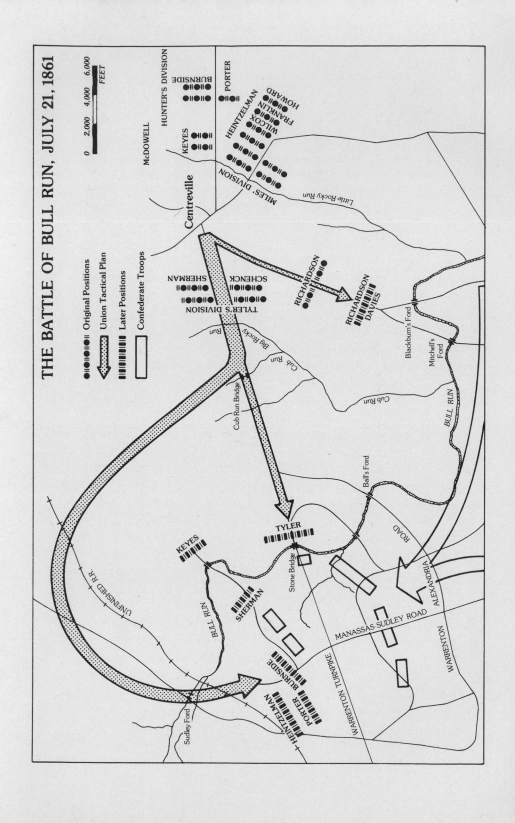

THE BATTLE OF BULL RUN, JULY 21, 1861

FEET
0 2,000 4,000 6,000

Original Positions
Union Tactical Plan
Later Positions
Confederate Troops

McDOWELL

HUNTER'S DIVISION

BURNSIDE
PORTER

KEYES

HEINTZELMAN
WILCOX
FRANKLIN
HOWARD

MILES' DIVISION

Little Rocky Run

Centreville

SHERMAN
SCHENCK
RICHARDSON

TYLER'S DIVISION

RICHARDSON
DAVIES

Blackburn's Ford
Mitchell's Ford

Cub Run
Big Rocky Run

Cub Run

BULL RUN

Cub Run Bridge

Ball's Ford

TYLER

ROAD

Stone Bridge

ALEXANDRIA

KEYES

BULL RUN

UNFINISHED R.R.

SHERMAN

MANASSAS-SUDLEY ROAD

BURNSIDE
PORTER
HEINTZELMAN

WARRENTON TURNPIKE

WARRENTON

Sudley Ford

distance from our camp to Centreville was a mile, thence to the turning point beyond Cub Run a long mile and thence to Sudley's Springs across the upper ford, by the circuitous road, about seven miles. Without obstructions we should reach Sudley's Springs easily, about an hour after sunrise.

The night was clear and the moon was full. The command was in good spirits and it was a great advantage to our militia and volunteer regiments to be brigaded with the regulars for their example of steadiness and discipline. Burnside's brigade led the way and it seems incredible that we did not reach Centreville, a distance of one mile, until 4.30 A.M. and it was nearly six o'clock when our column turned to the right beyond Cub Run. About an hour after turning to the right the roar of cannon down the stream behind us announced that the demonstrations below had begun and they gave to our march a needed exhilaration. From the point of leaving the turnpike we should have marched to Sudley's Mill, seven miles, in two hours and a half at most; but owing to the slow and intermittent movements of the brigade in front, four hours were consumed in making it. With that wasted hour and a half there fled an opportunity of the same sort as that which was lost by the same commander [i.e., Burnside] at Antietam a year later and prevented a complete and triumphant success on that bloody day.

About 10 o'clock A.M. there came once more to our division a definite and prolonged halt. The road on which we were standing passed along the verge of gentle heights, wooded on our right, but overlooking a cultivated valley on our left beyond which were low, wooded hills a mile away. A low cloud of dust in that direction attracted our attention, and, mounting a fence I could see with a glass a long, moving column of troops and discern their glistening bayonets and mounted officers. It was moving in a direction which would cross our line of march not far in front of the head of our column. Colonel Porter at once directed me to go to the head of the column and report the fact to Colonel Hunter. Hastening to the front I found the division commander with Colonel Burnside seated by the shaded springs enjoying a luncheon which was spread on the ground under the trees. Making my report, which did not seem to disturb him in the least, he requested Captain W. D. Whipple, his Adjutant General, to go and examine the matter. Whipple and I got out of the woods to the left as quickly as possible and, riding to an eminence near by, made out distinctly the approaching column and its flags. Hastening back, Captain Whipple told Colonel Hunter of the enemy's approach and direction, and orders to move on were given.

Returning to Colonel Porter and acquainting him with the situation, he sent me again to the head of the column to note the first place where his brigade could break out of it and pass to the front. At the head of the column now in motion I found the 2d Rhode Island led by Colonel [John S.] Slocum, and Captain Whipple and I assisted him in carrying out our suggestion to deploy the first two leading companies as skirmishers, and the Colonel rode gallantly forward with them and was lighting a cigar as I saw him for the last time. Within an hour he was mortally wounded. Coming to an opening in the woods to the right, through which could be seen fields beyond, I awaited Colonel Porter with his brigade. The skirmish fire of Burnside's advance could now be heard. When Colonel Porter arrived, the head of his brigade turned out to the right and hastened through the opening woods toward the fields.

Then the first cannon was heard to our front and left, and two seconds later a round shot came hurtling through the woods, tearing through the leaves and branches, thumping against trees and finally striking the ground within ten paces in front of us with the most intensely vicious sound imaginable. It seemed to have breath and brought with it a voice that the dullest man in ranks could hear and understand. It was the welcome of the spirit of all evil at the threshold of our first battle—an instantaneous expression of infinite wickedness.

With the permission of Colonel Porter, I hurried forward out of the woods into the open fields to ascertain the position of the enemy and select our own. When I got out on to the open I saw Captains J. B. Fry and W. D. Whipple racing like a pair of thoroughbred hunters over the high rolling fields, halting now and then to sweep the topography with their eyes. Joining them, they instantly gave me their *coup d'oeil* and instructions where to form the brigade. To our left, toward the south, the cultivated fields, with here and there a clump of trees, sloped gently down over half a mile to the Warrenton turnpike where the foot of opposite slopes were met rising to woodlands beyond. The enemy was already deployed along the Warrenton turnpike, the shrubbery and fences of which afforded him considerable protection. His right was strengthened by a grove. Batteries appeared in position along the crests behind his line from which all sorts of projectiles were thrown upon the ground in front of the position our brigade was soon taking at a double-quick step. Oh! for only the odd half hour of the hour and a half which had been uselessly lost in our march. Had we been on the field an hour sooner and well deployed we could have prevented the enemy taking any position and have routed him on his arrival and first attempt to form lines. That the enemy did not prevent our formation for attack is something to our credit, but also demonstrated that, but for the timely discovery of his approach, we should have met him with the chances greatly against us. It was to be seen by a glass that the enemy's forces were handled with celerity and precision.

Our brigade was quickly formed in line with the 27th New York on the left, then United States Marine Battalion, 14th New York, 8th New York and the Battalion of Regulars on the right, with cavalry extended to the right and rear. [Charles] Griffin's battery, one of the finest in the army, moved out in front of the center and opened fire upon the enemy's batteries with an effect that awakened frequent cheers along our line. Fragments of shell from the enemy reached our position during the formation and one of them striking a soldier of the 27th on the head causing him to drop his arms and go bounding about like a decapitated chicken— a singular phenomenon that I have never again observed.

Just as we were throwing out our line of skirmishers for an advance, came Captain W. D. Whipple, Assistant Adjutant General of the division, and reported to Colonel Porter that Colonel Hunter was wounded and had been carried off the field, and that he reported to him as senior officer. Porter went to the left of our brigade to be near the center of the division and there met Colonel Burnside, who came tearing up on a foaming charger, and saying with hysterical excitement, "Porter, for God's sake let me have the regulars. My men are all being cut to pieces."

Colonel Porter, who was always calm and clear headed, asked, "Colonel Burnside, do you mean to say that the enemy is advancing on my left?"

"Yes," said Burnside, "and you will be cut off if you can't stop him."

Colonel Porter then reluctantly directed me to have Sykes' battalion fall out and report to him on the left of the line, and then said he to me, "Look after this brigade yourself."

Sykes fell out from the right and marched to the left. I have ever believed this shifting of Sykes' battalion from the right of the line after the battle had begun, on account of the personal stampede of Burnside, as one of the fatal errors of that day. Two hours later Sykes returned to the right across a lost field of battle to hold the enemy in check while the broken army was leaving. Griffin had silenced the enemy's batteries and compelled them to retire. The head of Heintzleman's division appeared beyond our left; Sykes attacked and carried the grove in front of Burnside, driving the enemy out. Burnside's brigade, with the exception of the 2d New Hampshire Regiment, was entirely out of the action after Sykes' attack.

Our brigade advanced steadily, except the 27th on the left, which became excited and enraged by its casualties and rushed madly down the slope upon the enemy where its Colonel received a gunshot wound in the thigh and about sixty men were palled *hors de combat* and the gallant Major J.[Joseph] J. Bartlett took the command. Our cavalry dashed out on the right and took some prisoners, among whom was General George Steuart of Baltimore. Griffin moved farther to the front and [James B.] Rickett's regular battery came to join him. Our brigade had reached a line beyond that first occupied by the enemy. Tyler's division had crossed Bull Run and was engaged on Heintzleman's left. The 14th New York was extending to the right to cover ground lost by the 8th which had been broken up owing to the absence of Sykes' battalion from the right. Whipple and I had arranged five regiments to move forward with Griffin's and Rickett's batteries and meanwhile [Richard] Arnold's battery on the middle ground found an effective position.

Up to this moment everything had been favorable, when to our amazement we saw Griffin's and Rickett's batteries limber up and move on up the slopes without supports. A round shot struck Whipple's horse on the breastplate and went through him lengthwise leaving his rider on foot for a while. I rode quickly to the moving batteries and ascertained that they had received orders from General McDowell through Major Barry, chief of artillery, to move up onto the crest of the slope in front. Seeing General McDowell riding across the field toward the right, I rushed to him and explained our plan and pointed out the danger the batteries were incurring. He raised both hands and in a weary voice said, "Go and give any orders you deem necessary, Mr. Averell."

I then hurried up the Marines and Fire Zouaves from Heintzleman's division to the support of the batteries and pushed the 14th New York on the right into the woods. Then hastening to the batteries which had reached the crest and gone "into battery" and loaded, I found General Heintzleman by the side of Griffin, discussing with him the character of a line of men forming not over two hundred and fifty yards in front in the edge of the woods. Griffin's men were at the lanyards and he wished to give the command "fire." Heintzleman thought they were our own troops in front and appealed to me. The crest swelled up a little between the batteries and the line in question, so that the men in line could not be seen below their knees. With the naked eye I could see them dressing to the right and making side steps. From their uniforms I decided at once and said, "they are the enemy," and advised Griffin to fire. Heintzleman was on my right and, extending his left arm, laid his hand on my right to check me and exclaimed, "No, no! They are our men."

At that instant down came the line of small arms of the enemy to a level; we heard the command "fire," and experienced a sensation like that of passing through an imaginary seive. Heintzleman gave an expression of pain as a ball passed through his wrist near my arm and it seemed to me that every horse in the batteries sank down with many of the men. The horses attached to the line of caissons in rear started down the slopes at a frightful pace. The Marines delivered a desultory fire and broke away in spite of their gallant officers, one of whom with eight men was killed and two with seventeen men were wounded. The Fire Zouaves, who had been expected to make the Southern army quail when they should get a chance to indulge in their bent toward ruthless destruction, huddled together firing a few guns in the air and then ran like scared dogs. The slopes behind us and our first position were covered in a few minutes with the variegated uniforms of our disorganized regiments and not a few of them lay scattered about, quite still, on the ground. As I was descending the slope I remember passing Major Zeilin of the Marines, who was walking leisurely along with his sword drawn in his right hand, and as he would pass a mullain stalk or tall weed he would take the trouble to cut off its head with a right or left cut accompanying the blow with a half audible curse. The brave old gentleman was working off his grief and mortification at the conduct of his recruits.

The 27th New York promptly reformed on our first position facing the enemy and served as a nucleus for the gathering of other regiments. Sykes' battalion under that ideal soldier marched steadily across the field to an eminence in the middle ground on our right and held everything within range at a respectful distance while Porter's brigade was reformed. The brave old Major [James] Wadsworth, with revolver in hand, said to Whipple and myself, "Gentlemen, I am ready to lead any regiment against the enemy that will follow me." A number of division and brigade commanders collected on our left, around McDowell, a silent, smitten, waiting group. General McDowell said, "Gentlemen, it seems evident that we must fall back to Centreville. Colonel Porter you will please cover the withdrawal with your division."

Colonel Porter turned and directed me to see the order executed. When I went along our line to give the proper orders, men of the 27th raised an appealing—an angry cry, "We are not whipped, don't let us go away." Some raised their clinched fists in the air and demanded to be led again to the front. Alas! brave hearts, it was too late.

That had happened, which by every law of cause and effect, should have happened. An army unready and unfit for battle had been pushed to a humiliating defeat. Wherever there had been a chance for this splendid manhood to win, the control of an idiot or an imbecile had intervened to prevent it. Yet in a higher, aye, in the highest sense we had won, but we did not begin to understand until seventeen months later that this misfortune and other and greater ones which followed it were all to win the success of a supreme necessity to the Union of States, the freedom and dignity of labor, which was then hidden from us in the dim unknown. The plan of the battle was excellent, its dilatory execution with lack of tactical experience defeated it. The enemy's troops were handled with celerity and their small-arm fire was far better than ours. There was not sufficient cavalry to reach the enemy's communications; what we had barely sufficed for the orderly duties of the army. The active use of an additional regiment of cavalry might have prevented the junction of Johnston and saved us two days' delay, the 19th and 20th, in ascertaining the enemy's position, and on the field it could have struck the enemy's left and rear early in the battle with startling results. What happened in the retreat and how it became a disorderly rout are matters of record.

My own distress was very great and my dominating grief was the fear that our country would be divided. That battlefield is impressed on my memory as no other is. I drew from memory the topographical map of it which appeared with McDowell's report and is now in the official Atlas accompanying the Official Records of the Union and Confederate armies. It was not found necessary to modify it by any subsequent instrumental survey. The scene of wrath and destruction at the bridge crossing of Cub Run defies description. The tangle, wreck and crash of men, well and wounded, but all wild with panic except the dead, animals, artillery and baggage wagons, all thrashed and pounded and penetrated by a relentless artillery fire from the enemy, made a picture to delight the court of his Satanic majesty. Poor Tillinghast was dying in an ambulance wrecked in the melee.

When I rode up the slope toward Centreville as the sun was setting, I saw a man standing as motionless as a statue on a large rock in a field gazing across the run toward the battlefield. On passing him I saw it was my faithful soldier-friend, Peter Kinney. His face was a picture of despair and he did not hear my voice until I had called to him several times. Then he was overjoyed. He had been waiting and watching for me until he had given me up and had been filled with remorse that he had lost sight of me.

In the report of Colonel Andrew Porter appeared these complimentary words of which I am proud:

Acting Assistant Adjutant General W. W. Averell sustained the high reputation he had before won for himself as a brave and skillful officer, and to him I am greatly indebted for aid and assistance, not only in performing with the greatest promptitude the duties of his position, but by exposing himself most fearlessly in rallying and leading forward the troops, he contributed largely to their general effectiveness against the enemy. I desire to call the attention of the Commanding General particularly to him.

We stopped at Centreville until about midnight in a vain effort to stem the current of men who had temporarily lost their manhood and most of the belongings of a soldier. Our brigade was pretty well assembled on their old camp ground and secured a few hours of needed rest. There was an attempted council of commanders at Centreville, but its inutility was so apparent it was soon abandoned. Colonel Porter and Colonel Franklin with their staffs rode in rear of our brigade. The night became cloudy and dark and all we could do was to follow the living stream. There was little talk and most of the horsemen fell asleep as they rode along. Late in the night Colonel Franklin and I found ourselves together, both quite overcome with fatigue. I do not remember who made the suggestion, but we turned out of the road into the thick woods a little way, unsaddled our horses, tied them to trees and, using our saddles as pillows and one saddle blanket as a bed, lay down and spread the other over us and slept soundly until broad daylight. Then saddling our horses we made haste out to the road and proceeded on our way.

After going a short distance, we met a Union soldier and asked him where he was going. He replied, "To Washington." We told him he was going in the opposite direction. He assured us he was right as he had not stopped since he had left Centreville and knew he had not turned around. Thankful for the correction of our error, arising from our failure to note and remember on which side of the road we had turned out, we soon saw the Capitol in the distance. Around the residence of Dr. [Thomas] Antisell, about a mile from the Long Bridge, was a cluster of horses and orderlies. Dismounting and entering we found a number of our division and brigade commanders enjoying a hot and bountiful breakfast to partake of which we required no repeated invitation. From Colonel Porter who was present I received orders to go to Arlington and reestablish our brigade in its old camps and resume life, pickets and shelter. All of our brigade which had come in together had been halted here to rest and to gather up stragglers as they came in.

It had been raining for several hours, and as I rode along the dreary mile I had yet to go, the lack of sunshine and life presented the sharpest and darkest contrast with the aspect of the surroundings on the day of our departure only six days before. But gloomy as it was, it harmonized with our feelings. As I approached Arlington House there was no life nor sound except that of the birds twittering in the dripping branches. A few untied horses with drooping heads among the trees and sleeping orderlies lying prone on the ground betokened the return of some weary souls from Bull Run. On the portico was the solitary figure of a large man sitting on a chair with his arm hanging over the back and his bare head bowed on his breast. His flushed face and stentorian breathing indicated profound slumber. At his feet lay a soiled helmet that had once been white and the metal lance head on top of it was broken off. It was McDowell's return.

[20]

Military Necessity

A
s if the lurid smoke of Bull Run had floated over and settled upon Washington and stifled the breath of its citizens on the 22d of July, so the political atmosphere was stifling to national hope on that day. The fresh recollections of the eighteen thousand baffled and beaten men who had been actually engaged, reinforced with the vivid imaginations of as many more who had been in sight or hearing of the battle, filled the city with consternation and dismay. The strange spectacle of doleful trains of ambulances laden with wounded, and of bloody bandages worn by hundreds who could walk, assisted to a public realization of the horrors of the event and awakened the wildest apprehensions of danger to the Capital. Those wise civilian counsellors who had pervaded the White House and the Congress three days before and with complacent assurance had maintained the cry "on to Richmond" now skulked in silence or with bated breath whispered to each other alarming rumors of imminent perils. Like a flash of summer lightning which makes a landscape visible in the night, so the awful calamity brought to the public mind a clear apprehension of war. Instant *military necessity* was apparent and imperious.

General George B. McClellan was summoned from the theatre of his brilliant Union conquests in West Virginia on July 22d. Meanwhile the most energetic measures were taken to reestablish, strengthen and multiply the defenses on the Virginia side of the Potomac.

General McDowell was at first completely broken in spirit. Late on the dreary morning of the 22d, after our brigade had been reencamped

303

and cavalry pickets sent out, I found myself quite ready to accept another invitation to breakfast which had been prepared for General McDowell at the Arlington House. He spoke but little in a broken effeminate voice and exhibited an indifferent appetite. It was not until I had aroused him to a sense of our immediate danger by telling him that a corporal's guard of Confederate troopers riding across country could have captured him and his escort before my arrival, that he began to recover from the inanition of his dire misfortune and to think and act. Colonel Andrew Porter was placed in charge of our immediate defenses in front of Arlington and pickets were very soon posted as far out as Bailey's Cross-Roads and on a line from that point to the Chain Bridge above Georgetown. Outposts and supporting main guards were established and abatis and additional field works rapidly constructed. Several new regiments came over the Potomac to join our forces, among which I remember the 22d, 30th and 35th New York on the 25th, and the DeKalb regiment on the 26th.[1] All the troops were rigidly inspected and regular drills were begun.

During these feverish and dreadful hours and days, the genius of Thomas A. Scott, Assistant Secretary of War, blazed along the railways and telegraph lines of which he assumed control. Orders were flashed to Governor [Andrew G.] Curtin at Harrisburg, and to every other point where troops were in readiness, to put them on cars and rush them to Washington. One or two armed vessels were ordered to Alexandria to command its approaches and all the crossings of the Potomac up to Chain Bridge were covered by the most reliable regiments, which rounded up the multitude of demoralized volunteers and sent them to convenient camps which had been promptly established where cooked food was kept ready for the men of each regiment. As food was forbidden to them elsewhere than in their own camps, hunger soon assembled and reorganized the dispersed and despondent thousands; and after refreshment and rest, their restoration to tranquillity, hope and resolution was rapid. Confidence on the Virginia side soon began to replace uneasy forebodings. A system of signals was put in operation by which Headquarters could be kept *en rapport* with the line of outposts. The general defense was perfected and united to Alexandria. Revolt in Baltimore was at once throttled by a concentration of troops in that city and the stringent measures of repression which were promptly applied.

---

[1]The DeKalb Regiment was the 41st New York Infantry.

On the morning of the 22d Thomas A. Scott allowed only the message of General Scott to General McClellan, then at Beverly, West Virginia, to go East, which stated that, "After fairly beating the enemy and taking three of his batteries, a panic had seized McDowell's army, and it was in full retreat on the Potomac." But after two or three days the direful extent of the national disappointment at Bull Run began to spread through the North with lists of names of killed and wounded, and then the mills that made crape received encouragement which kept them in motion.

General McClellan assumed command of the division of the Potomac on the 27th of July and preparations for the organization of the Army of the Potomac were begun. In his second general order issued on July 30th, Colonel Andrew Porter was appointed Provost Marshal in Washington. He was relieved of his command on the Virginia side by General Erasmus D. Keyes with 1st Lieutenant Herbert A. Hascall, 4th Artillery, as Chief of Staff. I remember Surgeon [George M.] Sternberg of the Medical Department came into camp that day from Centreville whence he had escaped from the enemy.

The Capital was at that time in a frightful state of misrule. It was not the beautiful city it has since become. Its streets were without pavements and deep with dust which filled the air in dry weather, and when wet, the mud and sloughs rendered them almost impassable. Frequent trains of army wagons, moving through the streets without any general regulation or order, subjected all other vehicles to intolerable delays and constant danger. Life and property were to a great extent at the mercy of gangs of thieves and all kinds of prowling criminals who found a convenient mask for their depredations in the noisy carousals of hundreds of unruly and disorderly volunteers absent from their regiments. The hotels were crowded with officers who were away from their duties without authority.

It was this laxity of discipline and neglect of military duty which first attracted the attention of our new commander and caused the appointment of Colonel Porter to the arduous duties of Provost Marshal. This was a new office in our service and it was necessary to define its duties. In Washington they were generally as follows:

The preservation of good order and the suppression of anything that would disturb it.
Suppression of gambling houses and disorderly resorts.
Regulation of hotels, markets and places of amusement.

Searches, seizures and arrests.
Obtaining information from the enemy.
Preventing information reaching the enemy.
The conduct of the secret service of the Government.
Passes of citizens or Express Companies for the conduct of business.
Complaints of citizens as to the conduct of soldiers.

In the field the duties were extended beyond the limits of the camps of the army and, on the march, included the enforcement of orders forbidding depredations on private property.

All the regular infantry near Washington, a battery of artillery and a squadron of cavalry, were detailed for these duties under the Provost Marshal. This force was so stationed as to most conveniently perform its duties as Provost Guard and at the same time be always in readiness to go quickly to any threatened point on the outskirts of the city, which was important in consideration of the many vulnerable points that then, and for a short time afterward, existed in our environment, especially on the Maryland side.

The headquarters of the Provost Marshal with its several offices were established in the Corcoran block on "I" Street above Vermont Avenue. The residence of Hon. Reverdy Johnson then stood in a large lot on the corner of the streets named. We lodged and had our meals at a pleasant little house nearly opposite our headquarters, kept by William Wormley, who was the first gentleman I ever saw who was not embarrassed by being a mulatto.[2] He was a very remarkable man who enjoyed the friendship of many prominent people. Mr. John Van Buren of New York and Mr. Charles Sumner of Massachusetts, belonging to different political parties, always stopped with Wormley and telegraphed him when they were coming. He had portraits of both presented to him, the one of Sumner being of life size, in oils. Generous in every direction where want appealed, Wormley acquired wealth and afterward founded the great hotel of his name. At his funeral in after years I saw in attendance all the prominent ladies and gentlemen of Washington and of the Army and Navy in the city.

---

[2] Wormley (1819-1884) was a prominent Washington hotel owner and caterer. His establishment, the Wormley House, on I Street near Fifteenth, had an international reputation and attracted many prominent people. In 1868, Wormley accompanied Reverdy Johnson, a former Maryland senator and United States attorney general, to England. Johnson served as the American minister while Wormley was the steward at the American legation.

Wormley had a hard task to care for us for we worked day and night. Our headquarters were never closed. Patrols of cavalry and of infantry soon cleared the city and no officer nor soldier was permitted to be absent from his command without written authority which must state the reason of his absence. If visiting the city on public business he must have an order from his brigade commander. A few extra prisons were employed. I remember two: the "Old Capitol" and the 13th Street prison. General McClellan in his report says, "Washington soon became as quiet as any city in the Union."

Many residents with strong secession predilections, business relations and social alliances with Southern people abandoned their homes, some of them at a sacrifice, and found their way into the Confederacy; but many remained for a time and assumed a variety of political attitudes. Some were quiet, discreet persons who tried the impracticable role of neutrality. Others with daring assurance admitted they were secessionists who proposed to take no active part in the war, while the most dangerous professed openly the most loyal Union sentiments but secretly seized every opportunity to carry valuable information to the Confederate authorities. Active agents of the enemy permeated society and pervaded the departments, whose business it was to furnish him with information of our doings. In spite of all our watchfulness and precautions, intelligence of our progress in organization, movements of troops and position of our works under construction in some unaccountable manner quickly found its way into the camps of the enemy at Manassas.

We had under our control and general direction an alert and skillful detective force of about one hundred and sixty persons under the personal direction of that matchless detective, Allen Pinkerton, then known as Major E. J. Allen, the father of those noted detectives, Robert and William Pinkerton. Of all the really efficient and loyal detectives I have ever seen, Allen Pinkerton or Major Allen was the greatest. He was a Scotchman by birth, strongly built, with large chest and powerful arms. His complexion was bronzed, forehead broad and wide with prominent developments indicating the keenest perceptive faculties. His eye was remarkable. Quiet and dreamy when in repose, but when absorbed in an exciting quest the pupil would dilate and contract as in the eye of a cat and as he neared his prey their intense burning gleam together with his quick, feline motions reminded one of a tiger. He was utterly fearless and had been known to enter a dark room alone to arrest an armed desperado. He had the mysterious faculty of rendering himself invisible while passing along a street. He knew by a wonderful intuition the ways and habits of all criminals and after letting them run for a few days could go by an unerring instinct to their hiding place. When engaged in conjecture as to the route of a criminal, he had a manner of moving the index finger of his right hand like detective Bucket in "Bleak House." His force was composed of all sorts and conditions of men and women. A few appeared as accomplished ladies and gentlemen who lived in good style at the hotels and contributed to the social gayeties of the capital. Then there were correspondents of distant journals—some foreign, contractors, priests, hackdrivers, pedlars, organ grinders, domestic servants and beggars.

We caught many common spies and penetrated the conclaves of conspirators, yet we could not get at the source of the higher, reliable and dangerously valuable information which was conveyed to the enemy. Sometimes our movements and reconnaissances that were ordered at the front were so promptly met, and sometimes prematurely responded to, that we knew the enemy's news gatherer must be someone who was in daily contact with, and had the confidence of, the highest officials. We knew that when the news was sent, the messenger must cross the Potomac at some point. Every crossing was watched day and night for fifty miles up and down the river.

At last our vigilance was rewarded. One dark night a man came across the Potomac in a skiff near Port Tobacco, Maryland, and immediately fell into the hands of two of Pinkerton's men, who, acting as secession friends brought him safely to our headquarters. He was the bearer of a letter to a Mrs. B. who lived in secluded apartments over a glove store near the corner of 13th Street and Pennsylvania Avenue. The Confederate messenger was sent to the 13th Street prison where he was shortly joined in the same cell by another prisoner, one of Pinkerton's force, to get his confidence and experience, while another "operative" took the letter after its examination to Mrs. B. The messenger was secluded in Mrs. B.'s apartments while she carried the letter to the residence of a prominent counsellor at law on "I" Street below Seventeenth. The counsellor had gone south leaving his wife and two grown daughters behind. The letter was taken by one of these ladies without delay to the home of Mrs. Greenhow on Sixteenth Street between "H" and "I" and quite near our headquarters. So the trace was broken in order that, if only one person should be apprehended, the others might escape suspicion. Every stage of the letter's progress was attended by Pinkerton's operatives and a detective, technically called a "shadow," was left on each house.

Mrs. Greenhow was a woman of rare abilities, thoroughly acquainted with Washington, its surroundings and its society, a brilliant, cultivated lady of varied accomplishments and withal a keen politician with a large acquaintance in diplomatic circles. Mr. Greenhow, her husband, was a translator and cipher writer in the State Department. This lady had established in a modest but attractive way *un petit salon* where she received visits from the highest government officials and most prominent society people as well as from travellers and men of affairs. She also frequently made calls on public functionaries of all grades in political, civil and military life. Every one with whom she came in contact was "shadowed" through all the diversities and complexities of their social acquaintance. Her house and that of the counsellor's wife were quickly bereft of servants, who going forth on errands failed to return, and their places were filled with Pinkerton's domestics seeking situations. From these, frequent reports of everything going on in these houses were received through the "shadows."[3]

After a brief time a letter was taken by Mrs. Greenhow to the counsellor's wife who carried it to Mrs. B. on the Avenue, and when night had settled down the precious missive was brought to our headquarters. The letter was voluminous and written in a combination of two ciphers which Pinkerton's cipher man unravelled. It was a complete report of existing and projected defenses around Washington, armament in place and expected, proposed strength of garrisons, troops recently arrived and on the way, even the proceedings and proposed measures of the military committees and the condition of foreign affairs. Also an abstract of official reports of forces in the West and much information that was known to but few persons. When this was laid before General McClellan, his amazement was unbounded. Some of the information was news to him, especially the political portion.

A letter was then written in the same ciphers containing the most recent published news of the day together with some misleading information and forwarded over the route ascertained from the imprisoned messenger by his fellow captive and addressed to the *nom de guerre* of an officer on the staff of the General commanding at Centreville.

While the Confederate General was inditing his reply, Pinkerton's

---

[3]A good parallel to Averell's narrative is in John Bakeless, *Spies of the Confederacy*, pp. 28-41.

messenger, whose name I remember was Applegate,[4] was making good use of his eyes and ears in the enemy's camp. The reply which was returned contained explicit requests as to the information desired by the Confederate General. This proved exceedingly interesting to General McClellan for it is almost as important to know what your enemy lacks as what he possesses. Here the game ended by making "traps" of the houses of those conspirators: that is, they were secluded in their homes and whomsoever called upon them was admitted and detained. Thirty-five persons were gathered at the house of Mrs. Greenhow. Some of them were of sufficient distinction to be brought directly to our headquarters where a few were asked to remain until the "trap" was opened. Among them was a member of the military committee of the Senate who had been innocently beguiled through his sympathies into furnishing reassurances to a lovely, loyal woman who seemed painfully distressed about the safety of Washington.

I may not mention from whom the accurate military information was obtained; the principal ones are dead—loyal but indiscreet persons who received an effectual caution. Fragments of an interesting correspondence were found unconsumed in a stove in Mrs. Greenhow's house, which when put together revealed the sources and destination of information of vital importance. There was some question as to which Department, that of State or War, should have charge of these arrested conspirators, and it was decided that they should be regarded as State prisoners and a commission consisting of General John A. Dix and Edwards Pierrepont afterwards disposed of them.

It was deemed necessary to lay the reports of this matter before the President and as General Porter was absent in Philadelphia on account of illness it became my duty to present them. There were several gentlemen with the President, Mr. Seward and Colonel Thomas A. Scott being among them. The question of the immediate disposal of the arrested conspirators was discussed and I ventured to suggest that they be sent to Fort Ontario at Oswego, N.Y., where there were spacious and comfortable quarters somewhat isolated and easily guarded. Mr. Lincoln remarked immediately that it was too near Canada and a temptation would be

---

[4]Samuel Applegate may well have been a double agent in the Civil War. Bakeless, *Spies of the Confederacy*, p. 58.

presented to their friends there to communicate with them which might lead to difficulties, and after a moment's reflection he said, "These people are so fond of the South, suppose we send them down there."

Mrs. Greenhow after two or three days' enforced seclusion in her own house was transferred to the 13th Street prison and later on to the Old Capitol Prison where she remained through the winter of 1861-2. This implacable enemy of the Union denounced the government to her guards and visitors in the most violent and opprobrious terms at every opportunity and in some mysterious maneuver was successful in sending important political and military information to the enemy. The remarkable clemency and magnanimity that the government displayed toward this vindictive and dangerous woman should be remembered to the honor of the Administration.

At the first report of the arrest of Mrs. Greenhow to the President, someone inquired, "Why wouldn't it be well to strike higher and arrest the most prominent people here who are believed to be secessionists?" The name of the mayor, James G. Berret, was mentioned. It was stated that there was no evidence against him. But, it was argued, he was a Marylander and his associates and friends in Maryland required an example. Let them know that we will no longer tolerate enemies among us, the political effect throughout the North would be excellent. A Union man could not live in the South outside a prison a moment; should we be less tolerant of secessionists right here in Washington where they can be most dangerous? It was evident that the conspiracies and weaknesses that were disclosed in the reports which I had presented had disturbed and alarmed the Administration. The revelation conveyed a reflection, not devoid of sting, upon the town-meeting style of running a government in time of War. It provoked a resentful feeling which manifested itself in a passionate desire to stamp out all anti-union sentiments in the North and to imprison or exile all persons who might or should entertain them. When I left the President and his counsellors, no conclusion had been reached nor orders made.

Mayor Berret was a gentleman of most distinguished appearance with an erect figure above six feet in height and of perfect proportions, supporting a fine head well poised. The easy and agreeable courtesy of his manners and the bright, frank expression of his fine gray eyes, altogether made him notable among the handsome men of his time, and he was then about thirty-eight years of age. While General Mansfield had commanded the forces in Washington, the Mayor had obtained the old Capitol as a comfortable and secure prison and had harmonized the activities of his police force with those of the military.

At 11 o'clock that same night, August 23d, Colonel Thomas A. Scott, Assistant Secretary of War, brought to me the order of the Secretary to arrest Mayor Berret and send him to Fort Lafayette, New York Harbor. I detailed Lieutenant Wilson for the duty and Major Allen (Pinkerton) called the mayor to the door of his residence on "H" Street between Fourteenth and Fifteenth streets, while Colonel Scott went with me into the hall to identify the mayor and to see the order executed with as little discomfort to him as the circumstances admitted. The mayor had retired but accepted the situation promptly, yet with the remark that there was "no reason on earth for such action." He remained at Fort Lafayette only about twenty days when the President ordered his release and had a personal interview with him.

All the persons who were guiltily implicated in the Greenhow conspiracy and treasonable acts were sent to the Old Capitol Prison where they remained until the spring of the next year when they were transferred to Fort Monroe whence after two months longer incarceration they were set at liberty beyond the Union lines in Virginia on their parole that they would not return north of the Potomac during the war. I believe Mrs. Greenhow shortly afterward got into trouble in New Orleans and was confined to Ship Island by order of General B. F. Butler. It may be remembered that Mrs. Greenhow escaped thence and went to London on a mission for the Confederate government, and that she afterward returned on a blockade runner which entered the harbor of Wilmington in a dark night and that sitting on or leaning over the rail she fell overboard and sank. It was supposed that she was weighted with foreign gold as she never rose again.[5]

One of the methods of obtaining information from the enemy which

---

[5]Rose O'Neal Greenhow was the Confederacy's most famous female spy. In May 1862, she was sent to the Confederacy where she was treated as a heroine. Jefferson Davis told her, "But for you there would have been no Battle of Bull Run." She then toured the South but did not visit New Orleans, then occupied by federal troops. In August 1863, she left Wilmington, North Carolina, for Europe. While abroad her book *My Imprisonment and the First Year of Abolition Rule at Washington* was published in London. Returning to the Confederacy on 30 September 1864, her ship ran aground off Wilmington. She and two Confederate agents, fearing capture by the federal blockading fleet, requested a rowboat to put them ashore. This boat capsized in the waves and she was drowned— legend says she had gold tied around her waist. Her body was brought to Wilmington where she was buried with military honors.

was carried on successfully for some months was as follows: Major Allen informed me one day that a lady, of whom he gave me a personal description, would probably enter the office sometime in the next twenty-four hours and inquire for me and on seeing me would ask direction to a certain place, and requested me to quietly show her to one of his inquisition rooms and send for him. It happened as indicated and a prepossessing, bright-eyed, lady-like little woman appeared, and when Major Allen had arrived she proceeded to pull off her fine linen undersleeves, which were double and voluminous, and when opened and spread out displayed a sketch of the enemy's field works about Centreville and other points and the distribution of his forces, armament and the topography, with an abstract of returns and general information. This had been prepared by one of Allen's men who was in the rebel camps supplying officers with gold and silver insignia of rank, such as stars and braids for their coats and hats, which they were glad to have at a moderate price. These were furnished by us in small quantities, so as to make the journeys more frequent, and the thread and other fastenings and a variety of light trinkets were also sent by this woman who with her husband placed them on the officers' uniforms. Those ornaments were selected which pertained to the higher grades in order to bring the "operative" in contact with those officers having the most information. It was interesting to listen to the personal descriptions of this clever woman and her repetition of conversations she had heard while plying her needle with great pains in order to occupy time. Her journeys were made from Washington through Kentucky to the Virginia and Tennessee R. R. and thence to her waiting customers. She, of course, carried all the newspapers and such other innocent aids and comforts as she could. Our "safe guard" carried her without detention to the point of crossing the lines. We had two or three such operatives constantly at work in the Confederate Armies.

On the 12th of August the Provost Marshal received an order early in the morning, signed by Simon Cameron, Secretary of War, directing him to arrest Charles J. Faulkner forthwith and confine him in the jail of Washington City. Hon. Charles James Faulkner had been the United States Minister at the Court of France and had but just returned from his mission and was then putting up at Brown's Hotel. General Porter asked me to execute the order in person on account of the distinguished character of Mr. Faulkner. Taking a carriage and a mounted orderly, I called at the hotel and sent up my card. Mr. Faulkner received me in his private parlor with a pleasing courtesy of manner and speech. He was a man of medium height, clad in black frock coat, vest and trousers, immaculate linen with a standing collar and plain black necktie—the general make up of an ideal statesman of fifty years. His clean-shaven face had that high refinement which comes through generations of gentle people and its changeful expressions indicated a life-long intercourse with clever and intellectual men and women. Without taking a proffered seat I said to him, "If you will kindly read the paper I hand you it will inform you of the occasion of my visit."

As he read the order of the Secretary to General Porter, his frame stiffened up suddenly and a pallor came down his high forehead and spread over his face and thin lips. When read, he dropped the hand which held the paper and, raising the other, said in a steady voice of earnest solemnity and with an expression of face and eyes which was aimed beyond and above me, like an appeal to the nation: "I protest against this order as an outrage upon my rights as a citizen of the United States. I have never by thought, word or action been disloyal to the government I have had the honor to represent at the Court of France. I protest against the arrest and the ignominy of being confined in a common jail." When this impressive outburst was over he said to me calmly, "I am at your service, Sir."

Then I advised him to pack a portmanteau with such things as he would require for a week and arrange his baggage so that I could send for it and have it cared for. We drove to the jail and leaving Mr. Faulkner in the carriage I obtained an entrance. The assault upon my senses when I had entered its portals I can never forget. The cells were crowded and the corridors filled with grovelling, wallowing, howling, obscene beasts in wrecked and wretched human forms of all colors, reeking with indescribable stenches and unspeakable filth. The first instant in this unmitigated inferno was sufficient for me. For the first and only time in my army life I willfully disobeyed an order or rather felt it my duty to delay obedience until these horrible conditions were reported. Reentering the carriage I directed the driver to take us to our headquarters, explaining to Mr. Faulkner that there was no room for him in the jail. He could never know what crowded horrors were therein. On the way I bethought myself of Major Willard, commanding the 8th United States Infantry of the Provost Guard, who had temporarily taken a small house on New York Avenue, and I called there and ascertained that he had a nice furnished room on the second story. I informed the Major of my order and requested him to take charge of Mr. Faulkner by order of General Porter and to send for his baggage.

It was a great relief to unburden my mind to General Porter, who listened with a growing indignation which quickly became red-hot, and under its impulse we went to see the Secretary of War, with whom he was personally acquainted being from the same State. General Porter could cut deeper with less language, when laboring under a finely controlled rage, than any man I ever knew. He showed the Secretary the order and asked him if he had any idea what it meant. The Secretary replied it was simply to arrest Mr. Faulkner and put him in jail as a State prisoner. Then General Porter said what I cannot undertake to repeat. Its substance reduced to unimpassioned English was that the government could take his commission then and there, but no authority could require him or his officers to do an inhuman act, that if Mr. Faulkner was a State prisoner the United States Marshal was the proper officer to make the arrest, but if he was a prisoner of war he was entitled to the proper treatment of a prisoner of war, which, it was evident to him, the Secretary did not appreciate nor understand. It was torrid while it lasted and the upshot of it was that Mr. Faulkner was sent to Fort Lafayette. It was generally understood that the arrest had been made in retaliation for the arrest and imprisonment of a personal friend of the Secretary by the Confederates shortly after the Battle of Bull Run.

My duties brought me frequently into official intercourse and somewhat confidential relations with General McClellan whom I saw for the first time when he assumed command of the Division of the Potomac. There were a few prominent commanders evolved by the Civil War who resembled him in many respects, but they were men who had required development and exhibited growth and improvement as their experiences increased. But McClellan seemed to me to set out in his great career with a completed character and with faculties fully perfected. A few others of subordinate rank on the Union side made a near approach to him in the fullness of their powers and the exalted excellences of their characters which inspired and maintained an unfailing esteem in the minds of all virtuous men who knew them. But none possessed a personality as glowing and faultless as McClellan. On the Confederate side there were similar lofty characters and among those I knew Robert E. Lee, Albert Sidney Johnston, and Joseph E. Johnston, who were pre-eminent examples of the same class of great American soldiers in whom the brutifying tendencies of war had no effect.

Of all the great commanders with whom I ever had official or personal relations, McClellan was easily the chief in the comprehensiveness and readiness of his intelligence. With unfailing patience and absolutely tireless energy, he exercised his amazing executive ability with a refreshing earnestness of manner, totally devoid of egotism or affectation, that was wonderfully winning to all who came near him. There were days when he was in the saddle riding around the defences of Washington from sunrise until sunset studying and supervising continuous or connected works over fifty miles in extent and at evening would resume his office duties with unabated vigor until midnight. Only those who have seen it done can imagine the herculean labor required in organizing an army of a hundred and fifty thousand men of all arms with all its staff departments and reducing it to obedience, discipline, fighting efficiency and mobility.

All competent and unpreduciced men who have read the memorandum submitted by General McClellan to President Lincoln at the request of the latter on the 4th of August, 1861, must at once admit that his measurement of the full proportions of the great impending conflict between the North and the South and of the necessities for immediate and adequate preparations for its successful prosecution on the part of the government, was the first ever made, and that it was timely, exact, comprehensive and truly prophetic was fully demonstrated by subsequent events. That paper was the egg from whose incubation sprang the Grand Army of the Potomac. And if it were known that that memorandum, involving an issue so momentous as the life of this nation, was written at a single sitting without pause, those who have read or shall read it would bow in profound acknowledgement of the genius who wielded the pen. It came to the sorely tried soul of the President like the dawn of day to the anxious master of a rudderless ship off a dangerous lee shore.[6]

The General's headquarters during the summer and autumn of 1861 were in the Wilkes' Mansion, corner of "H" Street and Madison Place. One warm night about nine o'clock I was leaving them after a short interview with the General, when Mr. Lincoln came across Madison Place alone in a pair of old fashioned leather slippers and wearing a long brown

---

[6]McClellan's memorandum to Lincoln on August 1861 was his proposal on how to win the war. In addition to efforts in Kentucky, Missouri, along the Mississippi River, western Virginia and a naval blockade, he proposed the main army in Virginia to have 273,000 men. He said that he realized this force was large but he proposed "to re-establish the power of its government, and to restore peace to its citizens, in the shortest possible time." Furthermore, McClellan predicted, "I propose, with the force which I requested, not only to drive the enemy out of Virginia, and occupy Richmond, but to occupy Charleston, Savannah, Montgomery, Pensacola, Mobile and New Orleans, in other words, to move into the heart of the enemy's country, and crush out the rebellion in its very heart." See George B. McClellan, *Report of Maj.-Gen. George B. McClellan, Aug. 4, 1863*, pp. 43-47.

linen "duster" without coat, vest or necktie, and entering headquarters without inquiry or announcement, he mounted the stairs and walked into McClellan's room on the first floor front. The windows were wide open and the room wall lighted. Across Madison Place was Lafayette Park whose shrubbery in the darkness would afford concealment to any person desiring to escape observation, so that the President was an easy mark for the pistol or rifle shot of an assassin.

Returning, I found my class-mate Colburn who was a favorite staff officer and always near the General, and we went across the street and waited until the President came out when we took him in charge and walked home with him to the White House. We ventured to tell him he had no right to do that sort of thing but he turned it aside by remarking that the war was over the other side of the river. Without any protection an assassin could have killed him, or two or more men could have captured him that night without risk to themselves. I at once saw Marshal Lamon, the faithful friend of the President, and gave him a serious warning of what might be the fearful consequences of such carelessness of the President's safety. It was of no use to speak to Mr. Lincoln about it for he would forget it immediately if he heeded it at all. It was such fatal carelessness as this which permitted the tragic end of his life.

Marshal Ward H. Lamon was one of the notable characters of that time. Tall and remarkably well built, weighing about two hundred and forty pounds, he was one of the most muscular and active men I ever saw. He could stand erect and turn a somersault and alight in the same tracks from which he had sprung with ease. He generally carried arms and was always prepared for an encounter but never used any weapons. On one of those occasions of a difficult arrest, he struck a powerful, desperate man who fell senseless and bleeding at the nose and from his ears. It was thought for some time the blow had been fatal. Lamon, deeply regretting the result, went to the President and told him all about it. After Mr. Lincoln had heard him he said, "Well, Marshal, the next time you find it necessary to strike a man, do take a club or something that will not hurt him so much."

There was a gentleman much about the White House at that time who bore so strong a likeness to Mr. Lincoln that he in after years stood as a model for the statue of the President now in the old chamber of the House of Represenattives. He was from Illinois and his name was Leonard Sweat and known as a close friend of the President. He came often to see me on special matters and on the 7th of August came on the part of the

TEN YEARS IN THE SADDLE

President to offer me the Lieutenant Colonelcy of an Illinois Volunteer Cavalry regiment of which Mr. Lincoln was going to make Mr. T. Lyle Dickey, his former law-partner, the Colonel. Judge Dickey came to Washington and called to see me on the 9th of August with my old friend Colonel Emory, who had been made Lieutenant Colonel of the 6th United States Cavalry. Several of my best friends advised me to accept the proffered Lieutenant Colonelcy and by the "backsight" of after years it seemed probable that I made a mistake in declining it. It would have taken me far away from Washington and the repressing and overslaughing political influences which hindered the promotion of regular officers who did not know how, or did not care, to avail of them. In the West there was more freedom of action and successes were not immediately forgotten. Colonel Dickey did not remain long in service and the field was then left open to his Lieutenant Colonel.

During the time I was engaged on Provost duty in Washington, a little over two months in the summer and autumn of '61, my time was most thoroughly engrossed with a variety of duties, yet it was possible to seize a few odd hours for social enjoyments rendered extraordinarily alluring by conditions which had never before existed in this country and will never be repeated. Washington seemed at that time like the vivid and brilliant cup of an enormous social orchid around which the calyx of a great army of an hundred and fifty thousand men was forming. Many of the busy-bees, big-bugs and butterflies of humanity visited it for the pleasing stimulation and intoxication of its intense sensations or for the coveted nourishments of fortune there to be found in the golden pollen of the treasury. Everything was in motion, topics changed daily, often hourly. Expectation stood tiptoe on every threshold. Yesterday was stale, the day before ancient, and the last week legendary.

The families of the cabinet officials and the prominent members of Congress and of the Army and Navy constituted the main social body, to which the foreign legations contributed an interesting auxiliary. This highly intelligent and representative social nucleus was greatly augmented and enlivened by an ever-changing contingent of visitors who brought to it a yet more complete cosmopolitan character. There was no time nor inclination for extravagant entertainments. Never did social life depend more exclusively on the personal qualities, individual characteristics and accomplishments of the men and women who maintained it than at Washington during the organization and growth of the Army of the Potomac. There was a natural, if not necessary, evolution of the *salon* in the houses of many social leaders where clanking sabres and jingling spurs were often heard. The beautiful and gifted daughter of the Secretary of the Treasury presided over her father's mansion whence there gently flowed political influences, far reaching and potential.[7] Almost any evening one might find at the house of General Andrew Porter, distinguished social exemplars of many capitals drawn thither by the brilliant social attractions of its gracious mistress who was generally assisted by two or three estimable ladies who were her guests.

The ancient Carroll mansion, always a fashionable centre, had an additional stimulant to social animation in the wedding of the eldest daughter to Captain, afterward General, Griffin of the Army. One of the Senators from Rhode Island maintained a charming home. Colonel Thomas A. Scott and the Camerons of Pennsylvania, the Schonbergers of Cincinnati and Mr. Charles Knap, the great gun maker, Mr. Clem Hill and the Prussian Minister, Baron Von Gerolt, all had pleasant and attractive houses in which the ready welcome of friends was brightened by lovely young ladies. Governor [William] Dennison of Ohio, the Postmaster General [Montgomery Blair], and Senators [Ira] Harris of New York and [Milton S.] Latham of California maintained establishments notable for their charming hospitality. Among the visitors to the Capital and the surrounding army who became widely known and distinguished for his philanthropy and practical sympathy among the sick and suffering in the hospitals was Mr. Clement B. Barclay of Philadelphia. Señor Romero was then an entertaining and agreeable young gentleman well known. The French princes—de Joinville, Comte de Paris and Duc de Chartres—and other members of McClellan's staff, Hudson, Radowitz, McMahon, Raymond, Biddle and Russell found rest and social recreation in the later hours of the evenings.[8]

A number of the officers of the Army of the Potomac had their

---

[7]Kate Chase Sprague (1840-1899) was the daughter of the widowed secretary of the treasury, Salmon P. Chase. Kate served as her father's official hostess. Extravagant tastes led her to the wealthy senator from Rhode Island, William Sprague, and they were married on November 12, 1863, in a glittering ceremony. Her husband's wealth was used to promote her father's presidential aspirations. Financial difficulties and hints of adultery by Kate led to a divorce in 1882. She died in poverty, spending her last years raising chickens and selling milk.

[8]In 1861 the three French noblemen came to America to observe the first major war since Napoleon. The Prince de Joinville was the son of King Louis Phillipe while the Comte de Paris and the Duc de Chartres were the sons of the Duc d'Orleans, brother of the king. They were given the honorary rank of captain and were assigned to McClellan's staff, serving as aides-de-camp during the Peninsular campaign. They performed gallantly under fire during the Battle of Gaines Mills (June 27, 1862). After the war they returned to France where the Prince de Joinville produced a fine painting of the Battle of Gaines Mills and the Comte de Paris wrote a four-volume history of the Civil War.

families domiciled in Washington whence they would occasionally lend their welcome presence in social excursions to the camps.

The steady development of strength and discipline of the army furnished the burden of popular thought. Frequent reviews of divisions in rapid succession awakened in the troops and in the public mind a consciousness of their increasing coherency and mobility. On September 12th the first of these public reviews began with General Fitz-John Porter's division composed of the brigades of [George W.] Morell, [John H.] Martindale and [Daniel] Butterfield. The general officers of other divisions were present and those who had seen the jolly little army that had been sent to Bull Run in July remarked that it was now easy to understand the cause of our defeat. When this series of reviews was completed our lines were advanced, on the 28th, to Munson's Hill. The moral effect of this upon the army was of great benefit. It enabled it to strip itself of all useless impedimenta and encumbrances which had been accumulated and a feeling of confidence of first importance was generated. One of the reviews, which took place on the 24th, was of two thousand cavalry and seven light batteries east of the Capitol and was electrifying in its dash and precision.

The most rigid discipline and attention to duty was enforced throughout the army and was generally accepted with satisfaction. I can recall but one or two instances of notable insubordination. A regiment encamped on the heights, out Fourteenth Street, North, openly mutinied on August 14th and drove its officers out of camp.[9] General McClellan applied an effectual remedy instantly. By his order the infantry regiments of the Provost Guard and a section of a battery and squadron of cavalry were marched to the vicinity of the mutineers' camp, and one regiment formed line on the east facing their camp and drove all the men of the mutinous regiment out into the road at the point of the bayonet and there formed them in line. Then, I, as Acting Assistant Adjutant General, read to them the special order of the General Commanding, in which he recited their conduct and properly characterized it and accepted the issue they had made with military authority. He then ordered that the chief mutineers should be pointed out by their officers, that they should be put

---

[9]The regiment in question was the 79th New York Infantry. For more details on the mutiny, and the punishment subsequently imposed, see William Todd, *The Seventy-ninth Highlanders, New York Volunteers, in the War of the Rebellion, 1861-1865*, pp. 56-67.

in irons and sent forthwith to the Dry Tortugas off the coast of Florida and there be confined during the remainder of the war, and that the colors should be taken from the regiment and placed in the War Department and not restored to it until it had shown by its conduct in battle that it was worthy to carry them.

To say that the mutinous regiment seemed paralyzed were stating it mildly. There was a low cry like a protesting moan from those nearest the colors when they were taken away. Then the officers were directed to pass along the ranks and point out the leaders in the mutiny. This was done and about forty men were at once put in irons and marched away without a word of good-bye down to the wharf and put on board a vessel sailing for New Orleans and stopping at the Dry Tortugas. The officers were then directed to march the regiment to its camp. This was better than a court-martial and death, which would not have subserved the purpose as well. And it was the last show of any disposition to mutiny thereafter, except a threatened mutiny in Colonel [Edward D.] Baker's California regiment a week after, which was instantly quelled.

Just a month later the regiment which had been deprived of its colors distinguished itself by good behavior in a reconnaissance at Lewensville, Virginia, and its colors were restored, and not long after, the exiles to the Dry Tortugas were brought back to their regiment.

On the 2d of October there was an imposing military funeral for the venerable Commissary General [George] Gibson who had died on September 30th. The escort consisted of a battalion of infantry under Major George Sykes, four pieces of artillery under Captain Griffin and a squadron of cavalry under Captain [William B.] Royal. General Scott was too feeble to attend and I remember Mr. Gibson Hunt and his sister were the chief mourners.

The Senators and Representatives in Congress from the State of New York had recommended twelve gentlemen from that state for the appointment of Brigadier General of Volunteers. Seven of these were graduates of the Military Academy who had been in civil life. From the beginning to the end of the war, those graduates of the Academy who had been for some years in civil life after graduation appeared to have a great advantage over those who had remained continuously in service, in the way of promotion. They had been among politicians and knew how to reach them. They at least had their acquaintance and also the assurance to look out for their own interests with them. Regular officers as a general thing depended solely upon the merit of their services and indulged the hope that it would be recognized in due time. However, the political consideration which the graduates of the Military Academy enjoyed was fairly measured by the notable fact that Blenker received the greatest number of votes, only [John J.] Peck and [Abner] Doubleday receiving an equal number.

About the 7th of October I was in the office of the Assistant Secretary of War to make my usual morning report and was leaning against the wall waiting until other business was disposed of when a delegation of citizens from the other side of the Potomac came in to ask protection for the depredations of [William H.] Young's Kentucky Cavalry of which regiment there had been frequent complaints. Colonel Scott remarked, "I wish to God I could find a Colonel who could take care of that regiment and make it behave properly."

I stepped forward at once and said, "Colonel, I am your man."

He asked, "Are you in earnest, young man?"

"Perfectly so," said I.

On the same day I received the following order:

> War Department,
> Adjutant General's Office,
> Washington, Oct. 7, 1861.
>
> Special Orders)
> No. 272.)
>
> Leave of absence until further orders is granted 1st Lieutenant W. W. Averell, 3d Cavalry, to enable him to take command of the 3d Regiment Pennsylvania Volunteer Cavalry—late Young's Cavalry.
>
> By order,
> (Signed) L. Thomas,
> Adjutant General.

On the 10th I was mustered in as Colonel of the 3d Pennsylvania Cavalry.[10] I was succeeded in my office as Acting Assistant Adjutant General to the Provost Marshal General by Captain James McMillan, 2d Infantry, an accomplished officer of the class of '56 and an old friend from

---

[10]Although William H. Young himself came from Kentucky, the overwhelming majority of his "Kentucky Cavalry" came from Pennsylvania. When Young was replaced with Averell, the regiment assumed a Pennsylvania Volunteer designation. Although it was actually the first volunteer cavalry regiment to be recruited from this state, two subsequent regiments enlisted before its name was changed, hence the official designation of the "Third Regiment Pennsylvania Volunteer Cavalry."

Livingston, an adjoining county to my native county, Steuben, in New York.

Thus terminated my service as a staff officer. My commission as Colonel did not arrive from the Governor of Pennsylvania until the 21st of October, and I remember there was an unusually startling sensation on that day caused by the death of Colonel Baker in a fight up about Leesburg, Virginia. Baker was a Senator from California of remarkable eloquence whose warm personal friends included the President.[11] On one occasion he had entered the Senate Chamber in full uniform, dusty from the field, and took part in a debate with dramatic effect.

A perusal of Colonel Cogswell's report concerning the Balls Bluff disaster, in which the gallant Colonel Baker lost his life, will clearly show that, with all his superb qualifications of an illustrious political career and his personal courage, he was utterly unfitted, by complete ignorance of the elementary principles of military tactics required in the presence of the enemy, to be entrusted with the command of a brigade or even of a regiment in battle.[12] That he had not also any understanding or experience of discipline, or the ability to inculcate or enforce it, had been already exhibited on the 20th of August when Provost Marshal, General Andrew Porter, was ordered to take a light battery, a squadron of cavalry and as many companies of infantry as he might deem necessary and put down a threatened mutiny in Colonel Baker's California regiment and to fire upon them if they refused to obey. It was only this readiness to suppress the mutiny which prevented it. A regiment reflects the military character and abilities of its Colonel as surely and truly as a good mirror reflects a human face. It was no reproach upon the Colonel, nor yet for that matter upon the regiment, but it brought a deep and sinister reflection upon those heedless and shortsighted men whose influences were permitted to sway and control the appointing power in a vain endeavor to unite a high political renown with a blare of military glory off hand.

This was only one small but notable illustration of the disastrous

---

[11]Baker was actually a senator from Oregon. He recruited and led a "California regiment" composed of recruits from New York and Pennsylvania. It was so named due to the monetary support it received from Californians, but its official designation was the "71st Pennsylvania Infantry." Baker's remains were buried at the Presidio of San Francisco, California.

[12]The official report of Col. Milton Cogswell of the 42nd New York is not as critical of Colonel Baker as Averell alleged. See U.S. War Department, *The War of the Rebellion; a Compilation of the Official Records of the Union and Confederate Armies*, vol. 5, pp. 320-23 (hereinafter cited as OR).

consequences of a policy which persistently ignored the experiences of ages and scorned and derided military science and art. In the main body of the Army of the Potomac all officers were required to take a rigid course of tactical training and to acquire a thorough experience in company, regimental, brigade and division duties, and boards of officers were appointed for their examination as to fitness. It was a wonderful school and those volunteer officers who were graduated from it, with their lives, saw as clearly and deplored as deeply in the later years of the war as did regular army officers at the beginning, the waste of life, time and treasure which ensued from the policy which wasted the lives of Colonel Baker and his men and deprived the Congress of a gifted and brilliant member.

The fitting corollary to this incident was the subsequent surprising and inexplicable arrest of General Charles P. Stone, commanding the Corps of Observation to which Colonel Baker's regiment belonged, and his incarceration in Fort Lafayette and Fort Hamilton 189 days with communication forbidden with any person, and without preferred charges, or any allegation of crime and of course without trial or conviction, and at the end of that time, his release with no orders as to what he should do— whether he should consider himself on leave or report somewhere for duty. No response was accorded to his many applications for a copy of any charges against him. The military committee of Congress on the conduct of the war is on record as instigating the arrest and the Secretary of War, Edwin M. Stanton, as ordering it. Whether these despotic proceedings were intended, as the French were pleased to interpret the execution of Admiral Byng, *"Pour encourager les antres,"* or, as a diversion of the public mind from the real cause of the calamity, will ever remain a mystery.

General Charles P. Stone was a graduate of the Military Academy of the class of 1845 and had received two brevets, when brevets were deemed an honor, for gallant and meritorious conduct in battle in the Mexican War. He was an officer of high scientific attainments and large experience. He had come to the front as early as January in 1861 and rendered most essential service in organizing and disciplining the District of Columbia Volunteers and guarding the Baltimore and Ohio Railroad, the only railway communication of Washington with the North at that time; and he had been continuously in important commands up to the time of his arrest. Some months after his release, he was returned to duty, in May 1863, and appointed Chief of Staff to General N. P. Banks in the Department of the Gulf and received the surrender of Port Hudson, and afterward served before Petersburg, Virginia, until September 1864. After the war he went to Egypt where he remained eleven years as Major General in the Egyptian Army and Chief of Staff to the Khedive. His last public work, which was completed but a short time before his death, was the building of the pedestal for the statue of "Liberty Enlightening the World" in New York Harbor.

A singular divinity shaped the ending of General Stone's work on earth which should not escape recognition by a people so fond of building extravagant monuments to its ideals. There, in full view of Forts Lafayette and Hamilton wherein this loyal gentleman and faithful soldier lay six months an unaccused prisoner in this land of liberty, his final handiwork stands a colossal satire upon that episode in his life, of which unrecognized purpose the builder was as unconscious as the blocks of granite he put together. When men build, better than they know, they seem to adjust the purposes of God. The last time I saw General Stone was as his guest at the dedication of the *Statue of Liberty* and the impression of the scene was deep and lasting. His steamboat had approached Liberty Island as near as the encircling throng of sea and river craft would permit, and "God's Daughter," majestic and weirdly glorious in broken sunlight, was looking down upon us from above an enshrouding bank of fog which concealed her pedestal from view. When the General with a group of friends gathered on the deck forward and kindly listened to my reading of John Boyle O'Reilly's beautiful poem written for the occasion and published in the *New York World* that morning.

Poet and builder and nearly all his guests of that occasion are gone. The memory of Colonel Baker, the Senator from California, endures worthily in marble at the Capitol, John Boyle O'Reilly's in a classic slab in Boston, while the memory of General Stone will linger for a while a transitory reminiscence about the foundations of "Liberty Enlightening the World."

21

Cavalry

As these reminiscences will run through the incidents and episodes of my experience in the military service which have left the deepest impressions on my memory, and as my service was chiefly in cavalry operations, it will enlighten the understanding of those readers who may not have had occasion to acquaint themselves with the organization, history and uses of cavalry, if a brief statement of them be made.

Cavalry, from its earliest organization and use to a time long after the invention of gunpowder and the introduction of firearms, was that part of an army which was trained to maneuver and fight exclusively on horseback. Its organization was the "Squadron" and its only weapon, the sabre. By rapidity of movement, quickness of evolution and solidity of formation, it could become, as under the great Seydlitz, an intelligent and furious projectile which no infantry, with its smooth-bore, short-range, muzzle-loading guns, could withstand. With all the infantry changes that have occurred from match-lock muskets to breach-loading, magazine, long-range rifles, cavalry has been compelled to make corresponding modifications in its arms and tactics. It has long since ceased to be a projectile, except against cavalry. Its firearms have been increased in range, improved in readiness and accuracy of aim and rapidity of firing; and the men have learned to fight dismounted. During the Civil War a skirmish line of dismounted cavalry, armed with the Spencer magazine-rifle, often stood off and sometimes drove an equal or stronger skirmish line of infantry.

Cavalry, when employed with light horse-batteries and well instruct-ed in fighting dismounted, was capable of independent action of great importance, as was gloriously illustrated by General John Buford the first day of Gettsburg when with a quick *coup d'oeil* he recognized the supreme value of the position as a battlefield and covered it obstinately until that other heroic commander, General John F. Reynolds, came to his assis-tance with the first corps, and together they resisted the onset of the enemy until the field became available to the concentrating corps of the Army of the Potomac.

Reliable information of the enemy's position or movements, which is absolutely necessary to the commander of an army to successfully conduct a campaign, must be largely furnished by the cavalry. The duty of the cavalry when an engagement is imminent is specially imperative—to keep in touch with the enemy and observe and carefully note, with time of day or night, every slightest indication and report it promptly to the com-mander of the army. On the march, cavalry forms in advance, flank and rear guards and supplies escorts, couriers and guides. Cavalry should extend well away from the main body on the march like antennae to mask its movements and to discover any movement of the enemy. Without this kind of work, strategy is impossible. Cavalry should never hug the army on the march, especially in a thickly wooded country, because the horses being restricted to the roads, the slightest obstacle in advance is liable to cause a blockade against the march of infantry, as happened in '64 in the Wilderness campaign where on a critical occasion our infantry was pre-vented by a blockade of cavalry in the road from gaining an advantageous position before the enemy should reach it and an appalling loss in killed and wounded was the result. In camp it furnishes outposts, vedettes and scouts. In battle it attacks the enemy's flanks and rear, and above all other duties in battle, it secures the fruits of victory by vigorous and unrelent-ing pursuit. In defeat it screens the withdrawal of the army and by its fortitude and activity baffles the enemy.

Another splendid illustration of good cavalry work was given by General Buford on the 29th of August, 1862, at the second Battle of Bull Run, when he counted seventeen regiments of the enemy's infantry pass-ing through Gainsville, Va., to our left and reported it to General Fitz-John Porter, thus enabling that General to so place and handle his divi-sion of ten thousand men as to hold the Confederate General Longstreet's corps of twenty-five thousand men from attacking the left flank of our army while it was engaged with "Stonewall" Jackson's corps.

A deplorable instance of the disaster and disgrace which may follow neglect or inefficiency of cavalry work when battle is imminent was afforded at the Battle of Chancellorsville, when the cavalry commander remained about the headquarters of the army and failed to observe and report the movement of Stonewall Jackson's corps on its way to crush our right wing.[1]

The vigilance of cavalry protecting an army in position is always of most vital importance; the lack of it has sometimes led to great and humiliating surprises like that which befell our army on the first day of Shiloh in '62 and that at Cedar Creek at the Shenandoah Valley in October, '64.

In addition to these active military duties of the cavalry, it receives flags of truce, interrogates spies, deserters and prisoners, makes and improves topographical maps, destroys and builds bridges, obstructs and opens communications, and obtains or destroys forage and supplies. The regularity, certainty and good order with which the several corps of the Army of the Potomac with a train of baggage wagons forty miles long were transferred from the Chickahominy to the James River during seven days of battle in '62, were chiefly due to the accurate topographical maps which had been drawn from surveys and sketches made of the intervening country by officers of the 3d Pennsylvania Cavalry, under my command, during the fortnight preceding the movement, which gave to General McClellan a better knowledge of the fields of action than the Confederates possessed.

During our Civil War our cavalry inaugurated a novel expeditionary service, which was popularly known as "Raid." Its purpose was to destroy the enemy's communications and resources behind his lines in the interior of his country, to draw his forces out of position, and to divert and distract his attention. The stupendous effects which may result from the operations of a small force engaged in such service was demonstrated by the "Salem Raid" in December, 1863, when a cavalry force of twenty-five hundred men, with a four gun horse-battery, left its camp on the Balitmore and Ohio railway in West Virginia, and penetrated the enemy's country over two hundred miles through violent winter storms, and destroyed a section and several bridges of the Tennessee and Georgia railway and the winter supplies of the Confederate General Longstreet, then operating against Burnside in Eastern Tennessee, and drew away

---

[1]Averell is referring to the actions of Brig. Gen. Alfred Pleasanton whose cavalry failed to detect Lt. Gen. Thomas J. (Stonewall) Jackson's daylight march across the Union front during the Battle of Chancellorsville. Once in position on Maj. Gen. Joseph Hooker's exposed right flank, six Confederate brigades routed the unsuspecting Union troops.

from the enemy's main army in Virginia over twenty thousand men in a fruitless endeavor to intercept and capture the invaders.

The history of the cavalry of the United States army began in 1833, when the first regiment of dragoons was organized. The second regiment of dragoons was organized in 1836 but its designation was changed to "Regiment of Mounted Riflemen" in 1842. This change of name was so obnoxious to the regiment, although it was then but six years old, that its original designation was restored in 1844. The Regiment of Mounted Riflemen was organized in 1846 at the beginning of the Mexican War. The organization of the First and Second Regiments of cavalry took place in 1855. These five regiments comprised all the Cavalry of the regular army when the Civil War began in 1861.

Previous to 1861 the unit of administration was a regiment of ten companies. The field officers were one Colonel, one Lieutenant Colonel and two Majors. A company consisted of one Captain, one First Lieutenant, one Second Lieutenant and eighty-four enlisted men. Two companies united formed a squadron, the tactical unit for maneuver, and was commanded by the senior Captain. When two or more squadrons were united, a field officer commanded.

The arms were carbine or rifle, sabre and revolver and their equipments, saddle, bridle, lariat, nose bag, saddle bags, camp utensils, rations and forage, extra horseshoes and nails, grooming tackle and ammunition.

In 1861 the regiment was increased to twelve companies and an additional Major was added.

In August, 1861, an ill-advised act of Congress changed the designations of the two regiments of Dragoons and of the Rifles into First, Second and Third Cavalry, and of the old First and Second cavalry into Fourth and Fifth, and the strength of each was increased to twelve hundred men. At this time the old Dragoons and Rifles were so dispersed in the Far West, and the regular army had become so completely submerged by the inundation of volunteers for the war, that no voice was heard in protest against an act which wiped out the time-honored regimental names with the romantic and heroic history which had distinguished them—the glory and inspiration of the oldest mounted regiments —forever. War, even with its best justification—the promotion or preservation of civilization, the defence of liberty or maintenance of a nationality—needs to cloak itself with all the glamour that bedizened panoplies, waving banners, tossing plumes, martial music, prancing squadrons and thundering cannon can lend to hide its essential and hideous brutality;

A RAW CAVALRYMAN.

Sketches of cavalrymen from The National Tribune, *Washington, D.C., Thursday, May 29, 1890. Accompanies an article by Major Frank W. Hess, "Voluntary Cavalry."*

A YEAR AFTERWARD.

and above its most murderous vortices of death and destruction must be spread the alluring bewitchment of glory. Regiments lose a great inspiration when they lose names that have been glorified.

In European countries the general term cavalry includes cuirassiers, dragoons, lancers, hussars and so forth, and so might our cavalry regiments have retained their distinguishing, original names with their administrative cavalry number and thus have preserved their history. The horse is all that remains of original cavalry that is useful; the sabre has become a cherished and honored badge which is essential to ceremonial occasions. The various and picturesque designations of English regiments have never been changed and the emblazonments upon their standards and emblems upon their accoutrements commemorate the meritorious services of each regiment in all parts of the world. Upon the mess tables of the officers of English regiments may always be seen pieces of plate that are emblematic of illustrous service in India, Africa, at Quebec, in the Peninsula, the Crimea, Egypt and elsewhere, that commemorate events which happened, perhaps, before the oldest living officer was born.

A young officer or recruit when joining such a regiment is at once penetrated with the influence of its heroic records and his character and conduct must take an accordant shape. A regiment that does not cherish its record lacks history or character.

At the beginning of our Civil War our five regiments of mounted troops were distributed by companies and squadrons along both slopes of the Rocky mountains from British North America to Mexico. None had ever been engaged in battle as a regiment excepting the Rifles in the Mexican War and the First Cavalry under Colonel Sumner against the Cheyenne tribe of Indians in 1857. The experience, therefore, of the oldest and best officers of cavalry had been limited generally to the command of a Captain, or at the highest of a Major, in active operations against an enemy. The companies were generally separated so long a time and at such great distances from regimental headquarters as to become almost independent of regimental administration and to be regarded as the unit in respect to it. An Act of Congress, approved July 11, 1862, was the first to make mention of "troop" in our cavalry organization and subsequent acts repeated it, but the designation "company" was used in the army until May 16, 1881, when the Adjutant General ([Richard C.] Drum), upon the ground that the legal designation was "troop," directed that it be used in all official papers, orders, etc., instead of "company."

The cavalry required in the main army of operations as estimated by General McClellan on August 4, 1861, was twenty-eight mounted regiments.

To enable the non-military reader to appreciate the amount of arduous work that was to be done in the short time that was available to create and set one hundred and sixty-eight squadrons in the field, it is necessary to take a brief consideration of the material from which the cavalrymen of the opposing armies were to be drawn and shaped into a fighting force.

Men of the Eastern and Middle States were not accustomed to the saddle, as were the men of the Western and Southern States. Young men from the North and East, whether from the town or country, were more used to driving than riding. They were also quite as unaccustomed to the use of firearms as to horsemanship and none had ever seen a sabre and very few a revolver.

The breadth of plantations in the South and the social conditions that had existed through generations before the war had encouraged the use of the saddle and made good horsemen. Their habits of hunting and fetes and tournaments had developed horsemanship to a high degree of excellence. The use of firearms was also quite common. In the West the energies of the men of the new generations who had carried the frontier beyond the Mississippi required good riders.

These considerations should make it readily understood that when the Northern and Southern armies in Virginia began about the same time the organization of cavalry forces, the Army of the Potomac had, in many important respects, by far the greater obstacles to overcome in their training. It was only in equipment and arms that the North enjoyed any advantage. It must then be easily admitted that to teach a young citizen from the North or East, who had never been astride a horse, how to saddle him and ride him at all gaits, over all kinds of country, to perform properly all the multifarious duties of caring for his horse and his equipments, arms and ammunition, and finally to use his sabre, revolver or carbine against the enemy with confidence and skill, would require much more time and labor than was necessary in the Confederate army.

Soon after the organization of volunteer regiments of cavalry and before the men had learned to ride or to use their arms, or to be handled in evolutions of the simplest elementary character, the newspapers began to wonder why our Union cavalry did not show more enterprise, and cavalry officers who were working day and night were obliged to endure the jibes and derision of the press for more than a year. The ideals of the press and people regarding cavalry were correct enough but they were a long way off from the realities. The weakness of a body of untrained cavalrymen is in proportion to their strength in numbers.

The leading officers who created and drilled the volunteer cavalry of the Army of the Potomac from the school of the trooper dismounted up through the platoon, company, and regiment to the division were W. W. Averell, David McM. Gregg and George Bayard. These all became Brigadier-Generals of cavalry and commanded the first three divisions of volunteer cavalry that were formed. Brigadier-General John Buford commanded the brigade of regular cavalry.

The most efficient and distinguished Colonels of cavalry who assisted with energy and zeal in the work of its creation were Duffié, First Rhode Island; Horace Binney Sargent, First Massachusetts; John B. McIntosh, Third Pennsylvania (succeeding Averell); Benjamin F. Davis, Eighth New York; Judson Kilpatrick, "Harris Light"; Farnsworth, Eighth Illinois; and di Cesnola, ——New York.[2] All these became Brigadier-Generals, excepting Davis who was killed as a Colonel at Beverly Ford, Va., in '63. Neither Stoneman nor Pleasanton ever drilled any volunteer cavalry.

The brief narration of my service as Colonel of the Third Pennsylvania cavalry will give an idea of the work required to convert twelve hundred loyal and liberty-loving pedestrians into a regiment of cavalry equal in precision and rapidity of maneuver and fighting efficiency to any regiment of regular cavalry in the army.

---

[2]Alfred N. A. Duffié (1835-1880) was born in Paris and had served in the French army as a lieutenant of cavalry. He came to the United States in 1859 and, at the outbreak of the Civil War, he offered his service to the Union. He was commissioned a captain in the 2nd New York Cavalry, "Harris Light Cavalry." In March 1863, he fought with Averell at Kelly's Ford.   **Horace Binney Sargent** (1821-1908), colonel of the 1st Massachusetts Cavalry, was assigned to Averell's brigade in 1863 and was active in this command until May of that year. Sargent was then ordered to Louisiana where he was seriously wounded during the Red River campaign.   **John B. McIntosh** (1829-1888), a graduate of Annapolis, resigned from the navy after the Mexican War but reentered military service during the Civil War. He fought at Kelly's Ford, and had a distinguished military record.   **Benjamin F. Davis** (1832-1863), a West Point graduate, was a colonel of the 8th New York Cavalry in 1862. He was killed in action June 9, 1863.   **Judson Kilpatrick** (1836-1881) organized a regiment of the 5th New York Cavalry and participated in nearly every important cavalry operation in the East. In 1864-65 he led a cavalry division in Sherman's campaigns through Georgia and the Carolinas. **Elon J. Farnsworth** (1837-1863) enlisted in his uncle John Farnsworth's regiment of the 8th Illinois Cavalry in 1861, after which he served on the staff of Gen. Alfred Pleasanton. On July 3, 1863, Farnsworth was killed while leading a hopeless charge against the Confederates.   **Luigi (Louis) Palma di Cesnola** (1832-1904), the son of an Italian count, came to New York in 1860. In October 1861, di Cesnola enlisted in the 11th New York Cavalry and was then assigned to Averell's command in Virginia with the rank of colonel of the Fourth New York Volunteer Cavalry. Di Cesnola participated in the famous battle at Kelly's Ford and was later awarded the Congressional Medal of Honor for conspicuous leadership and bravery in the Battle of Aldie.

22

The Third Pennsylvania Cavalry

T he regiment to which I was appointed Colonel had been organized at Philadelphia in July and August, 1861. It had been
known up to the time of my appointment as "Young's Kentucky
Light Cavalry," from the name of its first Colonel, William H. Young, of
Kentucky. He was mustered out on October 31st, the same day that I
assumed command. He was a picturesque and notably adventurous man
who had taken part in the unfortunate expedition of the notorious filibus-
ter, Walker, into Nicaragua, sometime in the fifties. One of the companies of the regiment had been recruited in Washington city but all the
others were composed of Pennsylvanians: hence its new designation, 3d
Pennsylvania Cavalry.

The twelve companies of the 3d Pennsylvania were scattered in
bivouacs on the Virginia side of the Potomac from a point opposite
Georgetown down to Alexandria. This dispersion did not permit any
proper regimental administration while it had prevented discipline and
afforded no opportunities for instruction beyond that of the company.
Quite naturally, complaints of irregularities had brought the regiment
under the notice of the War Department which by a fortunate chance led
to my appointment as its Colonel. My experience of two years at the
Cavalry School as an instructor and my service in the Mounted Rifles on
the frontier enabled me to realize the amount of work that lay before me.

When I was mustered into service as Colonel of the 3d Pennsylvania
Cavalry at the War Department on October 10, 1861, I had never seen an
officer or a man of the regiment. I determined to assemble it and assume

335

command on the last day of the month which would be muster day, and I would have to call the name of every officer and man in the regiment and to see them face to face which would be the most complete and satisfactory introduction I could have. However, I was curious to have a glimpse of the officers and men immediately and anxious to have their muster rolls properly prepared for their first muster for pay. So one day I set out, well mounted, with an orderly carrying blank muster rolls, to visit the long line of bivouacs of the companies of my regiment.

The beginning and ending of incidents or episodes in human life are longest remembered, and so I can easily recall the varied impressions made upon my mind during my ride that day. I was beginning the life and service of a Colonel of Volunteers. I had already assumed the double-breasted coat with the double row of buttons and exchanged my old shoulder straps with a single bar for new ones with an eagle. Having always been so completely subordinate in my army life and service, and having looked upon the rank of Colonel as so exalted and as requiring such long experience and conspicuous and acknowledged ability, I had never dreamed of reaching a higher grade than that of Major. Now I suddenly found myself travelling a new tangent in my projected and accepted military career, and I became keenly sensible of new and greater responsibilities than I had ever felt before. Since the Battle of Bull Run my time had been so thoroughly occupied with my duties in Washington that I had been able to make only two or three brief visits to the Virginia side of the Potomac to witness the review of a division, but my present errand promised to afford me an opportunity to see a larger part of the Army.

I remember it was a sunny Indian summer morning and the blue haze which haunts the shores of the Potomac in the autumnal season filled the browning woodlands with inviting suggestions of quiet solitudes and dreamy repose. But the spell of this enchanting landscape, which held the eye, was broken soon after I had crossed the Potomac, by the hearing of trumpet calls mingled with the music of military bands at practice from all directions and the rattle of small arms firing in target practice like the patter of heavy rain drops on a roof before a coming storm. This portentous suggestion was strengthened by the occasional rolling thunder of distant heavy guns testing ranges along the field works and fortifications surrounding Washington. This was the chorus of the titanic forge in which, under the hand of a mastering military genius, a hundred and fifty thousand men were being welded into a loyal, obedient, irresistible engine of destruction which was to become the bulwark of the nation and to make its name, "Army of the Potomac," illustrious and immortal.

I found the companies of the 3d Pennsylvania enjoying a jolly, gypsy sort of life in picturesque bivouacs, well chosen for the comforts of shade and the convenience of the three essentials of a cavalry camp; viz., wood, water and grass. Some of the men were engaged in athletic sports, some with cards and a few with newspapers. The general appearance of the men was very encouraging. They were young, strong and radiant Americans, the majority of whom were from the country towns and farms. Many of them, by their bearing and manners, showed the habits of good associations. But the appearance and behavior of several of the officers were not promising. It was easy to see that some of them should exchange places with some of their men in the ranks for the advantage of the service.

I selected a wide, grassy slope, easily drained, for a camp in Virginia, a mile from the Aqueduct Bridge. The site was convenient to water and to the transportation of supplies and adjacent to broad and rolling fields, well suited for cavalry exercises. With the assistance of a detail from the Provost Guard in Washington, the camp was laid out precisely in accordance with Army Regulations. New Sibley tents, picket lines, ten days' rations and a supply of forage were all brought on the ground on the 30th of October. The field officers' tents were pitched and a large commissary tent supplied with benches and blackboards for a school was set up near the Colonel's tent. A tall flagstaff, with a set of flags, ready for raising, completed the preparations. To secure exemption from complaints about subsistence, which are inevitable with new troops without experience in the preparation of food in camp, I had obtained the appointment of an ex-Commissary Sergeant who had served ten years in the 8th U.S. Infantry, but was yet young, as 1st Lieutenant and Quartermaster and Commissary of my regiment. This assured immediate instruction in cooking and regularity of accounts.

Orders had been issued assigning my regiment to General Fitz-John Porter's division which was composed of the brigades of Generals Morell, [John H.] Martindale and Butterfield whose camps were a mile or two further out. This assignment was very agreeable to me as I regarded General F. J. Porter as the most accomplished and most nearly faultless soldier and gentleman I had ever known. He had been one of our instructors of artillery and cavalry at West Point in the time of my class, and cadets, who are the keenest observers of the characters and abilities of the professors and instructors, had looked upon Major Porter as an ideal soldier and gentleman. They valued a word of commendation from him as the highest encomium they could receive. He had been graduated from the Military Academy in 1845 in a class of men of whom a large proportion became highly distinguished in the military service of their country, such as Generals William F. (Baldy) Smith, T.[Thomas] J. Wood, Gordon Granger, Charles P. Stone, John P. Hatch, David A. Russell, Thomas G. Pitcher, Henry Coppée, J.[John] W. Davidson, E. B. Hunt and others.[1] After my graduation my personal acquaintance with General Fitz-John Porter never failed to sustain the high ideal I had first formed of him. He was a remarkably handsome man. His form and perfect proportions, his unaffected dignity of manner, his ease and grace of action, whether walking or riding, his unfailing courtesy and gentleness under all circumstances; all these attributes, dominated by an impassability like that which characterized the Duke of Marlborough could not fail to command attention. Longstreet, the great Southern General who had the experience of opposing him in strategy and tactics, said after the close of the war that Porter had all of the qualifications of a Field Marshal.

But to return to my work of Colonel. On the morning of the 31st of October, 1861, all the companies of the 3d Pennsylvania Cavalry assembled at the camp with their muster rolls ready. When the picket lines had been put up and the horses tethered to them and fed, and the new Sibley tents had been pitched in twelve parallel streets, and the flag staff raised and the flag hoisted, the regiment was assembled in line in front of the tents facing the flag and my order assuming command was read. It was the first time the regiment had ever been a part of such a spectacle. The men had set up a beautiful white town, as if by magic, which was to be their home until the next spring. The unconscious germination of an *esprit de corps* began at that moment. A regular muster then took place with due formality and care. The camp was named "Camp Marcy" in honor of General Randolph B. Marcy, an old and valued friend of mine in frontier service who had conducted explorations in the Far West in the early days, was a great hunter of big game, and had written most entertaining narratives of wild western life. His family was one of the best known and most highly esteemed in the old army. One of his daughters was the wife of General McClellan.

---

[1]Averell mistakenly listed Henry Coppée and Edward B. Hunt among the other generals. Coppée served gallantly in the Mexican War but spent the pivotal Civil War years as military secretary to Maj. Gen. Darius N. Couch and as editor of the Philadelphia-based *Military Magazine*. Hunt, also of the class of 1845, rose to the rank of major before dying from an accident on October 20, 1863.

Fortunately, there was at least one bugler in each company and the one most capable among them, named Seaman, who could sound all the calls, was at once appointed chief bugler, and I have recorded his name because he afterward made it worthy of mention. All of the officers were, after supper, called to a camp fire in front of my tent and the chief bugler sounded the "officers' call" before them two or three times so that it might be recognized and obeyed. A copy of cavalry tactics was given to each officer with the lesson marked for the next evening, and I made known to them my purpose to make the regiment, in its drill, discipline and fighting efficiency, equal to any regiment of regular cavalry in the army and that I should not form an opinion of the qualifications of any officer until the end of three weeks. It was easily perceived that the mention of regulars had not fired their ambition. At the beginning of the war there were some irritations engendered between volunteers and regulars by thoughtless and inexperienced officers and men of both. The volunteers were not inclined, at first, to regard with favor a discipline and obedience that seemed to them humiliating and servile, and they did not pretend to salute their officers, nor did the officers generally desire or expect military courtesies of that kind, and the associations of officers with the men out of ranks were quite naturally what they always had been at home. But in a remarkably short time the one hundred and fifty thousand volunteers of the Army of the Potomac all became regulars and the fifteen thousand regulars of the old army in some measure leavened the mass and all differing characteristics disappeared in the process.

All the work of establishing the camp, mustering the regiment, detailing and mounting guard, opening adjutant's office and company records filled up the time of the first day of my command, but it was only pastime compared with the work done in the days which immediately followed. We began at the beginning with lessons and drills. I personally drilled the officers an hour and a half in the morning and the same time afternoon and required them to apply the same drill at once to the men.

On the first occasion of drilling the officers, the men gathered in front of their company grounds and indulged in audible criticisms of their officers with friendly freedom; and I was really glad to hear it for a reaction was set up in the officers which made for discipline when they came to apply the drill to the men. The evening school was conducted as was a section room at West Point only there was more time used by the instructor in explanations and lecture. The adjacent fields were daily covered with officers and men going through all the schools from trooper dismounted upward through the school of the platoon, company and squadron, and later to that of the regiment mounted.

Within a week after taking command of the 3d, the 8th Pennsylvania Cavalry was ordered to report to me, and these two regiments constituted the first brigade of volunteer cavalry that was formed in the war. My duties were considerably increased as the Colonel of the 8th was thoroughly incompetent as a cavalry man of any grade. It was a most promising body of officers and men with the exception of the Colonel.

About this time a Board for the examination of cavalry officers was established in Washington that met once a week. I was detailed as a member of it. Colonel J.[James] H. van Alen was president of this board. He had brought a cavalry regiment to Washington from New York. The regiment crossed the Potomac, and the Colonel took a house in Washington, gave charming dinners and was appointed president of the board above mentioned. The fact that he had seen no military service and knew nothing of cavalry, even theoretically, did not prevent him making a very imposing president. The Colonel was a well-groomed, typical club man, who in a fresh and very becoming uniform looked like a living picture full of high lights. His speech was impressive and deliberate and two rows of glistening white teeth seemed to give precision to his utterance.

The invariable mode of procedure was, when an officer to be examined had been called and had entered the room, generally manifesting more or less trepidation, Colonel Van Alen would address him, naming his grade and saying, "You have been ordered to appear before this board for an examination of your qualifications as a cavalry officer. Colonel Averell, will you please conduct the examination?"

Lieutenant Colonel Judson Kilpatrick and a few other competent young officers were members of the board. This examination was of immense benefit to the cavalry service. The idle and shiftless dependents of influential, social or political connections could not hold a commission without proper qualifications.

After three weeks the alternative of resignation or examination by the cavalry board was presented to seven officers of my regiment including three Captains. From time to time others followed and several applications were pressed for each vacancy. The choice of many young gentlemen from Pennsylvania was afforded who came nearest to satisfying my ideal that an officer of cavalry should possess the superior qualifications which would make him a leader of his men. It was not easy to find such for the 3d, but no mistakes of judgement were made in the selection of such candidates as

Henry King of Pittsburgh, Walter and Charles Newhall, and Charles Treichel of Philadelphia, and others who were well-educated young gentlemen, some of them the finest cricketers in the country. A large proportion of vacancies were satisfactorily filled by the promotion of young gentlemen from the noncommissioned officers of the regiment. These promotions encouraged a gratifying emulation in discipline and efficiency, the effects of which were felt and seen in the ranks. It has been a great satisfaction to me that several of the young volunteer officers who sprang from the ranks of my regiment received commissions in the regular army after the war and rose by their merit to a higher rank: as Colonel Edward M. Heyl, Major Frank W. Hess, Captain C.[Charles] A. Vernou.

One vacant captaincy was notably filled to my satisfaction and to the great advantage of the regiment by the appointment of ex-Sergeant James W. Walsh, who had served two enlistments as Orderly Sergeant in the United States Regiment of Mounted Riflemen. He had been highly esteemed by the officers of that regiment as an ideal soldier. The company to which he was appointed in the 3d Pennsylvania quickly became a model for the others. It was pleasing to see how soon the officers and men of the regiment came to regard him with the highest respect and now, nearly forty years after, there is no officer of the 3d Pennsylvania more fondly remembered by its survivors than Lieutenant Colonel Walsh.

After a fair trial of a fortnight, the Colonel of the 8th was ordered before the Board for the examination of cavalry officers and my classmate, Captain David McM. Gregg, of the 6th United States Cavalry was appointed to fill the vacancy which ensued. Although Gregg had been my senior in our class rank, he served with me during that time as faithfully and subordinately as he could have served had he been of a younger class. He not only divided the general duties with me but brought that comradeship which is a welcome comfort to a hardworking Colonel of cavalry.

Like the enjoyment of a parent in the growth and development of his children was my satisfaction in watching the rapid changes which attended the conversion of an unwieldy assemblage of loyal citizens into a well-disciplined, instructed and easily maneuvred regiment of cavalry. The loose and various movements of the individual were disappearing and the alert, erect and graceful carriage of the soldier were becoming uniform and habitual. The men were proud of the discipline they were learning. They saluted their officers and in their deportment and in the performance of their duties began to feel that self-respect which is born of discipline. Within sixty days the details assembled for guard mount at a gallop and the time from the sounding of "boots and saddles" to the "assembly" was reduced to a minimum for parades. Officers from several parts of the army came to witness the brigade drill for which it had been necessary to create tactics, as up to that time none had been known in our country for a brigade of cavalry.

The men had surrounded Camp Marcy with a high hedge of ever-green shrubbery with arches over the entrances.

Although there was not an idle hour during the day amid the stress of drills, study, recitations and guard and picket duties, the benefits of reasonable recreation were not neglected. Under proper guidance the camp was occasionally illuminated during the evening with hundreds of candles and the taste and skill of the men were exhibited in attractive decorations. A general "stag-dance" interluded with music, songs and choruses would bring spectators and visitors from other camps. On some such evenings the school tent was arranged and decorated for my officers to receive and entertain guests. My old friend Wormley, the caterer in Washington, would produce the requisite collation with all needed appointments on the shortest notice.

On one of these occasions, Mr. George Bancroft, the historian, with General and Mrs. McDowell and Miss Kate Chase, the daughter of the Secretary, and General Wadsworth and some of his staff were among our guests. The general officers of our division kindly brought their bands to furnish music and on one evening General Butterfield brought three of them. Mr. Bancroft took the deepest interest in the growth and develop-ment of the Army of the Potomac. He had gleaned the battlefields and martial records of nations in search of data for history and here he could observe every detail of the creation of a great army *ab initio*.

The Chaplain, Rev. Dr. Moses Hunter, was the only officer of the regiment who had any leisure. He was a very learned theologian from Detroit, Michigan, where he had been an esteemed teacher in a seminary. The Biddle family of that place had procured his appointment as Chaplain to my regiment. It was necessary to promote the Chaplain's mission work by such influences as I could bring to bear upon it, for cavalry men, when hardworked, were not easily enthused with theological disquisitions of an eschatological character. The first Sunday after the Chaplain's arrival only about fifty men fell out upon notice after morning inspection to attend divine service. The regiment was dismissed and the men repaired to their tents. The second Sunday, after about the same number had fallen out, the remainder, about ninety-five percent of the regiment, were marched out to the drill ground and there formed in close column in squadrons dismounted, at parade rest; and the Adjutant read to them the Articles of War, with instructions to go into the Regulations of the Army if the Articles gave out before the Chaplain closed. The third Sunday three or four hundred men seemed to prefer divine service where they could sit on the ground at their ease while the remainder stood in ranks and listened to the Articles of War and the good Chaplain remarked, after service, that he felt much encouraged with his work. The number inclined to attend religious services never exceeded seventy-five percent of the regiment, the remainder adhering to their preference for the Articles of War, until inclement weather caused the discontinuance of the service.

An unexpected and surprising compliment was received by me on November 21, 1861, in a letter, viz.:

> Adjutant General's Office,
> Washington, Nov. 20, 1861.
>
> Colonel W. W. Averell, Vol. Cav.,
>
> Dear Sir:
>
> General Thomas desires me to say to you, that there is a vacancy in the Adjutant General's Department, which he will be happy to offer to you, if agreeable to you, on condition that you enter at once on the duties of the corps, and relinquish your present command in the volunteers.
>
> Yours very truly,
> J. P. Garesché,
> Asst. Adjt. Genl.

In acknowledging this I expressed my thanks for the high consideration it implied but respectfully declined the offer as it was my opinion that I could be of more service to the country in the line of duty I had adopted. When I handed in my reply, it was intimated to me that it was the intention of the Department in case of my acceptance to assign me to duty with General McDowell as his chief of staff. This was another inviting tangent in my life and it is impossible to say whether my decision was wise or unwise, but my sense of duty was reinforced by my inclinations.

The belt of country between the picket lines of the Army of the Potomac at this time and those of the enemy, some fifteen miles in length by two to five miles in breadth, presented an ideal field for the exercise of young cavalrymen in the duties of outposts, patrols and vedettes, by which object lessons were furnished and confidence acquired. Men who had performed a tour of duty at the front for twenty-four hours had something to think about; and if shots were exchanged, which was not unusual, they learned more in one day, sometimes in an hour, about the business of a soldier than would be acquired in a month of drills and recitations. Within this belt the Confederate Cavalry had every advantage to be derived from friendly inhabitants and knowledge of the country, and ours suffered from occasional surprises and carefully laid traps.

The only serious mishap to my regiment occurred on November 25th, less than a month after I had taken command. The usual detail of a squadron, under Captain Charles A. Bell, had reported to General F. J. Porter for orders and had gone forth with a guide and examined the country in front and was returning to our lines when it was suddenly attacked in a narrow, wooded road and thrown into disorder, by six companies of the First North Carolina Cavalry, under Colonel Robert Ransom, Jr. Our loss was one man killed, half a dozen wounded and about a dozen missing. All Captain Bell had to show for results were two captured horses and equipments, one of which, with blood upon the saddle, had evidently belonged to an officer.

On investigation I learned that Captain Bell in returning to the lines had no advance guard. As a lesson it was made more impressive by requiring the immediate resignation of Captain Bell, who was very soon after appointed a Lieutenant Colonel of a new cavalry regiment and as he afterward assured me it was upon the commendatory fact that he had been a Captain in the Third Pennsylvania Cavalry.

The "War Governor" of Pennsylvania, Andrew G. Curtin, the Hon. David Wilmot and many other prominent Pennsylvanians often visited the camps of my brigade. Of all physical qualifications of men, that of height I believe the most essential, or at least it seems the most common among leaders in political life. I have observed that all the striking, influential or dominant leaders of thought on public questions, whom I have known or seen, were nearly all tall men.

Governor Curtin was a tall and handsome man who never failed to impress all who knew him with his patriotism, earnestness, zeal and sincerity. It was fortunate for the nation that the great State of Pennsylvania had such a Governor during the Civil War. With great executive ability, untiring energy, long foresight and convincing eloquence, he moved and inspired his people as no other man could. The visits of the Governor to my camps made for the good of the public service, as his judgement was enlightened with regard to the requisite qualifications for good officers of cavalry and mistaken appointments were avoided.

The men were kept so completely occupied that there were few infractions of rules, and disorderly conduct caused by drunkenness was extremely rare. There was a serious annoyance after the first payday in the wild and delirious conduct of a score of my men. The cause was soon ascertained to be an itinerant Jew with a light wagonload of the vilest, deadly imitation whiskey put up in bottles which he had been supplying to my men from a covert place in a thicket of pines not far from camp. A Sergeant of the Guard with a patrol brought the Jew and his outfit to my headquarters. In answer to questions he declared the liquor to be good whiskey but that he had never drank any of it. Then, in spite of his resistance and protestations that he would not and could not drink it, that it would kill him if he did, he was compelled by a few of the orderlies to swallow two or three drinks of his stuff. The bottles were smashed against a rock and the staggering wretch was put in his wagon and driven down to the ferryboat to Georgetown. The Corporal of the Guard, who had taken him down, reported on his return that the peddler was "dreadful sick," which gave me the pleasing assurance that the punishment had fitted the crime. There was never any more annoyance of that kind around Camp Marčy.

Early in December an incident occurred which illustrated the inability of a trained political mind to separate the rules and regulations of an army from the methods of political life. Hon. Simon Cameron, Secretary of War, was noted for the fidelity of his friends. His public life had extended back to the times of General Andrew Jackson and no friend ever forsook his loyalty to Mr. Cameron. This was largely due to the fact that Mr. Cameron never forgot his friends. One morning, a man named Perry Martin called at my tent with a note of introduction from the Secretary saying he wanted to be Sutler of the Third Pennsylvania Cavalry. I told him that the place had been filled, that the Council of Administration of the regiment had some time before nominated a worthy man and that I had appointed him in accordance with Army Regulations, and that the Officer of the Day inspected his store and list of prices daily and that his report was favorable to the Sutler whom I did not personally know.

The next morning Martin appeared again at my tent and said, "I am authorized by the Secretary to say that you can have anything you want if you will put out your Sutler and put me in." I asked him if that was all.

He said it was. Then I told him to get out of my tent, and he left. The Secretary sent for me and asked if the matter "could not be arranged between my Sutler and Martin." I told him the present incumbent was not my Sutler; he had been appointed Sutler of the regiment in accordance with the Regulations which contained a paragraph in its preface signed by Simon Cameron, Secretary of War, forbidding any departure from them. On the third day I received the following note:

War Department,
Washington,
Dec. 3, 1861.

Colonel W. W. Averell,

Sir:

The Secretary called again in my room today, and desires to have Perry Martin placed in position as Sutler under his commission from him. Please give this matter your attention.

Very respectfully,
Thomas A. Scott,
Asst. Secy. of War.

The order of the Secretary was immediately carried out. Colonel Scott laughed as he told me about it afterward, saying that the Secretary spoke of me as "that obstinate young Cavalry Colonel who stood up against the Secretary of War." From the point of view of a practical politician I had neglected an opportunity. Had I told Mr. Martin, when he made the offer, that when I received my commission as Brigadier General he should be Sutler of my brigade, I could have ordered new shoulder straps with a star within twenty-four hours. But I should have gone through life with the consciousness that the promotion had been bought and that I had taken unfair advantage of my comrades. Now, I have the satisfaction of seeing my name in the Army Register, where it will remain until I die, among a list of only nine Brigadier Generals who received commissions for specific distinguished services. I had to wait only nine months for it.

An interesting and agreeable experience of "finding bread cast upon water, after many days" occurred one day in Camp Marcy. A Captain of a volunteer artillery regiment came riding into camp in uniform, followed by a mounted orderly, and dismounting in front of my tent was admitted. He was a tall, fine, soldierly looking man, and there was something about his face and manner that I dimly recognized, but I could not recall him.

With a little emotion, which he could not repress in his voice, he said, "Colonel, you don't remember me. I was your company clerk in the Rifles in New Mexico," and then his voice broke altogether; and taking a camp stool at my bidding, he put his hands over his face for a moment until he had recovered his composure and then went on to say, "I knew you would be gratified to know that I had kept my word with you." He had never taken a drink since our settlement of that matter in 1857. I had him stay to dinner with me and enjoyed his visit very much. He became a field officer before the close of the War.

The best remembered military event of the winter of 1861-2 was the grand review at Bailey's Crossroads. The field was a broad amphitheatre, favorable at any part for a view of the whole, and the spectacle of a vast, organized host of eighty thousand men in masses of divisions with the artillery and cavalry of each division attached and all its banners floating in the sunlight was the grandest and most inspiring I ever beheld. General McClellan, with his staff, rode rapidly along the fronts of divisions awakening the wildest enthusiasm as he passed. Then the army passed in review before President Lincoln and the Commander-in-Chief [McClellan]; and as the ground trembled under the steady tread of the endless columns of disciplined soldiers and the air throbbed with the music of countless bands, the all pervading feeling was an enthusiastic and ardent admiration for the man who had created the Army of the Potomac.

In the realization of all observers, even the most experienced officers, the army was born that day. Everyone in and around Washington that had felt the throes of a tremendous and vigorous growth going on about them since the first of August and those who had visited the busy camps and attended the inspections and reviews of divisions had formed no adequate conception of the army as a whole. Not one had ever seen an army of over eighteen thousand men together except General McClellan, who had visited and studied the armies of Europe. Out of nothing and with the bleeding and dispirited fragments of McDowell's little command after Bull Run as a nucleus, this splendid army of one hundred and fifty thousand men, together with forty miles of garrisoned fortifications around Washington had been created in six months. The eyes of all spectators, and even of the army itself, were suddenly opened, as were the eyes of the young man who beheld the mountain full of horses and chariots round about the prophet of Israel.

This review immediately produced very important political effects, some of them not altogether beneficent. As I turned out of the column at the review to stand beside President Lincoln and General McClellan while my brigade was passing, I remember seeing Mr. [William] Russell of the *London Times*, talking with the Prussian minister, Baron Von Gerolt and his daughter, who, with other ambassadors had correspondents, manifested a lively interest in the spectacle. What they saw and felt was soon made known to their respective governments and people, and no doubt exerted a moral and political influence favorable to our cause. Its impression as a spectacle was not the chief purpose or desired effect on the army. It furnished needed tactical instruction and experience regarding time and space in the movement of large bodies of men and horse with their batteries. The capacities of roads for marching and of fields for maneuvre were practically tested.

There was an innovation of the cavalry guidon displayed by the 3d Pennsylvania Cavalry that day which ought to be recorded. It may well be regarded as the merest trifle in the imposing pageant of a grand army review, but it was of great importance in battles and the record of the 3d is entitled to its mention. At the first Battle of Bull Run we had experienced some hesitations and perilous delays in opening fire, by the difficulty of distinguishing Confederate flags from the guidons of the cavalry owing to their similarity of shape and colors. So, previous to the review, I purchased twelve United States flags with the dimensions of the regulation guidon and had the ends forked or cut into a swallow-tailed shape, and the 3d Pennsylvania Cavalry was the first regiment that carried the guidon that was afterward adopted in the United States Cavalry.

This grand review, together with the completed chain of garrisoned fortifications around Washington, clearly demonstrated that the military necessity which had filled the Capital with consternation and dismay after the first woeful disaster at Bull Run was now fully satisfied, and it was realized that the seat of government was now permanently secured from the danger of capture.

Ours being an industrial type of government and not militant, as are most of those of Europe, and our little army having been detailed at sentinel Army Posts on the distant frontier, our people had never seen it, or hardly any portion of it. There had been no organized National Guards such as we have today. The people generally regarded the beplumed general who could form a militia parade as possessing all the necessary abilities to command an army in war. The President and his cabinet and the men who composed the military committees of Congress, although prominent and experienced politicians among whom were a few states-men, had no knowledge of the many requirements of a general officer.

The first and most conspicuous acts of the government were to appoint Major-Generals from civil life, for instance N.[Nathaniel] P. Banks and Benj. F. Butler, of Massachusetts, and Robert Schenck, of Ohio. These were the ablest and most prominent of the civilians appoint-ed to the highest grade in the army, but their military history is largely a record of blunders and disasters. Butler's plan of attack on an outpost at Big-Bethel, Va., wherein it was arranged that two columns should approach the point of attack from opposite directions through a thick wood on a dark night and the necessary consequence of each column mistaking the other for the enemy and spending a little time in killing each other and less in becoming thoroughly demoralized, was the first display of this kind of military ability. The use of a powder-boat to blow Fort Fisher off the earth in the night, and which only succeeded in awakening pretty nearly every man in the garrison, was another of Butler's military inventions. The campaigns of Banks in the Shenandoah Valley and on the Red River furnished deplorable wastes of men and material. Schenck was one of five of the greatest leaders in political affairs and his first military blow as a General was amazingly unique, being a reconnaissance of Vienna, Va., upon a railway train running backward into the enemy's line. He was rewarded afterward by the administration for the novel calamity that ensued by being placed in command of the Department of West Virginia, at long range from his headquarters in Baltimore.

The Congressional "Committee on the Conduct of the War" had already begun to investigate every military operation and to suggest or constrain executive action. The condition of security of the Capital encour-aged and strengthened this untoward and meddlesome interference not only with the organization of the army but also with the strategic operations.

No organization for work or war can be efficient without a single directing head. If the unit of control of military operations be multiplied, disorders, delays, disasters and waste of life and treasure will inevitably follow and responsibility will become elusive. When the history of the Civil War shall be written with full intelligence of the truth and the adequate ability and courage to tell it, it will be clearly shown how, during three long tedious years of alternate hope and discouragement, all the direful results imaginable followed the want of united action and design.

Newspaper correspondents pervaded the camps of the army and every item of personal or public interest that could be gleaned by them was published within a few hours. As the Confederate Army of Northern Virginia at Manassas received our newspapers with but little delay, the Confederate leaders and government were kept about as well informed of the conditions existing in the Army of the Potomac as the editors of the Northern press. As early as January, 1862, there began to appear editorial expressions of impatience at the delay of active operations in the field. The lesson of Bull Run seemed forgotten, editorial suggestions became more and more urgent and, toward the end of January, quite clamorous.

Then Mr. Lincoln, who was always remarkably responsive to popular sentiment, yielded to these manifestations of impatience and on the 27th of January issued the President's War Order No. I, naming the 22d of February to be the day for a general movement of the land and naval forces of the United States. General McClellan was then the Commander-in-Chief of the armies of the United States and was the unit of general military control, and he first saw this order in the newspapers. It occasioned amazement and deep regret in the Army of the Potomac. It was the only topic for several days. But few seemed able to divine its inspiration and none to accept its propriety. Everyone knew that it was impossible of execution. All opinions that I heard and recollect agreed that it was untimely and futile. It is, however, pregnant with historic significance.

There were two insuperable conditions opposed to the execution of the order by the Army of the Potomac. It had been named "Army of the Potomac" on August 20, 1861, when it was in its infancy and it was only five months old when this war order was issued. McDowell's little army of thirty odd thousand men was about three months old when it occupied five days in marching twenty-five miles in fine summer weather and over hard ground to get across Bull Run to fight a serious battle when it was so untrained that but a small portion of it could be easily maneuvered or could handle its arms with efficiency; and broken, bleeding and humiliated it flocked off the field. Now here was a young and yet growing army of over a hundred thousand men. The newer regiments and batteries would have been more embarrassing on the march or in battle at this time than any other impedimenta. At least two or three months were yet required to get them into any sort of condition to be handled as soldiers.

The other condition was that from New Year's until spring the ground occupied by the enemy in our front with all its approaches was impracticable, if not impossible, for military operations. The eastern slopes of the Blue Ridge to the Bull Run mountains afford a better footing, but eastward of these the bottom was hub deep during this season of the year. This latter condition was found to exist when we tried it over two months after this time. And many times later on this condition was made distressingly apparent to the Army of the Potomac and memorably so in the "mud campaign" of Burnside about the same date, January 24, the next year near Fredericksburg, when the whole army was stalled in the mud and the horses of the cavalry became disabled with sore backs carrying boxes of "hardtack" to it for its subsistence. It may be remarked here as affording some light for a proper consideration of the popular charge that was made against General McClellan at this time that he was "too slow," which stigma upon his military reputation has become historical, that he moved the Army of the Potomac when it was young and untried earlier in the spring and later in the fall than any other of its commanders. He moved it on the 10th of March and was relieved from its command on the 5th of November. General Grant moved the same army two years later, when its soldiers had become the tried and seasoned veterans of many great campaigns and battles, on the 4th of May and was encamped before Petersburg on the 4th of July, built huts for the winter and lay there for over nine months without a murmur from the press or the government and at that time the general control of all military operations had been accorded solely to him.

The newspapers after having published the daily record of the organization and growth of the army, now began to chronicle the indications of an early movement, and this had the effect of bringing throngs of visitors to Washington to make their adieux to their friends in the army. The enemy, of course, had the news as we found out a few days later, and the army at Manassas began packing and transporting its surplus supplies and unnecessary material back toward Richmond.

Among the people who had made their residence in Washington during the winter on account of the presence of the army, there began now to be observed a social flutter such as agitates migratory birds when making ready for a long flight. Some of the most interesting and attractive people in the world swarmed on Washington. Parties of residents, visitors and tourists were daily visiting our camps. The capital was humming with an unprecedented social ebullition of all sorts of men and women, from town and country. Conventionalities were left outside the sentinels' posts. The emotions of parents, brothers, sisters, and sweethearts started the unhindered tear in many a soldier's eye.

In the camps of my brigade, our surplus personal belongings were cleared out and stored and our impedimenta reduced to a minimum. On March 2d General F. J. Porter, accompanied by General Butterfield and Major [William N.] Grier ("Old Billy Grier") of the United States Cavalry, reviewed my brigade and witnessed some field maneuvers with expressions of approval and satisfaction. My brother visited me during the off hours of the same day and was entertained with glimpses of army life, remaining with me over night and the next day.

On the 4th I was called to General Fitz-John Porter's headquarters at Hall's Hill and found General McClellan there. He and General Porter were alone together. I was asked if I could take my brigade and go around the enemy's army by his left or western flank and destroy the railway bridges across the Rappahannock at Rappahannock Station and at Fredericksburg. I replied that I would like to try. The map was carefully studied and distances estimated. The enemy's cavalry was thought to be doing picket duty along the front of his line with the main body near the railway and not more than one regiment covering his left flank.

It would be necessary for my brigade to march between twenty-five and thirty miles due west to get clear of the enemy's left flank and as many more to the first bridge and over thirty miles thence down the river to the second bridge. The movement would be related to a movement of the Army of the Potomac. It was thought best that I should make half the distance to the first bridge during the night as affording a better chance to get by the flank without encountering any considerable interference, and when once beyond the flank no serious obstacle might be expected.

The position of the enemy had been pretty accurately learned from scouts, spies and prisoners, but the responsibility of making the first march of a great but untried army to attack an enemy who had defeated our first onset seemed fully appreciated. *C'est le premiere pas qui coute.* It was fully considered, and although nothing was settled, the outline of the plan of action as I recollect it was that I would start early in the night and at daylight next morning a strong feint should be made on the enemy's right; and the whole army moved forward to attack the enemy's left where the condition of the ground and the topography were more favorable for maneuvering a large force; and it would also have the important advantage of being in the direction of the enemy's communications. The attention of a large portion of his cavalry would probably be diverted from my expedition. A brief signal code by salvo and lines of communication were projected. My brigade was kept in readiness to move at shortest notice, but I heard nothing more of the project until three or four days afterwards. When this

* * *

The manuscript ends here. The editors believe that Averell did finish this chapter but that the last pages were destroyed by accident.

The main body of the Army of the Potomac was on its way via ship to the Virginia peninsula. The Third Pennsylvania Cavalry along with other units were a diversionary force on the back of the main Confederate defense. *The History of the Third Pennsylvania Cavalry* describes the movement:[2]

It was before daylight on the tenth day of March, 1862, that the bugles sounded "Forward" and amid the rolling of drums and hastening of staff officers back and forth through the camps, indications were everywhere that the Army was on the move at last. We of the Third were hastened out past the camps of Infantry, to the picket line, and there were ordered to lead the advance of the Army of the Potomac to Centreville and Manassas, in company with the Eighth Pennsylvania Cavalry, under Colonel D. McM. Gregg. So away we went, soon arriving at Fairfax Court House, without meeting anyone to oppose us; out then on the Centreville road, until we halted in sight of a line of frowning guns, which we expected every moment to belch forth fire and shot upon us. Here Colonel Averell dismounted two companies of the Third to advance as skirmishers toward the fortifications on the hill, while the balance of the regiment and the Eighth Pennsylvania stood ready to support them. We were more than gratified, however, when we found no one to resist us. The enemy had gone, and the guns remaining *en barbette* were only harmless wooden logs—"Quaker guns," the newspapers dubbed them.

We were now upon ground from which our army had been driven on the disastrous day of the Battle of Bull Run, and we moved forward with great caution. But "Go ahead!" was the command, and we obeyed. After leaving Centreville we found all the country beyond denuded of woods and fences, and not a tree standing. This enabled us to get a good view ahead for some distance. The day was waning, however, and we were anxious if possible to get to Manassas, which was some miles beyond Bull Run. A message

---

[2]Rawle, William Brooke, *et al. History of the Third Pennsylvania Cavalry, Sixtieth Regiment Pennsylvania Volunteers in the American Civil War.* pp. 36-38.

from the rear came to us at this time to halt, and as we sat in our saddles we saw the sun go down on those fields, which in the previous summer had so copiously absorbed the blood of friend and foe. When we were ordered to go forward darkness had fallen, and the huts and other camp buildings inside the fortifications at Manassas were ablaze. We could see the forms of men moving between the flashes of light, and thought, of course, that some of the enemy were destroying what they supposed we would want as shelter. We marched on until we had entered the fortifications, rode around the burning buildings, and then retraced our way back to Centreville, where we camped for the night. We felt a peculiar gratification as we meditated over our experience of the day, for we had the honor to be the first Union troops to enter Centreville, cross Bull Run, and take possession of Manassas.

The fact that the Third Pennsylvania was given the advance in the first forward movement of the Army of the Potomac was evidence of the confidence in it and the regard for it felt by General McClellan. What it accomplished, and the fuss made over it, strikes us in the light of our later experience as rather trivial.

The Third Pennsylvania Cavalry returned to camp near Washington on 15 March 1862; the regiment boarded the transports at Alexandria on 25 March and arrived three days later at camp near Hampton, Virginia.

23

With the Cavalry on the Peninsula— April–August 3, 1862

I n the Peninsular campaign of 1862 there were employed fourteen regiments of cavalry, entire or in parts, and two independent squadrons. Considerably over half this force was composed of volunteers, and had been in existence about six months. In the regular cavalry three years had been regarded as necessary to transform a recruit into a good cavalryman. The amount of patient and persistent hard work required to convert twelve hundred untrained citizens, unaccustomed to the care of a horse or to his use under the saddle, and wholly inexperienced in the use of arms, into the semblance of a cavalry regiment in six months is known only to those who have done it.

The topography and soil of the peninsula presented a most difficult field for cavalry operations. From Fort Monroe to Hanover Court House there was hardly a field with sufficient scope for the maneuvers of a single regiment of cavalry. After a rain the deep alluvium became, under the tread of horses, a bed of mortar knee deep. The forests between the York and the James rivers were filled with tangled thickets and unapproachable morasses. The tributaries of the rivers, mostly deep, crooked and sluggish, become more tortuous as they approach their confluence, and the expanse of floods is converted by evaporation into stagnant swamps. A heavy rain in a few hours rendered these streams formidable obstacles. Above this dismal landscape the fierce rays of the sun were interrupted only at night, or by deluges of rains, so that men and animals were alter-

355

nately scorched and drenched. These conditions made cavalry operations in this region affairs of squadrons.

The cavalry had been organized into a division under General George Stoneman, Chief of Cavalry, and distributed by assignment to the corps of the army, excepting the cavalry reserve under General P. St. George Cooke and that portion which was attached to general headquarters. During the month of the siege of Yorktown not an hour was lost which could be applied to cavalry instruction. Alertness and steadiness soon characterized our cavalrymen. No incident was fruitless. When grindstones were procured and the sabres of my regiment were sharpened at Hampton, it produced a similar effect upon the men.

Few but cavalry names reached the ears of the army on the day of the evacuation and pursuit [May 4, 1862]. Stoneman and Cooke, on the right, with the 1st and 6th Regulars, struck cavalry, infantry, batteries, redoubts, and ravines, and pushed their attack with audacity. Cavalrymen galloped around field-works. We soon heard of the gallantry of Colonel Grier, Major Lawrence Williams, Captains Sanders, Davis, Baker, and others in cavalry charges, and that the French Princes were among the first in the advance. Lieutenant-Colonel Grier, commanding the 1st ("Old Billy Grier, the *bueno commandante*"), had led a charge and engaged two of the enemy in personal combat, wounding one and himself receiving a wound. Then came tidings of the dash of Chambliss and McLean leading Hancock's column and crowding the left center of the enemy's line, and soon the Third Pennsylvania Cavalry met the enemy in the woods and drove him out with skirmishers and canister, and cleared our left toward the James of the enemy's cavalry under Stuart. During the following day the cavalry were spectators of the battle at Williamsburg (except the Third Pennsylvania actively engaged on our left), and were only occupied with the rather serious business of procuring food for the horses.

Although pursuit was again undertaken on the morning of the 6th by squadrons of the Third Pennsylvania and Eighth Illinois Cavalry and was continued for four miles, and five pieces of artillery were recovered and some prisoners were captured, it came to a dead halt from necessity. During the succeeding twenty days the cavalry swept the country in advance of our marching army by day and hovered around its bivouacs by night.

When the army was in line about seven miles from Richmond, on the 25th of May, I was directed to communicate with the gunboats on the James River at City Point. Lieutenant Davis, of the Third Pennsylvania,

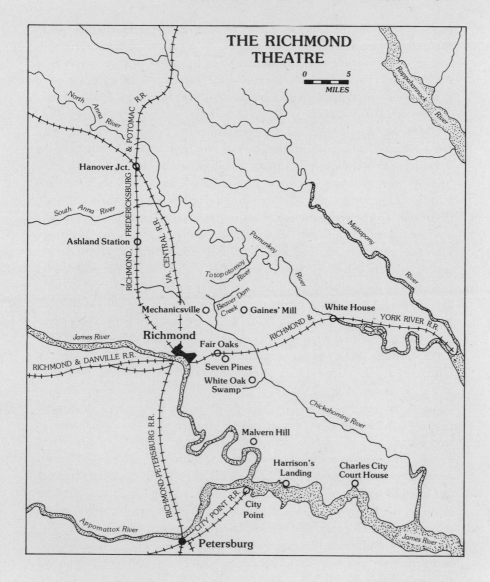

with ten men, was selected for the duty, and he made his way along various roads infested with the pickets and patrols of the enemy to the bank of the James, where, taking a skiff, with two Negroes, he went on board the *Galena* and communicated to Captain Rogers the position of the army, and received from the Captain a statement of the position of the gunboats.

On the 27th, not satisfied with the picnic appearance of our front on our left, south of the Chickahominy, I reported its perilous condition to McClellan, who at once sent Colonel N. B. Sweitzer of his staff to me, and together we rode to the front. As a result, orders were given at once for slashing the forest, and positions for batteries and outposts were determined—precautions which, three days later, disclosed their value in the Battle of Fair Oaks.

On the same day (27th) we were scratching the ground away up to our right at Hanover Court House, in invitation to McDowell to come down from Fredericksburg. Almost within his sight and quite within his hearing, the principal northern gate to Richmond was set ajar—the Virginia Central and the Richmond and Fredericksburg railroads were destroyed. In the resultant mêlée about Hanover Court House, the cavalry, under Emory, Royall, Lawrence Williams, Chambliss, Whiting, Harrison, and Arnold, and Rush's Sixth Pennsylvania, aggressively attacked infantry, captured whole companies with arms, swept right, left, and rear and generally filled the idea of cavalry activities in such a battle.

General Lee assumed command June 1st. On the 13th he announced himself, through his cavalry in Stuart's raid around our army. This expedition was appointed with excellent judgement, and was conducted with superb address. Stuart pursued the line of least resistance, which was the unexpected. His subordinate commanders were Colonels Fitz Lee, W. H. F. Lee, and W. T. Martin, all intrepid cavalrymen. It was an easy thing to do, but being his first raid, Stuart was nervous and, imagining perils which did not exist, neglected one great opportunity—the destruction of our base of supplies at the White House. Had he, at Garlick's, exchanged purposes with his detachment, sending it on the road home, while he, with the main body, bent all his energies to the destruction of our base of supplies, we might have had something to lament even had we captured his command. On our side were developed many things to be remembered with pride, and one thing to regret with mortification. The memories are glorious that not a single vedette or picket was surprised, and that never was outpost duty more honorably and correctly performed than by Captain W. B. Royall and Lieutenant McLean of the Fifth United States Cavalry. They met the enemy repeatedly, and the Lieutenant gave his life, and the Captain was prostrated with sabre wounds in resisting Stuart's column. The killing of the dashing Confederate Captain Latane and several men with the sabre, and the checking of the invading forces for an hour attest the courage and devotion of Royall and his picket. We had to regret that there was no reserve to the outpost within supporting distance, and that when the reserve was alarmed in its camp, precious time was lost by indirections. This raid of Stuart's added a new feature to cavalry history. A similar expedition, however, had been projected previously. Just before the Army of the Potomac advanced on Manassas, in March, '62, in a conference with General McClellan, it was suggested that I should take my brigade, consisting of the Third and Eighth Pennsylvania Cavalry, the first brigade of cavalry formed in the war, and go around the enemy, then at Manassas, destroying the bridge at Rappahannock Station, and that at Fredericksburg; but the immediate movement of the enemy from Manassas prevented its being carried out.

Our General's plans were not disturbed by Stuart's raid, and two days after it was over, the Third Pennsylvania Cavalry crossed the Pamunkey River on our right and rear, ascended to King William Court House and Ellett's Mills, burned the bridge and ferryboat, and a schooner and other boats, and a storehouse containing thirty thousand bushels of grain. Scouts were pushed out many miles in quest of news of Jackson's coming. This was the last extension of our hands towards McDowell, for Jackson came sooner than he was expected, on the 26th, the day upon which a general advance had been determined and the Battle of Gaines's Mill was opened.

McClellan met and mastered the occasion. Alert, radiant, and cheerful, he stood out in front of his tent in his shirt-sleeves nearly all day of the 26th listening to his army. To the north, across the Chickahominy, his clipped right wing, environed with our cavalry, was sullenly retracting its lines to the position at Gaines's Mill. Stoneman, with infirmities that would have kept a man of less fortitude in hospital, was in the saddle confronting Stuart's cavalry and covering the White House Landing.

The ensuing night was without rest for the cavalry. The strain of the following day to help the Fifth Corps to hold its ground until dark will never be forgotten, it was not devoid of heroic cavalry effort. Fragments of the reserve under General Cooke stood massed in the valley of the Chickahominy on its left bank. About 5 P.M., when it was evident that we were being pressed on the right and left of our line by all the force the enemy could bring into action against Porter, and that we were not likely to be able to resist his attack, the cavalry was moved from its masked position to the edge of the hill and placed in a formation to charge, should charge seem likely to do good. It was there exposed to the enemy's fire, and must either retire, advance, or be destroyed. In a few minutes the order to charge was given to the Fifth Regulars, not three hundred strong. Chambliss, leading, rode as straight as man ever rode, into the face of Longstreet's corps; and the Fifth Cavalry was destroyed and dispersed. Six of the seven officers present and fifty men were struck down. Chambliss, hit by seven balls, lost consciousness, and when he recovered found himself in the midst of the enemy. The charge at Balaklava had not this desperation and was not better ridden. Chambliss lay on the field ten days, and was finally taken to Richmond, where he was rescued from death by the kind care of Generals Hood and Field. In this battle there were two and a half squadrons of the Fifth and two squadrons of the First United States Cavalry, three squadrons Rush's Lancers (Sixth Pennsylvania Cavalry), and one squadron Fourth Pennsylvania (Colonel Childs).

Two or three weeks before this several officers of the Third Pennsylvania Cavalry—Newhall, Treichel, W. E. Miller, and others—penetrated the region between the Chickahominy and the James, taking bearings and making notes. Their fragmentary sketches, when put together, made a map which exhibited all the roadways, fields, forests, bridges, the streams, and houses, so that our commander knew the country to be traversed through the seven days far better than any Confederate commander.

On the evening of June 27, my pickets from Tunstall's Station and other points were called in, and at 6:30 A.M., on the 28th, the regiment crossed White Oak Swamp, leading Keyes's Corps, and advanced to the Charles City road. Lieutenant Davis was again sent to communicate with the gunboats on the James.

At daylight on the 29th, Captain White's squadron, with two hundred infantry and two guns, was sent to picket and hold Jones's Bridge on the Chickahominy. About 9 A.M. my scouts reported a regiment of the enemy's cavalry advancing in column about a mile away. Some woodland intervened. Between this and my position was an open field a quarter of a mile across. A picket was quickly posted at the higher edge of the wood, with orders to fire upon the enemy when he should come within range and then turn and run away, thus inviting pursuit! On my position two guns were already placed to enfilade the road, and a few squadrons held in readiness to charge. The enemy came, was fired upon, and the picket fled, followed by the enemy in hot pursuit. Upon arriving within two hundred yards of our position, the picket quitted the road through the gaps in the fences made for that purpose, thus unmasking the enemy's column; the two guns of Major West fired two rounds, and two squadrons, led by Captains Walsh and Russell, of the Third Pennsylvania, were let loose upon the enemy, and over sixty of his officers and men were left on the ground, whilst the survivors fled in great disorder toward Richmond. The command was the First North Carolina and Third Virginia Cavalry, led by Colonel Lawrence Baker, a comrade of mine in the old army. The Third Pennsylvania lost one man killed and five wounded.

After this affair I galloped back to see General McClellan, and found him near a house south of White Oak Swamp Bridge. Near him were groups of a hundred officers eagerly but quietly discussing our progress and situation. So soon as McClellan descried me, he came with the Prince de Joinville to the fence where I dismounted. After telling him all I knew and had learned from prisoners and scouts, I ventured to suggest that the roads were tolerably clear toward Richmond, and that we might go there. The Prince seemed to exhibit a favorable interest in my suggestion, but the General, recognizing its weakness, said promptly, "The roads will be full enough tomorrow"; and then earnestly, "Averell, if any army can save this country, it will be the Army of the Potomac, and it must be saved for that purpose." The General rode to the front with me, and reconnoitered the ground in all directions. In the afternoon, with Hay's regiment of infantry and Benson's battery, I established our outposts and pickets within one mile of New Market, where we were first touched with some of the enemy's infantry during the night. On the 30th, there were battles on our center and right; and having joined the Fifth Corps, I proceeded to Malvern Hill in the evening and rode over the field with Captain Colburn, my classmate and the favorite aide of McClellan, and made a topographical sketch of the position, which was of some use afterward in posting the infantry and artillery as they arrived.

During the night of the 30th, the General commanding asked me for two officers for hazardous service. Lieutenants Newhall and Treichel, because of their intimate knowledge of the country, were sent to communicate with our right and center, and a second time that night made their way for a mile and a half through the enemy's camps.

During the battle of July 1 (Malvern Hill), my cavalry was deployed as a close line of skirmishers with drawn sabres in rear of our lines, with orders to permit no one to pass to the rear who could not show blood. The line of battle was ready and reserves of infantry and artillery in position some time before the enemy came in force and developed his attack. There were some preliminary bursts of artillery, but the great crash of all arms did not begin before 6 P.M. It lasted about two hours. The Commanding

General, with his mounted staff, was standing on the plateau in front of the farmhouse at the rear verge of the hill, a conspicuous group, when a round shot from the enemy struck the ground a few yards directly in front of him and threw dirt and gravel over the little group around him. General Porter, with whom I was riding, had just started toward the front when he turned and said to McClellan, "General, everything is all right here and you are not needed; if you will look after our center and right that would help us here more than you can by remaining." Then we separated from them and rode toward our left at Crew's house. The wounded were already coming away from the lines.

When the battle was over and the field had become quiet, the cavalry bivouacked half a mile in rear of the line of battle. Men and horses were too tired to do aught but sleep for hours. At midnight I found myself in the saddle with a cup of hot coffee held to my lips, a portion of its contents having scalded its way down my throat. When awakened I was informed by the Duc de Chartres that General McClellan desired to see me. We found him near by in a little orchard by a camp fire, giving orders rapidly to his generals and staff officers. When my turn came, McClellan said, "Averell, I want you to take command of the rear guard at daylight in the morning and hold this position until our trains are out of the way. What force do you want?" I asked for just enough to cover the front with a strong skirmish line. The orders were given for Buchanan's Brigade of Sykes's Division, Fifth Corps, to report to me at daylight, and also a battery.

At daylight the cavalry advanced toward the front. There was a fog so dense that we could not see a man at fifty paces distance. Colonel Buchanan was met with his staff returning from the front on foot, their horses being led. He informed me that the enemy was threatening his pickets, and advancing on both flanks. I asked him to halt his command until further orders, and galloped to the front, where our line of battle had been the night before. I could see nothing, but could hear shrieks and groans and the murmur of a multitude, but no sounds of wheels nor trampling horses. I ordered the line re-established with skirmishers and a squadron of cavalry on either flank. Colonel Hall, with the Second Regiment Excelsior Brigade, also reported for duty, and took position in the line. The battery not having reported, some cavalry was organized into squads, resembling sections of artillery, at proper intervals behind the crest. By this time the level rays of the morning sun from our right were just penetrating the fog, and slowly lifting its clinging shreds and yellow masses. Our ears had been filled with agonizing cries from thousands before the fog was lifted, but now our eyes saw an appalling spectacle upon the slopes down to the woodlands half a mile away. Over five thousand dead and wounded men were on the ground, in every attitude of distress. A third of them were dead or dying, but enough were alive and moving to give to the field a singular crawling effect. The different stages of the ebbing tide are often marked by the lines of flotsam and jetsam left along the seashore. So here could be seen three distinct lines of dead and wounded marking the last front of three Confederate charges of the night before. Groups of men, some mounted, were groping about the field.

As soon as the woodland beyond, which masked the enemy, could be clearly seen, I offered battle by directing the infantry lines to show on the crest, the sham sections of artillery to execute the movements of going "into battery, action front," and the flank squadrons to move toward the enemy until fired upon. All these details were executed simultaneously at the sound of the trumpet. The squadrons had not proceeded three hundred yards when they were fired upon and halted. At the same time, a horseman from among those on the field approached our line with a white flag. An aide was sent to meet and halt him. The Confederate horseman, who was an officer, requested a truce of two hours in which to succor their wounded. I was about to send a demand that his request be put in writing, when I reflected that it would be embarrassing for me to reply in writing, so word was sent to him to dismount and wait until his request had been submitted to the Commanding General. In the meantime the scattered parties of the enemy withdrew hastily from the field to the woods, and there was some threatening desultory firing on my flanks, killing one man and wounding another. After waiting thirty minutes, word was sent to the officer with the flag that the truce was granted, and that their men could come out without arms and succor their wounded. I had no idea that the flag was properly authorized, else there would have been no firing on my flanks, but time was the precious thing I wished to gain for our trains which crowded the bottom lands below Malvern. My squadrons were withdrawn to the line, the infantry lay down, while officers took position in front of the line to prevent conversation with the enemy. In a few minutes thousands of men swarmed from the woods and scattered over the field. I kept myself informed by couriers of the movements of our army and trains, and had already sent officers to reassure our rear of its security, and also to bring me back a battery of artillery. Captain Frank with his battery responded. I sent a request to General

Wessells, commanding Keyes's rear brigade, to select a good position about two miles in my rear in case I should need a checking force when the time for withdrawal should come. That excellent soldier had already chosen such a position and established his brigade in line of battle.

When the quasi-truce had expired, at the sound of the trumpet, the line resumed its attitude of attack, and the officer with the flag again appeared with a request that the truce be extended two hours. After a reasonable wait, answer was returned that the time was extended, but that no further extension would be granted. I had come on the line at 4 A.M., and these maneuvers and truces had consumed the time until after 9 o'clock. The Army of the Potomac was then at its new base on the James, and all its trains were safely on the way there, with Keyes's Corps some miles below in my rear awaiting the enemy. So when the extended truce had expired, my command, with the exception of the cavalry, had left the field. Our dead and wounded, about twenty-five hundred in number, had been cared for during the night. Not above a dozen bodies could be found on our field during the truce, and these were buried. Twelve stalled and abandoned wagons were destroyed, and two captured guns which could not be removed were spiked and their carriages were broken. The Third Pennsylvania Cavalry which had led the Army of the Potomac across White Oak Swamp, now saw its last serviceable man safe beyond Malvern Hill, before it left that glorious field, about 10 A.M., July 2. A heavy rainstorm was prevailing. When everything movable was across Turkey Bridge, it was destroyed by my rear squadron. My command passed through Wessells's lines about noon, and the lines of General Naglee a little later. Everything was now quiet and in good order, and the Third Pennsylvania proceeded to camp at Westover after dark.

The Eighth Pennsylvania Cavalry, under Colonel D. McM. Gregg, had scoured the left bank of the Chickahominy, on the 28th, and had swum the river to the right bank, rafting its arms across at Long Bridge. He subsequently picketed the front of our center and right on the 30th, and on July 1 and 2—an extremely important service. The Fourth Pennsylvania Cavalry, after its efficient service, at and about Gaines's Mill, during the day and night of the 27th of June, performed similar duties with General McCall at Charles City road on the 30th. The Eleventh Pennsylvania, Colonel Harlan, which, on the 13th, had covered the White House Landing during Stuart's raid, on the 28th joined Stoneman on similar duty and retired with him.

Colonel Farnsworth, Eighth Illinois, after his active participation in covering our right wing on the 26th, and guiding trains and maintaining steadiness of lines on the 27th, guided Keyes's corps to the James River below Malvern, on the 29th, and assisted the Eighth Pennsylvania in covering that corps on the 30th and 1st of July. The Second United States Cavalry and McClellan Dragoons, under Major Pleasanton, escorted Colonel B. S. Alexander, of the Corps of Engineers, on the 29th, to Carter's Landing on the James. Captains Norris and Green, of the Second, performed scouting service in the direction of the Chickahominy and Charles City Court House, after the arrival of the regiment on the James. And so ended the first lesson of the cavalry service of the Army of the Potomac.

Near the White House, on the morning of the 29th of June (at the very time that the Third Pennsylvania Cavalry was repelling the First North Carolina and Third Virginia Cavalry at Willis' Church, south of the Chickahominy), Stuart received a note from General Lee asking for his impressions in regard to the designs of the Union Army. He replied that there was no evidence of a retreat down the Williamsburg road, and that he had no doubt that it was endeavoring to reach the James. On the 30th, while we were establishing our advance on Malvern Hill, Stuart, north of the Chickahominy, was directing his cavalry columns toward the bridges of that river behind us. Had the disposition of his forces been reversed at the outset, and had he, with his main body, gone to Charles City road and obstructed and defended the crossings of White Oak Swamp, he could have annoyed and perhaps embarrassed our movements. Finally, had his cavalry ascertained on July 1, any time before 3 P.M., that the center and right of our lines were more vulnerable and favorable to attack than the left, the enemy need not have delivered the unsuccessful and disastrous assault on Malvern Hill, but, while maintaining a strong demonstration at that point, might have thrown two or three corps upon our center below Malvern with hopes of dividing the Union Army. Undoubtedly Gregg and Farnsworth, with the Eighth Pennsylvania and Eighth Illinois Cavalry, would have successfully prevented the reconnoissance of our center and right, but that it was not attempted was a discredit to Stuart's cavalry.

At Harrison's Landing, General Stoneman having taken sickleave and General Cooke having been relieved, on the 5th of July I was appointed acting Brigadier-General and placed in command of all the cavalry of the Army of the Potomac, and at once issued orders organizing it into a

Colonel William W. Averell and staff of the 3d Pennsylvania Cavalry. Westover Land-ing, Virginia, August 1862. Left to right: Lt. W. H. Brown, Lt. H. H. King, Averell, Lt. Phillip Polland. Photograph by Alexander Gardner. (Courtesy Library of Congress)

cavalry corps, and the history of the cavalry brigades was begun. Stone-man, returning the same day, resumed command, and I took the First Brigade, composed of the Fifth United States, the Third and Fourth Pennsylvania, and the First New York Cavalry.

Active scouting followed in the direction of Richmond and up the Chickahominy. On the 3d of August I crossed the James, with the Fifth United States and Third Pennsylvania Cavalry, to explore the ways to Petersburg, encountering the Thirteenth Virginia Cavalry in a charge led by Lieutenant McIntosh, of the Fifth United States, supported by Captain Miller of the Third Pennsylvania. The enemy was driven over seven miles, and his camp and supplies destroyed.

All the successes and sacrifices of the army were now to be worse than lost—they were to be thrown away by the withdrawal of the army from the Peninsula, instead of reinforcing it.

24

Conduct of the War

No true story of the war can ever be written with an exclusive consideration of the military operations alone and without a careful study and estimate of the tendencies and strength of all the forces which were involved in its prosecution—moral, social, political and military—the resultant of which dictated the conduct of the war. It is not my present purpose to undertake the telling of such a story. This is intended to be simply a record of reminiscences from which cannot be omitted recollections of a question which has been a subject of controversy since 1861, and which will continue to be discussed so long as the Army of the Potomac is remembered.

Let us take a brief retrospect of the stupendous military problem which was presented to the country in July, 1861, and endeavor to make a resolution of the controlling forces involved therein. The purposes of the impending conflict had been clearly and authoritatively defined and declared by both the North and the South; and after the firing on Fort Sumter the people of both sections had become firmly united in their respective determinations: the South to make secession with independence an accomplished fact, and the North to defend and maintain the Union of States. The resources of neither side were yet well understood, nor had any reasonable estimates been made of the forces that would probably be required by each for the prosecution of the war. The military population of the North, by the eighth census (1860) which enumerated all white male inhabitants between eighteen and forty-five years of age was 4,559,872; and of the South it was 1,064,193. The military population of the South could yield to military service a much larger proportion of its numbers than could be spared from that of the North for the reason that it had a colored population adequate to perform the agricultural labor.

The South promptly proceeded to muster and organize all her energies for the development of her military power, the control of which was wisely entrusted, under a military President, to military officers of the greatest military ability and with the largest military experience. Such an organization, so controlled, evolved a prodigious military strength which was measured by the force required to break it, namely: 2,145,370 men (including the strength of the regular army which at the beginning of the war was 16,442), and more than three thousand millions of dollars. The North enlisted nearly one-half of its military population. Had the South employed only one-half of its military population it would have numbered in its ranks 532,096 soldiers, but no compilation has ever been prepared from which any reliable statements can be made concerning the number of troops employed on the Confederate side. It has been estimated at 600,000. The total number of men who lost their lives from all causes in the Union Army was 359,528, of whom 67,058 were killed in action. The total Confederate loss has been estimated at 133,821 killed and died of wounds, and diseases,—the number killed in action being 51,425.[1]

That the soldiers of the opposing armies possessed equally the soldierly qualitites of courage, fortitude and endurance has never been questioned by those who fought with either. Northern soldiers were generally better fed, clothed, armed and equipped than those of the South, and it has always been claimed and allowed that the Federal artillery was far superior in quality and efficiency to that of the Confederates. These facts naturally give rise to the question, "Why was this mighty preponderance of numbers required by the North?"

It is admissible from a military point of view to regard the whole Confederacy, when ready for war, as a vast entrenched camp, defended at every point where an attacking army could be supplied and maintained, and, as such camp, requiring largely superior forces to assail it successfully. Also, as the defending forces might be transferred with celerity by interior lines of communication from one point to another, or from one

---

[1] Averell's figures are generally correct. For a more complete discussion of numbers see Thomas L. Livermore, *Numbers and Losses in the Civil War in America: 1861-65.*

army to another, according to the necessities of the defense, the lack of strength due to the paucity of numbers might be thus largely made up, while the cost of arms, equipments, and supplies for the lacking numbers would be saved. Then again, an army operating on the defensive in its own country and familiar with its topography and with friendly inhabitants, enjoyed advantages which were equivalent to a considerable proportion of the preponderant numbers. But however important and valuable all the conditions mentioned might have been, and undoubtedly were, to the Confederates, they were far more than overbalanced by the Federal control of the sea where it washed the shores of Southern states, and by the blockade of their ports. Thus environed, time, which consumed and exhausted supplies which could not be replenished, became the greatest enemy of the Confederacy. Hence, two or three grand sorties were desperately made which terminated at Antietam, Gettysburg and Nashville. The Confederate armies withstood the assaults and incursions of these tremendous odds during four long years until their subsistence and supplies were exhausted and no more men were available to recruit their wasted ranks.

In a conversation which I had with a venerable and intelligent colored man on my first visit to Richmond after the surrender, in reply to my question how the women and children subsisted in the city during the last days of the Confederate army at Petersburg, he said, "They lived on the leavings of the army, sir,—on what the soldiers could spare them."

"Well then," I asked, "what did the soldiers live on?"

"Why bless your soul, sir! they lived on the leaves of the trees!"

In his description of the destitution which had prevailed, the old man mentioned that the ladies of Richmond were in such need of clothing that petticoats were not uncommonly made of gunnybags. I do not believe this picture of the privations of the South at the time of the surrender was much exaggerated.

The military strength of the North at the close of the war had not been measured—it seemed immeasurable; for on the first day of May 1865, after the surrender, the names of 1,000,516 armed men were on the Union rolls, of which enormous force 797,807 were reported "present for duty" not including the Navy. Over 300,000 of this number had been enlisted just before the surrender.

The total number of Confederate soldiers captured, including those who were surrendered, was 464,169. Add to this number the total Confederate loss in killed and died of wounds and diseases and it would appear that the aggregate Confederate strength employed had been 597,990 which is only 2,010 short of 600,000.[2]

After a consideration of these statistics and conditions by an intelligent student of history who had, however, no knowledge nor experience of military affairs, he would naturally, if not necessarily, come to the conclusion that one Southern soldier must have been equal in efficiency to at least three Union soldiers. But without further consideration of the advantages enjoyed, or disadvantages suffered, by either belligerent, and admitting that the seasoned soldiers of both sides were equal in efficiency as was proved in many a hard fought battle, there are many thoughtful, patriotic people who apprehend that the cause of the prolonged failure of the Federal forces to overcome the resistance offered by the Confederate armies, and the excessive expenditure of human life, treasure and time by the Federal government in accomplishing that object will eventually, when truth and reason prevail, be found, wholly or chiefly, in the unmilitary conduct of the war.

In view of the means which were so promptly and lavishly provided by a patriotic people, and the appalling waste of them in futile battles and untoward military operations, the prosecution of the war on the part of the Union, had it been conducted as was the Confederate resistance only by educated military officers, untrammelled by political or other interfering influence, then its conduct should have covered their names with everlasting shame and disgrace. In the ultimate analysis of history there will inevitably be found among the component influences, the resultant of which shaped the conduct of the war, a persistent, selfish, unpatriotic, political purpose, which modified, misdirected, thwarted, hampered and delayed purely military operations, which should have been entrusted to the exclusive control of military men. In the days of imminent peril to the Capital, this purpose lay *perdu*, but when security was restored it resumed a control limited in its extent and activities only by political expediency. This alone will account for the necessity for preponderant numbers and for the undue length of time consumed in the war and for the enormous expense which necessarily followed. Although not occupying a high nor a conspicuous position, my intercourse with men who were prominent in government affairs and with officers of all grades in the army gave me opportunities to learn something of the conduct of the war, whether

---

[2] *Ibid.*

military, political or mixed, and a few rays of light upon the subject may glimmer out of my recollections.

Let us recall the earliest manifestations of the disposition of the politicians to influence the direction of military affairs. In the early appointments of prominent politicians to the highest grades in the volunteer army there seemed to be an implication, unproclaimed perhaps, that all the military genius, talent and experience of the regular army had left it to join the Southern Confederacy—that there was a lack of that supreme military ability requisite to direct the operations of armies, with which the South was so well supplied. Hundreds of regular army officers with years of experience and the best military education the world affords were left in subordinate positions, while political favorites, devoid of military knowledge or experience, were given important commands. It was only in hours of deadly peril that this heedless political playing with war was suspended.

Again, let us revert to the first grand review of the Army of the Potomac. On an ample field 80,000 men in masses of divisions were assembled with the artillery and cavalry of each division attached. The field was a broad amphitheatre, favorable at any part for a view of the whole, and the spectacle of such a vast organized host, with its standards floating in the sunlight, was the grandest and most inspiring I ever beheld. General McClellan, with his staff, rode rapidly along the fronts of divisions, awakening the wildest enthusiasm as he passed. Then the army passed in review before the President and the General-in-Chief, and as the ground trembled under the steady tread of the endless columns of disciplined soldiers and the air throbbed with the music of countless bands, the all-pervading feeling was an enthusiastic and ardent admiration for the man who had created the Army of the Potomac.

In the realization of all observers, even of the most experienced officers, the army was born that day. Those who had visited its busy camps and attended the inspections and reviews of divisions had formed no adequate conception of the army as a whole. Not one had ever seen an army of over 18,000 men together, except General McClellan, who had visited and studied the armies of Europe. Out of nothing this splendid army had been brought forth in six months. Taking the weakened and dispirited fragments of McDowell's little command, after the Bull Run disaster, as a nucleus, an army of 150,000 men had been fashioned out of raw material and supplied and equipped with all the wonderful instruments of modern warfare, and the great marvel was where was all this immense material—the small arms, field guns, seige and garrison artillery, ammunition, equipments, tents and clothing—obtained, how was it assembled, and how in such brief time had this mighty host acquired the discipline and skill to handle themselves and their arms with such celerity and precision? Everyone in and around Washington had felt the pulsations of momentous preparations and the throes of a tremendous and vigorous growth going on about them since the 1st of August, but on the day of the grand review at Bailey's Crossroads the eyes of all spectators, and even of the army itself, were suddenly opened, as were the eyes of the young man who beheld the mountain full of horses and chariots round about the prophet of Israel.

If properly handled, here was the highest exponent of the immeasurable military power of the North, and with all sorts of handling—good, bad, and indifferent—it ever remained the loyal, indestructible bulwark of the Union. All other Union armies were more or less expeditionary forces to whose greatest achievements the Army of the Potomac contributed by its detachments. At its first grand review it represented, together with forty miles of garrisoned fortifications around Washington, the work of McClellan for six months. And in that Army, then and ever after, it cannot be denied, love for "Little Mac," as the soldiers called him, and faith in his genius were animating forces which endured to the end. They survived all the calamitous misdirections of party expediency. The loyal subordination to constituted authority which it learned from the example and precepts of its creator and master carried it obediently and steadily through fields, where strategy had been abandoned, without a murmur from its wasting ranks save that which came from expiring breaths and flowing blood. Eleven thousand men uselessly stricken down in twenty minutes to satisfy the rage of a balked and baffled commander, regardless of tactical or strategical expedients, was only one attestation to the original and abiding character and training of the Army of the Potomac.

This review, together with the grand environment of completed defences, clearly demonstrated that the Capital was secure. *Up to this time not a word of criticism had been heard unfavorable to McClellan.* His campaign in West Virginia had been vigorous and successful. He had met political and military conditions never before presented in this country and had mastered them promptly and with consummate ability. The creation of the Army of the Potomac, fully equipped and instructed in so brief a period, was an achievement unparalleled in history. His energy and executive force, his glowing personality and spotless life and character, his exceptionally useful military studies, experience and success seemed to signalize him as the genius of the Nation's purpose. From the 27th of July up to this time McClellan had been supreme in the direction of military affairs. He had been made General-in-Chief. His Herculean grasp of the military situation was the daily theme of the Northern press and his name was on every tongue. It was the floodtide of his career. The ebb now set in, which, at the end of another six months, left him stranded, alone, on a dock at Alexandria, without a soldier to command.

In order to comprehend how and why this happened it is necessary to take a brief retrospect of the political condition which existed at that time. We must recollect that the new Republican party had come into the government upon the inauguration of Mr. Lincoln, who was elected President by a plurality vote which was but a little above one-third of the total popular vote cast at the Presidential election in 1860.[3] The leaders of a new party are always essentially radical and have the strength and intrepidity of all pioneers. The inauguration brought into the government a group of radical politicians who in a short time, through unresisted growth, became political giants who subordinated every public effort and aspiration to the successful perpetuation of the power of the political party which had thus come into the government on the vote of a minority of the people.

Fortunately for their eager purpose, the first gun fired at Fort Sumter united the people of the North in a fixed determination to save the Union, and the means for destroying its enemies were promptly and generously furnished to the government. Political lines disappeared and they who had been the chief opponents of the new party at the election were now the first to proffer their services to the President. The ghastly enormity of the charge—that a group of politicians entrusted with the government did determine to utilize the means so generously placed at their disposal during the supreme stress of war in order that the control of the government might eventually be secured and perpetuated by and for their party —would be incredible were it not impossible to believe that there can be an effect without a cause and that there could be any cause which would be adequate to the actual effects which were produced in the prosecution

---

[3]In the election of 1860 there were four candidates. Out of a total of 4,689,568 popular votes cast, Lincoln received 1,865,593 or 39.78 percent. The total number of electoral votes in 1860 was 412; Lincoln received 180 or 43.69 percent. See U.S. Bureau of the Census, *Historical Statistics of the United States, Colonial Times to 1957*, p. 682.

of the war save a meddlesome political interference with military operations. It is the only cause that is consistent with the records. It was the only cause that was competent to the effects.

It needed no experience of presidential elections reaching farther back than the election of General Zach. Taylor after the Mexican War to foresee that whoever, as military commander, should lead our armies to victory and to the final success of the Union cause and satisfy the patriotic hopes of the people would become a popular idol whose election to the presidency could not be prevented. McClellan's brief and unrestrained domination of military affairs had "irked the very souls" of these ambitious partisans; but when the Capital had been secured and they apprehended the great army might be ready to move, they aroused their cherished purposes, which though dormant had gained strength by careful organization; and the party entered upon a daring political career which overcame all opposition, even of majorities, and maintained its supremacy for twenty-three years.

The first thing necessary to be done was to place the party leaders in position to control the President through the most important channel, the War Department. Hon. Simon Cameron, the Secretary of War, was a statesman of the old school and a patriot who recognized nothing on earth above his country. He was not the man for them to attempt to engage in the promotion of their purposes. In Edwin M. Stanton they found precisely the man they required. To secure his appointment as Secretary of War in Mr. Cameron's place and to be assured of no opposition from the friends of General McClellan, for whom Mr. Lincoln had at that time a ready and friendly ear, Stanton professed to the President the warmest admiration and friendship for General McClellan and his family. Stanton had not come in with the new party, but had, on the contrary, gone out of public life with the preceding Democratic administration of James Buchanan. He hungered for a future. He spent his time at first in finding fault with the new administration and in ridiculing Mr. Lincoln. A letter which he wrote to his late chief, Mr. Buchanan, on the 26th of July, shortly after the first Bull Run disaster, throws a glaring light on the condition of his mind at that time. He attributed the disaster to "Republican interference with army operations," and "to Lincoln's running the machine." He predicted the "loss of the Capital, national bankruptcy and general ruin." Singularly enough he said, "a change in the War Department was not unlikely."

Stanton possessed an extraordinary combination of qualities and characteristics. He was a social and political chameleon. Of medium height, with abundant muscle, a florid complexion, half concealed by a dark, flowing beard, and prominent eyes, which upon occasion lent to his manners the suggestion of a bulldog, he had exhaustless energy and great executive ability for the largest affairs. His gifts of cunning and duplicity would have made the diplomacy of Machiavelli seem unsophisticated. The force of his personality was immense and his audacity unlimited. He was reckless in his eagerness to satisfy his insatiable personal ambition. And withal he was a moral and physical coward. He submitted to being bearded in his office with the door locked by officers whom he had outraged. On one occasion it was the gallant old General [Marsena R.] Patrick who compelled him to apologize. On another, the chivalrous and courteous General Harry Naglee.

His amazing abilities must be acknowledged when we consider how a man with such a character and antecedents made himself Secretary of War in Mr. Lincoln's cabinet. His stepping stone was Secretary Chase, who then exercised a controlling power in the cabinet. "Who pays, rules" was applicable to the Secretary of the Treasury. The sword is powerless without the purse. The transcendent talents displayed by Mr. Chase in providing an average of two millions of dollars a day for war expenses with such ease as to leave him leisure to acquaint himself with the details of every department of the government made him a power. He was not devoid of an exalted political ambition. It was he who lent an ear to the designing Stanton's aspirations and arranged the Russian mission for Mr. Cameron.

Other conditions seemed to conspire to aid the meddlesome partisans in their project to overcome the chief obstacle in the way to a successful promotion of their scheme. An unfortunate illness took hold of McClellan, who had broken down under the tremendous strain of overwork, which rendered it impossible for him to know the extent and strength of the organized attack upon him, or to counteract the undermining influences which were operating on the mind of the President. The insidious and disquieting suggestions of the Cabal produced an uneasiness in Mr. Lincoln's mind which led him to the uncommon and inconsiderate action of sending, without the knowledge of General McClellan, for some of his division commanders to confer with him and some members of his cabinet concerning the operations of the Army of the Potomac. General McClellan, who was now convalescing from his fever, being informed by Stanton of the proposed conference, was driven to the White House and presented himself at the conference. When requested to unfold his plans and purposes before the meeting, General McClellan declined unless the President should give him an order in writing so to do. Mr. Lincoln, acting without advice, had the discretion to refrain from giving the order. McClellan had already learned that to disclose his plans, or even his thoughts, was to advertise them to the enemy in our front. His military instincts forbade him participating in this caucus style of conducting military operations.

The fact was that the Army of the Potomac was really not ready to move into a campaign until some time after the roads had become impassable and no movement was practicable until spring. But the men would become better seasoned, disciplined and instructed as soldiers by two or three months longer experience in camp. Additional time was absolutely necessary to the preparation of the newer regiments and batteries. A young army cannot be dragged through the clogging discomforts of a winter campaign and brought into contact with the enemy with that vigor and high *morale* which are so essential to success in its first battle. Had the enemy been acquainted with McClellan's plans, then detachments from the army confronting us would have been thrown against our several lodgments on the southern coasts and the enemy would have been saved the expense of their maintenance in their army of northern Virginia. All our forces along the immense front, from the Potomac to the Mississippi, were daily gaining strength and improving in condition. All the possible economies of war, of life, treasure and time would be better satisfied. But no! Bull Run was forgotten! The army must move! The early whispers of the alleged dissatisfaction of the administration with the "slowness" of McClellan had found their way into the press and under partisan inspiration they had grown bolder and louder until they became clamorous for a movement of the army.

Mr. Lincoln, always remarkably responsive to popular sentiment, now yielded to an intense public impatience which had been cleverly and widely wrought up and which would brook no delay, and a fortnight after Mr. Simon Cameron had given place to Stanton, on January 27, 1862, just six months to a day after General McClellan had been placed in command, the President, without the knowledge of the General, issued his first war order, as follows:

PRESIDENT'S GENERAL WAR ORDER NO. 1.

Executive Mansion,
Washington, January 27, 1862.

ORDERED, that the 22d day of February, 1862, be the day for a general movement of the land and naval forces of the United States against the insurgent forces. That especially, the army at and about Fortress Monroe; the Army of the Potomac; the Army of Western Virginia; the Army near Mumfordville, Kentucky; the Army and flotilla at Cairo; and a naval force in the Gulf of Mexico be ready to move on that day that all other forces, both land and naval, with their respective commanders obey existing orders for that time, and be ready to obey additional orders when duly given.

That the heads of departments and especially the Secretaries of War and of the Navy, with all their subordinates, and the General-in-Chief, with all other Commanders and subordinates of land and naval forces will severally be held to their strict and full responsibilities for the prompt execution of this order.

Abraham Lincoln.

This order may seem ineffably puerile but it is really pregnant with historic significance. It is the most competent, relevant and incontrovertible evidence that can be produced to demonstrate the partisan inceptions, insidious evolution and successful encroachment of the political conspiracy which perverted the military conduct of the war.

Abraham Lincoln is one of the greatest American ideals. His remarkable qualities, the vehement epoch and conspicuous peculiarities of his life, and the supreme pathos of his death have touched the imagination of the world. It has been said that, "To him who only thinks, life is a comedy and to him who only feels, life is a tragedy," To Lincoln, life embraced the most awful tragedy and broadest comedy. His thought grasped immortality in the noblest, most solemn, and imperishable phrases of our language, and the current of his daily life rippled with numberless incidents of his irrepressible humor. Thought and feeling, together, plumbed his soul in the proclamation of emancipation. Americans jealously and reverently guard the precious ideals they have built up, and history will find it more and more difficult to discover traits of the original individual which have long since been dismissed from memory as irrelevant, if not impertinent.

I had several opportunities to meet Mr. Lincoln and of all men I ever saw he compelled the closest observation. His personality exhibited various dissimilar and inconsistent characteristics and his mind widely differing phases. Whatever the subject under consideration only a part of himself seemed attentive to it. The various and arduous occupations of his youth and early manhood had perhaps left their different and indelible impressions which might have effected a sort of polygenesis of his character. The loftiest mountain displays the greatest inequalities and varieties of light, shade, color and meteorological phenomena from its glistening summit to the profound shadows of its foundations. A tall, typical American, this rugged and picturesque man, responding to an early Western environment, had been reared in an atmosphere of patriotism and had become a strong, logical thinker, a popular lawyer and a very great debater.

When he came to the executive chair at the opening of the war he brought not the slightest knowledge nor experience of military affairs. He knew nothing of the organization of the army nor of the regulations or customs of the military service and at first he revealed no conception of the value of a military education, training and experience in time of war. Consequently, he was unable to discriminate between the military counsel of the ablest General and the empirical suggestions and advice of irresponsible politicians. There were many "Sir Oracles" and military doctrinaires in those days to fill Mr. Lincoln's mind with disquietude and alarm. The momentous exigencies of war with the unavoidable and tremendous responsibilities attending them when devolved with almost unlimited power, on such a man so unwary and perplexed as the President, might lead without surprise to the development of variable determinations, uncertainties, and even inconsistencies. What would be affirmed or promised by him today might be denied tomorrow. At this time, when the exercise of his enormous executive powers and functions were in embryo, Lincoln was an easy prey to the crafty Stanton and his coadjutors.

The order above quoted reveals his utter ignorance or disregard of any rule of action, custom or courtesy in promulgating a general order affecting the army, in such a way that its General-in-Chief should first see it in the newspapers, and it further exhibits an indifference to the flagrant indignity and deep humiliation that was then put upon the General-in-Chief. The famous Papal Bull was quite as effective upon the comet as was this order upon military operatons, but the Bull, in time, left a mocking reproach upon the Pope while this order brought no reflection upon the President, for he was now in accord with the public sentiment which had been created by the conspirators; and moreover, the order correctly represented the general ignorance and heedlessness that prevailed regarding military operations.

I could relate some incidents of the meetings of the party leaders, which took place almost daily in a sort of club or coterie, indicating their methods and purposes, but one will be sufficient as an illustration. When the Army of the Potomac was before Richmond and the question of reinforcing it was under discussion, a prominent Senator opposed it and remarked, referring to McClellan, "This young man's wings must be clipped"; whereupon Senator Dixon, of Connecticut, made the inquiry, "Am I to understand that it is the sense of this conference that General McClellan is not to be allowed to take Richmond because of its effect on parties? For myself I do not care for its effect on parties, all I want is a restoration of the Union"; and then he left the room.

Whether the party encroachments be considered step by step or in their ultimate fruition, it will be long remembered how this minority party grew strong and stronger, how it assumed the loftiest and most vehement patriotism, how it soon became tyrannical and fierce, and sometimes bloodthirsty, as in the sequences of Balls Bluff and of the second Bull Run disaster, and finally how it consolidated itself and became great through terrorism. Marquis de Tocqueville said in his philosophic and prophetic work, *Democracy in America*, that "there was no tyranny like that of a majority," but he had not dreamed in his philosophy, although it was keen and profound, of that more cruel tyranny which was to come from the *coup d'état* that our Civil War permitted a minority to spring on the government of the United States.

From the time of his convalescence General McClellan saw the dark cloud lowering on the bright prospects of the Army and his heart was greatly troubled, but he uttered no complaint nor reproach. That he felt and realized the dreadful impending calamities that were inevitable to the political interference with the conduct of the war was revealed one day as he was returning from General [Frederick W.] Lander's funeral, by a remark which he made to his friend, General Franklin: "When I saw Lander's peaceful face I thought that were it not for my duty to my country and to my family I would have wished myself in his place."[4]

At this crisis in his career General McClellan committed his first great mistake. He should at once have offered his resignation and made

---

[4]Lander died on 2 March 1865 from a "congestive chill."

known the reasons. We can conjecture that in the event of its acceptance the voice of the Army would have been heard, echoed from one hundred and fifty thousand homes in the North, and that an ebullition of resentment would have been provoked in and about Washington which would have paralyzed the activities of the conspiring partisans, and McClellan would have been placed in a position to have prescribed a proper conduct of the war. And here also was revealed the complete lack of a quality in McClellan's character which has often been a helpful and sometimes a winning component among the qualities of great Generals, namely: political acumen. His genius was purely military. He had clear and matured views with regard to the co-ordinate powers of the government, and with reference to the supreme principle of the concentration or diffusion of political power, which creates two parties in all constitutional governments, Federalism and Democracy—he was a Democrat.

This was the pith of the trouble. He was above all, a sincere patriot; and his ambition, aims and efforts were comprised in the single word "duty." He was quite indifferent to the influence, or even acquaintance, of men who made a business of politics. He was invariably courteous, refined and engaging in his manners, but his incessant official occupations and his domestic tastes and habits effectually precluded opportunities for political associations. In his spiritual nature, religion was an ever living force. No man ever heard him speak an idle or profane word. His absolute unselfishness and ingenuousness led him to credit and trust men and to promote their welfare, some of whom turned with the tide and not only deserted his friends but joined his enemies. He had many faithful friends among public men but their touch with the administration was slight.

With the keen political traits and sagacity of a Marlborough he might have enlisted and controlled a following that could have sustained him against the machinations of his political enemies. Mr. Montgomery Blair was always his friend. Mr. Seward was too much occupied with the foreign correspondence, which he made illustrious, to take any political initiative or even to interest himself much in the business of other departments. Secretary Chase early adopted General McDowell as his protégé and military mentor. But it would not have been a difficult task for McClellan to have secured the friendship of Mr. Chase and to have neutralized the unfriendly influence of McDowell and suppressed Stanton. McClellan was constitutionally self-reliant and, as I have always thought, too subordinate.

It has been stated by a writer of great intelligence and commanding influence that, "when Lincoln recalled McClellan to the command of the defence of Washington, he had to do it against the united voice of his cabinet and against the *protests* of almost, if not quite, a united party *in Congress and in the Country*." On the contrary, it was well known that the Cabinet was only united in its dismay at the situation, with a disordered, disheartened army falling back on the Capital, with Pope and McDowell in the advance, and quailed with consternation at the imminent peril which threatened the government and that measures had been taken for the personal safety of the Administration.

The true reason for the recall of McClellan was expressed in the President's words addressed to him, "General McClellan, you are the only man who can save Washington." The estimation in which McClellan was held throughout the country was partly measured by the presidential vote of 1864, after two years of obloquy had been heaped upon him. In a popular vote of 4,024,792, McClellan's was only 203,822 short of a majority of that vote over that for Mr. Lincoln, and the party in power had full control over the elections, particularly of the army vote.[5]

I have sometimes indulged myself in dreaming of the probable results which would have ensued had the Federal administration imitated that of the Confederacy to some extent by placing such a man as General W. B. Franklin at the head of the War Department, McClellan as General-in-Chief, Fitz-John Porter in command of the Army of the Potomac, with Generals Buell, Thomas and Rosencrans in the Mississippi Valley. The General-in-Chief, with an assured and intelligent support, could in that case have visited and studied every field of projected operations during the winter of 1861-2, and when the spring opened have launched the various forces in concerted, but not advertised, movements upon the Confederacy with the prospect of complete success before the next winter. But the sadness which generally attends any consideration of the "might have been" is here relieved by the conviction that the Union could never have been permanently restored without the universal freedom of labor throughout the land. The people might not have been ready to

---

[5]Averell's Democratic bias and bitterness towards the Lincoln administration are clear throughout this chapter. Actually, Lincoln received 403,151 more popular votes than McClellan in the 1864 election (Lincoln 2,206,938; McClellan 1,803,787). This gave Lincoln a handsome victory with 55.03% of the popular vote. His margin of the electoral vote was even more impressive with 67.52% of the votes cast (Lincoln 212; McClellan 21; not voting 81). See U.S. Bureau of the Census, *Historical Statistics*, p. 682.

approve it. They were not quite ready for it when it did come, but "it might have been" made acceptable even with a correct and undelayed conduct of the war.

No one who is able to discern in the grandeur and power of this Republic a world embracing purpose will now gainsay that the redemption of the land and all its people from human slavery was a supreme and inevitable necessity to the endurance of the United States. And as there never was a redemption of a man or of a people without a crucifixion, it may be that we should accept the sacrifices of the war, however unnecessary, unjust, inhuman and brutal some of them appeared, as parts of an infinite scheme whose mysterious complexities we may not comprehend nor penetrate. Nevertheless, we are not relieved from the duty of studying causes and effects without prejudice or passion.

[EDITORS' EPILOGUE]

During the summer of 1862 on the Virginia peninsula, picket duty replaced campaigning while the deadly weather took a heavy toll on the army. Averell was struck down with the "Chickahominy fever"—a type of malaria—and was unable to participate in the Antietam campaign. He complained of his illness to his brother Oscar: "I was quite ill then [September 10] with the Malarial fever and sort of typhoid which exhibits itself in congestive headaches and in a general dislocation of all ones joints."[1] Averell rarely complained of his health, but he must have been severely ill at this time to warrant the arrival of his sister, Lucy Crandall, to nurse him. Lucy wrote to their parents concerning William's health: "He is out of his head the most of the time and very weak. He will not let me be out of his sight day nor night—I have not had a night's rest in five weeks. It is the Billious diarrhea that set in and it has him down very low." Lucy asked their father to send herbs including "red raspberry leaves."[2]

In February of 1863, General Hooker, who had been appointed commander of the Army of the Potomac on January 26, reorganized the cavalry. For the first time a separate cavalry corps was established under

---

[1]W. W. Averell to O. J. Averell (September 15, 1862), NYSL, box 1, folder 7.
[2]L. Averell Crandall to H. Averell (November 28, 1862), NYSL, box 1, folder 7.

the command of Maj. Gen. George Stoneman. The three divisions were commanded by Averell, David McM. Gregg and Alfred Pleasanton with a brigade of regulars under John Buford. To display the new organization, Hooker conducted a grand review for President Lincoln who "saw the face of the country swarm with cavalry, and apparently an endless stream of horsemen pouring from every avenue leading to the parade ground."[3]

One of the few true cavalry fights of the war occurred soon after at Kelly's Ford on the Rappahannock River. Averell's force had been embarrassed on February 25, 1863, when a small force of Confederate cavalry under his old friend Fitzhugh Lee captured 150 soldiers and challenged Averell with a note: "If you won't go home, return my visit and bring me a sack of coffee." On the 16th of March Averell, with about 3,000 men, saw his chance to rout Lee's cavalry. As usual, the Confederates had spotted the Union movement and quickly moved to cover the crossing on the Rappahannock. The Union cavalry found them there the next morning. The order to cross was given and the Union army was successful in fording the river at Kelly's Ford. Instead of continuing this momentum, Averell ordered his cavalry to stop and wait for the Confederates on the edge of a broad, open field well-suited for cavalry action. With only about 800 men Lee approached the field, observed by federal scouts.

Averell handled Lee's spirited charges well, though hardly brilliantly, since he had almost four times as many men. With skillful use of artillery and excellent battlefield control by Brig. Gen. Alfred Napoleon Duffié, Lee's cavalry was forced to fall back. Averell's caution again took the upper hand as he waited more than thirty minutes before pursuing the Confederates. By that time Lee had regrouped and awaited Averell. For a second time Averell did not attack. Instead, when his force neared Lee's, Averell ordered it to assume another defensive position. Lee again attacked, only to be repulsed by a glorious mounted Union cavalry charge. A brief sabre clash occurred and the defeated Confederates left the field, fearful of another pursuit by Averell. They had little reason to be afraid, for like McClellan, Averell decided prudence and reorganization should not be forfeited to the chance of total victory. Averell permitted the troops to withdraw unmolested, although he left Lee a sack of

---

[3]Rawle, William Brooke, *et al.*, *History of the Third Pennsylvania Cavalry, Sixtieth Regiment Pennsylvania Volunteers, in the American Civil War*, p. 187.

Major-General Fitzhugh Lee. (Courtesy Library of Congress)

coffee with a note: "Dear Fitz: Here's your coffee. Here's your visit. How do you like it?"

Averell and the Union cavalry were considered successful by most observers. The young general had taken an unruly lot of boys and molded them into cavalrymen. The historians of the unit, although calling him "our martinet of a colonel," later recalled:

He was an excellent drillmaster, with proper views of what constituted real discipline. Instruction in a systematic manner, with a view of preparing these men for the service expected of them, was commenced and persistently followed in the most industrious and painstaking manner. . . . Squad drill, troop drill, battalion drill followed each other in such rapid succession as to make his head swim, and a detail for a scout or picket duty in the presence of an active and industrious enemy was hailed as a "sweet day of rest."[4]

Gen. Benjamin Butler, whom Averell detested as one of the worst political generals, called Kelly's Ford, "the best cavalry fight of the war." Secretary of War Edwin Stanton telegraphed Hooker following the battle: "I congratulate you on the success of Averell's expedition. It is good for the first lick. You have drawn first blood. . . . Give my compliments and thanks to Averell and his command."[5]

In order to divert the enemy's attention before his campaign against Chancellorsville, General Hooker ordered Averell's cavalry division to attack in the direction of Gordonsville south of the Confederate army. This general raid against Richmond, known as Stoneman's Raid, was the first independent Union cavalry action in the war, but it failed to divert the Confederate's attention from the main army. Except for destruction of some rebel property and severance of communication between Robert E. Lee's army and Richmond, little damage was inflicted. Furthermore, the cavalry was unable to rejoin the army until May 6th, thus missing the major battle at Chancellorsville. During this interlude the cavalry enjoyed "two beautiful farms, land very fine" as they allowed their horses to graze near the deserted village of Stevensburg. Averell himself had been recalled on May 3rd to scout the army's right flank for a field capable of cavalry action. When he reported that none was apparent, Hooker disgustedly removed him, fearing his caution.

General Hooker had placed great emphasis on the possible results of Stoneman's Raid for the entire Chancellorsville campaign. He had sent a dispatch to Stoneman stating that the general "desires you to understand that he considers the primary objective of your movement the

---

[4]*Ibid.*, pp. 23, 200.
[5]OR, Series I, vol. 25, part 2, p. 148.

cutting of the enemy's connection with Richmond by the Fredericksburg route, checking his retreat over those lines, and he wishes you to make everything subservient to that object." Hooker emphatically stressed the necessity of active campaigning. "Let your watchword be fight, and let all your orders be fight, fight, fight, bearing in mind that time is as valuable to the general as the rebel carcasses."[6]

Averell, too, had received a copy of Hooker's orders. When his cavalry division had reached the Rappahannock on April 29th, Averell found the river swollen. Although he admitted that "the force of the enemy and the defenses upon the other side were insignificant," Averell refused to order his men across because he feared many might drown. Subsequently he crossed at Kelly's Ford, site of his successful cavalry fight of a month before. Continuing south to the Rapidan where he estimated that the force of the enemy was too strong to attempt a crossing, he returned to his camp. As Hooker's chief of staff, Maj. Gen. Daniel Butterfield, succinctly summarized to Lincoln, "Averell's division returned; nothing done; loss of 2 or 3 men."[7]

While writing to Brig. Gen. Lorenzo Thomas, the adjutant general of the army, Hooker explained his reason for removing Averell:

It is unnecessary for me to add that this army will never be able to accomplish its mission under commanders who not only disregard their instructions, but at the same time display so little zeal and devotion in the performance of their duties. I could excuse General Averell in his disobedience if I could anywhere discover in his operations a desire to find and engage the enemy. I have no disposition to prefer charges against him, and in detaching him from this army my object has been to prevent an active and powerful column from being paralyzed in its future operations by his presence.[8]

He was initially ordered to report to Washington but was later told to go to Philadelphia to serve as a mustering officer. On his way there, Maj. Gen. Robert Schenck, badly in need of a cavalry organizer for the volunteer forces in western Virginia, requested that Averell be transferred to his Middle Department. Averell was given command of the Fourth Separate Brigade headquartered in Weston, West Virginia, near the middle of the new state. Schenck told Averell that his new command,

---

[6]*Ibid.*, part 1, pp. 1066-67.
[7]*Ibid.*, part 2, p. 421.
[8]*Ibid.*, part 1, pp. 1072-73.

is intended to be, as far as it can be properly made so, a mobile force, and your service will be to keep that region of West Virginia between the [Baltimore and Ohio] railroad and the Kanawha line clear of the enemy, preventing his invasions, and supporting and cooperating with Brigadier-General [Benjamin F.] Kelley, commanding on the line of the railroad, and with Brigadier-General [Eliakim P.] Scammon, commanding on the Kanawha and Gauley Rivers.[9]

When he arrived in West Virginia, Averell again was faced with a widely separated command. His cavalry and infantry, chiefly West Virginia volunteers, were scattered about the center of the state. He immediately began to reorganize and concentrate the command. Within eighty days he brought together 3,000 men, reorganized them and gave them fresh horses and new equipment.

In the summer of 1863 West Virginia still had not completely separated itself from Virginia. Groups of Confederate supporters remained, especially in the eastern part of the state, and Averell was ordered to drive them out. Equally important was the destruction of the supply line to Confederate forces in eastern Tennessee. During the last half of 1863 Averell participated in three major expeditions.

The first foray, from the 5th to 31st of August—known as Averell's Raid—was directed at Staunton, Virginia. Before this raid he had received orders informing him that the destruction of his command "would not be considered a loss in the hazardous undertaking." Averell's forces destroyed a Confederate saltpeter works near Franklin, West Virginia, and fought an unsuccessful engagement with a superior Confederate force at White Sulphur Springs. Losses suffered in this battle forced Averell to retreat to Beverly, but the raid was successful in destroying more than $5,000,000 of Confederate supplies.

Arriving at Beverly, Averell's brigade waited until November 1st to participate in another action. In cooperation with a brigade under General Duffié, they moved south against a Confederate force near Lewisburg. Duffié's brigade captured this town on November 7th. Locating a large Confederate force of about 7,000 at Droop Mountain near Lewisburg, Averell and his brigade, with about half that number of men, drew up a defensive line on the mountain. Here they defeated the last major Confederate force in West Virginia under Gen. John Echols. In a speech given on the fifteenth reunion of his cavalry division, Averell remembered

---

[9]*Ibid.*, part 2, p. 502.

"Desperate hand to hand combat between Union cavalry, commanded by Gen. Averill (sic), and Stuart's rebel troop, at Kelly's Ford, on the Rappahannock, Va., March 17. From a sketch by an officer." Frank Leslie's Illustrated Newspaper *(April 4, 1863).* *(Courtesy Library of Congress)*

that day: "The enemy came at us and in four hours we had them on the go. I never experienced a happier moment in my life than when we went into the works. And the troops felt the same way. I remember one Irishman jumping up and exuberantly yelling, 'the thirty-fourth fight and the first victory.' "[10] Despite the victorious outcome, Averell's forces had suffered severely and were forced to return north to Winchester.

The third major expedition which Averell undertook that year was

[10]Averell's scrapbook and unidentified newspaper clippings in the Dascomb Collection.

from the 8th to 25th of December, against the Virginia and Tennessee Railroad near Salem, Virginia. This raid would be the most successful of the three. With relatively small loss to his own force, Averell captured 200 prisoners and 150 horses.

At Salem three depots were destroyed, containing 2,000 barrels flour, 10,000 bushels wheat, 100,000 bushels shelled corn, 50,000 bushels oats, 2,000 barrels meat, several cords leather, 1,000 sacks salt, 31 boxes clothing, 20 bales cotton, a large amount of harness, shoes and saddles, equipments, tools, oil, tar, and various other stores, and 100 wagons. The telegraph wire was cut, coiled, and burned for half a mile. The water-station, [railroad] turntable, and 3 cars were burned, the track torn up, and the rails heated and destroyed as much as possible in six hours. Five bridges and several culverts were destroyed, over an extent of 15 miles. A large quantity of bridge timber and repairing materials were also destroyed.

With a great deal of satisfaction Averell concluded his report to the general-in-chief, Henry W. Halleck, "My command has marched, climbed, slid, and swam 355 miles since the 8th instant."[11]

The weather was more of a hazard on this third raid than the enemy. Four days after his first report to Halleck, Averell now safely back at Beverly reported, "With frozen feet forced marches were made in frost and snow and through swollen streams by my noble soldiers, without a murmur. For three days my guns were dragged, almost entirely by the men, over roads so slippery that horses could gain no foothold, and some limbs were broken and men otherwise injured by their falling."[12] During this raid Averell experimented with a rocket code to insure communication with other federal troops in the valley. Unfortunately, while the brigade was crossing a river, all of Averell's rockets became soaked and useless. Capt. Ernst A. Denicke, Averell's chief signal officer, recommended waterproof cases in the future.

In March, 1864, the Department of West Virginia was reorganized. Averell was given command over half the Union cavalry in the state and placed under Maj. Gen. Franz Sigel. Averell set up his headquarters in Martinsburg at the northern or lower end of the Shenandoah Valley. Because it had been a major route between the north and the south since

---

[11]OR, Series I, vol. 29, part 1, pp. 924-25.
[12]*Ibid.*, pp. 924-25.

the eighteenth century, both sides carefully guarded and strongly contested control over the valley throughout the Civil War. Averell's division was ordered to establish a line of outposts from the Shenandoah River to Back Creek and to patrol the area within sixty miles of Martinsburg. Averell was upset over his inability to obtain adequate supplies—especially horseshoes—for his new command. In April he received permission to meet with the new commanding general of the United States Army, Ulysses S. Grant, to request more horses and the new Spencer or Burnside carbines. Although Grant was sympathetic, he could do little for the young cavalry commander.

As when he had received the command of the Third Pennsylvania Cavalry two-and-a-half years before, Averell now found the officers of his cavalry division inadequate. On March 1, 1864, he complained to General Thomas:

My brigade commanders have neither the rank nor the experience required to fit them for the important duties that are devolved upon them; duties which are the more onerous because of the inefficiency of their subordinates. The results are want of discipline, neglect of duty, and waste of precious time and valuable material thus far, and I have apprehensions of more serious results in the future. In former times years were considered necessary to bring a new cavalry regiment to a servicable condition; latterly an assemblage of men from all classes and conditions of civil life are as soon as mounted on horses called cavalry, and expected to perform the duties that legitimately belong to that arm. More especially in cavalry than in any other arm does everything depend on the officers who should be energetic, industrious, intelligent, and persevering. I regret to say that in my command where one can be found making progress a dozen can be seen standing still.[13]

Averell, however, was gaining a reputation among the enemy. His frequent raids had set the Confederates off-balance, and they were unable to rest as long as Averell's cavalry could move about so freely. Robert E. Lee, in a letter to the Confederate president, commented that their cavalry was "worn down by their pursuit of Averell."[14] A month later Lee again spoke of Averell's successes in a letter to Gen. Samuel Jones. "General Averell, by the last reports of scouts in the valley, was at Martinsburg with his cavalry." Lee warned Jones that, "I think it probable, however,

---

[13]*Ibid.*, vol. 33, p. 701.
[14]*Ibid.*, p. 1061.

from the success that has hitherto attended his expeditions, that whenever the weather permits they will be renewed. Every preparation ought now to be made to resist them. The main cause of his success appears to me at this distance to be owing to the terror with which he has inspired the troops. As soon as his approach is announced his progress is neither retarded [n]or watched." Jones, however, disagreed and on February 19, 1864, told Lee:

I have not observed the terror with which you seem to think Averell has inspired the troops in his front. I was with them during the late raid [the December raid when Averell struck the Virginia and Tennessee Railroad] and did not observe in them any indications of terror; on the contrary, they exhibited, amidst great difficulties and hardships enthusiasm and eagerness to meet the enemy, and if Averell had persevered in his attempt to return by the Sweet Springs I believe his command would have been captured or destroyed.[15]

The overall impression given by the Confederate reports is that they were very concerned with Averell's movements. Moses S. Hall, a lieutenant colonel of the West Virginia volunteers, summed up his intelligence of Averell's important role in the state: "Deserters and refugees are coming in daily," Hall wrote to General Kelley on January 30, 1864. "They also state that General Averell is a terror to them; more so than even Stonewall Jackson was to us. A rumor of his approach is equal to death to them. His departure from West Virginia would be joyful news to them."[16]

Averell's cavalry raids in the Shenandoah Valley were effective in harassing the enemy and disrupting the railroads. In early May, 1864, when Averell left Logan Court House, West Virginia, on an expedition against the Virginia and Tennessee Railroad, an unidentified newspaper clipping provided a breathless account of Averell's successful raid:

The cavalry raid of that dashing and gallant officer, Gen. Averill [sic], made from Charleston, West Virginia, May 8, was undoubtedly one of the most hazardous and brilliant of the war. It was, too, successful. All and more of the usual dangers of field and flood were encountered—rivers were swam, forests penetrated, mountains scaled, unknown regions traversed, enemies met. For upwards of sixty miles of the mountain travel there was nothing but precipitous

---

[15]*Ibid.*, pp. 1141; 1156.
[16]*Ibid.*, p. 446.

bridle-paths, and for that distance did the men on foot drag themselves and their horses up and down. But seven days' rations and proportionate ammunition had been taken. For eighteen days . . . the command were unheard of by their friends. After the 11th their ammunition was exhausted, and but for the fortunate capture of a rebel train on the 9th, they would have been without food: as it was they were seven days on half rations. They had ridden, walked, forded, swam, climbed and fought during the raid of three hundred and fifty miles, exhibiting an endurance and heroism challenging the admiration of the world of chivalry.[17]

At Cove Mountain Gap on May 10th, Averell's troops met a large Confederate force under Gen. John Morgan. A gallant cavalry fight lasting several hours left the Confederates in control of the field. General Morgan wrote his wife that "Averell fought his men elegantly, tried time and time again to get them to charge but our boys gave them no time to form."[18] The newspaper report noted that, "Gen. Averill [*sic*] was constantly in front of the first column, and on its falling back, at the front of the command, encouraging and stimulating it to the noble heroism displayed, by his own fearless exposure and dauntless courage."[19] During this fight Averell received a glancing wound on his forehead by a musket ball. Blood gushed profusely from this wound, and he went to the rear where his head was bandaged. Then he quickly returned to the front to lead his force.

Averell was not lacking in personal bravery. An admirer later wrote a poem entitled "Averell's Raid." Although some of the historical facts are incorrect, the last stanzas sum up Averell's reputation among both the rebels and his own men.

> Now my kind rebels no use for to talk,
> For Averell he is now the cock of the walk,
> For when he goes raiding by night and by day,
> If you'l take my advice, you'l keep out of his way.
>
> If you had been present when on the last raid,
> To have seen the great conduct of Averell's brigade,
> They being well mounted and horses that are tough
> Hurrah for your railroad, we'll soon tear it up.[20]

---

[17]Ledger book, pp. 50-53; NYSL, box 10.
[18]Quoted in Shelby Foote, *The Civil War, A Narrative*, vol. 3, p. 246.
[19]NYSL, box 10.
[20]NYSL, box 8, folder 7.

Early in the spring of 1864, Averell suffered a relapse of his fever, aggravated by his head wound. Shortly after his recovery from these infirmities, a large Confederate force undertook an offensive campaign in the Shenandoah Valley. Ten thousand Confederates under Gen. Jubal Early raided Maryland and Pennsylvania and penetrated to the very gates of Washington. For the third and final time in the war, the Pennsylvania town of Chambersburg was captured, but this time it was burned to the ground when the residents refused to pay the Confederate ransom. Much of the Union cavalry, including Averell's division, was south on raids, and the remaining federal forces were unable to stop Early's offensive. Although Averell himself rushed back to Martinsburg by railroad, he was unable to prevent the enemy from crossing into Maryland. Partly as a result of this Confederate success, but more because of revised Union plans, Maj. Gen. Philip H. Sheridan was appointed to command all the Union troops in the Shenandoah Valley. The president apparently desired that Grant himself assume command in this area, but Grant convinced Lincoln that Sheridan would be able to handle the situation.[21]

On August 1, 1864, Sheridan took over the command in the Shenandoah Valley. The new general found that despite more than three years of war, the Union forces remained concentrated in the lower (northern) end of the valley. Occasionally, successful raids would be made up the valley (southward), but the Confederates were still able to move with impunity as shown by Early's recent raid. A week after his appointment Sheridan was made commander of the entire Middle Military District to include the departments of Washington, the Susquehanna and West Virginia. Along with Sheridan came most of his old staff, including Alfred T. A. Torbert, his chief of cavalry. Since Averell's date of rank preceded Torbert's, Sheridan anticipated trouble.

A new type of commander had come into prominence, not only in the Shenandoah Valley, but throughout the Union army as men like Grant, Sherman, Sheridan and Thomas replaced McClellan, Burnside, Hooker and Halleck. The older order had relied on training, preparation and caution, while the new would demand sacrifice, decisiveness and success. Conflict seemed inevitable, not only in the

[21]See Philip H. Sheridan, *Personal Memoirs of Philip Henry Sheridan, General, United States Army*, vol. 1, p. 463.

military but in the nation as a whole, as a new, more vigorous and powerful social, political, economic and military order gained control. Averell would fall victim to this transformation.

On the day Grant appointed Sheridan to command the Middle Military District, he advised, "Do not hestitate to give commands to officers in whom you repose confidence, without regard to claims of others on account of rank. If you deem Torbert the best man to command the cavalry, place him in command and give Averell some other command, or relieve him from the expedition, and order him to report to General Hunter. What we want is prompt and active movements after the enemy, in accordance with instructions you already have."[22] On August 26, 1864, Grant gave Sheridan one of the most extraordinary orders in United States history: "Give the enemy no rest. . . . Do all the damage to railroads and crops you can. Carry off stock of all descriptions, and negroes, so as to prevent further planting. If the war is to last another year, we want the Shenandoah Valley to remain a barren waste."[23] Men from a different era with a gentleman's code of warfare would find it difficult to adjust to such an idea.

Despite the change in command, Averell continued to complain about his supplies, especially the lack of proper mounts, and offered excuses to the new commander why he could not fight the irregular forces of the enemy near Charlestown. He was unable to stop the enemy at Shepherdstown and fell back to Hagerstown, Maryland. Sheridan's doubts about Averell seemed to be confirmed, as was his decision to promote Torbert to the command of all the cavalry in the Middle District with Averell under him. This decision was interpreted by Averell as a personal affront. Later he would complain that "Major-General Sheridan illegally assumed the prerogative of the President of the United States and ordered me to report to a junior officer on the 23rd of August without any just cause."[24]

Averell's dissatisfaction did not endear him to Sheridan, who by now had decided to remove Averell as soon as the first reasonable opportunity arose. A successful attack against retreating Confederates

---

[22]OR, Series I, vol. 43, part 1, p. 719.
[23]Quoted in Bruce Catton, *Grant Takes Command*, p. 361.
[24]OR, Series I, vol. 43, part 1, pp. 500-1.

on September 7, 1864, delayed this removal. Averell's cavalry surprised the enemy at Oldfields, three miles east of Moorefield, West Virginia, routing and dispersing the cavalry brigades of John McCausland and Bradley Johnson. Twenty-seven officers were captured, including General Johnson who later escaped, and 393 enlisted men. In addition, the Union force took four guns "complete with limbers and caissons, large quantities of small-arms, and 400 horses and equipments." Averell's force had only 7 men killed and 21 wounded.[25] This lopsided victory stayed Sheridan's hand.

The following day, however, a reunited Confederate force challenged Averell and he retreated back toward Martinsburg. "Sheridan sent word to Averell by an aide-de-camp that he would take the hair off any man's head who ran train to Martinsburg without his orders to do so."[26] Once again a substantial Union victory had been compromised by indecision.

Averell felt his honor had been impugned and on September 13, 1864, he requested an official investigation by Grant into the charges being circulated against him.

Since I have been in this department I have unfortunately incurred the displeasure of a few small politicians, and they have left no stone unturned to injure me publicly and privately. The most atrocious slanders have been circulated regarding my official conduct and private character. I have endured the contumely that these few active enemies have heaped upon me with indifference until the present time, conscious of the rectitude of my conduct and always reliant upon the confidence of my superiors and the respect of my comrades. But recently I have become aware that the mind of General Grant has been poisoned by these slanderous reports and his judgment prejudicial against me. I think it is my duty now to request an investigation.[27]

On September 19, after being defeated by Sheridan near Winchester, General Early withdrew his command up the valley and formed a strong defensive line near Strasburg on Fisher's Hill. As Sheridan prepared to meet Early on September 23, 1864, he warned Averell to demonstrate some decision. "I do not want you to let the enemy bluff you or your command," Sheridan warned, "and I want

---

[25]*Ibid.*, p. 3.
[26]*Ibid.*, part 2, p. 56.
[27]*Ibid.*, p. 79.

Major-General Philip Henry Sheridan, commander of Union forces in the Shenandoah Valley. (Courtesy Library of Congress)

you to distinctly understand this note. I do not advise recklessness, but I do desire resolution and actual fighting with necessary casualties, before you retire. There must now be no backing or filling by you without a superior force of the enemy actually engaging you."[28]

Sheridan's forces won a substantial victory as the infantry charged up the sides of Fisher's Hill. Early lost over 1,200 men, more than

[28]*Ibid.*, part 1, p. 505.

double Sheridan's casualties. More importantly, the Confederate force was broken and it rapidly retreated as Sheridan shouted, "Forward! Forward everything! . . . Go on, don't stop, go on!"[29] Unfortunately, Averell's natural caution had taken hold. Two days after the battle Sheridan removed him. Sheridan explained his action in a letter to Grant two days later: "I have relieved Averell from his command. Instead of following the enemy when he was broken at Fisher's Hill (so there was not a cavalry organization left), he went into camp and let me pursue the enemy for a distance of fifteen miles with infantry, during the night."[30]

This second removal from command was something Averell would never forget and could never forgive. Sheridan's dismissal was a living cancer within him, as evidenced by an occasion five years later when they accidentally met. Because the meeting occurred at a public function Averell was unable to show his contempt, but he quickly assured Sheridan that, "I was the victim of a grievous wrong or great mistake and I cannot permit you to entertain the impression from our exchange of civilities this morning that I am willing to resume friendly intercourse with you until some explanation from you of your actions on the occasion I have referred to has been received by me."[31]

Not all observers agreed with Sheridan's reasons. A *New York Herald* reporter gave details of Averell's dismissal and reported possible political intrigue behind it.

This order [relieving Averell] caused a universal feeling of amazement in this army, and it is generally thought that some question of rank between General Averill [*sic*] and General Torbert is involved, the former being the ranking officer, but the latter chief of cavalry of this military division. Averill's division officers and men exhibited their devotion to him by the most marked demonstrations. The officers, who seemed to love him as an elder brother, shed tears at his departure, and as the general rode along the lines for the last time the men greeted him with the most enthusiastic cheers and many expressions of affection.

General Averill called the officers together and addressed them, enjoining upon them to continue as energetic and attentive in the future as they had been in the past, and to yield the same obedience to his successor as they had to him.[32]

---

[29]Quoted in Mark Mayo Boatner, *The Civil War Dictionary*, p. 281.
[30]OR, Series I, vol. 43, part 2, p. 171.
[31]Dascomb Collection.
[32]*The New York Herald*, September 27, 1864, p. 1.

Sheridan's action shattered Averell in a way that physical damage incurred by bullets or fever during the war had not. For the rest of his life he would try to refute this action and gather evidence to substantiate his belief that the removal was politically rather than militarily motivated. The action particularly galled the proud Averell late in life when he reflected on his military service and saw his record indelibly blemished by this incident. Shortly after Averell's removal, his brother heard from a friend that Secretary of War Stanton had not approved of Sheridan's action and had expressed "great admiration" for Averell. The secretary said he would wait for a full report before he took action, but Stanton never did take any action.[33] As early as July, 1865, a personal friend of Averell's, Will Rumsey, the son of the congressman who had appointed Averell to West Point, wrote that he had heard secondhand a remark by Sheridan "that the greatest mistake he [Sheridan] made in the valley was relieving Genl Averell."[34]

When Averell was collecting his papers to write his memoirs, he contacted numerous officers to substantiate his version of the dismissal. The fullest statement came from William Blakeley, a Pittsburgh lawyer and former lieutenant colonel of the Fourteenth Pennsylvania Cavalry which had been under Averell's command in the Shenandoah Valley. In 1873, at a dinner with Sheridan at the Monongahela House in Pittsburgh during a reunion of the Society of the Army of the Cumberland, Blakeley asked Sheridan why he had removed Averell. Sixteen years later, Blakeley reported Sheridan's reply "in substance."

When I [Sheridan] was assigned to the command of the "Middle Military Division" I had determined in my own mind to make General Averell my Chief of Cavalry. I know him to be a thorough Soldier, and his success in the valley had won for him the position as the leading cavalry officer in the service, and with his knowledge of the country, he was in my judgment well qualified for this position.

In consulting with General Grant in relation to my new field, he specially requested me to assign General Torbert to that position.

I called General Grant's attention to General Averell, and his rank and services, but General Grant without making any objections to General Averell insisted upon General Torbert's being assigned to the position.

General Averell outranked General Torbert, and refused to serve under him and suggested to me that I should relieve him (Averell) from his command. This I refused to do, and said to General Averell that all his orders

---

[33]H. J. Raymond to O. J. Averell (October 6, 1864), NYSL, box 2, folder 2.
[34]W. Rumsey to W. W. Averell (July 21, 1865), NYSL, box 2, folder 2.

would be given direct to him, and I would not ask him to serve under Torbert. This arrangement was satisfactory to General Averell, and it worked well for a time but afterward, I found it impossible to successfully direct the movements of my army without a Chief of Cavalry. I was compelled to relieve General Averell against my judgment, and personal preference. I regarded Averell as a superior officer over Torbert. I have always regretted my action on General Averell's account and also for the reason that General Torbert failed to come up to the standard, and I was finally compelled to assign General [Wesley] Merrit to this position.[35]

Capt. Thomas R. Kerr, who had furnished this letter to Averell, wrote his own account substantiating Blakeley's. Kerr remembered speaking to General Sheridan in 1867 in Pittsburgh, and, according to Kerr, Sheridan "said he never done anything he regretted so much." Kerr gave the name of another witness to this conversation and urged Averell to write for substantiation. Finally, Kerr encouraged Averell to write his own version of the incident.[36]

Averell's orders had not only removed him from command, they also directed him to go to Charlestown, West Virginia, and stay there. At Averell's request the orders were modified to permit him to return home to Bath for convalescent leave. With this banishment to his home, Averell's military career was ended. He sat out the rest of the war recuperating from severe dysentery, malaria, his head wound, and a seriously damaged ego.

Averell's friends attempted to have him assigned to the Department of the Gulf as commander of the Union Cavalry in Texas. For at least six months there seemed to have been some support for this move, but Averell was never given official encouragement.[37] A former Pennsylvania Republican congressman, John Covode, had told Averell almost a year before, "I went to the President at the request of my son George to say that you was the best cavalry officer they ever had in the Potomac Army and that you should be made a Major General. The President replied that you should be."[38] The president was true to his word. On March 13, 1865, Averell was promoted to brevet major general of volunteers. Shortly before, Averell had been told he would not receive the appointment in the Department of the Gulf, and that

[35]W. Blakeley to T. R. Kerr (March 18, 1889), NYSL, box 5, folder 12.
[36]T. Kerr to W. W. Averell (March 18, 1889), NYSL, box 5, folder 12.
[37]Letters in NYSL, box 2, folder 3.
[38]J. Covode to W. W. Averell (February 8, 1864), NYSL, box 2, folder 2.

General Henry Halleck, the army chief of staff, did not even want him to come to Washington.[39]

On May 18, 1865, Averell's resignation was accepted, and for the first time in fourteen years he was a civilian. (Ironically, in 1880 Averell tried to regain his rank on the technicality that his resignation had been accepted by the secretary of war rather than the president. He requested Alexander Ramsey, President Rutherford B. Hayes's secretary of war, to restore him "to the rank to which I am now entitled" in order to gain a better pension. Averell's request was denied.[40])

William Averell was not a failure during the Civil War; he was a victim of change. He had been just what the army needed early in the conflict—disciplined, capable and cautious. He took untrained horsemen and molded them into a cavalry force of which any commander could be proud. Although his attitude made him appear at times to be a martinet, his men eventually understood and appreciated the need for discipline. Indeed, Averell like McClellan always was remembered with warm affection by his men. For the rest of his life Averell received friendly notes from the men he had commanded, and he was asked to head more than one veterans' association. By 1864, however, the Union army needed decision and resolution even more than discipline and training. The excuses of unpreparedness would no longer hold. The president and the commanding general were demanding that the rebellion be crushed. To reorganize following battle was a luxury that could no longer be tolerated. Averell, only thirty-one years old, had risen too high, too fast. He could not adapt his methods and tactics to the changed nature of the war. As the colonel of the Third Pennsylvania Cavalry he had found a role that suited his temperament and abilities, but, unfortunately, he was not permitted to remain in that post.

The days and weeks that followed General Averell's return to his home in Bath were marked by a pattern that had already been established during his active military service. Averell had not limited himself to the daily routine and demands of military life; he had supplemented his military career with a number of businesses and

_____

[39]J. C. Kelton to W. W. Averell (February 23, 1865), NYSL, box 2, folder 3.

[40]Averell's printed request to be used as a congressional bill may be found in the Dascomb Collection.

speculative endeavors in the burgeoning coal, iron ore, oil and lead silver fields.[41] By the time Averell resigned from the army on May 15, 1865,[42] he was well into another career. Fellow officers and friends who sent their regrets and good wishes to Averell over the "Sheridan Affair" frequently made references to his oil and coal interests.[43]

Accounts of the general's non-military enterprises during this period are clearly stated in letters from Horatio Frank Averell, a New York "Counsellor at Law and Advocate in Admiralty," to General Averell dated March 7, 1864, August 11, 1865, and in a very detailed letter of July 15, 1864:

On the 24th May Oscar [Averell's brother] D. M. Barnes (City Editor N.Y. Times) and myself started for the oil regions described in your letters upon the subject but upon reaching Point Pleasant [West Virginia] a coal project was presented to us and thinking it more feasible than oil our energies were thereafter primarily centered upon it.

After reaching Charleston [West Virginia] we made the acquaintance of Capt. Gregg Chaplain in 7th Pa. Cav. and he, Oscar and myself (making also provision for ¼ for yourself if desired) entered into a contract to lease for oil on the Great Kanawha for 15 miles covering bottom lands from Charleston that far below and according to Gregg's theory, embraces the "Great Oil Basin"—

The coal lands we had in view lie at and near the mouth of the Pocotalico River which you remember empties into the Gt. K. [sic] just above Red House Shoals.

I left Charleston on my return on 6th June and the arrangement was that Oscar should remain and secure contracts for coal lands and leases for oil while I came on and reported to capitalists here what we had discovered with a view of securing the necessary means to purchase land etc., etc.

As soon as I returned I laid the matter of our project in coal before Henry J. Raymond (of the Times) W. Carson and your friend Sibley. . . .

Last Saturday [July 9, 1864] I had an interview with Raymond and W. Riggs (of Jerome, Riggs and Co.) and they are ready to put in $30,000 or even more.[44]

In the late spring of 1865, prior to his resignation, Averell had

---

[41]H. F. Averill to W. W. Averell (August 11, 1864), NYSL, box 2, folder 4.

[42]Averell Diary, 1865 (May 15), "Resigned—left N.Y. 5 A.M. for Phila.," Dascomb Collection.

[43]G. Crook to W. W. Averell (October 22, 1864), NYSL, box 2; W. Rumsey to W. W. Averell (November 11, 1864), NYSL, box 2, folder 1.

[44]Dascomb Collection. The cover of this twelve-page letter is marked "strictly private. This letter will please be forwarded to the General unopened."

[45]Averell Diary, 1865 (April 20, 22), Dascomb Collection.

visited a coal mine and an oil refinery.[45] On June 19, 1865, freed
from his military responsibilities, he wrote in his diary, "Met some of
the Directors of the Averill Coal and Oil Co," and at a directors'
meeting a resolution was passed approving the general's estimates of
the coal project. The development of this coal-mining venture was
totally entrusted to William W. Averell's organizational, engineering
and business skills. This was to absorb much of General Averell's time
and energy for the next year. He was personally involved with surveying the coal lands acquired, the building of a railroad, the blasting
of rock and stone for better access to and development of the mines,
and the acquiring of men and equipment. Sandwiched between were
quick trips by railroad to New York City with the company's directors, including Henry J. Raymond, editor of *The New York Times*,
who had invested in the company.

General Averell's role in the development of the Averill Coal and
Oil Co. is quite clear in B. Franklin's letter of October 3, 1865:

Last week I was in at Jerome and Rigg's and saw Jerome. He seemed pleased
with the way things are going on under your sway. I saw your . . . reports
. . . and I think that you are getting on well. Your contracts for iron alone
has [*sic*] certainly saved a good deal of money for the company, and your idea
of getting the machinery made at Pittsburgh, as far as possible, strikes me as
very good.

I presume . . . you must have everything in nearly working order. The
question as to whether it is better for the company to sell the coal at the levee
or take it to market on the Ohio below, which you appear to propose, is one
which I think were I in your place, I would settle for myself at present. You
can judge better where you are, than anyone here could. . . . I am sorry that
you and the Supt. do not get on together. It is hard for a man to play second
fiddle after he has had full swing. . . . Of course you are supreme as
President, but I believe that you will find it to your interest and comfort to
have someone just like the Supt. who will carry on the details of the concern
with merely general directions.[46]

This early vigorous effort to achieve a business success with the
Averill Coal and Oil Co. was the real beginning of the general's entre-
preneurial career. Nonetheless, within a year, despite his determined
efforts, the Averill Coal and Oil Co. was in serious financial and
operational trouble. Moreover, bickering and criticism were fraying the

---

[46]Dascomb Collection.

personal relations between the directors and Averell, as noted in his diary on May 13, 1866: "Saw Raymond and told him that our business affairs should not interfere with personal regards."

Throughout this project and all of his later business undertakings, General Averell was to travel often and widely, meeting many old military friends and acquiring new contacts such as Townsend Harris and David Dudley Field.[47] He always kept a sharp eye open for promising projects and new business opportunities for himself and his many associates.

In September of 1866, Averell was informed confidentially that he was to receive the appointment of consul general to British North America at Montreal.[48] Despite voluminous correspondence and day-books, there is no hint of how, and through whose good offices, he received his appointment to Montreal. Nonetheless, President Andrew Johnson did appoint Averell, and he served in this post from October 2, 1866 to June 1, 1869.

General Averell's letters and diaries covering these years of consular service present a detailed, interesting account of his official duties as well as his personal and social activities. The Montreal society in which he moved included the important personages in Canada, and from them he learned of several opportunities for investment. But he had learned to be discerning. As he wrote to his father, Hiram Averell, shortly after arriving in Montreal, his work was largely routine and the financial rewards meager:

The principal duty of the Consul aside from politics is to certify invoices of shipment to the States for which he receives a fee of $2.50 which goes to the government. The fees amount to about $10,000 a year at this place. . . . I don't think there is any money to be made from the office as I am obliged to support a style of living which is expensive. Several of the prominent citizens have called upon me and everyone tells me lies and offer his advice. All they say is heard with attention but I make up my own mind. The principal subjects of national importance are the reciprocity treaty which was abrogated as you know or died out, the Annexation and the Fenians.[49]

---

[47]Townsend Harris (1804-1878), a New York merchant, was United States consul general to Japan from 1855 to 1862. He was instrumental in bettering Japanese-American relations in these early years.

David Dudley Field, (1805-1894), an outstanding American lawyer and law reformer, served as counsel for Jim Fisk and Jay Gould in the Erie Railroad litigation in 1869; he also defended William March "Boss" Tweed in 1874-1875.

[48]Averell Diary, 1866 (September 29), Dascomb Collection.

[49]W. W. Averell to H. Averell (November 26, 1866), Dascomb Collection.

After a year as consul general at Montreal, Averell requested of Secretary of State William Henry Seward that he be appointed United States minister plenipotentiary to the Republic of Mexico.[50] Almost immediately a flow of letters of recommendation in support of Averell's application for the Mexican mission reached Secretary Seward's desk, while two letters were addressed to President Andrew Johnson. On December 2, 1867, General Averell noted in his diary, "Called on the President." Nothing else is written or noted about the results of the Johnson meeting or Averell's reaction to it.

Two of the most interesting statements of support for Averell came from Thomas A. Scott and Charles Knap. Scott, vice president of the Pennsylvania Railroad in 1860 and later president from 1874-1880, began his letter to Seward with, "I had a long talk with Mr. Stevens [Thaddeus Stevens, Speaker of House of Representatives and longtime member of the House from Pennsylvania] today—particularly in regards to our Railway projects to and through New Mexico on their way to the Pacific on a South of the 35th parallel." Scott not only continued to present Stevens's views on the "Great Railway enterprise for the development of Mexico" but also pressed the need for a treaty with Mexico in order to protect American citizens and property in that country. Scott explained that the key to the success of the Mexican mission would be to have

a man who would take hold of and appreciate fully this enterprise—it might be carried through successfully—thus doing much to improve the facilities and intercourse between the two countries—I am sure if you send General Averill [sic]—(the present Consul General of Canada) to Mexico he would be equal to all emergencies and effect this matter—he is a man of rare administrative ability and trustworthy to the highest degree—I took the liberty of calling at your house hoping to see you and explain in person as desired by Mr. Stevens.[51]

Scott had also written an earlier letter (December 1, 1867) to Mr. Seward on behalf of Averell.

Charles Knap, apparently a close friend of the president, wrote to Johnson on behalf of General Averell. After the usual general statements of praise to be found in letters of recommendation, he closed

---

[50]W. W. Averell to W. H. Seward (November 21, 1867), Dascomb Collection.
[51]T. A Scott to W. H. Seward (December 13, 1867), National Archives, Diplomatic Section, Applications and Recommendations.

with "I ask as a *personal* favor that General Averell receive the appointment."[52]

Of the twenty-one letters of recommendation supporting Averell's Mexican application, those from Scott and Knap and one from Daniel Posley, representative from the Third Congressional District of West Virginia, reached Seward and Johnson after Averell's December 2nd visit.

In spite of such loyal support, Averell did not receive the Mexican appointment. He continued to function responsibly as consul general in Montreal, and at the same time was actively involved in new business enterprises. He traveled widely in Canada checking property for iron-ore deposits while continuing to broaden his contacts with a number of professional and business people. His Daybook for 1868 contains an extended list of stock transactions, particularly buying and selling of Erie, Pennsylvania, and Central Railroad issues, and playing the gold market.[53]

The inauguration of Ulysses S. Grant to the presidency on March 4, 1869, meant that Averell's consulship would very likely be awarded to one of the new administration supporters. But for whatever reason, General Averell decided he would like to continue at that post. Consequently, he made a strong bid through William Halsey, who had influence with the Grant people. Halsey wrote to Orville E. Babcock, Grant's personal secretary, requesting that Averell be granted a stay as consul general at Montreal.

Babcock's reply was quick and to the point:

I shall do nothing to prevent Averill's [*sic*] remaining at Montreal, and will on your account say a good word, but I must say I am afraid he would have to go on account of the ground he took against the General after the Chicago Convention. He went to New York to nominate someone against him.[54]

Undaunted by the abrupt end of his consular career, Averell immediately turned his full attention to several areas of business, some of which he had explored during his consulship. By the end of Sep-

---

[52]C. Knap to His Excellency, The President (December 9, 1867), National Archives, Diplomatic Section, Applications and Recommendations.

[53]Averell Diary, 1868, Dascomb Collection. Listed on two memoranda pages of this diary.

[54]O. E. Babcock to W. Halsey (March 8, 1869), Dascomb Collection; Averell Diary, 1869 (March 12), "Rec'd letter from Wm Halsey enclosing one from O. E. Babcock stating that he thought I would have to go out of this office."

tember, 1869, he had acquired an iron mine in Canada. He also began experimenting with a process for cast steel which he called the "Trenton Experiment." The process was sufficiently successful for Averell to apply for a United States patent on September 15, 1869.[55]

Like all of the general's other major enterprises, this steel-making project necessitated a search for backing. Averell obtained capital wherever possible, especially from military friends and powerful connections in investment and finance, including Jay Cooke, Thomas C. Durant, Jay Gould and Thomas A. Scott.[56]

Not content with one mine and one metallurgic process, General Averell also became interested in the industrial possibilities of fibrous asbestos—an early claim suggested it as a base for making paper and leather.

A different mineral soon occupied his attention, however. In the fall of 1870 Averell became interested in asphalt. The rapid urbanization of America, especially in the northeast, was creating demands for a cheap but reliable street-paving material. Ever on the lookout for a new product which could both benefit the people and earn a substantial financial reward for its developer, Averell set out on November 18 to see pavement laid by a Belgian engineer-chemist, Edward J. De Smedt,[57] at 20 North Washington Square, New York City, and at Newark, New Jersey. The general saw "—some 500 yards—badly cracked and somewhat disintegrated after one year, but ascribed to imperfect materials and unsuitable machinery."[58] Bad as the pavement appeared, Averell was convinced of the potential of asphalt, if he could

---

[55]Averell Diary, 1869 (September 15), Dascomb Collection.

[56]Thomas A. Scott (1821-1883), president of the Pennsylvania Railroad, came into prominence by efficiently transporting Pennsylvania troops at the beginning of the Civil War, while serving as first assistant secretary of war in charge of government railroad lines and transportation. Scott and Averell were close personal friends.

Jay Cooke (1821-1905), American financier, founded Jay Cooke and Company which marketed Civil War loans of the Union government. After the war he turned to railroad bonds.

Thomas C. Durant (1820-1885), a leading figure in the building of American railroads. He was a powerful lobbyist during congressional debate of the Railroad Acts of 1862 and 1864, and organized the famed Credit Mobilier. Durant was a friend of Averell's as well as a business associate.

Jay Gould (1836-1892), was an American capitalist who typified the "Horatio Alger" legend of the post-Civil War years. A bold speculator, Gould defeated Cornelius Vanderbilt for control of the Erie Railroad by stock manipulation.

[57]Edward J. De Smedt, a Belgian analytical chemist, was a graduate of the University of Brussels and an employee of James L. Graham at whose home he had a laboratory for experiments with an artificial street pavement. From March 1, 1870, to February 7, 1871, De Smedt received seven patents for asphalt pavement from the United States Patent Office.

develop the right formula of materials and a method to lay it properly.

At this time, the directors of the Grahamite Asphalt Pavement Company elected William Woods Averell president of the company. On February 16, 1871, Averell had notified James Lorimer Graham, Esq., a director of the company, that "I am willing to undertake the duties of President provided that"[59]—and a list of five conditions followed having to do with stock issued to him, capitalization of the company, and maintenance of harmony. As president of the company, the general first undertook an analysis of the De Smedt·formula, the machinery used in laying the pavement, and the paving techniques. He then began a series of experiments to improve them. He developed better pavement-laying techniques and culminated long years of effort and experimentation by being granted a United States patent on January 14, 1878, entitled "Improvement in Asphaltic Pavements."[60]

Always careful to obtain other opinions, Averell followed his analysis of the De Smedt process with a series of asphalt experiments. He invited General McClellan, his lifelong friend, and Generals Quincy A. Gillmore and Horatio G. Wright, of the Army Corps of Engineers, to check his pavement specimens in the presence of a reporter from James Gordon Bennett's *New York Herald*.[61] The reporter's witnessing of the pavement experiment was important to Averell since Bennett had stated that "a mcadam or granit [sic] road [is] the best."[62] Apparently the *Herald* did prepare a piece on the general's asphalt experiments, for Averell recorded in his diary that he had stopped at Bennett's office and "corrected the article on pavement."[63] Some favorable publicity, especially from a valuable contact like Bennett, would certainly reward his effort.

Averell continued to search for support and financing of his experiments. During this period he tried to interest Commodore Cornelius Vanderbilt in the project. Averell's diary records his meeting

---

[58]"Memo Averell's Pavement during Experimental Period," p. 1, Dascomb Collection; Averell Diary, 1870 (November 18, 21), Dascomb Collection.

[59]W. W. Averell to J. L. Graham, Esq., (February 16, 1871), NYSL, box 2, folder 6.

[60]Averell Papers, NYSL, box 4, folder 2.

[61]James Gordon Bennett (1841-1918), namesake of the founder of the *New York Herald*, became editor of the *Herald* in 1867. He financed the Stanley expedition into Africa to find Livingstone and supported the ill-fated G. W. De Long arctic expedition. In 1883 he organized the Commercial Cable Company to handle European dispatches.

[62]Averell Diary, 1871 (March 10), Dascomb Collection.

[63]*Ibid.*, March 13.

with the legendary entrepreneur: "Interviewed Commodore Vanderbilt on the subject [asphalt pavement] who knew nothing about it and thought a dirt road best."[64]

General Averell would not let himself be deterred by such attitudes, but he knew he would have to prove his case. His private papers and business correspondence for this period are filled with technical, legal and other details relating to asphalt. Moreover, his diaries or daybooks record his persistent seeking of street-paving contracts. To convince skeptics, he laid several test strips of asphalt pavement at Battery Park, Central Park, and Fifth Avenue in New York City.

As a consequence of these activities Averell was in and out of prominent politicos' offices in New York City, Albany, and Washington, D.C. Governor Hoffman and Lieutenant Governor Beach of New York gave Averell a hearing, and Beach, while presiding over a session of the New York State Senate "extended the privileges of the floor to me [Averell]."[65] On this same visit to Albany, Averell "saw Mr. Tweed about pavement 10 A.M. Had a glympse of those unknown —Sweeney and Connelly. . . . Tweed seems a very clever business man."[66] Six days later, after another meeting with "Boss" William M. Tweed, the general wrote, "Saw Tweed 3½ P.M. and got permission to lay pavement in Warren Street."[67]

By 1873 business differences with James L. Graham, a partner in the Grahamite Asphalt Pavement Company, resulted in Averell's organizing the Grahamite and Trinidad Asphalt Company. The general "raised $40,000 by the sale of stock."[68] As was not infrequently the case in nineteenth-century business practice, the new company's name was similar to its predecessors and many of its employees and stockholders were retained.

The year 1873 is remembered in American economic history for the beginning of a severe depression. Even before the financial panic struck in the fall, Averell was hard pressed. His experiments were

---

[64]"Memo Averell's Pavement during Experimental Period," p. 1, Dascomb Collection; Averell Diary, 1871 (March 9), Dascomb Collection.

[65]Averell Diary, 1871 (March 22), Dascomb Collection.

[66]*Ibid.*, March 24.

[67]*Ibid.*, March 30.

[68]"Memo Averell's Pavement during Experimental Period," p. 2, Dascomb Collection.

going poorly and he was so short of cash that he sold some oil property stocks; he wrote "[stocks] off 5% so that prospect of selling part stock is coarse."[69] To save the Grahamite Asphalt Company the backers asked Averell to put back into the company treasury a substantial block of his stock to be used as collateral to raise cash. Averell called on Jay Gould and Commodore Vanderbilt, endeavoring to place some pavement stock, but to no avail.[70]

Thus, Averell had firsthand knowledge of the developing economic and financial crisis. The New York money market, the primary source of finance capital in the country, was drying up. Then came the failure of commercial houses, climaxed by Jay Cooke and Company's closing its doors in September and the New York Stock Exchange suspending all trading for ten days.

Along with others, Averell was battered by the Panic of 1873. Yet his faith in asphalt never faltered. During the winter of 1873-1874, despite a lack of investor interest, he organized the New York and Trinidad Asphalt Company for importing asphalt from Trinidad, the source of prime asphalt material.[71] He continued his asphalt experiments and lobbied in Albany, Washington, D.C., and Philadelphia for paying contracts.[72]

One prime contract received by Averell was for the repaving of Fifth Avenue in New York City. Since this required special action from the New York State legislature, Averell spent much time in 1875 lobbying for this bill. To support his cause he supplied affadavits on the superiority of his asphalt, newspaper editorials[73] and even a petition from dozens of Fifth Avenue residents.[74] The names of such prominent citizens as August Belmont, William H. Vanderbilt, James G. Bennett, and Russell Sage appear on the petition.[75] However, the

[69]Averell Diary, 1873 (February 11), Dascomb Collection.

[70]Ibid., March 22.

[71]"Memo Averell's Pavement during Experimental Period," p. 5, Dascomb Collection.

[72]Averell Diary, 1875 (March, April, May, June), Dascomb Collection.

[73]New York Commercial Advertiser (September 4, 1875), Averell Papers, NYSL, box 9, folder 8.

[74]Copy of Petition, Averell Papers, NYSL, box 3, folder 7.

[75]August Belmont (1816-1890) was a prominent banker, financier and diplomat.

William H. Vanderbilt (1821-1885), son of Commodore Vanderbilt, augmented the family fortune and served as president of the New York Central Railroad. He gave liberally to Vanderbilt University and to the College of Physicians and Surgeons in New York City.

James G. Bennett (1841-1918) was publisher and editor of the New York Herald.

Russell Sage (1816-1906), American financier, was associated with Jay Gould and was active in stock speculation in the post-Civil War period. He was particularly interested in an elevated railway system in New York City.

bill encountered the opposition of Tammany Hall chieftain John Kelly.[76]
Averell, after a meeting with Kelly, recorded in his diary: "Tammany
frightened . . . and in real danger of loss of power. Rome and Rum
rule New York so far as the Democratic Party is concerned."[77]
Averell's reference to the Democratic party in New York City being
ruled by "Rome" and "Rum" antedates the Reverend Samuel Burchard's politically damaging remarks during James G. Blaine's
campaign for the presidency in 1884.[78] Averell's ill-concealed aversion
to the Irish-dominated Tammany machine persisted beyond the immediate issue. In 1878 Kelly and his Tammany Hall organization
would deny Averell their endorsement of his bid for the House seat
from the 8th Congressional District of New York.[79]

Throughout 1875 and 1876, Averell, De Smedt and their partners
were active in the city of Philadelpha and in the nation's capital,
laying a test strip of pavement on Pennsylvania Avenue. The
Washington pavement test was a tedious, tiresome round of dealing
with Congress and the commissioners of the city. It was not an easy
nor totally successful struggle for Averell despite his constant efforts to
bring pressure to bear in high places.[80]

As the financial crisis eased in 1879 and 1880, General Averell
was charged with an infringement of patent rights by Edward J. De
Smedt, his former employee. De Smedt cited Averell with interference
for seven patents issued from March 1, 1870, to February 7, 1871.[81]
Averell responded in a detailed statement which outlined his asphalt
pavement experiment, the subsequent patent granted on January 14,
1879, and his particular duties with the company, including the
following statement: "During these years from 1870 to 1879, although
nominally the president of the company, I had been the company. . . .

[76]John Kelly (1822-1886) was a politico and "Boss" of Tammany Hall following William M.
Tweed's fall from power. Referred to as "Honest John," he reorganized Tammany in 1874 and his
iron-handed rule saved the organization as a political force. Kelly is credited with the organization of
a system to assess candidates and office holders for the support of the Tammany machine and to the
profit of the leaders.
[77]Averell Diary, 1875, (April 29), Dascomb Collection.
[78]Reverend Samuel D. Burchard, a tactless Presbyterian clergyman from New York, in the
presence of Republican candidate James G. Blaine, referred to the Democrats as "the party of Rum,
Romanism and Rebellion," thus offending the large Irish vote in New York State. Blaine lost New
York by a scant thousand votes.
[79]W. W. Averell to J. Kelly (November 2, 1878), NYSL, box 4, folder 7.
[80]Averell Diary, 1876, 1877; Averell Papers, Dascomb Collection.
[81]*Copy of Preliminary Statements of E. J. De Smedt and W. W. Averill (sic): U.S. Patent Office
Interference: De Smedt v. Averill. Subject–Asphalt Pavements.* Averell Papers, NYSL, box 4, folder 8.

I raised all the money, obtained all the work, and all the opportunities to make the experiments, and paid De Smedt summer and winter, whether work or not."[82]

The De Smedt patent dispute was resolved by a complicated settlement involving, as interested third parties, Amazi L. Barber and James McLain.[83] The case was settled out of court by the creation, through complex exchanges of stock and capital, of the American Asphalt Pavement Company, and the patent action was set aside. Little did Averell realize that the settlement of the De Smedt infringement proceeding would, within four years, lead directly to litigation against Barber and would continue for nearly twenty years before a decision could be reached.

The American Asphalt Pavement Company was incorporated under the laws of New York State on April 21, 1880, and the board of directors elected General Averell president with a three-man executive committee headed by Amazi L. Barber. The executive committee was given full power to transact all the business of the company.[84]

In less than a year the two heads of this mongrel creation were at odds. Questions of patents and royalties and other internal differences led Barber to organize the Barber Asphalt Paving Company. In 1883 Averell sued for infringement of his patents and won a judgment against the Barber Company.[85] There were fifteen days of delays, appeals and referee awards. Finally, in 1898, the Appellate Division of the New York Supreme Court upheld an award in Averell's favor for $466,401.18 and modified the judgment by increasing the amount to be paid by Barber by $102,905.15 with accrued interest from January 1, 1888.[86] The total amount of the award to Averell approximated $700,000.

[82]*Ibid.*, p. 15.

[83]Amazi L. Barber was an employee of Averell's who later as a director of the American Asphalt Pavement Company controlled the overall operations of the company to General Averell's financial disadvantage. Using Averell's patents, Barber organized the A. L. Barber Paving Company, which by the 1890s had become the largest asphalt-paving company in the United States.

James McLain, a Washington, D.C. attorney, was associated with A. L. Barber *et al.* in the effort to neutralize Averell's participation in the contracts and profits derived from laying asphalt pavement under the patents issued to Averell on January 14, 1879.

[84]W. W. Averell's Handwritten Account of the Barber litigation, p. 4, Averell Papers, Dascomb Collection.

[85]*Ibid.*, pp. 6-8.

[86]*Reports of Cases Heard and Determined in the Appellate Division of the Supreme Court of New York*, vol. 24, pp. 53-58.

Interest in late nineteenth-century innovations, especially in the communications field, also attracted Averell's interest. Consequently, he developed and perfected an asphaltic conduit for an underground electrical system for which he received a United States patent on July 21, 1883.[87] Two years later, the United States Patent Office acknowledged the receipt of Averell's "petition, specification and drawings for your alleged Improvement in Method of an Apparatus for Telephonic and Telegraphic Communication."[88]

Undated sketches in Averell's hand as well as letters refer to this device as a "Waterphone." Although Averell corresponded with several groups working with communications, Thomas D. Conynham of the Hazard Manufacturing Company was unable to convince him to market the waterphone. Conynham arranged several demonstrations and requested Averell's presence, but the general was either hestitant or unwilling to accommodate his backers in this effort.[89]

Whatever misgivings Averell might have had regarding the waterphone project, his asphaltic conduit for underground electrical systems did gain recognition. A long editorial on the subject of underground "electric subways" praised Averell's ,engineering, mechanical skill, inventiveness, and, particularly, his conduit. The editorialist felt that benefits would accrue to society by adopting the Averell conduit system for use in telegraphic, telephonic and illuminating purposes. The low cost of Averell's conduit would reduce the

cost to so low a figure as to place it within the means of every druggist and corner grocery store, as the easiest and cheapest medium of communication with customers . . . an Averell conduit would reduce the distance between New York and Philadelphia to 16 miles [sic] . . . while it would possess the inestimable advantage, for financial, speculative, diplomatic and detective purposes of being absolutely and inviolably secret.[90]

The Averell conduit did bring the general some measure of notoriety and success, if not a large income.

Despite General Averell's almost constant preoccupation with the post-Civil War economy, he never lost interest in politics. In part, this was simply good business, since he had learned how politicians could

---

[87]Averell Papers, NYSL, box 9, folder 6; Copy of patent (July 21, 1883), Dascomb Collection.
[88]United States Patent Office patent copy receipt, Dascomb Collection.
[89]T. D. Conynham to W. W. Averell (July 11, 13, 16, 1888), Dascomb Collection.
[90]Editorial, New York, Tuesday, June 1, 1886—Newspaper unknown, Dascomb Collection.

assist or block his various enterprises. However, Averell also exhibited a longtime dissatisfaction with the Republican party. Therefore, in national politics at least, he usually supported Democrats. He received countless requests from several states to campaign for Democrats but seemed reluctant to do so except for former military men such as Gen. George McClellan in 1864 or Gen. Winfield S. Hancock who opposed James A. Garfield in the 1880 presidential race.

In the 1880 presidential campaign, General Averell was an active participant. In late October, with the campaign reaching its final days and with the outcome in doubt particularly in New York, Averell wrote: "Left New York at 7 P.M. on a special car with General McClellan, and General Crook and General Sterling (?) and Colonel Jones on the Erie Railroad for tour through the black Republican counties from Elmira."[91] When Hancock lost to Garfield, Averell blamed John Kelly of Tammany Hall. A mere 21,000 more Democratic votes could have carried New York for Hancock, and with its thirty-five electoral votes, the presidency. It is no wonder Averell could write, "Great indignation among democrats against Kelly and Tilden."[92] In earlier diary comments, Averell had expressed a dislike for Samuel J. Tilden, former governor of New York, who had been a presidential candidate in 1876.

With the passing years Averell would remain a steadfast Democrat. On November 2, 1896, he wrote in his diary: "The political campaign is now over and tomorrow's election day. The result seems to depend on Illinois, Indiana, Michigan, Minnesota and Iowa. I am doubtful if the people shall succeed against the enormous power of money and elect Bryan." Late on election night, November 3, he added: 'The election passed off quietly and the returns up to 10 P.M. indicate the election of McKinley of Ohio. The power of money was too great for the people. Untold millions have been lavished on the contest by the Republican Party."

William Woods Averell's personal life was a full one socially and culturally. His extensive and frequent travels brought him a wide

---

[91]Averell Diary, 1880 (October 27), Dascomb Collection.
[92]Ibid., November 3. Samuel J. Tilden, governor of New York in 1874, led a reform group which helped bring down the "Tweed Machine" in 1872 and launched Tilden to be the Democratic presidential candidate in 1876.

circle of friends, acquaintances and associates. He was as much at ease with the political, diplomatic and wealthy people of his day as he was with his military and close personal friends. Although Averell was away from his family and home in western New York for so much of his active career, he returned frequently to visit and maintained family ties by letter. He displayed a genuine concern for his sisters, Sarah, Lucy, and Martha, and his brother Oscar James Averell. Oscar was actively involved in the coal, oil and asphalt projects and served as a lobbyist and a promoter of Averell's interests in Albany, N.Y., Washington, D.C., and wherever his services were required. On occasion he sought to obtain capital for the general's enterprises.

On September 24, 1885, at age fifty-three, General Averell married an English widow, Kezia Hayward Browning. There were no children from this marriage, but the general and Kezia bestowed much of their parental interest on the youngest of his sisters, Sarah Averell Dascomb and Lucy Averell Henica.

In 1888, with Grover Cleveland in the White House, General Averell was reinstated in the United States Army by a special act of Congress and placed upon the retired list. This return to the army list was, the culmination of a dogged, continuous effort by Averell to achieve some degree of restitution—at least, in his view—for his removal from command by Sheridan twenty-four years before. The reinstatement also brought him an appointment as assistant inspector general of Soldiers Homes. In this post, the first he had held with an assured income since leaving his consular post in Canada, General Averell was required to travel to these hospitals, to evaluate conditions for the care and treatment of the veterans, to write detailed reports and to struggle (as always) for appropriations.

In 1898, after ten years as an assistant inspector general, Averell resigned. Two years later, on February 3, 1900, he died.

Throughout both his military and civilian careers, William Woods Averell demonstrated the diversity, innovation, and imagination necessary to achieve preeminence. Unfortunately, his excessive trust and lack of ruthlessness did not befit this tumultuous period in American history and prevented Averell from finding such recognition. The general's military experience, however, instilled a determination and perseverance that governed his life and enabled him to overcome temporary reverses.

The Sheridan incident, although painful, did not result in a life

Kezia Hayward (Browning) Averell. Born in 1839 in Surrey, England; married Averell on September 24, 1885, in Bath, New York.

of frustration, overwhelming self-pity and despair. However much the removal from command rankled Averell's pride, he and his friends always insisted he had been the victim of the political generals in the Union army and in Washington. Nonetheless, once into civilian life, Averell's wide-ranging interests, established during his military years, were able to grow in the booming economy of the post-Civil War "age of enterprise." He did not sever connections with his military friends but often turned to them for help in financing and in gaining preferment or support for his several business enterprises, inventions and engineering projects. At the same time Averell widened his contacts to include individuals in the speculative and investment community whose established success could be helpful.

William W. Averell ca. 1890.

General Averell's business career in some ways reflected his military career. He not only had a potential for success but did achieve brilliant successes; however, these achievements failed to bring him wealth or eminence. He was a product of his times—desirous of material success, energetic and diligent in his efforts—but he was never able to match or become one of the "captains of industry" of this age.

Averell's failures in both military and civilian life tend to obscure his ability as an organizer and administrator and his inventive and imaginative qualities. There is little evidence even from his critics to suggest that the general was regarded as lacking ability. Rather, Averell emerges as a knowing, farsighted person who, because of a weakness or trait in his character, lacked or chose not to be motivated by the "root hog or die" philosophy that prevailed in these years.

How does one measure the life of William Woods Averell—military officer, inventor, engineer and entrepreneur—in light of his successes and failures and within the context of his time? Perhaps the answer can be found in the following comments from Averell's letter to his younger sister Martha, whose personal problems had been unburdened upon brother Willie in a letter from older sister Sarah.

Just here I rec'd Sarah's letter mailed the 2nd inst. am obliged to laugh at the troubles which came temporarily upon you. . . .

Did you ever read that little story "How to make the best of it?"

The philosophy which is there briefly enunciated should be called to *your* aid and support.

In the course of some twenty years I have had some steep hills to climb—there is no man of my position in the army who has had as much to contend against—

My youth, want of influential friends and wealth have conspired against me, but I believe I am now a few lengths ahead of all competitors—and I am not at the end yet—

Now the secret of my success is this. I have been blessed with a little foresight and I have *fixed purposes* and notwithstanding the efforts of my rivals and enemies I manage to row my own boat—Men with great political influence closely connected with the Administration, men of wealth and genius have been pitted against me, but through everything I have seen and worked my way.[93]

---

[93] W. W. Averell to Martha Averell (April 5, 1863), Averell Papers, NYSL, box 1, folder 7.

Bibliographic Notes

Compared with military, political, diplomatic and business associates of his time, William Woods Averell has failed to attract the attention either of Civil War scholars or of those devoted to research of the postwar economic revolution to 1900. This neglect of Averell is understandable partly because his memoir, *Ten Years in the Saddle*, although known to be partially completed, did not come to light until 1965. In 1967 William E. Dascomb, a great grandnephew of William Averell, with the help of one of the editors, discovered a substantial number of Averell's papers, personal and business correspondence, daybooks and various other materials. Despite the acquisition of this material, the Averell documents were fragmentary and scattered. Large blocks of material covering Averell's military, consular and business activities were missing.

By 1968 ten boxes of uncatalogued Averell manuscript material had been found in the New York State Library at Albany. This resource— catalogued in 1976—yielded much additional primary data covering Averell's life and supported much of the information contained in the William E. Dascomb collection.

Recently, three reels of microfilm covering the years of Averell's service as the United States consul general to British North America were received from the Diplomatic Section of the National Archives.

William E. Dascomb provided the editors with leads to new possible sources of manuscript materials. As a consequence, more Averell documents were traced to two private collections at Bath, New York, the site of the general's home. This material, however, has not been used in the preparation of this work.

Only part of the manuscript material in the Dascomb Collection has been organized and catalogued. There still remains a large volume of papers, letters, patent applications and patents, legal briefs, etc. dealing with General Averell's many and varied business, political and personal affairs from the Civil War to his death. Undoubtedly, valuable discoveries will be made in these and other collections.

Secondary Sources

Articles

Allen, R. S. "Pinos Altos, New Mexico," *New Mexico Historical Review*, 23 (1948), 302-32.

Amsden, Charles. "The Navaho Exile at Bosque Rendondo," *New Mexico Historical Review*, 8 (1933), 31-50.

Boehm, Robert B. "The Unfortunate Averell," *Civil War Times Illustrated*, 5 (August, 1966), 30-36.

"Dick" [Captain William Dickinson]. "Reminiscences of Fort Defiance, 1860," *Journal of Military Service Institution of the United States*, 4 (1883), 90-92.

Eckert, Edward K. "The McClellans and the Grants: Generalship and Strategy in the Civil War," *Military Review*, 55 (June, 1975), 58-67.

————. "William W. Averell: Sheridan's Scapegoat General?," *By Valor & Arms*.

Ellison, Samuel. "Memoir of a Kentuckian in New Mexico, 1848-1884," J. Manuel Spinosa, ed. *New Mexico Historical Review*, 13 (1938), 1-13.

Hess, Major Frank W. "Volunteer Cavalry, the First Cavalry Battle at Kelly's Ford, Va.," (Washington) *The National Tribune* (May 29, 1890), 1-2.

Heyman, Max, Jr. "On the Navaho Trail: The Campaign of 1860," *New Mexico Historical Review*, 26 (1951), 44-63.

Meyer, M. C. "Letters of a Santa Fe Army Clerk," *New Mexico Historical Review*, 40 (1965), 141-64.

Morgan, M. R. "Memories of the Fifties," *Journal of the Military Institution of the United States*, 37 (1905), 147-67.

Reeve, Frank D. "The Government and the Navaho, 1846-1858," *New Mexico Historical Review*, 14 (1939), 82-114.

Rhodes, Charles D. "Averell, William Woods," *Dictionary of American Biography*, 1 (New York, 1928), 441-43.

Sword, Wiley. "Cavalry on Trial at Kelly's Ford," *Civil War Times Illustrated*, 13 (April, 1974), 32-40.

"West Point," *Scribner's Monthly*, 4 (July, 1872), 257-84.

Books

Ambrose, Stephen E. *Duty, Honor, Country: A History of West Point*. Baltimore: Johns Hopkins Press, 1966.

Avery, Clara A. *The Averell-Averill-Avery Family—A Record of the Descendents of William and Abigail Averell of Ipswich, Massachusetts*. 2 vols. Cleveland: Press of Evangelical Publishing House, 1914.

Bailey, Lynn R. *The Long Walk: A History of the Navajo Wars, 1846-1868*. Los Angeles: Westernlore Press, 1914.

Bakeless, John. *Spies of the Confederacy*. Philadelphia: Lippincott, 1970.

Bancroft, Hubert H. *History of Arizona and New Mexico, 1530-1888*. Volume 7 of *The Works of Hubert H. Bancroft*. San Francisco: The History Company, 1889.

———. *History of the North American States and Texas. Volume 2, 1801-1889*. Volume 16 of *The Works of Hubert H. Bancroft*. San Francisco: A. L. Bancroft and Company, 1889.

Bandel, Eugene. *Frontier Life in the Army, 1854-1861*. Translated by Olga Bandel and Richard Jente. Edited by Ralph P. Bieber. Volume 11 of Southwest Historical Series. Glendale, Calif.: The Arthur H. Clark Company, 1932.

Bearss, Edwin C. and Arrell M. Gibson. *Fort Smith: Little Gibraltar on the Arkansas*. Norman, Okla.: University of Oklahoma Press, 1969.

Bender, A. B. *The March of Empire: Frontier Defense in the Southwest, 1848-1860*. Lawrence: University of Kansas Press, 1952.

Boatner, Mark Mayo, III. *The Civil War Dictionary*. New York: D. McKay Co., 1959.

Brackett, Albert G. *History of the U.S. Cavalry*. New York: Harper and Bros., 1865.

Brooks, Clinton R. and Frank D. Reeve (eds.). *Forts and Forays: James A. Bennett, A Dragoon in New Mexico, 1850-1856*. Albuquerque: University of New Mexico Press, 1948.

Butler, Benjamin F. *Butler's Book*. Boston: A. M. Thayer and Co., 1892.

Casson, H. N. *History of the Telephone*. Chicago: A. C. McClurg and Co., 1910.

Catton, Bruce. *Glory Road*. Volume 2 of *The Army of the Potomac*. Garden City, N.Y.: Doubleday, 1952.

———. *Grant Takes Command*. Boston: Little, Brown, 1969.

Century Magazine Editors. *Battles and Leaders of the Civil War*. 4 vols. New York: The Century Company, 1888.

Clancy, Herbert J. *The Presidential Election of 1880*. Chicago: Loyola University Press, 1958.

Cochran, Thomas C. *Railroad Leaders, 1845-1890: The Business Mind in Action*. Cambridge, Mass.: Harvard University Press, 1953.

Cochran, Thomas C. and William Miller. *The Age of Enterprise: A Social History of Industrial America*. New York: The Macmillan Company, 1942.

Coggins, Jack. *Arms and Equipment of the Civil War*. Garden City, N.Y.: Doubleday, 1962.

Congressional Quarterly. *Members of Congress, 1789-1970*. Washington: Government Printing Office, 1971.

Cooke, Jacob B. *The Battle of Kelly's Ford*. Providence, R.I.: The Society, 1887.

Cullum, George W. *Biographical Register of Officers and Graduates of the U.S.M.A.* New York: D. Van Nostrand, 1868.

Curtis, E. S. *The North American Indian*. 20 vols. Norwood, Mass.: The University Press, 1907-1930.

Dale, Edward Everett. *The Indians of the Southwest: A Century of Development Under the United States*. Norman, Okla.: University of Oklahoma Press, 1949.

D'Arcy, William. *The Fenian Movement in the United States, 1858-1886*. Washington: Catholic University of America Press, 1947.

Danis, William W. H. *El Gringo, or New Mexico and Her People*. New York, 1856: Santa Fe: The Rydal Press, 1938.

DeForest, John William. *A Volunteer's Adventures: A Union Captain's Record of the Civil War*. Edited by James H. Cronshore. New Haven, Conn.: Yale University Press, 1946.

Dornbusch, Charles E. *Regimental Publications and Personal Narratives of the Civil War*.

[*Military Bibliography of the Civil War*]. 3 vols. New York: New York Public Library, 1961-1969.

DuBois, John Van Deusen. *Campaigns in the West, 1856-1861.* Edited by George P. Hammond. Tucson: Arizona Pioneer Historical Society, 1949.

Dunn, J. P. *Massacres of the Mountains: A History of the Indian Wars of the Far West, 1815-1875.* New York: Harper and Bros., 1886.

Foote, Shelby. *The Civil War: A Narrative.* 3 vols. New York: Random House, 1958-1974.

Forman, Sidney. *West Point: A History of the United States Military Academy.* New York: Columbia University Press, 1950.

Fox, William F. *Regimental Losses, 1861-1865, in the American Civil War.* Dayton, Ohio: Morningside Bookshop, 1974. Reprint of 1898 edition published by the Albany Publishing Co., Albany, New York.

Frayer, Robert W. *Forts of the West.* Norman, Okla.: University of Oklahoma Press, 1965.

Freeman, Douglas S. *R. E. Lee: A Biography.* 4 vols. New York: Scribner, 1934-1935.

Giddens, Paul. *The Birth of the Oil Industry.* New York: Macmillan, 1938.

Grodzinsky, Julius. *Jay Gould: His Business Career, 1867-1892.* Philadelphia: University of Pennsylvania Press, 1957.

————. *Transcontinental Railroad Strategy, 1869-1893.* Philadelphia: University of Pennsylvania Press, 1962.

Hassler, Warren W., Jr. *George B. McClellan, Shield of the Union.* Baton Rouge, La.: Louisiana State University Press, 1957.

Heitman, Francis B. *Historical Register and Dictionary of the U.S. Army.* 2 vols. Washington: Government Printing Office, 1903.

Hofstadter, Richard. *Social Darwinism in American Thought, 1860-1915.* Philadelphia: G. Braziller, 1945.

Holbrook, Stewart H. *The Age of the Moguls.* New York: Doubleday, 1953.

Hoopes, Alban W. *Indian Affairs and Their Administration with Special Reference to the Far West, 1849-1860.* Philadelphia: University of Pennsylvania Press, 1932.

Janson, H. W. *History of Art.* Englewood Cliffs, N.J.: Prentice-Hall, 1971.

Jones, Stanley L. *The Presidential Election of 1896.* Madison, Wis.: University of Wisconsin Press, 1964.

Kaempffert, W. *History of Invention.* 2 vols. New York: C. Scribner's Sons, 1924.

Kirkland, Edward C. *Industry Comes of Age: Business, Labor and Public Policy, 1800-1897.* New York: Henry Holt and Co., 1961.

Kluckhohn, Clyde and K. Spencer. *A Bibliography of the Navaho Indians.* New York: J. J. Augustin, 1940.

Kluckhohn, Clyde and Dorothea Leighton. *The Navaho.* Cambridge, Mass.: Harvard University Press, 1946.

Lane, Wheaton J. *Commodore Vanderbilt.* New York: Knopf, 1942.

Leech, Margaret. *Reveille in Washington, 1860-1865.* New York: Harper, 1941.

Lewis, Lloyd. *Captain Sam Grant.* Boston: Little, Brown and Co., 1950.

Livermore, Thomas L. *Numbers and Losses in the Civil War in America: 1861-1865.* Boston: Houghton Mifflin and Company, 1901.

Long, E. B. with Barbara Long. *The Civil War Day By Day: An Almanac, 1861-1865.* Garden City, N.Y.: Doubleday, 1961.

Lowe, Percival. *Five Years a Dragoon.* 2nd edition edited by Don Russell. Norman, Okla.: University of Oklahoma Press, 1965.

Luomala, Katherine. *Navaho Life of Yesterday and Today.* Berkeley, Calif.: University of California Press, 1938.

McClellan, George B. *Report of Maj.-Gen. George B. McClellan, August 4, 1863.* New York: American News Co., 1864.

McClellan, George B., Major General U.S.A. *Report on the Organization and Campaign of the Army of the Potomac: To Which Is Added an Account of the Campaign in Western Virginia.* New York: Sheldon and Co., 1864.

McKnitt, Frank (ed.). *Navaho Expedition: Journal of a Military Reconnaissance from Santa Fe, New Mexico, to the Navaho Country Made in 1849 by Lieutenant James H. Simpson.* Norman, Okla.: University of Oklahoma Press, 1964.

Mendelowitz, Daniel M. *A History of American Art.* New York: Holt, Rinehart and Winston, 1960.

Miles, Nelson A. *A Personal Recollection of General Nelson A. Miles.* Chicago: The Werner Company, 1894.

Miller, Francis T. (ed.). *The Photographic History of the Civil War.* 10 vols. New York: The Review of Reviews, 1911.

Miller, William (ed.). *Men in Business.* Cambridge, Mass.: Harvard University Press, 1952.

Moore, Frank. *The Rebellion Record: A Diary of American Events, with Documents.* New York: G. P. Putnam, 1862-1868.

Near, Irwin W. *History of Steuben County, New York and Its People.* Chicago: The Lewis Publishing Company, 1911.

Nevins, Allan. *The Emergence of Modern America, 1865-1878.* New York: The Macmillan Company, 1927.

Nicolay, John G. and John Hay. *Abraham Lincoln: A History.* Volume 9. New York: The Century Company, 1890.

Prime, William C. *McClellan's Own Story: The War for the Union.* New York, 1887.

Prucha, Francis P., S. J. *A Guide to the Military Posts of the United States.* Madison, Wis.: State Historical Society of Wisconsin, 1964.

Rawle, William Brooke, *et al. History of the Third Pennsylvania Cavalry, Sixtieth Regiment Pennsylvania Volunteers in the American Civil War.* Compiled by the Regimental History Committee in accordance with a Resolution of the Third Pennsylvania Cavalry Association. Philadelphia: Franklin Printing Company, 1905.

Reports of Cases Heard and Determined in the Appelate Division of the Supreme Court of New York. (New York: Banks and Brothers, 1898), volume 24, pp. 53-58.

Rister, C. C. *Border Captives: The Traffic in Prisoners by Southern Plains Indians, 1835-1875.* Norman, Okla.: University of Oklahoma Press, 1940.

Rowell, John W. *Yankee Cavalryman: Through the Civil War with the Ninth Pennsylvania Cavalry.* Knoxville, Tenn.: University of Tennessee Press, 1971.

Sandburg, Carl. *Abraham Lincoln: The War Years.* 4 vols. New York: Harcourt, Brace and Company, 1939.

Sheridan, Philip H. *Personal Memoirs of Philip H. Sheridan, General of the U.S. Army.* New and enl. ed., with an account of his life from 1871 to his death, in 1888, by Brig.-Gen. Michael V. Sheridan. New York: D. Appleton and Company, 1902.

Shippee, L. B. *Canadian-American Relations, 1849-1874.* New Haven, Conn.: Yale University Press, 1939.

Simon, John Y. (ed.). *The Papers of Ulysses S. Grant.* Volume 1, 1837-1861. Carbondale, Ill.: Southern Illinois University Press, 1967.

Sobel, Robert. *Biographical Directory of the United States Executive Branch, 1774-1971.* Westport, Conn.: Greenwood Publishing Company, 1971.

Strait, Newton Allen. *Alphabetical List of Battles, 1754-1900.* Washington: 1905. Detroit: Gale Research Co., 1968.

Strode, Hudson. *Jefferson Davis: American Portrait.* New York: Harcourt, Brace, 1955.

Swinton, William. *Campaigns of the Army of the Potomac.* New York: C. B. Richardson, 1866.

Taylor, George R. and Irene D. Neu. *The American Railroad Network, 1861-1890.* Cambridge, Mass.: Harvard University Press, 1956.

Todd, Frederick P. *Cadet Gray: A Pictorial History of Life at West Point as Seen Through Its Uniforms.* New York: Sterling Publishing Co., 1955.

Todd, William. *The Seventy-ninth Highlanders, New York Volunteers in the War of the Rebellion, 1861-1890.* Albany, N.Y.: Press of Branlow, Barton and Co., 1886.

Underhill, Ruth. *The Navajos.* Norman, Okla.: Oklahoma University Press, 1956.

U.S. Bureau of the Census. *Historical Statistics of the United States, Colonial Times to 1957.* Washington: Government Printing Office, 1960.

U.S. Congress. *Biographical Directory of the American Congress, 1774-1961.* Washington: Government Printing Office, 1961.

————. House Executive Document, No. 24, 36th Congress, 2nd Session, Volume 6 (1860), Serial 1097, "Indian Disturbances in New Mexico."

U.S. War Department. *The War of the Rebellion: A Compilation of the Official Records of the Union and Confederate Armies.* 130 vols. Washington: Government Printing Office, 1880-1901.

Upton, Emory. *The Military Policy of the United States, 1839-1881.* New York: Greenwood Press, 1968.

Utley, Robert M. *Frontiersmen in Blue: The United States Army and the Indian, 1848-1865.* New York: Macmillan, 1967.

Warner, D. F. *The Idea of Continental Union: Agitation for the Annexation of Canada to the United States, 1849-1893.* Lexington, Ky.: University of Kentucky Press, 1960.

Warner, Ezra J. *Generals in Blue: Lives of the Union Commanders.* Baton Rouge, La.: Lousiana State University Press, 1964.

————. *Generals in Gray: Lives of the Confederate Commanders.* Baton Rouge, La.: Louisiana State University Press, 1959.

Watson, T. A. *The Birth and Babyhood of the Telephone.* New York: Information Department of American Telephone and Telegraph, 1934.

Williamson, H. F. and A. R. Dunn. *The American Petroleum Industry: The Age of Illumination.* Evanston, Ill.: Northwestern University Press, 1959.

Index

Albuquerque, New Mexico Ter., 108, 118, 120, 132, 145, 146, 151, 186, 192, 199,209, 211, 223ff; trip to, 226, 227

Alexander, Barton S., 365

Alexandria, Virginia, 5, 276, 304, 335, 354, 375

Allen, Major E. J. *See* Pinkerton, Allen

Allen, Jesse K., 21, 39

Alley, John W., 119

American Asphalt Pavement Company, 414, 414n

Anderson, Robert H., 45

Anderson, William W., 203, 221

Antietam Creek, Md., Battle of (17 Sep 1862), 5, 371, 385

Antisell, Thomas, 301

Apache Indian Tribe, 108, 117, 137. *See also* Gila Apaches, Mescalero Apaches

Applegate, Samuel, 310, 310n

Arbuckle, Fort, Indian Ter., 4, 249ff

Arkansas River, 89, 91, 97ff, 104ff, 230, 257; Big Bend of, 232

Arizona, Territory of, 107, 120, 154, 226n

Armijo, Don Louis, 135

Armijo, Gov. Manuel, 135

Armistead, Frank S., 243

Army of Northern Virginia (C.S.A.), 350, 378

Army of the Potomac (U.S.A.), 4, 7, 56n, 173, 279, 324, 328, 329, 333, 337ff, 355ff, 369, 373ff, 377, 385; McClellan assumes command, 305; McClellan's reorganization of (1861-62), 316ff

Army of Western Virginia (U.S.A.), 379

Army Register, 226, 346

Army, Union (1861-65), 4, 10, 53, 68, 69, 120, 214n, 239, 330, 365, 370ff, 393, 418

Army, U.S.: camp life, 101, 158, 184, 188, 195, 198-99, 342; Corps of Engineers, 365, 410; enlistment, 281ff; equipment and uniforms, 80, 145, 173f; food, 96, 187, 188, 198-99; garrison life, 76, 130ff; medical care and disease, 94, 97ff, 145ff, 305, 385; recruitment, 275ff; regulations and discipline, 60f, 64, 94, 130ff, 174f, 305f, 339, 343ff, 388; tactics (Indian wars), 178ff, 188ff, 193ff

Arnold, Richard, 298, 358

427

The Editors: Nicholas J. Amato is Professor of History at St. Bonaventure University in New York and has written numerous historical articles. Edward K. Eckert, Associate Professor of History at St. Bonaventure, is the author of *The Navy Department in the War of 1812* and many articles on military and naval history.